Over the Rainbow

Over the Rainbow

໒

Queer Children's and Young Adult Literature

Edited by

MICHELLE ANN ABATE

and KENNETH KIDD

The University of Michigan Press • *Ann Arbor*

Copyright © by the University of Michigan 2011
All rights reserved
Published in the United States of America by
The University of Michigan Press
Manufactured in the United States of America
⊗ Printed on acid-free paper

2014   2013   2012   2011   4   3   2   1

A CIP catalog record for this book is available from the British Library.

Library of Congress Cataloging-in-Publication Data

Over the rainbow : queer children's and young adult literature /
    edited by Michelle Ann Abate and Kenneth Kidd.
        p. cm.
     Includes index.
     ISBN 978-0-472-07146-3 (cloth : alk. paper) — ISBN 978-0-472-
05146-5 (pbk. : alk. paper)
        1. Children's stories, American—History and criticism.
     2. Children's stories, English—History and criticism.   3. Young adult
fiction, American—History and criticism.   4. Young adult fiction,
English—History and criticism.   5. Gays in literature.
     6. Homosexuality in literature.   I. Abate, Michelle Ann, 1975–
II. Kidd, Kenneth B.
     PS374.H63O84   2011
     810.9'9283—dc22   2010047504

Acknowledgments

In April 2009, Eve Kosofsky Sedgwick died. A pioneer of LGBTQ studies and queer theory, Sedgwick was the author of seven books, four edited collections, and numerous essays and articles. Over the course of her long career, her work helped to produce as well as to popularize the academic study of nonheteronormative gender and sexual identities. Her contribution to the field cannot be overestimated. Sedgwick's death marks an important milestone in the history of the LGBTQ movement and forms a sad signpost to a year that commemorated both the fortieth anniversary of the Stonewall Rebellion and the publication of the first book for young readers that explicitly addressed the subject of homosexuality.

Sedgwick began her essay "Queer and Now," from her volume *Tendencies* (1993), with the powerful opening sentence: "Motive: I think everyone who does gay and lesbian studies is haunted by the suicides of adolescents." Such is certainly true for both of us and likely for many of the scholars represented here. We would extend Sedgwick's comment, arguing that the production, dissemination, and consumption of books for young readers with queer content can save lives. It is our hope that this collection honors this fact, while it simultaneously seeks to hasten its end. We look forward to the day when the lives of queer youth—along with those who support, document, and advocate for them—are no longer under physical or cultural assault.

We are grateful to many colleagues, family members and friends who both supported and assisted at various points with this project. First and foremost, we'd like to thank the authors of the essays contained in this volume for their time, their cooperation, and—most of all—their insightful work. The fall 1998 special issue of *Children's Literature Association Quarterly* on LGBT children's literature edited by Kenneth was made possible by Marilynn Olson, Claudia Nelson, Gillian Adams, and Teya Rosenberg, then editors of the journal. Four essays featured in that volume are reprinted here (see "Publication History" for more information). At the invitation of Jack Zipes and Louisa Smith, Kenneth also guest-edited a special issue of *The Lion and the Unicorn* on sexuality and children's literature, in which appeared Jody Norton's essay on transchildren, also reprinted here. Thanks to these and other colleagues for their confidence and support.

We have also incurred many individual debts. Michelle would like to extend her thanks and appreciation to Matthew Prickett, who reformatted essays, helped with correspondence and especially the securing of permissions, and kept the spirit of the project alive. If this book chronicles the past history of LGBTQ studies in children's literature, then Matt surely embodies its future.

Michelle is also indebted to her partner, Rachel MacKnight, whose love, support, and companionship provides not simply personal and professional encouragement, but also—taking a cue from Sedgwick once again—the core of that concept: courage itself.

Finally, Michelle would like to dedicate this volume to Marijane Meaker (M. E. Kerr), who has been a pioneer in LGBTQ-themed literature as well as children's and young adult literature for more than five decades. All of us LGBTQ writers, scholars, and individuals who have come after are deeply indebted to your bravery and brilliance.

Similarly, Kenneth would like to acknowledge the invaluable assistance of doctoral students Marina Hassapopoulou and Kevin Sherman, who also helped with essay reformatting and editing. Their hard work and patience are much appreciated.

Kenneth's life is enriched by his alternative family, headed up by Martin Brooks Smith and including Edmund, Zeke, Casey, and Phoebe. Martin's love and support make life all the more beautiful. A big thank you to Byron, Doris, Kathryn, and Lyn, and to the Smith/Provencher clan, especially Carolyn and Allison, who have welcomed him into their homes and hearts.

We're getting there. It's definitely worth the trip.

Contents

᠃

Introduction

§▲

MICHELLE ANN ABATE AND KENNETH KIDD

The year 2009 marked the fortieth anniversary of the Stonewall Rebellion in New York City, widely considered the beginning of the LGBTQ political movement in the United States. It was also the anniversary of John Donovan's young adult novel *I'll Get There: It Better Be Worth the Trip*, the first such novel to openly address homosexuality. *Over the Rainbow* is inspired by these two anniversaries. This volume gathers together significant essays on queer children's and young adult literature published in the wake of the progressive social politics as well as developments in literary-theoretical studies of the last several decades. As more titles with queer energies were published, and as lesbian/gay studies and then queer theory found traction in the academy, scholars began turning their attention to children's and young adult texts. They did so all too aware of the homophobia and erotophobia surrounding (often structuring) the discourses of youth. Most of these scholars work in children's literature studies, itself a relative newcomer to the academic scene. For various reasons, then, it took some time for lesbian/gay-oriented and queer-theoretical treatments of children's literature to emerge.[1]

Although other groupings might work just as well, we have arranged the essays according to the kinds of children's texts or forms with which they are primarily concerned. Part 1, "Queering the Canon," features essays that revisit classic or historical works of children's and young adult literature from the perspective of lesbian/gay studies or queer theory. These essays seek to establish that queerness is central rather than marginal to the literary heritage, at once questioning and shoring up the canon conceit. The essays in part 2, "After Stonewall," focus on the cultural politics of post-1969 texts explicitly about lesbian/gay issues, often designed to educate readers about lesbian/gay families. Part 3, "Queer Readers and Writers," features essays advocating and modeling queer theories of children's textuality by way of its ostensibly queer readers and writers. We move therefore from established writing or canon to contemporary writing to readers themselves, in and around texts that seem more cultural than literary per se, such as fan fiction and computer games. The chronology we follow here is the chronology of the primary subject matter, which corresponds somewhat to changes in critical discourse. This organization underscores the long and varied tradition of queer children's narrative as well as the three major kinds of interpretive work undertaken thus far. We intend these parts to be interrogative as much as descriptive: what makes a canon? what has happened "after Stonewall"? and who might be "queer readers and writers"?

The essays range in original publication date from 1997 to 2010. For readers interested in their chronology, a publication history is provided at the book's end. Had we grouped the essays by chronology or critical method, most of the essays in part 2 would have appeared first, as the earliest work on queer children's literature was concerned primarily with the first wave of explicitly themed lesbian/gay (not yet bisexual or transgendered) literature. Most of the essays in part 2 were published in the 1990s, three of them in the same 1998 special issue of *The Children's Literature Association Quarterly*, guest-edited by Kenneth. Most of these essays, like other work published in that period, take a lesbian/gay-identified rather than a queer-identified approach. One manuscript reviewer commented that the essays in part 2 seem dated, and while we very much admire them, their ostensible datedness is an intriguing issue, perhaps reflecting the ostensibly datedness of a gay-affirmative rather than a more contemporary and avowedly queer sensibility. Lesbian/gay-identified essays tend to be invested in the relationship between identity politics and the politics of representation in a homophobic culture. But not all such essays were published before queer-oriented essays. Crisp's piece on *Rainbow Boys*, very much concerned with the politics of gay affirmation, first appeared in 2008, whereas Martin's essay on queer reading practices dates to 1997. What might it mean to update a sample, especially in a book designed to pay tribute to the past as well as inspire future work? How faithful should we be to chronology, given recent work on queer temporality?

The issue of canon is also tricky. One 1998 essay, that by Nelson, is included in part 1 because it deals with pre-Stonewall literature, if from a lesbian/gay studies perspective. But British boys' magazines are not so much canonical as historical (part of our "literary heritage"). What about Fisher's *Understood Betsy,* once well known, now less so? Inness's essay on Nancy Drew, focused on the lesbian reader and hence included in part 3, might also fit in part 1, in the sense that Nancy Drew enjoys a certain kind of cultural-historical if not exactly canonical prestige. Bernstein's essay is placed in part 1 because it queers a familiar if not canonical text, *Harriet the Spy,* but the essay is arguably queer theory, with its claim that age, like other identity markers, can be queered. Within the world of online Harry Potter fanfiction distinctions are made between "fanon" and less legitimate or literary or beloved stories; is this a queering of the canon or another remodeling? In short, within these three categories, we have made certain calibrations based on topic, method, and chronology.

Another reason for putting queer before lesbian/gay literature in the volume is that while 1969 may well serve as a beginning point for the latter, what we're calling "queer children's literature" predates and may outlast the LGBTQ movement. The word "queer," which first emerged in English in the sixteenth century, has long meant "strange," "unusual," and "out of alignment," even as it has been linked to non-heteronormative sexuality since around the turn of the twentieth century. The term has an interesting history in relation to Anglo-American children's literature. In children's titles from the late nineteenth and early twentieth centuries, the term "queer" appears not infrequently and has a range of associations, among them the strange, the fantastic, the animal, and the aristocratic. Edward Eggleston's 1884 *Queer Stories for Boys and Girls,* for instance, is a collection of stories "not entirely realistic in their setting, but appealing to the fancy, which is so marked a trait of the mind of girls and boys."[2] The queer folk of E. H. Knatchbull-Hugessen's *Queer Folk: Seven Stories* (1874) are fairies and other magical creatures, whereas "queer" refers to animals in such texts as Harriet Beecher Stowe's *Queer Little People* (1867), Olive Thorne Miller's *Queer Pets at Marcy's* (1880), and Palmer Cox's *Queer People with Wings and Sting and Their Kweer Kapers* (1895). In some titles, royalty and queerness overlap, as in *The Queer Little Princess and Her Friends* (1888) and

Queer People Such as Goblins, Giants, Merry Men, and Monarchs (also 1888). In these narratives, children are often linked to the assorted queer creatures they love. As some contributors to this collection emphasize, children are referred to as "queer" in not a few established classics, including Burnett's *The Secret Garden* (1911) and MacDonald's *At the Back of the North Wind* (1871). These usages follow the general understanding of "queer" at the time as meaning odd, eccentric, or singular, often but not always negatively so. By the early twentieth century, however, such usage tapered off as "queer" became more pejorative and more closely associated with same-sex attraction and gender-bending behavior. The *OED Online* cites examples of that association from 1914 forward. Only much later, in the wake of the progressive movements of the 1960s and 1970s, was "queer" reclaimed or resignified as a term of personal and collective pride. "Queer" still means eccentric and singular, even as it also calls forth and performs a nonheteronormative sexual and culture identity. While some adults may believe in queering children's literature, the term itself has yet to make a comeback within the field, except at the level of literary criticism.

"Queer" defies definition, indeed is the antidote to definition in any easy or clear sense. The term at once fortifies and dismantles the notion of a stable or knowable self, in relation to gender and sexuality especially but not exclusively. The best-known academic description of "queer" is likely that of Eve Kosofsky Sedgwick, as "the open mesh of possibilities, gaps, dissonances and resonances, lapses and excesses of meaning when the constituent elements of anyone's gender, of anyone's sexuality aren't made (or *can't* be made) to signify monolithically."[3] Whereas Sedgwick's earlier work in *Between Men* was more aligned with feminist critique and gay liberation, her subsequent books *Epistemology of the Closet* and *Tendencies* form the basis of queer theory in the early 1990s, along with key works by Judith Butler and Michael Foucault.[4]

Understanding children's literature as queer rather than more narrowly as lesbian/gay broadens the interpretive possibilities. For example, many pre-1969 texts for children and young adults avoided the term "queer" but were nonetheless engaged with issues of queer desire and identification. Not a few Anglo-American classics and even genres are homosocial and even homoerotic, and thereby also queer. Victorian and Edwardian narratives routinely idealized the world of "chums." Romantic friendship is at the heart of many texts, from *The Wind in the Willows* to Lucy Maude Montgomery's *Anne of Green Gables*, both published in 1908. These are just a few of the classic children's texts that seem queer to the contemporary eye. "While, to a large extent, the terms 'homosexual,' 'gay' or 'lesbian' and 'queer' successively trace historical shifts in the conceptualisation of same-sex sex," Annamarie Jagose reminds us, "their actual deployment has sometimes been less predictable, often preceding or post-dating the periods which they respectively characterize."[5]

For better and for worse, the emergence of lesbian/gay literature seems easier to chart. Michael Cart and Christine Jenkins report that since 1969, about 200 novels with LGBTQ content have appeared, most of them in the United States, with sixty-six titles published between 2000 and 2004 alone.[6] Homosexuality has become nearly a mainstream topic in YA literature, with publishers more willing to support such and librarians and teachers evaluating and promoting titles through book awards and other mechanisms.[7] Thematic and structural parallels between the YA novel and the coming-of-age narrative for adults made for a fairly easy adaptation of the YA genre. As Michelle has recently suggested, in an essay not reprinted here, the lesbian pulp novel also inspired and even metamorphosed into the young adult novel in the case of one prominent author, Marijane Meaker, who under the pen name Vin Packer wrote a series of lesbian pulps (notably *Spring Fire*) before turning to young adult literature as M. E. Kerr. Michelle proposes that Kerr's 1994 YA novel *Deliver Us from Evie* reworks the 1950s conventions that shaped *Spring Fire*.[8] Many of these YA texts feature white, middle-class protagonists, affirm homophobic stereotypes, or end in violence and death, as Jenkins's analysis of the genre (included in this volume) suggests. The first young adult novels about AIDS, M. E. Kerr's *Night Kites* (1986) and Gloria Miklowitz's *Goodbye, Tomorrow* (1987), emphasize homophobia and AIDS-phobia (rather than homosexuality) as social problems but still affirm certain stereotypes about LGBTQ people, sometimes through ostensibly affirmative characters and plots. Writers working in the gay-affirmative tradition include Nancy Garden, Keith Hale, A. M. Homes, Norma Klein, Ron Koertge, Isabel Miller, and David Rees. Inspired partly by postmodernism, some authors go beyond the affirmative mode and dwell on the aporias of life, love, and identity, as with Francesca Lia Block's metafictional Weetzie Bat series.

While the LGBTQ teenager can be imagined and even brought into the light of day, not yet so for the lesbian/gay first-grader. The bulk of

LGBTQ literature for younger readers has focused on lesbian/gay parents or uncles. The children's picture book has been much more resistant to LGBTQ theming, in large measure because of the prohibition against the representation of any sexuality, much less queer sexuality, especially in childhood. In the late 1980s, Alyson Press launched a children's series dubbed Alyson Wonderland, featuring such texts as Lesléa Newman's *Heather Has Two Mommies* (1989) and Michael Wilhoite's *Daddy's Roommate* (1991), which took center stage in the "Children of the Rainbow" curricular debate in New York City. Then as now, most lesbian/gay-affirmative picture books evacuate sexuality from the family portrait, and refer only obliquely to HIV and AIDS. Persistent is the belief that sexuality, and especially homosexuality, threatens the essence of childhood, as McRuer's essay on AIDS-themed picture books, reprinted here, makes clear. Even ambitious undertakings such as these are circumscribed by familiar norms and mores.

McRuer's discussion focuses attention on the expectation that children's literature and especially lesbian/gay-affirmative writing for children and teenagers have educational value. For McRuer, these books teach the wrong cultural lessons as they go about the business of AIDS education. The young adult novel, derived from the more frankly titled "problem novel," tends toward didacticism, and this extends to LGBTQ variants of the genre. That's not to say that realism or fantasy don't have didactic tendencies; those tendencies are just more hidden. Queer children's literature both endorses and moves against a pedagogical or instrumentalist program, just as it both endorses and moves against the politics of identity affirmation, as expressed in more didactic works of lesbian/gay literature.

Recent social science writing on LGBT youth reflects and supports a general cultural trend toward queer—perhaps to the point of disappearance for the "gay teenager." In *The New Gay Teenager,* for instance, psychologist Ritch C. Savin-Williams notes the recent displacement of said teenager by more diverse queer youth identities such as "boidyke," "polygendered," "trannyboy," and "genderqueer." The book offers a critique of the use of "universal, linear sexual identity models to represent the lives of 'gay youth'" and then a hopeful forecast of the eventual insignificance—even banality—of same-sex identity and desire.[9] In this literature, affirmation and identity politics are routed away from the "labels" of first-wave lesbian/gay liberation. We see in children's literature the same trend toward queer characters, as well as a trend toward young such characters. Moreover, the authors of such books are now more likely to be out themselves as queer people. While David Levithan's *Boy Meets Boy* is set in high school, the novel begins with this line: "I've always known I was gay, but it wasn't confirmed until I was in kindergarten."[10] Among its cast of characters is Infinite Darlene, a drag queen who just happens to be the quarterback of the football team. *Luna,* Julie Ann Peters's story of a transchild, covers the life of Liam/Luna from age three to eighteen, including a difficult period of male-to-female transition during adolescence. In James Howe's *Totally Joe,* written for middle-school children, a charmingly gay male seventh-grader comes out to friends and family after getting a boyfriend. Both Levithan and Howe are out as queer authors; indeed, Levithan launched his writing career as such.

We'll be curious to see just how far back writers will be allowed to take queerness (will kindergartners come out? maybe a queer *Look Who's Talking*?). These books push lesbian/gay identity into queerness, and both into the forbidden zone of childhood. This is a heartening development, given that queer children's writers have long been closeted for fear of career damage. In an interview with Michelle, M. E. Kerr reports that after she came out in the 1990s—right after winning the American Library Association's prestigious Margaret A. Edwards Award for contributions to young adult literature—she experienced backlash in the form of fewer invitations to speak at public schools and libraries as well as instructions not to bring up the subject on the visits that were arranged.[11] Levithan, by contrast, has been welcomed into schools and libraries and is best known for *Boy Meets Boy.*

The essays in part 3 of *Over the Rainbow* dwell on the queerness of readers and writers as well as fictional characters. The emphasis shifts to narrative forms that might be said to queer literature, to complicate our notions about distinction, form, and value.[12] Martin recollects the queer child reading subject, while Norton entreats us *all* to be queer readers and writers, to strive "for a sublime realism of subjectivity—the kind of life-affirming, child-affirming psychosocial realism that not only recognizes, but celebrates diversities of gender, sexuality, race, and culture on the multiple intersecting planes of the polymorphous carnival of wonders we call childhood." Rounding out this section are Tosenberger's analysis of Harry Potter slash fanfiction, and Wood's essay on *eroge* computer games. In both cases, the line between reader and writer (or creator and gamer-player) is just as fuzzy as the lines between "straight" and queer, child and adult.

While scholars of children's narrative have made productive use of lesbian/gay studies and queer theory, the reverse is not true as yet. Queer theory has lately shown great interest in the figure of the child—we think especially of Lee Edelman's *No Future* (2004) and Kathryn Bond Stockton's *The Queer Child* (2009)[13]—but not so much in children's literature. There are some exceptions, beginning with Martin's essay reprinted here, and Michael Moon's work on Horatio Alger Jr.[14] Edelman talks briefly about the Harry Potter books and *Peter Pan,* and the important essay collection *Curiouser: On the Queerness of Children* takes its title and some inspiration from Lewis Carroll.[15] The typologies of queer childhood offered up by Stockton dovetail beautifully with certain children's texts and genres, but her archive is restricted to works for adults, albeit child-themed. If, as Michael Cobb remarks, "the child livens up queer theory," so might children's literature.[16] We hope with this volume to encourage a more dynamic relationship between queer theory and children's literature studies.

We want finally to thank our queer and queer-friendly colleagues, some of whose writing appears here, and some of whom sponsored conference sessions and special journal issues on the topic. We hope that the selections in this volume are sufficiently suggestive of the larger enterprise. There were too many wonderful essays available and not enough space or money to reprint them all. Gavin White and Roderick McGillis, for example, have written important essays queering the canon.[17] Gillian Adams has investigated homosociality and the fifteenth-century *Medici Aesop,* while Elizabeth Goodenough has explored Oscar Wilde's fairy tales in relation to suppressed sexualities and the Christian poetics of atonement.[18] Etsuko Taketani and Maude Hines have taken up nineteenth-century constructions of gender and sexuality, with Taketani focusing on the politics of cross-dressing in the work of Eliza Leslie and Catharine Beecher.[19] Looking at post-Stonewall Canadian young adult fiction, Benjamin Lefebvre uncovers and analyzes a disturbing narrative pattern in which secondary gay characters function as threats to heterosexual manhood and are given little to no existence of their own.[20] Lefebvre's essay, like Tribunella's in this volume, is concerned with the foreclosure of queerness in and around heteronormative masculinity. We would point also to Rebecca

Rabinowitz's "Messy New Freedoms: Queer Theory and Children's Literature" and to Melynda Huskey's "Queering the Picture Book," which offer compelling perspectives on queer theory and strategies of reading.[21] No one volume can do justice to the rich and varied scholarship that already exists or anticipate what will come next.

It's difficult to say where *Over the Rainbow* leaves us. On the one hand, we can see clear progress across the decades in terms of staking out and arguing for the significance of sexuality and singularity in and around children's literature. Queer children's literature is now not only a thinkable subject but a viable one professionally.[22] At the same time, understanding children's literature as queer means embracing trajectories and tonalities other than the lesbian/gay-affirmative and celebratory. While proud of the work done so far, we are curious about the work to come, which may or may not look familiar. Right now there's much discussion about queer theory's fate in the academy. Some critics have moved to other concerns and talk about queer theory in the past tense; others bristle at any suggestion that queer theory might be over or passé. We've seen already just how pervasive and problematic certain rhetorics of progress and "development" can be. At this moment, it seems, we must insist for practical and political reasons on the reality of queer childhood and queer children's literature while being alert to such metaphors and remaining open to possibility.

NOTES

1. Recognizing the difficulty of such designations, we use "lesbian/gay" to designate the first wave of academic work on same-sex topics (lesbian/gay studies) as well as the first wave of children's books with a same-sex focus or component (lesbian/gay children's literature). "Queer" is highly elastic and linked with the advent of queer theory and queer studies in the academy. We use "LGBTQ" to indicate lesbian/gay/bisexual/transgendered/queer people.

2. Edward Eggleston, *Queer Stories for Boys and Girls* (New York: Charles Scribner's Sons, 1884), n.p.

3. Eve Kosofsky Sedgwick, "Queer and Now," introduction to *Tendencies*, by Eve Kosofsky Sedgwick (Durham: Duke University Press, 1993), 8.

4. See Sedgwick, *Between Men: English Literature and Male Homosocial Desire* (New York: Columbia University Press, 1985), *Epistemology of the Closet* (Berkeley: University of California Press, 1990), and *Tendencies*; Butler, *Gender Trouble: Feminism and the Subversion of Identity* (New York: Routledge, 1991); Foucault, *The History of Sexuality*, vol. 1, *An Introduction*, trans. Robert Hurley (New York: Vintage, 1980).

5. Annamarie Jagose, *Queer Theory: An Introduction* (New York: New York University Press, 1996), 73.

6. Michael Cart and Christine Jenkins, eds., *The Heart Has its Reasons: Young Adult Literature with Gay/Lesbian/Queer Content, 1969–2004* (Lanham, MD: Scarecrow Press, 2006), 128. For other summaries and annotations, see Allan A. Cuseo, *Homosexual Characters in YA Novels: A Literary Analysis, 1969–1982* (Methuchen, NJ: Scarecrow Press, 1992); Alex Sanchez, "Coming Out: The Changing Content of YA Books," *Signal* 25.2 (2002–3): 32–35; Roberta Seelinger Trites, *Disturbing the Universe* (Iowa City: University of Iowa Press, 2004), 84–116.

7. The ALA's Gay, Lesbian, Bisexual, and Transgendered Round Table has sponsored the Stonewall Book Awards since 1971; better known are the Lambda Literary Awards or "Lammies," administered annually by the Lambda Literary Foundation.

8. Michelle Ann Abate, "From Cold War Lesbian Pulp to Contemporary Young Adult Novels: Vin Packer's Spring Fire, M. E. Kerr's Deliver Us from Evie, and Marijane Meaker's Fight against Fifties Homophobia," *Children's Literature Association Quarterly* 32.3 (2007): 231–51.

9. Ritch Savin-Williams, *The New Gay Teenager* (Cambridge: Harvard University Press, 2005), 3.

10. David Levithan, *Boy Meets Boy* (New York: Knopf, 2003), 1.

11. Michelle Ann Abate, "A Conversation with YA Novelist M. E. Kerr," *Children's Literature* 35 (2007): 195–96.

12. By and large we have chosen to focus on narratives rather than material objects such as dolls or toys; in so doing, we bypass such wonderful work as Regina Buccola's "Dusty, the Dyke Barbie," *Children's Literature Association Quarterly* 29.3 (2004): 228–52.

13. Lee Edelman, *No Future: Queer Theory and the Death Drive* (Durham: Duke University Press, 2004); Kathryn Bond Stockton, *The Queer Child, or Growing Sideways in the Twentieth Century* (Durham: Duke University Press, 2009).

14. Moon, "'The Gentle Boy from the Dangerous Classes': Pederasty, Domesticity, and Capitalism in Horatio Alger," *Representations* 19 (Summer 1987): 87–110.

15. See Edelman, *No Future*, 21. In their introduction to *Curiouser: On the Queerness of Children* (Minneapolis: University of Minnesota Press, 2004), editors Steven Bruhm and Natasha Hurley discuss Carroll's *Alice* books at some length. They also note that in books such as *Heather Has Two Mommies,* discussed in this volume by Elizabeth A. Ford, "we find sanitized middle-class worlds where the children are evacuated of any desires but those of creature comforts" (Bruhm and Hurley, xii).

16. Michael Cobb, "Childlike: Queer Theory and Its Children," *Criticism* 47.1 (2005): 120.

17. Gavin White, "Falling out of the Haystack: L. M. Montgomery and Lesbian Desire," *Canadian Children's Literature / Littérature Canadienne pour la Jeunesse* 102: 27 [2] (Summer 2001): 43–59; Roderick McGillis, "'A Fairy Tale is Just

a Fairytale': George MacDonald and the Queering of Fairy," *Marvels & Tales* 17.1 (2003): 86–99.

18. Gilliam Adams, "The *Medici Aesop:* A Homosocial Renaissance Picture Book," *The Lion and the Unicorn* 23.3 (1999): 313–35; Elizabeth Goodenough, "Oscar Wilde, Victorian Fairy Tales, and the Meanings of Atonement," *The Lion and the Unicorn* 23.3 (1999): 336–54.

19. Etsuko Taketani, "Spectacular Child Bodies: The Sexual Politics of Cross-Dressing and Calisthenics in the Writings of Eliza Leslie and Catharine Beecher," *The Lion and the Unicorn* 23.3 (1999): 355–72; Maude Hines, "Missionary Positions: Taming the Savage Girl in Louisa May Alcott's *Jack and Jill,*" *The Lion and the Unicorn* 23.3 (1999): 373–94.

20. Benjamin Lefebvre, ""From Bad Boy to Dead Boy: Homophobia, Adolescent Problem Fiction, and Bodies That Matter," *Children's Literature Association Quarterly* 30.3 (2005): 288–313.

21. Rebecca Rabinowitz, "Messy New Freedoms: Queer Theory and Children's Literature," in *New Voices in Children's Literature Criticism,* ed. Sebastien Chapleau (Lichfield, Straffordshire, UK: Pied Piper, 2004), 19–28; Melynda Huskey, "Queering the Picture Book," *The Lion and the Unicorn* 26.1 (2002): 66–77.

22. In addition to the proliferation of articles, another indication is the appearance of book-length studies such as Victoria Flanagan's *Into the Closet: Cross-Dressing and the Gendered Body in Children's Literature and Film* (New York: Routledge, 2008).

PART 1

Queering the Canon

❧ EVEN AS BOYS AND ESPECIALLY GIRLS are sexualized in Western mainstream culture—in popular fashion and advertising, for instance—they are still often presumed innocent of sexuality. If society is unwilling to imagine the sexual nature of young people more generally, then it is surely not ready to consider their tendencies toward nonnormative sexualities. Indeed, common conservative rhetoric in the United States asserts that lesbian teachers, same-sex parents, or gay Boy Scout leaders are intent on "recruiting" or "indoctrinating" the nation's children into sexual deviancy. Such language casts childhood and LGBTQ identity as mutually exclusive. Since children are ostensibly devoid of LGBTQ thoughts, feelings, or actions then, by extension, so are the narratives intended for them. Indeed, the very idea of a children's classic is often invoked in the context of nostalgia and a claim to innocence, functioning as a prophylactic against sexuality and other markers of presumptively adult identity.

The five essays featured in this section challenge the assumption that children's classics are innocent of sexuality and especially queer sexuality. They tease out queer elements of the narrative that suggest or stand in for sexuality. In so doing, they take part in a project that emerged in the wake of the 1970s lesbian/gay liberation movement and became a central preoccupation of latter-day LGBTQ studies: "queering the canon." While it became commonplace for critics to unveil the homoerotic undertones and narrative weirdnesses of movies like *Calamity Jane* and *The Maltese Falcon*, novels such as *The Talented Mr. Ripley*, or television shows such as *Batman* and *CHiPs*, such analytical moves came later to the field of children's literature. Entrenched denial about (homo)sexuality, combined with the phobic conflation of homosexuality with pedophilia, has made children's literature the final frontier for queer theory in some ways.

These essays span a ten-year period, 1998–2008, underscoring that the project of queering the canon is ongoing. Three of the literary texts under scrutiny date back to the first part of the twentieth century, while two are more contemporary. Although other scholars have since explored Alcott's *Little Women* in relation to lesbianism, notably Kathryn Kent in *Making Girls into Women*, Trites's essay on the subject remains foundational, and most likely, controversial, given the cherished place *Little Women* has long occupied in American culture. Even lovers of Baum's Oz books must admit they are a tad strange, but Pugh's essay powerfully highlights their queer utopianism. Tribunella's essay shows how queerness is both cultivated and managed in and around *A Separate Peace*. These essays challenge us to consider how queerness has helped underwrite canonicity; we cannot assume that queerness runs counter to literary or aesthetic value. Collectively, they also suggest the existence of a queer literary tradition of children's literature, at once questioning and shoring up the idea of the canon or the classic more generally.

These essays use "queer" as both a noun and a verb. Indeed, they evidence the broad spectrum of linguistic and sociopolitical meanings of "queer": from eccentric or strange, to gay, lesbian, and bisexual, to transgendered, transsexual, and—looking further ahead—genderqueer and beyond (postqueer?). In so doing, these essays demonstrate that queerness is hardly an unusual or alien element of narrative; rather, queerness may be something of a literary or cultural trope.

David and Jonathan—and Saul—Revisited

Homodomestic Patterns in British Boys' Magazine Fiction, 1880–1915

ả

CLAUDIA NELSON

Late-Victorian and Edwardian Britain offers an absorbing field of study for the historian of sexuality, in that it was at once aggressively opposed to behavior that it identified as "homosexual" and cordial to feelings that we would classify as "homoemotional." In the homosocial world of school, army, business, and clubs that existed around the turn of the century, middle-class men's closest relationships were often with other middle-class men; as Eric Trudgill points out, "Male friendship was a keystone of society."[1] Boys' fiction during this period likewise often appears designed to appeal to, or even help engineer, a reader who was most at his ease in a single-sex world.[2] Popular reading for male adolescents assured its audience that men might reasonably serve as the ultimate source and object of emotional drama and satisfaction in boys' lives, celebrating, in Beverly Lyon Clark's phrase, "a [male] bonding so effective that females are no longer necessary to enact the feminine."[3]

Clark and other investigators of homoemotional—or, as many argue, homoerotic—imagery in Victorian children's literature have understandably concentrated on the school story,[4] a fertile area for inquiry because romance in this genre necessarily comes from the exaltation of the passionate friendship between boys. But in focusing instead on adventure tales, the present essay seeks to change the terms under which such investigations are sometimes conducted by urging that we pay more attention to two things we already know. First, the school story is, of course, not the only genre within turn-of-the-century boys' fiction to celebrate male bonding; we need to consider the possibility that different genres may turn their explorations of these passionate ties to different ends. And second, while today we tend to view male homoemotionalism, homoeroticism, and homosexuality as three points on one continuum (a homoemotional but celibate person, some would claim, is simply a homosexual with inhibitions), this way of thought was by no means universally accepted by the Victorians themselves. As Jeffrey Richards observes, Victorian "manly love" must be considered in the context of "a centuries-old tradition of strong non-sexual male friendships," regarded by many commentators even at the sexually self-conscious end of the century as pure, uplifting, and socially valuable—certainly not as culturally transgressive.[5] Conversely, homosexual behavior between men was often associated with what we now refer to as "cruising": the brief and even anonymous sexual encounter between men who have no long-term emotional investment in each other.[6] In these circumstances, homoemotionalism or passionate same-sex friendship was not a preliminary stage in homosexuality, but its antithesis.

I propose that in late-Victorian Britain, at least as regards the marketing of the boys' culture of the era, the opposition between homosexuality and heterosexuality was less important than that between domesticity and antidomesticity—so that the marriage plot and "family values" could be validated even within dramas with an all-male cast.[7] To be sure, homosexuality, which was certainly a Victorian bugbear, was usually seen as antidomestic, as were self-serving activities such as stealing and cheating, all of which are often explicitly represented within boys' narratives as liable to damage the family. But homoemotionalism was not considered incompatible with domesticity, although we often see it in that light today, and for that reason it was more often celebrated than censured. For instance, as I have suggested elsewhere, homoemotionalism was the mechanism through which late-Victorian schools were consciously presented to the public as alternative "families" for the production of men, in which domesticity was to be translated into a male idiom rather than eradicated.[8] Indeed, even the male bonding that occurs within the adventure story, that apparently most antidomestic genre of Victorian boys' fiction, takes on a domestic cast.

Yet, unlike the school story, in which passionate friendship exists only between boys of the same age, the adventure typically constructs a triangle (or even a quadrangle) involving both adolescent and adult males. Thus adventure tales do not only investigate homoemotional- ism, whether by itself or in contrast with homoeroticism; they also com- ment, often unfavorably, on the father-son bond, offering a new vision of all-male domestic bliss that undermines older visions of patriarchal authority. In an era in which women were gaining ever more iconic force—writers lauded them as domestic goddesses, all-powerful moth- ers, and potential saviors of humankind—boys' fiction often offered its readers an alternative and potentially less threatening vision of the new family, imagining male emotional needs and ties as paramount. In this way, as Kenneth Kidd has suggested to me, such fiction may be said to constitute a liminal and idyllic space between the uncomfortable ex- tremes of a feminized private sphere and a masculinized public sphere. Boys anxious about their incipient entry into the competitive and an- tidomestic world of moneymaking could find in adventure stories a re- assurance that the supposedly separate spheres might be crossed to cre- ate a male homoemotional and domestic sphere that combined the best features of both its progenitors.[9]

During the period I will examine here—approximately 1880–1915— the adventure story was promulgated in a variety of forms, but partic- ularly through the boys' magazine serial, in which it was the dominant genre.[10] Different magazines targeted boys at different social and edu- cational levels, but even across class lines adventure stories tend to fol- low certain set patterns in their representation of homoemotional bond- ing: the conservative *Boy's Own Paper,* published by the Religious Tract Society, adheres to the same conventions that we see in lower-status, profit-oriented titles such as *The Boy's Journal* and *Pluck.* Three related narrative blueprints relevant to this investigation appear again and again and from magazine to magazine. One common story requires that an adolescent gradually win his father's regard by gaining the re- spect and love of an intermediary male or, more generally, by proving himself within his peer group. In the second, the protagonist frees him- self from the clutches of a predatory "false father" (there is usually no biological tie) and turns to the healthier love of a boy his own age. And the third shows the boy transferring his loyalties from one adult male to another. While such tales may imply that passionate love between fa- ther and son precludes the formation of homoemotional ties outside the family, it is also possible to find stories in which, to draw upon a bibli- cal paradigm, the love of David and Jonathan coexists with that of

David and Saul. In creating such spaces of coexistence, authors of adventures collectively suggest that for the boy reader of this period, homoemotionalism was, in a sense, the ultimate domestic value.

As homoemotional love stories, school stories often focus on the romance of sameness—the joys of bonding with someone of the same age, class, nationality, and race as well as the same gender. In *Tom Brown's Schooldays,* for instance, the narrator praises Tom and Arthur's love for each other but inveighs against friendships between older and younger boys, apparently because age differences are likely to lead to an overtly sexual exchange.[11] In contrast, the adventure tale derives much of its interest from offering its readers various combinations of difference, whether defined in terms of race, class, nationality, or generation: Robert Louis Stevenson's Jim Hawkins, Long John Silver, and Dr. Livesey and Rider Haggard's Allan Quatermain, Sir Henry Curtis, and Ignosi are representative. The idealized male figures who grace the covers and number heads of the popular boys' magazine *Chums,* for example, as Robert H. MacDonald notes,[12] are a mixture of young boys, older boys, and adult soldiers, perhaps celebrating the growth of the individual over time but more likely reflecting visually the same heterogeneity that the magazine's interior romanticizes. Indeed, it appears that the happy ending of the magazine-serial romance depends upon the elision of difference, which permits male individuals of wildly divergent backgrounds to dwell together in amity, just as more self-consciously "homosexual" texts of the period—E. M. Forster's *Maurice* (written but not published in 1913), say—often eroticize interclass or intergenerational bonds between men. What one narrator of 1890 decries as "the ugly barriers which the usages of society place between the gentleman and the workman"[13] often function as the real antagonist to be defeated.

Take, for instance, Gordon Wallace's serial "Cameron's Last Chance!" (*Boy's Journal* 1913), wherein a baronet, Sir Andrew Cameron, hires twenty-year-old Bart Elliott, who is poor but virile, to "make a man" of his effete nineteen-year-old son, Arthur.[14] Bart's task is explicitly to turn Arthur into a son of whom his father may be proud, so that Bart functions as a stand-in for Sir Andrew in the child-rearing process; that Bart's name is also the abbreviation for "baronet" is surely no accident. Over eight installments, and under Bart's guidance, Arthur achieves health, self-reliance, unselfishness, pluck, and domestic competence as an outback chef. He also finds gold deposits that might enable him to "shake off Bart Elliott and his cramping influences" and make him "independent of his father,"[15] but a fortunate amnesia saves him from an independence for which he is not yet ready, and his windfall is limited to 1,500 pounds surreptitiously bestowed upon him by Sir Andrew later in the story. Nevertheless, Bart is not only substitute father but also substitute brother and celibate spouse. In the final chapter, the three settle down in the outback as equal partners, the young men "like brothers" to each other and like "two sons" to Sir Andrew.[16]

Thus one of the serial's points is that being "bush-mates" in the single-sex world of the Australian outback erases the differences that separate men from each other in England, be they differences of class, as for Arthur and Bart, or differences of age, as for Arthur and Sir Andrew. Arthur, indeed, notes his desire to turn himself into Bart—"I've got to admire him so much that I've wanted to be like him for a long time"— to which his interlocutor replies that drawing closer to Bart means drawing closer to Sir Andrew: "No doubt your father would like to hear you talk that way."[17] The final chapter equates Arthur's successful achievement of Bart-like heroism with the literal recovery of the father; foiling a kidnapping, Arthur rides a log down a logging slide at fifty miles per hour, only to discover that the rescued victim is Sir Andrew. At the same time, measuring up to the father's standards of manliness means escaping the father's dominance, at least ostensibly. When the baronet "discovers" that his son has become financially independent of him through his own secret gift, he exclaims, "Good heavens above! Have you passed out of my hands altogether?"[18]

The story's happily all-male domestic ending indicates, of course, that the answer to this question is no. Rather, one gathers that the drawback of the unreformed father-son relationship (that unmediated by the passionate friend here represented by Bart) is its insistence on hierarchy. Once status discrepancies are erased, men can join together, building families in which there is no need for women to keep the peace.[19]

Other stories published in the *Boy's Journal,* and in other periodicals, offer variations on this theme of the son proving his manhood via another man in order to win the grudging admiration of his father. For example, the Guy Rayner serial briefly cited earlier, which starts out as a school story entitled "Harry Stanton: A Story of Real Life" and ends eight months later as a pirate tale called "In the Land of Furze and Bloom, or, The Search for the Hidden Treasure," focuses admiringly on the "more than brotherly love" shared by the adolescent heroes, which, according to the clergyman father of the title character, is "the most precious thing you can possess." It is this love that sustains them when the machinations of the school bully cause the clergyman to reject Harry and the fatherly headmaster to expel him from school, thus paving the way for the pirate adventure. Although Harry has earlier remarked of his father, "How dearly I love him. I would rather die than cause him trouble," he nonetheless must fight his way back into his father's regard, an effort that is facilitated by his ability to sustain a passionate friendship with a coeval.[20]

Another excellent example of this trope ran concurrently with "Cameron's Last Chance!" This is Nelson Power's "The Fighting Footballer; Or, The Sporting Chance," in which the son of an antisport mill owner turns professional athlete in order to save his father's fortune and effect a domestic rapprochement. Here the third member of the romantic triangle is of the father's generation and is characterized as "thought[ful] and sympathe[tic]," given to laying "a hand upon the young man's shoulder" affectionately,[21] so that we might expect the hero to transfer his loyalties to this more understanding "father." But in fact the story's ultimate goal is again an all-male egalitarianism that includes the biological father, who must shamefacedly admit, "I've never understood you; only in the last few days have I come to realize that you're a man, Jim—a man in the best sense of the word. But now we can let all the past be forgotten, and we'll work together shoulder to shoulder, boy, like good chums." This ending suggests that any form of male bonding is interchangeable with any other form: father and son *should* also be "chums." Jim's mentor tells father and son to "live happily ever afterwards!" and the narrator remarks that "if you go now to Rivermoor, you will find no more devoted couple than Arnot Steerman and his son." What we have here is not only a father-son bond but also a companionate marriage.[22] As such, it recoups domesticity—but not patriarchy—for the male.

Such narratives imply that the relationship between fathers and their adolescent sons is fraught with difficulty and works best when it can be filtered through some other male. Male domesticity, in other words, is a delicate work of art more than a natural state. Patricia Barnett observes that the stories published in boys' weeklies in the last third of the nineteenth century rely heavily on the romantic archetype of "the foster-child," which requires the boy protagonist to search for his true father, occasionally having simultaneously to protect himself against the figure of the "false father." She suggests that "this theme re-flects, psychologically, every child's fantasy of having exotic and mys-terious origins" and "encourage[s the] identification of the average reader with a mystic and triumphing super-hero who is never the ordi-nary mortal he seems to be."[23] My own inclination is to substitute for Barnett's Jungian approach one grounded in the social history of the period. It is noteworthy that the late-Victorian era, as I have argued elsewhere, often "viewed fatherhood . . . with considerable ambiva-lence, anxiety, and even hostility" and obsessively sought to find ways to define, reform, and control it[24]—in fact, to "search for [the] true fa-ther." While the foster-child paradigm is certainly as common within turn-of-the-century adventure serials as Barnett contends, we cannot afford to ignore the larger context of widespread concern about male parenting. Unable to find an uncomplicated and satisfying father-son relationship within the family as originally constituted, boys' authors focus on other forms of manly love that either substitute for the flawed father or point the way to the discovery of the father who is not flawed.

Thus in considering examples of the second type of story that pro-liferates in turn-of-the-century boys' magazine fiction, that in which a boy rejects a "false father" in favor of the love of another boy and thereby becomes reconciled with a "true father," we may find that such tales continue the critique of the father that underlies "The Fighting Footballer" and, to a lesser extent, "Harry Stanton" and "Cameron's Last Chance!" Sometimes, in fact, these stories treat the regeneration of the father-son bond in a rather cursory way, implying that the best kind of homoemotional domestic bliss is to be found in the more genuinely egalitarian bond that exists between hypermasculine and hyperfemi-nine boys. Such boys can serve each other as protectors and moral guides as well as loving companions, suggesting a relationship that is simultaneously that of parent and child and that of partners in a "mar-riage" that is asexual but nonetheless often characterized by physical expressions of affection.

Earlier adventure tales, such as the 1869 *Boys of England* serial "Mark Rushton," may locate the hypermasculine and the hyperfeminine in a single admirable body:

> So finely moulded were his form and features, so adolescent and even feminine in their grace, that the wags of the gun-room would sometimes venture to address him as *Miss* Rushton; but the taunt of

effeminacy always brought its practical refutation in the . . . swift and stinging bash of that strong little fist propelled by an arm, which, though as white and almost as delicately rounded as a girl's, was sprung with muscles of steel.[25]

Even the later stories, such as Gordon Stables's "The Rough Riders: A Story of the Rebellion in Cuba" (*The Captain,* 1899), may feature similarly androgynous heroes. Fifteen-year-old Arch is "handsome, certainly, but neither very tall nor very strong," despite his hidden muscles; still, on the battlefield "His shrill, treble, girlish voice inspired confidence." Arch's eighteen-year-old companion, Dod, is apparently in love not only with Arch's twin sister but with Arch himself, as "for the life of him Dod couldn't have told which he liked the better." The true father of this interesting ménage, replacing the biological fathers whose opposed political loyalties during the Civil War represent an early threat to their sons' mutual love, is Teddy Roosevelt, the "daring-looking and well-set-up king of the Rough Riders" who "loved his men, and was beloved by them."[26]

But a more typical ploy in the later narratives is the creation of a family constellation consisting of a criminal adult, a feminized boy of startling moral purity, and the adolescent protagonist who must decide between these rival models of masculinity—or, one might argue, between "bad" homoeroticism and "good" homoemotionalism. Thus while Louis Rousselet's "The Two Cabin-Boys" (*Boy's Own Paper,* 1881–82) features a worthy father, Pierre Riva, whose industry has made him "the most well-to-do man in the village" and whose "kindness, courage, and honesty [have] made him the most esteemed,"[27] it establishes as a more important character an adult who pretends to be driven by paternal feelings but who really has more dangerous drives to satisfy. Ostensibly this man's chief lust is for money, but in the context of sinister homosocial bonding it is interesting that the criminal, Dominique Martignes, endears himself to Daniel, the protagonist, by calling him "Ducky" and "my little one" and vowing eternal friendship: "Nothing annoys me so much as going on board without a companion. I won't take an engagement unless on the same ship as you."[28] Indeed, Dominique is the second "false father" to captivate Daniel; the first has caused Daniel's real parent to disown the lad when Pierre discovers that while Daniel was on a tobacco-smuggling expedition with Mateo, the older man shot a revenue officer. Intense bonds between predatory men and young boys, in other words, work to undermine male domestic bonds.

In contrast, intense peer relationships are all to the family's benefit. The task of the second cabin boy of the title, Penguin, a lad of "almost girlish appearance," is to supplant Dominique in Daniel's affections and restore the wanderer to his sorrowing parent. Penguin's own bond to the ship's captain, whom, he notes, "I love as my own life," serves as a model of what father-son connections ought to be even though no biological tie exists; but it is the love of the two boys that enables the reestablishment of domesticity via the reconciliation of father and son and Daniel's marriage.[29] Despite the many occasions upon which the cabin boys' love has some sort of physical expression, Rousselet makes clear that the good passionate friendship eases both patriarchal succession and heterosexuality. "Spiritual, transcendent and free from base desire," in Richards's phrase,[30] manly love creates an emotional climate that will encourage a high-minded approach to marriage in later life.

A final *Boy's Journal* series, Geoffrey Murray's "Mighty London!" (1913–14), provides another striking example of the difference between bad fathers and good ones and between inappropriate and appropriate forms of male bonding. Our story begins with Sam Sherlock, a brutish father who wants to punish his son, Allan, for following up the day's newspaper peddling by playing the violin instead of stealing. In the ensuing melee, Sherlock's wife (who is far superior morally to her husband) reveals that Allan is not their child after all, opening the way for the boy to find more attractive father figures. But although the first of these men, Arthur Stannard, appreciates Allan's musicianship, represents a higher social class, and offers to "be your father and mother too ... yes, and your tutor into the bargain," he turns out to be a gentleman jewel thief, the "guv'nor" of Sherlock's gang of thieves. When Allan objects to following in these criminal footsteps, Stannard retorts that he must obey: "Understand me, once and for all, you are mine—body and soul! Mine; d'you hear? You'll do my bidding and work my will, or else."[31] Allan's tortured reaction to the discovery of his new father's nature suggests that the struggle between criminal man and honest boy is simultaneously a struggle between deviance and pure manly love:

Arthur Stannard was a thief! Arthur Stannard! The man he had revered and worshipped—the man he was beginning to love as only man can love man, was a common scoundrel!

Fate, laughing at him, had led him straight from the clutches of one ruffian, who would have poisoned his soul[,] into those of another, far more cunning, far more clever, who assuredly would drag him down into perdition unless Allan could escape.

Forcibly returned to Sherlock, Allan finds himself once again in the "lovin' arms" of the "pore old father what you was so wicked as to run away from,"[32] a plot twist that suggests that one problem with the seductive criminal in this formula is that he represents a blind alley rather than a genuine escape from the false father.

Of course Allan eventually finds his true father, in the shape of his biological grandfather Thomas Merridew, and in accordance with all the dictates of romantic melodrama, Merridew is a courtly aristocrat of the highest probity, "almost worshipped" by the local villagers. The story of how Allan came to lose his family in the first place, however, rings interesting changes on the rivalry of true and false parent. Merridew had originally hoped to marry his daughter, Allan's mother, to Robert Garfield, orphan son of a merchant prince, but she preferred the poor but worthy Harry Standish. Standish, indeed, was the wiser choice, as Garfield was then revealed as a bankrupt knave primarily interested in his prospective bride's money. After she became (in rapid succession) a wife, widow, mother, and corpse, Garfield paid his groom Sherlock 300 pounds to steal the infant Allan and bring him up as a criminal; Garfield himself took the alias Arthur Stannard. This elaborate plot, hinging on Garfield/Stannard's obsession with corrupting his rival's son by establishing his ownership of the boy's "body and soul," implies that jealousy both sexual and financial is the consuming passion of the false father, whose deviance both disrupts the desirable all-male family and is thwarted in its turn by other worthy father figures—such as the "tall, soldierly-looking man, Chief Inspector Tanner, the famous head of the criminal department of Scotland Yard," on whose account Allan feels a quasi-sexual "sudden wave of mingled relief and gratitude surge through him." Tanner uses Allan as bait to attract the real object of his interest, the gang; in this tale, it seems that for good and bad fathers alike, the major function of the adolescent son is to serve as a pawn in their dealings with one another.[33] Unable ever to come into contact save through intermediaries such as Allan and, earlier, his mother, adult saints and adult villains are nonetheless passionately interested in connecting with their opposite numbers.

This summary of "Mighty London!" ignores the bond forged between Allan and Tom St. Cyr, Merridew's admirable foster son, who performs much of the detective work of the story; I pass over this relationship because this narrative's primary emotional energy seems to me to be situated in father-son bonds of one kind or another. Yet the existence of an important peer relationship is what differentiates serials such as "Mighty London!" and "The Two Cabin-Boys" from stories illustrating the final variation on the adventure's construction of homoemotional bliss, in which the triangle requires the boy hero to shift his loyalties from one father to another. This subgenre figures male domestic bonds as simultaneously unsatisfactory and deeply desirable, forcing the protagonists to audition applicant after applicant until a stable father-son bond is finally achieved.

One narrative that follows this pattern is G. A. Henty's "Facing Death: A Tale of the Coal Mines" (*Union Jack,* 1880), which traces Jack Simpson's rise from orphaned son of a miner to consulting engineer. This rise is accomplished by a series of swaps or add-ons wherein the protagonist exchanges one foster father for another of higher rank and loftier expectations, trading up to the success that we have learned to expect of the Henty hero. Jack's original foster father, Bill Haden, has taken in the two-month-old orphan reluctantly, at his wife's urging, and offers the promising lad little encouragement. Accordingly, when Jack is ten years old he fixes on a more useful mentor in the person of an artist who kindles the boy's ambition by passing on the wisdom he received from his own father: any working-class lad can "end by being a rich man and a gentleman." The artist promises to write to Jack annually to keep his ambition alive, and with this stimulus Jack is able to move on to a new mentor, the village schoolmaster Mr. Merton, formerly an outstanding student of mathematics at Cambridge. Jack's own Cambridge hopes are scotched, however, by labor trouble in the mines, in which his first foster father is heavily involved. While Bill is one of the strikers, Jack's sympathies are with management; significantly, the mine owner, Mr. Brook, has taken a fatherly interest in him. We then fast-forward to a mine explosion, in which Jack saves Mr. Brook and asserts his authority over Bill—whom he now calls "Bill" rather than "Dad." Twelve years later, Jack has married Mr. Merton's daughter, and the story ends with a family tableau: Jack, Mr. Merton, Mr. Brook, and the artist sit cozily around a table, while Bill and his wife are out of the picture, playing with Jack's children. Mr. Merton lives in Jack's house; Bill and Jane are relegated to a "pretty cottage just opposite to the entrance of the grounds."[34] Class tells.

In one sense "Facing Death" is about putting one's class origins behind one as quickly as possible: learning to "speak posh," reassigning one's loyalties to the dominant social group. Moreover, the homoemotionalism at work here seems far from homoeroticism. Unlike Rousselet's and Murray's sinister older men, Henty's good surrogate fathers do not call Jack "Ducky" or desire to own him "body and soul" in a way calculated to "drag him down to perdition"; unlike the good fathers we have seen in other stories, they do not even clasp his hand in a warm yet manly fashion. But "Facing Death" also seems designed as an attempt to get the middle-class reader to accept working-class boys as potential equals who may be blended into the middle-class "family" both through assimilation and through marriage. Jack's attractiveness is thus both his class difference from the reader (who would have expected a miner's son to be so perfect?) and the eventual erasure of this difference as Jack sits at the middle-class table and sends his origins across the street. Even so, and despite all the first-naming of Bill in the body of the story, we hear at the last that Jack "still affectionately calls [Bill and Jane] 'dad' and 'mother.'"[35] Just enough class difference is retained to render piquant our identification with Jack—presumably a homoemotional identification, since *The Union Jack*'s readers are predominantly boys.

Exchanges such as the ones performed in Henty's tale may also be motivated, at least ostensibly, by the death of the original father. Take S. Clarke Hook's "'By Nelson's Side': The True Story of Nelson's Famous Powder Monkey" (*Pluck,* 1894–95), in which the title character, Alec, loses his adored parent in battle but gains multiple father-substitutes, from Nelson himself to gunnery captain Jack Bell. The comportment of these two men toward Alec establishes the father's proper role: it is to comfort, protect, and nurture (all actions more conventionally associated with Victorian motherhood), while the son may reciprocate by prolonging the father's life. The all-male "domesticity" possible in the navy is, by Hook's account, so complete that no male-female ties are necessary for emotional satisfaction. Nor is the original father to be criticized, despite the narrative's need to replace him; when the ship's bully, Tally, calls Alec's father a coward and a fight ensues, Nelson adjudicates, stating flatly, "A braver man than your father never lived. You were utterly wrong, Tally, in speaking as you did to the boy, under any circumstances, and your assertion was untrue. I cannot punish a lad for upholding his father's honour." When the sea story eventually segues, in the inimitable fashion of the working-class boy's serial, into a narrative of detection, the villain's crime in burning down the house belonging to another of Alec's protectors, Harry Richardson, is the more heinous because the act has destroyed "many things that we value greatly because they belonged to my father," as Harry laments.[36] Treasured, even fetishized, material goods associated with the departed parent, such as favorite possessions or Alec's father's medal for bravery, stand in for that parent but also suggest the ease with which fathers can be added to or exchanged. Fathers are all the more desirable because they are fungible.

Not that sons are irreplaceable either. In a short story published in the somewhat more upscale *Chums* in 1892, "'Duty First!' The Story of Our Old French Master, by the Author of 'One of the Light Brigade,'" the schoolboy narrator, Bellamy, chafes under the burden of having to learn French until his teacher, Anatole Alsace, reminds him that "you must learn the great lesson of obedience to authority or you will never make a man." At this comment, "Bellamy looked up quickly, and the master saw that there was a chord in his nature which would vibrate under a skillful touch." A series of conversations between boy and man ensues, in which Alsace both tells Bellamy thrilling French war stories and signals his willingness to stand in for Bellamy *père:* "'Does your father smoke? . . . Then I suppose I may smoke too, without setting you a bad example.' . . . Smoking vigorously, until the room grew misty before the eyes of the delighted boy, Monsieur Anatole warmed with his subject . . . his text being always 'DUTY!'" After the eighty-four-year-old master heeds his country's call to arms during the Franco-Prussian War, leaving Bellamy with a parting kiss and a reminder that duty is all-important, the newspapers report that he is a baron with a field command. Alsace's forces capture a spy, who "prove[s] to be the Baron's only son, whose persistent profligacy had brought ruin on the family, and who now disgraced alike his father and his country's cause"; duty ever uppermost in his mind, Alsace has his son executed and subsequently loses his own life on the battlefield. Because he has been able to form a loving bond with Bellamy, however, Alsace does not die childless: the narrator assures us that the English son has learned the lesson of "duty before everything," even if the French son has not.[37]

Other stories vary this pattern of infinitely replaceable parts within the male family by suggesting the same accretive possibilities that exist within serials discussed earlier, such as "Cameron's Last Chance!" The difference is that instead of ringing down the curtain on a triangle composed of two postadolescent boys and an adult man, tales within this subset envision the happy ending as consisting of two "fathers" and a son. The emotional satisfactions of such a configuration are clearly just as rich as in the earlier type, however, as H. C. Crosfield's 1905 *Captain* serial "The Adventures of John Baywood" demonstrates. Set in the 1630s, this narrative focuses on how the title character is forced to leave Massachusetts and his stern father owing to the jealousy of Zephaniah Eccles, his rival for the affections of a young woman named Verity. John's deepest sadness seems to be elicited by separation not from his ladylove but from his father, since "there had never been any tenderness between us, yet now I knew that he was suffering more than I was." But John finds an unlikely substitute father in Barnabas Skeffington, the sea captain who shanghais him into his crew; while Skeffington lacks the senior Baywood's probity, he makes up for this deficiency inasmuch as he is "easily pacified, warm and faithful in friendship."[38]

This relationship, indeed, is all that sustains John when they find themselves enslaved on the island of Hispaniola—only "the Captain's friendship . . . redeems the time from being one of abject and hopeless misery," he reports—and gradually it succeeds also in redeeming Skeffington himself, who as a Cambridge dropout has the potential to embrace better careers than piracy. To put to rest the story that John has fled under his own steam, Skeffington testifies to having kidnapped him: "I love this lad Jack like mine own son, and I desire to make amends for the ill trick I was deceived into playing him." After the captain saves John's life three times, John is finally in a position to make up the quarrel with his father, who apologizes profusely for his lack of tenderness, and to marry Verity. But Verity herself makes clear who the real marriage partners are when she notes, "I verily believe that thou lovest Barnabas Skeffington more than me, thine own wedded wife."[39] Heterosexual ties in these tales exist primarily to signal the protagonists' full membership in the adult community—specifically, the community of adult men. It is the homoemotional ties between father and son or brother and brother that furnish the true romance.

While narrative patterns such as the ones identified here appear with startling frequency in turn-of-the-century boys' magazine fiction, they are by no means limited to that set of texts. Herbert Sussman, for instance, has identified within early Victorian fiction a "masculine plot" that focuses on "bonding with the father or more often a surrogate father. This process of bonding involves, first, ritualized rejection by the father, then acceptance by the surrogate father sealed by chaste bodily contact within carefully controlled rituals of male-male physicality"; it also involves a rejection of the marriage plot.[40] Sussman and James Eli Adams both see the "masculine plot," as expressed by such canonical writers as Carlyle, as "radically challeng[ing] Victorian domestic ideology" in ignoring the female.[41] But in the case of late-century mass-market writing for boys of the type that I have been examining here, I propose that what we see is rather a radical *acceptance* of domestic ideology, a contention that the masculine plot and the marriage plot can and should be combined. To return to Clark's point (cited at the beginning of this essay), the removal of women from a narrative and the contention that they are not the ultimate good need not imply a rejection of the values conventionally associated with femininity. Rather, the tales suggest an attempt to claim the domestic and the emotional for men, to recast in a single-sex mold values that we now prefer to define as heterosocial. Magazine adventure stories certainly tell boys that domesticity is difficult, that father-son relationships as "normally" constructed are flawed. But at the same time, they suggest that there is nothing so desirable as that staple of Victorian heterosexual romance, the companionate marriage and the happy egalitarian family. Perhaps it is only the modern reader who will consider it strange that the participants in that marriage and that family are all to be male.

NOTES

1. Eric Trudgill, *Madonnas and Magdalens: The Origins and Development of Victorian Sexual Attitudes* (London: Heinemann, 1976), 146.

2. In *Propaganda and Empire: The Manipulation of British Public Opinion, 1880–1960* (Manchester: Manchester University Press, 1984), 207, John M. MacKenzie hypothesizes that the reason that so much late-nineteenth-century boys' fiction describes a male-dominated world is that it was a literature that glorified war, a homosocial activity. Certainly combat of all kinds is a major feature of these stories, yet the reverse might equally be the case: authors focus on war in part because doing so allows them to glorify that male-dominated world.

3. Beverly Lyon Clark, *Regendering the School Story: Sassy Sissies and Tattling Tomboys* (New York: Garland, 1996), 212.

4. See, for instance, Kenneth Allsop, "A Coupon for Instant Tradition: On

'Tom Brown's Schooldays,'" *Encounter* 25.5 (1965): 60–63; Jonathan Gathorne-Hardy, *The Old School Tie: The Phenomenon of the English Public School* (New York: Viking, 1978), 177; Isabel Quigly, *The Heirs of Tom Brown: The English School Story* (London: Chatto and Windus, 1982).

5. Jeffrey Richards, "'Passing the Love of Women': Manly Love and Victorian Society," in *Manliness and Morality: Middle-Class Masculinity in Britain and America, 1800–1940*, ed. J. A. Mangan and James Walvin (Manchester: Manchester University Press, 1987), 117.

6. See Jeffrey Weeks, "Inverts, Perverts, and Mary-Annes: Male Prostitution and the Regulation of Homosexuality in England in the Nineteenth and Early Twentieth Centuries," in *Hidden from History: Reclaiming the Gay and Lesbian Past*, ed. Martin Bauml Duberman, Martha Vicinus, and George Chauncey Jr. (New York: New American Library, 1989), 195–211.

7. Since the original publication of this essay, Sharon Marcus's fascinating study *Between Women: Friendship, Desire, and Marriage in Victorian England* (Princeton: Princeton University Press, 2007), 29, has made a similar argument for women, suggesting, for instance, that to the extent that particular "nineteenth-century lesbian relationships resembled marriages," they enjoyed "a high degree of acceptance by respectable society."

8. Claudia Nelson, *Invisible Men: Fatherhood in Victorian Periodicals, 1850–1910* (Athens: University of Georgia Press, 1995), 141–69.

9. I do not mean to imply that this phenomenon was peculiar to Britain. In discussing the work of Horatio Alger, for instance, Michael Moon analyzes the twin currents of homoeroticism and homodomesticity in these boys' stories of Gilded Age America. Moon ascribes some of Alger's popularity to the tales' depiction of all-boy families as "idyllic, domestic, self-perpetuating, untroubled by . . . the 'threat' (to male supremacy) of female enfranchisement," noting that while this picture strikes us as odd today, it speaks to deep and widespread longings within its original nineteenth-century context. See "'The Gentle Boy from the Dangerous Classes': Pederasty, Domesticity, and Capitalism in Horatio Alger," *Representations* 19 (Summer 1987): 106–7. The question of cultural differences and similarities between mid-Victorian America and turn-of-the-century Britain is outside my scope here, but the extent to which the (homo)emotional preoccupations of Alger's novels resemble those of the British magazine stories I am examining suggests that the rigid gendering of our own ideas about domesticity and bonding is a comparatively recent phenomenon.

10. I focus this essay on the magazine serial adventure rather than on adventures first published in book form in part because still more than boys' fiction as a whole, the vast territory of turn-of-the-century boys' magazine fiction remains more or less uncharted by scholarly explorers. But readers acquainted with the canonical adventure stories of the period—many of which, from *Treasure Island* (1885) to *Prester John* (1910) and Frances Hodgson Burnett's *The Lost Prince* (1915), started life in serial form—may well see resemblances between the works I discuss here and those that remain in print today. For comment on the kinds of emotional patterns to be found in these better-known tales, see

Claudia Nelson, *Boys Will Be Girls: The Feminine Ethic and British Children's Fiction, 1857–1917* (New Brunswick: Rutgers University Press, 1991), 117–46. I discuss the ideology of the boys' magazine of this era at greater length in "Mixed Messages: Authoring and Authority in British Boys' Magazines," *The Lion and the Unicorn* 21.1 (1997): 1–19, in which I argue that editors typically preferred contributions whose attitude toward authority and hierarchy was ambiguous; such tales could thus appeal to both the socially powerful and the socially powerless.

11. Thomas Hughes, *Tom Brown's Schooldays,* ed. Andrew Sanders (New York: Oxford University Press, 1989), 233.

12. Robert H. MacDonald, "Signs from the Imperial Quarter: Illustrations in *Chums, 1892–1914*," *Children's Literature* 16 (1988): 45–46.

13. Guy Rayner (S. Dacre Clarke), "Harry Stanton: A Story of Real Life," *The Boy's Graphic* 1 (1890): 17.

14. Gordon Wallace, "Cameron's Last Chance!," *The Boy's Journal* 1 (1913–14): 29.

15. Ibid., 54; these related ideas are juxtaposed in the text.

16. Ibid., 245.

17. Ibid., 210.

18. Ibid., 245.

19. For instance, Benson, employed by Sir Andrew to check up on Arthur's progress, disguises himself as an elderly man because "I thought Cameron would be more interested in me" (Wallace, "Cameron's Last Chance!" 212). Once Arthur has waded into a gaggle of toughs assaulting this apparent "old man," "his hard, brown fists flashing like the piston-rods of a steam-engine" (Wallace, 208), Benson can reveal himself to Bart as the hale forty-year-old that he is.

20. Rayner, "Harry Stanton: A Story of Real Life," 3. That the language in these stories often seems by today's lights to be characterized by excess and melodrama may be one indication of shifting attitudes toward homoemotionalism, since in the nineteenth century it smacked more of cliché than of camp.

21. Nelson Power, "The Fighting Footballer; Or, The Sporting Chance," *The Boy's Journal* 1 (1913–14): 253.

22. Power, "The Fighting Footballer," 492. The 1891–92 serial "Axel Ebersen: The Graduate of Upsala," by André Laurie (*Boy's Own Paper* 14), varies this conflation of father-son love and married love. In Laurie's tale, the love and tutelage of a kindly schoolmaster (who says of the young Axel, "I felt I could have kissed him. . . . this young rascal, with his frank and gentle eye, had at once gained my heart, and . . . I already thought of the pleasure I should have in guiding him and instructing him" [150]) give the title character the skill he needs to become a surgeon. Axel practices his calling only once, to cure his distant but adored father after a head injury; he thus becomes effectively his father's "parent," giving "health to his father and sav[ing] his family from want." It is all because of Axel, and the early love between Axel and the schoolmaster, that Mr. Ebersen is "alert and vigorous, launching forth into the great enterprises for which he is so well fitted" (468).

23. Patricia Mary Barnett, "English Boys' Weeklies, 1866–1899," Ph.D. diss., University of Minnesota, 1974, 186–89.

24. Nelson, *Invisible Men,* 202.

25. Quoted in Barnett, "English Boys' Weeklies," 112.

26. Gordon Stables, "The Rough Riders: A Story of the Rebellion in Cuba," *The Captain* 1.5 (1899): 475, 480.

27. Louis Rousselet, "The Two Cabin-Boys: A Story of Adventure by Land and Sea," *The Boy's Own Paper* 4 (1881–82): 29.

28. Ibid., 62.

29. Ibid., 118, 155.

30. Richards, "Passing the Love," 93.

31. Geoffrey Murray, "Mighty London!," *The Boy's Journal* 1 (1913–14): 27, 108–9.

32. Ibid., 110, 193.

33. Ibid., 413, 322. Christopher Craft points to a very similar arrangement in *Dracula* (1897), in which, as he argues, Lucy and Mina "mediate and displace a more direct communion among males." Like "Mighty London!," Bram Stoker's novel "does not dismiss homoerotic desire and threat; rather it simply continues to diffuse and displace it." See Christopher Craft, " 'Kiss Me with Those Red Lips': Gender and Inversion in Bram Stoker's *Dracula*," *Representations* 8 (Fall 1984), partially reprinted in *Dracula,* ed. Nina Auerbach and David J. Skal (New York: Norton, 1997), 447. This pattern is not uncommon in turn-of-the-century popular fiction.

34. G. A. Henty, "Facing Death: A Tale of the Coal Mines," *The Union Jack* 1 (1880): 245, 312.

35. Ibid., 312.

36. S. Clarke Hook, " 'By Nelson's Side': The True Story of Nelson's Famous Powder Monkey," *Pluck* 1–2 (1894–95): 1.14, 2.13.

37. " 'Duty First!' The Story of Our Old French Master," *Chums* 1.7 (26 October 1892): 100–101.

38. H. C. Crosfield, "The Adventures of John Baywood," *Captain* 13 (1905): 7, 12.

39. Ibid., 103, 341, 494, 493.

40. Herbert Sussman, *Victorian Masculinities: Manhood and Masculine Poetics in Early Victorian Literature and Art* (New York: Cambridge University Press, 1995), 47.

41. James Eli Adams, *Dandies and Desert Saints: Styles of Victorian Manhood* (Ithaca: Cornell University Press, 1995), 63.

Queer Performances

Lesbian Politics in Little Women

۶&

ROBERTA SEELINGER TRITES

Early in *Little Women,* Jo March's "queer performances" scandalize her sister Meg.[1] Alcott often uses the word "queer" to describe Jo's (and her own) nonconformist behavior, but the adjective provides the contemporary reader with a punning metaphor that aptly sums up one of the most subversive elements of the novel, and the noun prefigures Judith Butler's arguments about the performative nature of gender. As Butler puts it, "That the gendered body is performative suggests that it has no ontological status apart from the various acts which constitute its reality."[2] Later, she advises her reader to think of gender "as *a corporeal style,* an 'act,' as it were, which is both intentional and performative, where *'performative'* suggests a dramatic and contingent construction of meaning."[3] Thus, Butler argues, gender is not a biological construct; it is a social one. Jo's most blatant act of conformism is her rejection of socially inscribed heterosexual gender roles; the text often describes her "performances" in masculine terms to express her androgynous nonconformity.[4] In Jo's refusal to perform her prescribed gender role lies a critique of heterosexuality that can be read as a strong affirmation of lesbian politics.

Gender roles rarely exist independent of sexuality. Certainly for Jo March, the assumption of a gender role also marks the assumption of a corresponding sexual persona. For example, when playing the villain in the play she and her sister perform early in the novel, Jo exerts a

33

predatory masculine sexuality over her sister Amy's passive femininity.[5] Several years later when Amy and Jo pay calls on a few friends, Amy admonishes her sister to "gossip as other girls do, and be interested in dress and flirtations, and whatever nonsense comes up."[6] Jo fulfills this ultrafemme role so well that Amy is appalled. As the only time in the text when Jo panders to "laughing gentlemen" in the way that a conventional heterosexual flirt would,[7] this passage demonstrates that sexuality is inseparable from gender role.

Jo performs the sexual role of the flirt simply by asserting her understanding of a societally sanctioned gender role. At various times in the text, Jo plays roles that are defined by lesbianism, by androgyny, by homosociality, by homoeroticism, and even, eventually, by heterosexuality. These shifting manifestations of female sexuality provide *Little Women* with a subtext that both destabilizes Victorian notions of sexuality and explores the nuances of lesbian community. To investigate the shifting permutations of lesbianism in *Little Women,* I will interrogate Alcott's own ambiguous sexuality and explore various theories that engage the myriad nuances of lesbian reading. The critical methodologies that lesbian theory offers the reader lead, then, to the possibilities of interpreting *Little Women* as a lesbian text.

Alcott a Dyke?

The 1995 publication of *A Long Fatal Love Chase* has foregrounded the sexual possibilities in the Alcott canon, but historically, most Alcott critics seem uncomfortable with issues of the author's sexuality.[8] Alcott herself cloaked whatever romantic experiences she had, expurgating her journals and burning myriad letters. Madeleine Stern's explanation of Alcott's self-censorship in the introduction to *The Journals of Louisa May Alcott* is representative of the tendency among critics to deny Alcott's sexuality: "That knowledge [of the fact that some of the journals have been destroyed or have vanished] naturally prompts the conjecture as to what has disappeared. References to sexual encounters? Unlikely. Had Alcott formed any close attachments of the kind, she would have woven them into her fiction rather than explicated them in her journals."[9] Stern's dismissal of Alcott's sexuality with a peremptory "unlikely" seems disingenuous in light of such journal entries as one in December 1865. What is left of the journal entry reads: "A little romance with Lladislas. W[isniewski]. [undeciphered]."[10] Beside the undecipherable passage, Alcott later wrote, "Couldn't be."[11] An endnote explains that this is the only place in Alcott's journals where she scratched out the entry so vigorously that she destroyed the paper.[12] The violence with which Alcott edited her words, however, admits the possibility of *some* sort of sexual encounter, despite Stern's efforts to bowdlerize Alcott's life.[13]

Elaine Showalter is one of a few critics who raise the possibility of Alcott's lesbianism.[14] But the critic sidesteps the issue when she concludes that *Little Women* is a paean to "egalitarian" heterosexual marriages.[15] Many critics, like Showalter, have been more interested in Jo's desire for independence than in her sexual desires, but the two are inextricably linked because Jo's independence is the direct result of her shifting sexual orientation. What is important in her rejection of Laurie's marriage proposal is her refusal to participate in the dependence inherent in nineteenth-century heterosexuality.[16] The various forms of lesbianism in which Jo participates provide her with the autonomy absent from conventional heterosexuality. Nevertheless, critics tend to ignore how much this type of sexual tension informs *Little Women* as often as they ignore Alcott's own sexuality.

Heterosexuality manifests itself in the novel in ways that seem almost parodies of Freudianism: the only male to whom Jo is attracted is an obvious reincarnation of her father. Alcott even describes that character's creation as a joke that catered to patriarchal conventions. On March 20, 1869, in a passage that demonstrates how Alcott wished to parody the social construction of gender roles, she wrote to Elizabeth Powell, then an instructor at Vassar: " 'Jo' should have remained a literary spinster but so many enthusiastic young ladies wrote to me clamorously demanding that she should marry Laurie, *or* somebody, that I didnt dare to refuse & out of perversity went & made a funny match for her. I expect vials of wrath to be poured out upon my head, but rather enjoy the prospect."[17] Alcott knows that Jo must perform within circumscribed limits, but she intentionally undercuts the legitimacy of that performance by making it seem comic.

Even though such narrative acts as Jo's marriage to a parody of her father distort the Freudian masterplot, critics including Ann B. Murphy, Anne Hollander, Madelon Bedell, Jerry Griswold, Shirley Foster, and Judy Simons insist on interpreting the novel as a tale that reinforces the hegemony of Freudian heterosexuality.[18] For example, Griswold quotes with approbation Bedell's description of Jo's cutting her hair as "a delicious father-daughter fantasy" because it supports his Oedipal reading of *Little Women*.[19] Griswold maintains that Jo's shearing has been in vain because no one ever wants or uses the money she has raised for her father. Thus, Griswold interprets the act as a completely unnecessary self-sacrifice performed solely to demonstrate the young girl's devotion to her father.[20] Griswold's immersion in post-Freudian thinking blinds him to other less heterosexist readings of the novel.

But to complicate matters further, Alcott's own pronouncements about gender often bordered upon a misogyny that would seem to preclude the possibility of her lesbianism. In 1860 she wrote in a letter to her friend Alf Whitman: "I was born with a boy's nature & always had more sympathy for & interest in them than in girls."[21] In 1868, shortly before publishing *Little Women*, Alcott wrote a similar passage in her journal: "Never liked girls or knew many, except my sisters, but our queer plays and experiences may prove interesting, though I doubt it."[22] There's that word "queer" again, this time also associated with playing. Here Alcott uses the word to cast herself and her sisters as characters who exist outside the expected norm for femininity: they are playing a role, but she defines that role for all of them as being one of otherness.

When noting some of the ambiguity surrounding Alcott's sexuality, Showalter cites Alcott's 1883 interview with Louise Chandler Moulton, in which Alcott asserts, "I am more than half-persuaded that I am a man's soul, put by some freak of nature into a woman's body . . . because I have fallen in love in my life with so many pretty girls and never once the least bit with any man."[23] Hardly the words of a misogynist, this passage provides us with an invitation to investigate Alcott's sense of her own sexual identity in terms of the concept of "inversion" popularized by sexologists Richard von Krafft-Ebing and Havelock Ellis. Precursors of Freud, sexologists argued that lesbians were people whose physical gender did not match their mental gender.[24] Significantly, however, the language of inversion—the idea of being a woman with a man's soul—was not popularized in America until the 1880s. It is quite conceivable that Alcott's language in the 1883 Moulton interview was influenced by a knowledge of the sexologists' notion of inversion. Having written *Little Women* twenty years before inversion was popularized as a psychological diagnosis, however, Alcott was something of a prophet of inversion as a concept.[25]

The contradictions embedded in Alcott's letter to Alf Whitman, in her journal, and in her interview with Moulton typify the ambiguity that surrounds Alcott's attitudes toward gender. In her thirties, she claimed never to have liked girls, but she never entered into long-lasting heterosexual relationships either; in her fifties, she said this was because she loved females more readily than she loved males. She did not like to write about females but wrote about them far more convincingly than she did about males; she seemed to loathe her own femininity but to worship it in her mother and sisters.[26] Understanding that Alcott felt her body and her mind to be the inverse of each other helps us to discern that Alcott lived with a shifting sense of her own sexuality. That ambivalence led her to destabilize Victorian notions of heterosexuality in *Little Women;* as a result, the text provides us with a kaleidoscope of possible interpretations regarding female sexuality.

Queer Theories

Some of the most interesting sexual politics in the novel surround Jo's female-centeredness, yet most critics have shied away from the meaning of Jo's passion for her mother and sisters.[27] Jo's devotion to these women is expressed most notably when she declares that "mothers are the *best* lovers in the world" and when she wishes that "I could marry Meg myself, and keep her safe in the family."[28] Nina Auerbach joins the ranks of those who deny the text's lesbian politics when she claims that Jo's proclamation about Meg is intended to express loyalty, not erotic love: "Allegiance is more important than sexuality."[29] But Jo's proclamations are rooted too firmly in the language of passionate love to pass for simple expressions of familial love. Lillian Faderman notes that such intense female relationships as those between Jo and her mother and sisters—what Faderman sometimes calls "romantic friendship"[30] and what Carroll Smith-Rosenberg calls "homosocial" relationships[31]—were so common in the nineteenth century that they were not regarded as pathological, as Auerbach's denial of the romance blatant in Jo's statement would indicate. Indeed, Victorians did not consider such relationships abnormal because they were "common enough to be a norm."[32] Faderman calls such "women-identified women" lesbians, regardless of whether or not they had genital contact with other women.[33]

Faderman's definition of lesbianism has come under attack by a number of lesbian theorists for being too inclusive. Lisa Moore, for example, critiques both Faderman and Smith-Rosenberg for "obscur[ing] the wariness and even prohibition that sometimes surrounded women's friendships, leaving us with a flattened notion of contesting constructions of female sexuality in late-eighteenth-century and early-nineteenth-century England."[34] Martha Vicinus thinks that calling all women-identified women lesbians "neglects both the element of sexual object-choice and of marginal status that was (and continues to be) so important in lesbian relationships.[35] But as Diana Fuss maintains, much of the purpose of lesbian (and gay) theory is "to call into question the stability and ineradicability of the hetero-homo hierarchy, suggesting that new (and old) sexual possibilities are no longer thinkable in terms of a simple inside/outside dialectic."[36] Bonnie Zimmerman argues that all definitions of lesbianism are politically motivated and can be useful within specific contexts.[37] And Reina Lewis problematizes the issue historically by acknowledging that "if we recognize the historical and cultural specificity of our current notion of sexual identity, then we must be prepared to find that same-sex relationships are differently defined and represented in texts from a different period or culture."[38] Thus, defining lesbianism in absolute terms seems to me a counterproductive reversion to heterosexist dialectics. Moreover, following Lewis, I find Faderman's and Smith-Rosenberg's definitions especially useful as a way to articulate the repression of female-female sexuality in the nineteenth century. Since overt sexuality was generally taboo in nineteenth-century Anglo-American children's texts, lesbian sexuality was perhaps double repressed. On the other hand, if lesbianism was not suspect in early Victorian culture, it might actually have provided an acceptable way for early Victorian writers to explore sexuality in children's books. Either way, I find Faderman's and Smith-Rosenberg's language pertinent to the identification of lesbian sexuality as it appears in the interstices of nineteenth-century children's literature.

As Alcott is definitely a "woman-identified woman," in Faderman's economy, Alcott is a lesbian writer. Alcott and her literary creation Jo March[39] both define themselves in relationships to other women; both care much more intensely about women than they do about men. Faderman makes note of the passionate friendships Alcott depicts in *Work*, "Happy Women," *An Old-Fashioned Girl*, and *Diana and Persis*.[40] *Work*, for example, ends with a multigenerational community of women-centered women clasping hands to show their solidarity. Faderman also describes Alcott's friendships with the sculptor Emma Stebbins and "her mate, a leading American actress, Charlotte Cushman."[41] Alcott's knowledge of such Boston marriages shows up in the relationship between two artists named Rebecca Jeffrey and Lizzie Small in *An Old-Fashioned Girl*. Faderman writes, "Although no biographer has yet been able to furnish evidence that Louisa May Alcott had such relationships herself, it is certain that she avoided heterosexual marriage . . . seeing it as incompatible with her goals.[42]

For my purposes, it is immaterial whether or not Alcott had sex with other women. It may be, as Showalter claims, "impossible to say whether [Alcott's] own spinsterhood was the result of a lesbian sexual preference unfulfilled in Victorian culture"[43] or indeed, impossible to say if her lesbianism might actually have been physically fulfilled. But it is not impossible to investigate the lesbian subtexts that exist in *Little Women*. Thus, I am far more interested in the enactments in *Little Women* of homosocial or passionate friendships that support a lesbian reading than I am in Alcott's sexuality. The central question I wish to investigate is this: Whom does Jo desire? For most of the novel, Jo's "primary emotional and erotic allegiance" is to women, for it is with women that she feels most.[44] Her homosociality often masks a homoeroticism that celebrates lesbian potential. When the empowerment of women is the result of homosocial passion as it so often is in *Little Women*, one of the sexual subtexts that emerges is distinctly lesbian.

Jo and Marmee

Carroll Smith-Rosenberg writes of nineteenth-century homosociality, "Women, who had little status or power in the larger world of male concerns, possessed status and power in the lives and worlds of other women."[45] Alcott's life and her fictional creations exemplify Smith-Rosenberg's point: as a woman in a world where female status was devalued, Alcott depicted in her fiction a homosocial female world wherein women could gain power denied them by the patriarchy. Bonnie Zimmerman also identifies the links among sexual orientation, female community, and creativity when she describes some of the shared tenets that inform much lesbian criticism: "Powerful bonds between women are a crucial factor in women's lives, and . . . the sexual and emotional orientation of a woman profoundly affects her consciousness and thus her creativity."[46] Thus, Alcott's lesbian sensitivity asserts itself in the creation of the woman-centered world of the Marches. In depicting this homosocial world, Alcott empowered herself and created powerful female characters whose strength derives almost entirely from other women. Jo's relationships with her mother and with her sisters and her intense desire to use these relationships to exclude the possibility of male relationships that might intrude upon their world exemplify how the passionate friendships of Victorian women were enunciated in literary fiction. Sifting through the many instances when Jo's homosociality cloaks the homoeroticism in her relationships with Marmee, with Beth, and with Meg, we can uncover lesbian patterns in *Little Women*.

The passion Jo feels for her mother typifies the homosocial connections between mothers and daughters in the nineteenth century. Smith-Rosenberg believes that the female world so many women experienced in that century originated in the same-sex networks that evolved as "the roles of daughter and mother shaded imperceptibly and ineluctably into each other, while the biological realities of frequent pregnancies, childbirth, nursing, and menopause bound women together in physical and emotional intimacy."[47] On a similar note, Catharine Stimpson describes the importance of mother-daughter relationships in lesbian fiction, for many lesbian novels are explorations of female communities that portray the mother-daughter relationship paradigmatically. Stimpson maintains that "a mother waits at the heart of the labyrinth of some lesbian texts"; she notes how often female characters engage the mother-daughter relationship as a way of experiencing both self-love and dependent love.[48]

While Stimpson delineates the recurrence of symbolic mother-daughter love in twentieth-century lesbian novels, Jo and Marmee enact the principle in a nineteenth-century text, for through her mother, Jo explores both her feelings about herself and her psychological dependence on women. All of the girls in *Little Women* "g[i]ve their hearts into their mother's keeping," but the reader knows more about Jo's heart being given to her mother than about any of her sisters'. From her mother's approbation, Jo gains the power of self-acceptance, especially notable when Marmee teaches Jo to accept (and repress) her anger. Much of the reason for Jo's intimacy with women occurs because she learns from her mother that only with other women is she allowed to express fully her feelings about such taboo subjects as anger. Because she has learned this lesson from her mother, Jo willingly immerses herself in female homosociety as Smith-Rosenberg defines it.

Analyzing a level of intimacy even more intense than homosociety,

Ann B. Murphy notes the homoeroticism in Marmee and Jo's relation-ship. She writes, "Marmee's seductive, loving presence, which creates a profound and inescapable homoerotic undercurrent throughout the novel, eventually subverts the appeal of heterosexual eroticism entirely, while the text utterly refuses to imagine or tolerate any other kind of desire. Thus while homoeroticism is never permitted direct expression, it dominates the action and feelings of the female characters."[49] Mur-phy points out that Meg reserves the first kiss after she is married for her mother and that Jo "rejects her mother's characterization of hetero-sexual love as 'the best love of all'" when she defines mothers as the best lovers.[50] Murphy puts her homoerotic reading of *Little Women,* however, in the service of a feminist psychoanalytic interpretation, maintaining that Jo cannot fully explore her heterosexual eroticism be-cause she lives in the "powerful shadow" of her pre-Oedipal attach-ment to her mother.[51] While Murphy's analysis reveals yet another di-mension of female sexuality at work in *Little Women,* she ultimately presents both strong mothers and homoeroticism as antithetical to what she implies is normal development.[52] Murphy problematizes Jo's heterosexuality, but she still insinuates that the lesbian possibilities in Jo and Marmee's relationship are suspect.

In actuality, the homoeroticism of their relationship gives them both strength. For example, in the opening chapter, Jo claims the sole power to protect and nurture Marmee, telling her sisters, "I'm the man of the family now papa is away, and *I* shall provide the slippers, for he told me to take special care of mother while he was gone."[53] Jo appropriates her father's role so that she can assert her possession of her mother. In sending Jo's father to serve in the Civil War, Alcott seems to be revising her own experience to emphasize the homosocial relationship between mother and daughter, for her own father never did conveniently leave to serve in the war so that his second daughter could play the role of husband. But for much of the novel, Jo willingly assumes many of the social roles of Victorian husbands: she wants to protect Marmee; she earns money to give to her mother; and—most important—she is her mother's chief confidante.

The intimacy that Jo and her mother experience affects them both profoundly. Of their shared confidences, Jo says, "It's so comfortable to say all I think to you, and feel so safe and happy here,"[54] and with her mother, she displays a physical affection she rarely displays with any-one else, kissing her and holding her close. Marmee reciprocates the intimacy, for only to Jo does Marmee reveal how her husband has effectively forced her to repress her anger. The revelation makes Jo feel "nearer and nearer to her mother than ever before."[55] Later, Marmee also tells Jo that John Brooke has asked to marry Meg before telling the young woman herself. Marmee makes clear that she gains as much strength from their relationship as Jo does when she tells her daughter, "I always feel strong when you are at home."[56] Marmee cannot depend on her other daughters to make her feel strong: "Now Meg is gone. Beth is too feeble, and Amy too young to depend upon; but when the tug comes, you are always ready."[57] The narrator refers to Jo and Marmee's intimate conversations as "sacred moments! when heart talked to heart in the silence of the night."[58] After Beth's death, only Jo's relationship with her mother relieves her grief: "Life looked more endurable, seen from the safe shelter of her mother's arms."[59] Jo's and Marmee's feelings for each other are certainly homosocial, but in their tendency to desire an isolation from other people lies a veiled homoeroticism that empowers them both.

Jo and Her Sisters

Other lesbian possibilities are at work in Jo's relationships with her sisters. The narrator even pairs the girls into couples early in the book: "Meg was Amy's confidant and monitor, and, by some strange attraction of opposites, Jo was gentle Beth's. . . . The two older girls were a great deal to each other, but both took one of the younger into their keeping, and watched over them in their own way."[60] Thus, from early in the text, Jo is paired first with Beth and then with Meg.[61] In both of these relationships, Jo often plays a masculinized role. From the very first page of the book, Jo rejects the restrictive Victorian gender roles that her sisters so comfortably execute. Her rejection takes the form of a performance: She acts like a boy. Jo's third statement in the opening chapter is followed by her "examining the heels of her shoes in a gentlemanly manner"; farther down the page she "put her hands in her apron pockets, and began to whistle."[62] When her younger sister Amy chides her for such "boyish" behavior, Jo admits, "That's why I do it."[63] Telling Jo she is "old enough to leave off boyish tricks," Meg joins Amy in her attempts to get Jo to recognize that she is "a young lady," but Jo adamantly refuses to play out her prescribed gender role, declaring: "I ain't! and if turning up my hair makes me one, I'll wear it in two tails till I'm twenty. . . . I hate to think I've got to grow up and be Miss March, and wear long gowns, and look as prim as a China-aster! It's bad enough to be a girl, any-way, when I like boy's games, and work, and manners! I can't get over my disappointment in not being a boy, and it's worse than ever now, for I'm dying to go and fight with papa, and I can only stay at home and knit like a poky old woman."[64] Beth consoles Jo, advising her to continue performing the masculine role she finds most comfortable: "Poor Jo; it's too bad! But it can't be helped, so you must try to be contented with making your name boyish, and playing brother to us girls."[65] Beth's understanding of Jo's frustration carries a deep significance, for she is the only character in the book who shares Jo's refusal to take part in the stifling Victorian marriage plot.

Several times, Jo makes clear that she never intends to marry; that is, she never intends to act heterosexually. In Book I, she "stoutly" declares that she and her sister Meg will be "old maids,' implicating her sister in her plans.[66] When Laurie teases Jo about the eventuality of a suitor carrying her off, she vehemently denies the possibility: "I'd like to see anyone try it."[67] Later she admits to him that she doesn't plan to have any heterosexual affairs because "I should feel like a fool doing it myself."[68] In Book II, just before Meg's wedding, Jo proclaims: "We don't want any more marrying in this family for years to come. . . . Nobody will want me, and it's a mercy, for there should always be one old maid in a family. . . . I'm too busy to be worried with nonsense, and I think it's dreadful to break up families so."[69] Jo's desire is directed to the women in her family, and she wants nothing more than for them to share the same desire. Jo also tells Laurie, "I haven't the least idea of loving [Professor Bhaer], or anybody else."[70] She then adds, "I don't believe I shall ever marry. I'm happy as I am, and love my liberty too well to be in any hurry to give it up for any mortal man."[71] And when Meg compares Jo to a chestnut burr—rough on the outside, but tender inside—Jo acerbically responds, "Boys go nutting, and I don't care to be bagged by them."[72] She decides, "An old maid, that's what I'm to be. A literary spinster, with a pen for a spouse, a family of stories for children, and twenty years hence a morsel of fame, perhaps."[73] Two recurring notes sound throughout Jo's explanations of why she will never marry: First, she recognizes that marriage will entail a loss of her personal power, and second, she does not wish to disrupt the sororal harmony of her home life. To "break up" this homosocial family and the power Jo has within it would be nothing less than "dreadful."[74]

Jo and Beth

Midway through the second half of the novel (at a point when Jo is still adamantly declaring her intentions to remain single), Beth echoes her sentiments: "I'm not like the rest of you; I never made any plans about what I'd do when I grew up; I never thought of being married, as you all did. I couldn't seem to imagine myself anything but stupid little Beth, trotting about at home, of no use anywhere but there. I never wanted to go away."[75] That is, Beth, too, never wants to leave the homosocial environment of her home, where she is loved, accepted, and empowered and where she is not subjected to the self-repression that a heterosexual marriage would demand of her. Beth expresses her "castle in the air" as a desire that "we may all keep well, and be together; nothing else."[76] Like Jo, Beth finds the potential disruption of their sororal world abhorrent.

Beth is especially afraid of any physical separation from Jo that would mark an emotional separation; Beth desires Jo's physical presence as much as Jo desires hers. This mutual desire implies a degree of homoeroticism. Beth tells Jo that she is glad her elder sister is not going to Europe: " 'Jo, dear, I'm very selfish, but I couldn't spare you, and I'm glad you ain't going quite yet,' whispered Beth, embracing her, basket and all, with such a clinging touch and loving face, that Jo felt comforted."[77] Beth calls Jo "comfortable" and easily falls asleep "cheek to cheek" with her sister.[78] Their mother recognizes the closeness of the bond between the two girls, admitting that Beth "will open her tender little heart to her Jo sooner than to anyone else."[79] Beth later corroborates their mother's assessment: "I can't speak out, except to my Jo."[80] Beth is silent in the text except through Jo; her longest pieces of dialogue all occur in conversation with Jo. She even says, echoing Marmee, "I feel stronger when you are here."[81] Jo loves her sister so passionately that she "burn[s] to lay herself upon the shrine of sisterly devotion" (325); Beth is "the dearest treasure she possessed."[82] Later, with a "silent kiss," Jo "dedicate[s] herself soul and body to Beth."[83]

Jo's passionate desire to possess her sister becomes most prominent in the chapters in which Beth is mortally ill. Terry Castle identifies the remarkable number of lesbian characters who are portrayed as ghosts.[84] She interprets this as a way the patriarchy mitigates its fears of lesbianism: "One woman or the other must be a ghost, or on the way to becoming one. Passion is excited, only to be obscured, disembodied, decarnalized."[85] Thus, as she is dying, Beth is described in spectral terms: Her face is "no paler, and but little thiner than in the autumn; yet there was a strange, transparent look about it, as if the mortal was being slowly refined away, and the immortal shining through the frail flesh with an indescribable pathetic beauty." Transforming Beth into a ghost frees Alcott to explore the subtleties of homoeroticism without alarming any Victorian censors. After this point in the text, Beth exists for Jo only as a disembodied memory, but one that she can fondle and caress without censure. Beth dies not to uphold the passivity of the Cult of True Womanhood but to veil the lesbianism fueling the novel.

During the lingering illness that leads to Beth's death, Jo finds a singleness of purpose in nursing her sister. The two live almost exclusively in each other's company, "preferring to live for one another" in part because Jo is "too wrapt up in her to care for anyone else; so they were all in all to each other, and came and went, quite unconscious of the interest they excited in those about them,—who watched with sympathetic eyes the strong sister and the feeble one, always together."[86] Jo reproaches Beth for not revealing that she knows she is about to die in language that indicates how empowering Jo finds their closeness: "How could you shut me out, and bear it all alone?"[87] After admitting that she loves Beth more than anyone in the world, Jo says in the voice of a lover, "I used to think I couldn't let you go; but I'm learning to feel that I don't lose you; that you'll be more to me than ever, and death can't part us, though it seems to."[88] The spectral lover Beth will endure even if the corporeal one cannot.

After Beth's death, Jo feels a "ceaseless longing" for her sister and is convinced that all the "light, and warmth, and beauty" are gone from her home[89] because Beth had given her an unconditional love that no one else can give her. With Beth, Jo could be strong without being condemned for being unfeminine; with Beth, Jo could be her "queer" self and still be not only accepted but also loved. With Beth gone, Jo has lost her greatest love. Beth's death is thus the single most important narrative event that leads to Jo's "compulsory heterosexuality," as Adrienne Rich would call it.[90]

Jo and Meg

Jo also mourns when her sister Meg decides to leave their homosocial world for a heterosexual marriage because Meg's emotional desertion of her sister is another narrative event that pushes Jo toward a stifling heterosexual relationship. From the beginning, the text borrows from the language of Victorian heterosexuality to describe the sisters' relationship: Jo loves Meg "very tenderly" and once professes that Meg "gets prettier every day, and I'm in love with her sometimes."[91] Such statements make it clear that Jo has no compunction about publicly expressing her feelings for her sister. Meg reciprocates Jo's tender feelings, although Meg's love for her sister seems at times more conditional than Jo's is. In the first half of the book Meg is often painfully conscious of the sexuality of which Jo is oblivious. Meg reminds Jo that she is a "young lady"[92] and repeatedly critiques Jo's unladylike behavior.[93] Jo may feign oblivion about the implications of her androgynous performances, but Meg criticizes them because she is so conscious of her sister's and her own sexuality. It is Meg who has protected Jo from interacting with "the Laurence boy" next door; she will not let Jo speak to him because she is so threatened by his sexuality.[94] Meg's role as the arbiter of sexuality reflects the text's consciousness of the import of Jo's "queer performances." That Meg is so aware of their sexuality makes clear that the textual incidences of Jo's "queerness" are no accident: Meg is the textual signifier who foregrounds Jo's incipient lesbianism.

When Jo first realizes that Meg is falling in love with John Brooke, Jo calls the relationship "horrid" and "ridiculous."[95] Jo fears that her sister is "drifting away from her into a world where she [cannot] follow."[96] Jo feels that she is an outsider to the Victorian marriage plot and that her sister's heterosexuality will immerse them both in the politics of exclusion. Jo is "disgusted . . . at the idea of anybody coming to take Meg away" and grieves over "the separation which must surely come some time, and now seem[s] very near."[97] Jo's grief represents a rejection of the Victorian idealization of marriage. She recognizes that the power she gains from her relationship with her sister will be lost once her sister shifts her intimacy to a relationship with a male. Jo tells her mother, "[Meg]'ll go and fall in love, and there's an end of peace and fun, and cosy times together. . . . Meg will be absorbed, and no good to me any more; Brooke will scratch up a fortune somehow,—carry her off and make a hole in the family; and I shall break my heart, and everything will be abominably uncomfortable."[98] Again, Jo's language casts her as Meg's lover. Jo asks her mother, "Why weren't we all boys? then there wouldn't be any bother."[99] Jo's rhetorical question paints her beliefs clearly: only women can share the type of fulfilling community that she and her mother and sisters share. She asks her mother to send John Brooke packing without telling Meg so that they can "all be jolly together as we always have been."[100] Jo feels threatened by Brooke, and she wants him out of their lives so that their idyllic and exclusive relationships will not be sullied.

When John later proposes to Meg, Jo declares impatiently, "John Brooke is acting dreadfully, and Meg likes it."[101] The text explains Jo's despair: she "found it very hard to see Meg absorbed in a stranger before her face; for Jo loved a few persons very dearly, and dreaded to have their affection lost or lessened in any way."[102] The sisters have known John for some time, so the narrator's calling him a "stranger" is a strong condemnation. John is alien to their homosocial world; he is the Other who can destroy the sisters' romantic friendship.[103] Jo tells Laurie, "You can't know how hard it is for me to give up Meg," meaning that Laurie can never understand the intimacy she has shared with her sister. Laurie tries to comfort her, saying, "You don't give her up. You only go halves," but Jo knows better. She answers Laurie, "It never can be the same again. I've lost my dearest friend."[104] Meg has bowed to the social conditioning that expects marriage of Victorian women. Jo—still strong enough to withstand this conditioning—resents the social imperative that deprives her of her daily intimacy with her sister.

The way the text describes Jo's reaction to the possibility of Meg's marriage makes clear why Jo detests the idea of heterosexual marriage. When she thinks that Meg has rejected John Brooke's proposal, she is appalled to discover that the opposite is true: "Going in to exult over a fallen enemy, and to praise a strong-minded sister for the banishment of an objectionable lover, it certainly *was* a shock to behold the aforesaid enemy serenely sitting on the sofa, with the strong-minded sister enthroned upon his knee, and wearing an expression of the most abject submission."[105] Women outside of heterosexual relationships can be "strong-minded," but they must be "submissive" within them. Jo accurately perceives such relationships as necessitating a loss of female power. She prefers "imaginary heroes to real ones, because, when tired of them, the former could be shut up in the tin kitchen [her writing desk] till called for, and the latter were less manageable."[106] Since women must be submissive in heterosexual relationships and men are not "manageable" (since they have all the power), a traditional Victorian marriage would offer little comfort to a woman used to being empowered in her close relationships. No wonder Jo resists the concept of marriage for so long!

Jo and Laurie

If Beth's death and Meg's marriage are two of the catalysts that lead to Jo's marriage, Laurie's behavior is the third. Laurie ultimately deserts Jo: not when he marries Amy, for by then he has already ruined his relationship with Jo. Instead, his defection occurs when he begins to flirt with Jo, when he betrays the equality of their androgynous relationship and begins to exert over her the masculine pressure endemic to Victorian heterosexuality. At first, Jo and Laurie's relationship is androgynous.[107] He calls himself "Laurie"—apparently an androgynous name at the time—to avoid the homophobic insinuations in his friends' calling him "Dora."[108] He shares many characteristics with the girls who live next door to him: like Meg, he is a romantic; like Jo, he is moody; like Beth, he plays the piano; like Amy, he is artistic. And as Showalter points out, in the original edition of *Little Women* before Roberts Brothers edited the text in 1880 to make it more conventional, Laurie is described in androgynous language: "He is both foreign and androgynous, with 'curly black hair, brown skin, big black eyes, long nose, nice teeth, little hands and feet, tall as I am.'"[109] In later editions, Laurie is less androgynous and is significantly taller than Jo,[110] but he still calls Jo "my dear fellow" and "a good fellow."[111] These appellations in the early part of their relationship demonstrate Laurie's commitment to treating Jo as an equal. And indeed, Jo and Laurie continue throughout most of the first book to play as equals: racing, skating, rowing, going to plays, writing for the family newspaper, and contemplating running away together. Sarah Elbert even calls Laurie the "fifth sister," and as long as he acts like one, the two share a friendship.[112]

Indeed, their early attraction is a strange one, and perhaps the relationship that most strikingly destabilizes Victorian notions of sexuality, for his girlishness and her boyishness provide the text with multiple layers of possibility. For example: If we interpret Laurie as feminized, as Elbert suggests, we can read nuances of a lesbian relationship in their friendship. If we interpret Jo as masculinized, we can read it as homosexual. Martha Saxton supports such a reading when she maintains that Jo rejects Laurie's proposal because "they are too much alike, too male."[113] Or if we interpret both characters androgynously, the relationship seems to be one of like attracting like, as if two inverts have found a perfect match. And finally, if we interpret them both asexually—as scores of traditional critics have—then we can erase the question of their sexuality from the text even more surely than Alcott eventually erases the possibility of Jo's lesbianism.

This much is certain: when Laurie ceases to perform as Jo's "sister," their closeness ends. Once Laurie begins to eschew his androgyny and enact his masculinity—as he first does when he sends for Marmee to come home from Washington and then inappropriately responds to Jo's gratitude by kissing her—Jo and Laurie cannot frolic together without Jo having to worry about Laurie's sexuality. After this, whenever Laurie flirts with Jo, he is trying to force her into the inherently subjugated role of playing belle to his beau, inflicting on her the inequality necessitated by the norms of Victorian heterosexuality. Jo refuses to marry Laurie precisely because she cannot yet play the role of dominated heterosexual hausfrau. She was much happier when their relationship allowed them the lesbian possibility of sexual equality.

Lesbian Dysphoria

Eventually, then, betrayed by Laurie and abandoned by Meg and Beth, Jo marries Professor Bhaer more out of desperate loneliness than anything else. Her first romantic expression of desire for Professor Bhaer is rooted much more solidly in this loneliness than in any declaration of heterosexual passion: "How I should love to see him, for everyone seems going away from me, and I'm all alone."[114] In fact, the entirety of chapter 42, "All Alone," is devoted to how lonely Jo feels. Their relationship, however, has its own embedded lesbianism, as Ann Murphy unwittingly demonstrates when she characterizes Professor Bhaer as feminine because he is "poor, alien, and powerless," even while he is simultaneously a patriarchal figure.[115] If, as Murphy argues, Jo marries Bhaer because she feels less threatened by the emasculated "nonerotic" professor than by Laurie's heterosexual eroticism, then she is practically participating in a Boston marriage with Bhaer.[116] In any event, Jo's sudden immersion in what initially appears to be a traditional love relationship adds yet another dimension to what the text communicates about female sexuality: Heterosexuality colonizes lesbianism.

In being sexually colonized by her marriage to Bhaer, Jo upholds the homosocial erotic triangle that Eve Kosofsky Sedgwick identifies as the defining relationship of nineteenth-century patriarchal fiction.[117] Sedgwick demonstrates how male characters in nineteenth-century fiction use a female character to maintain their homosocial bond with each other.[118] Masculine desire for a woman, in Sedgwick's reading, is actually displaced desire between men. So when Professor Bhaer finally shows up at the March household after a long separation from Jo, he uses as his excuse a desire to meet Mr. March. He directs his conversation—about the "burial customs of the ancients"—to Mr. March and "quenche[s]" Laurie in an argument, but barely speaks to Jo.[119] Bhaer and Jo are, of course, acting out the conventions of Victorian romance that require chaperonage and evasion in lovemaking. And the charade continues in the weeks to follow: "Everyone" recognizes that "Bhaer, while talking philosophy with the father, was giving the daughter lessons in love."[120] But despite being a Victorian convention—or even precisely because it *is* a convention—disguising the congress between two males by using a woman as the signifier of their desire marks the complete disintegration of the lesbian subtext of *Little Women*. The homosocial world of the March women has been destroyed and displaced by male homosocial relationships. The novel therefore displays what Terry Castle calls "dysphoric lesbian counterplotting" because "female homosexual desire" is defined as a "finite phenomenon—a temporary phase in a larger pattern of heterosexual *Bildung*."[121] Jo's lesbian desire has ostensibly been only a stage of her growth; she achieves maturity only when she participates in a male homosocial triangle.

In "Dismembering the Text: The Horror of Louisa May Aclott's *Little Women*," Angela M. Estes and Kathleen M. Lant observe that Jo experiences heterosexual love only after the text has effectively transformed Jo into Beth; Jo agrees to take Beth's place in their parents' home and thereafter becomes progressively more submissive and more willing to participate in a Boston marriage with Bhaer.[122] Estes and Lant demonstrate how many acts of textual violence Jo executes against herself: feeling as if she is cutting up her firstborn, Jo chops up her first novel to please publishers; she abandons Joanna, the doll with the name so similar to her own, whom she has mutilated; she burns her precious manuscripts and quits writing to please Professor Bhaer; and she cuts off her hair in the most memorable act of self-mutilation in the novel.[123] Although Estes and Lant attribute Alcott's repression of Jo to the necessary repression of strong women in the nineteenth century,[124] the destruction of the independent, energetic, and endearing Jo is also the destruction of the lesbian Jo. She must be punished for her queer performances because, as Butler puts it, "discrete genders are part of what 'humanizes' individuals within contemporary culture; indeed, we regularly punish those who fail to do their gender right."[125] The same held true for Victorian women. Thus, as long as Jo is a woman-centered woman, she is too powerful; she must be made to conform, to perform heterosexually.

After Beth's death, Jo tells her mother, "I'd no idea hearts could take in so many—mine is so elastic, it never seems full now, and I used to be quite contented with my family; I don't understand it."' Her mother replies, "I do," and "smile[s] her wise smile."[126] I understand it, too—but perhaps not the way Marmee does. With Meg and Amy married and Beth dead, Jo's heart *is* empty; all but one of her homosocial relationships has ended. Of course she feels lonely. And the only alternative Alcott was able to provide—bowing as she felt she must to patriarchal pressure—was Jo's immersion in the compulsory heterosexual marriage plot. It is significant, then, that Jo's self-mutilation and her subsequent textual murder are the only things that can prepare her for the heterosexual relationship that parodies Victorian marriage. As long as the sister Jo loves most lives, she exists textually in a homosocial relationship that is more convincing—and seems more satisfying—than any "stupid" marriage the author could arrange for her character.[127] But once Beth has died, Jo has little left of the lesbian community that has sustained her.

If readers feel betrayed by the ending of *Little Women*, it is because Jo betrays the homosocial female community she has proven is the only community worth sharing.[128] She is forced to sacrifice what she passionately desires to become the object of patriarchal homoerotics. Knowing that Alcott married Jo off to suit "per[v]erse publishers" doesn't help us accept Jo's father, either.[129] If anything, understanding that the economics of the patriarchy drove Alcott to distort her own artistic vision for her characters makes the ending of *Little Women* even more tragic. *Little Women*, then, is a quintessentially nineteenth-century lesbian text, for the patriarchy ultimately divides and conquers the women who empower each other through their love.

NOTES

I would like to acknowledge gratefully Beverly Lyon Clark for inspiring many of the ideas that inform this essay and for her help in revising this essay. I would also like to thank Francesca Sawaya and Torri Thompson for their insightful advice.

1. Louisa May Alcott, *Little Women*, ed. Elaine Showalter (New York: Penguin, 1989), 47.

2. Judith Butler, *Gender Trouble: Feminism and the Subversion of Identity* (New York: Routledge, 1990), 136.

3. Ibid., 139.

4. From beginning to end, the text describes Jo's rejection of traditional femininity as a matter of her acting masculine. Jo plays "male parts to her heart's content" in her family's dramatic productions (16); Laurie likes her "gentlemanly demeanor" (28); she refers to herself as a "business man—girl, I mean" (51), and she often likens herself to a boy or man (226, 322, 450). The people around her calmly accept her rejection of femininity; for example, Beth consoles Jo that she can at least act like their brother (3). Butler calls such "butch" performances as these a parody of the concept that gender identity is innate (*Gender Trouble,* 137). Emphasizing how ideologically rebellious gender nonconformity is, Monique Wittig claims: "The refusal to become (or to remain) heterosexual always meant to refuse to become a man or a woman, consciously or not. For a lesbian this goes further than the refusal of the *role* 'woman.' It is the refusal of the economic, ideological, and political power of a man" (*The Straight Mind and Other Essays* [Boston: Beacon, 1992], 13).

5. Showalter notes that the play the sisters stage, "The Witch's Curse," allows Jo to "dress like a man" and "make love to her sister" Amy (*Sister's Choice: Tradition and Change in American Women's Writing* [New York: Oxford University Press, 1991], 253).

6. Alcott, *Little Women*, 290.

7. Ibid., 291.

8. Terry Castle in *The Apparitional Lesbian: Female Homosexuality and Modern Culture* (New York: Columbia University Press, 1993) remarks that "when it comes to lesbians . . . many people have trouble seeing what's in front of them" (2) because "the lesbian represents a threat to patriarchal protocol: Western civilization has for centuries been haunted by a fear of 'women without men'—of women indifferent or resistant to male desire" (4–5).

9. *The Journals of Louisa May Alcott,* ed. Joel Myerson, Daniel Shealy, and Madeleine Stern, introduction by Madeleine Stern (Boston: Little, Brown, 1989), 32.

10. Ibid., 145. The material in brackets represents the editorial insertions of the editors of the journals.

11. Ibid., 148 n. 41.

12. Ibid.

13. Scores of similarly—if less violently—canceled passages in Alcott's journals indicate that she wanted to hide many of her personal relationships from posterity. For example, in 1879, Alcott three times mentions an ailing female friend "S.P.," even declaring once, "Poor S.P. failing fast. Not my fate yet" (*Journals*, 214–15). Alcott paid for S.P.'s medical treatment but never identifies her friend (220 n. 10). Alcott also tended to delete such information as "Sophy

B[ond] called" from an 1886 journal entry (285 n. 4). Since Alcott omitted myriad passages from her journals and letters that are clearly not sexual in nature, it is difficult to draw conclusions about why she was secretive about her relationships with women such as S.P. and Sophy Bond. But on the other hand, it is also quite possible that Alcott did have intensely romantic relationships.

Perceiving the lesbian potential in the Alcott biography, the Split Britches Company, a lesbian theater group, explored Alcott's "repressed lesbian desire" in their production *LITTLE WOMEN: The Tragedy* (Vivian M. Patraka, "Split Britches in *LITTLE WOMEN: The Tragedy*: Staging Censorship, Nostalgia, and Desire," *Kenyon Review* 15 [Spring 1993]: 7).

14. Showalter, *Sister's Choice,* 49, 63. After setting Laurie up as a "youthful sweet surrogate sister," Sarah Elbert goes on to describe Jo's sexual attraction to him in *A Hunger for Home: Louisa May Alcott and "Little Women"* (Philadelphia: Temple University Press, 1984), 162. Elbert then sidesteps her own potentially lesbian reading by arguing that Jo ultimately rejects Laurie because her love for him is primarily maternal (161); Jo must reject Laurie rather than carry out an "incestuous" relationship with him (156). Elbert's later edition of *A Hunger for Home: Louisa May Alcott's Place in American Culture* (New Brunswick: Rutgers University Press, 1987) repeats this thesis.

Charles Strickland remarks Alcott's ability "to acknowledge her bisexual feelings" when he also notes: "Although there is precious little evidence that she was a lesbian, it is undeniable that she felt strong erotic feelings toward her mother and toward other women. But she possessed erotic feelings toward men as well. . . . If a label must be affixed to her sexual orientation, it would be androgynous rather than lesbian" (*Victorian Domesticity: Families in the Life and Art of Louisa May Alcott* [University: University of Alabama Press, 1985], 108–9).

15. Showalter, *Sister's Choice,* 49, 57.

16. Ann B. Murphy also defines Jo's rejection of heterosexuality as related to her desire for independence, but Murphy seems to regret Jo's inability to participate in traditional heterosexuality: "Jo's rejection [of Laurie] is a self-defeating, pointless decision that denies her heterosexual erotic fulfillment" ("The Borders of Ethical, Erotic, and Artistic Possibilities in *Little Women*," *Signs* 15 [1990]: 568).

17. *The Selected Letters of Louisa May Alcott,* ed. Joel Myerson, Daniel Shealy, and Madeleine Stern, introduction by Madeleine Stern (Boston: Little, Brown, 1987), 125. Alcott's use of punctuation has not been regularized, nor has her spelling.

18. Murphy defines *Little Women* as an "oedipal narrative" ("The Borders," 579); I explore the nuances of her argument later in this essay.

Anne Hollander interprets "Jo's fear of sex" as one of the driving forces behind *Little Women* ("Reflections on *Little Women*," *Children's Literature* 9 [1981]: 31). Since Hollander accepts the Freudian notion that all art stems from a "basic erotic force" (33) and since so much of the novel explores Jo's writing, Amy's art, and Laurie's music, Hollander reads *Little Women* as commentary on sublimated sexuality.

Shirley Foster and Judy Simons come to a similarly sexual conclusion about

Jo's hair-cutting: "The episode can be read in Freudian terms as a reenactment of the experience of female castration" (*What Katy Read: Feminist Re-Readings of "Classic" Stories for Girls* [Iowa City: University of Iowa Press, 1995], 96).

Bedell, in fact, interprets the entire Alcott canon through a Freudian lens: "Many of her writings are concerned with the repeated theme of a romance between a child-woman and an older man; the latter often a guardian, an uncle or an older friend; in short, a displaced father. The theme is constant. It runs like a thread through her works, from the early sentimental short stories she published in her twenties, to the pseudonymous thrillers she wrote in her thirties, the children's novels of her mature period, and the later melodramatic works she began to revive as she grew old" (*The Alcotts: Biography of a Family* [New York: Potter, 1980], 241–42). In subsequent pages, Bedell makes clear that she considers the "older man" to be Bronson Alcott, rewritten as the love object in all of these fictions (242–45). The narrowness of Bedell's focus leads her to miss the primacy of female interrelationships in Alcott's works.

19. Bedell as quoted in Jerry Griswold, *Audacious Kids: Coming of Age in America's Classic Children's Books* (New York: Oxford University Press, 1992), 261 n. 10. See also 156–66.

20. Ibid., 158–61.

21. *Letters*, 51–53.

22. *Journals*, 165–66.

23. Alcott as quoted in Showalter, *Sister's Choice*, 48, and Elaine Showalter, introduction to *Little Women*, xiii.

24. See Carroll Smith-Rosenberg, *Disorderly Conduct: Visions of Gender in Victorian America* (New York: Knopf, 1985), 268–72.

25. Such writers as Radclyffe Hall (see Teresa De Lauretis, "Sexual Indifference and Lesbian Representation," *Theatre Journal* 40 [1988]: 155–77) and Carson McCullers (see Lori J. Kenschaft, "Homoerotics and Human Connections: Reading Carson McCullers 'As a Lesbian,'" in *Critical Essays on Carson McCullers*, ed. Beverly Lyon Clark and Melvin Friedman [New York: G. K. Hall, 1996], 220–33) found appropriating and revising inversion to be an empowering exercise.

26. As early as 1847, Alcott wrote of her sister Anna in her journal, "Father says, 'Anna's [journal] is about other people, Louisa's about herself.' That is true, for I don't *talk* about myself; yet must always think of the wilful, moody girl I try to manage, and in my journal I write of her to see how she gets on. Anna is so good she need not take care of herself, and can enjoy other people" (*Journals*, 61). In 1857, Alcott characterized her sister Lizzie as "sweet and patient always" (*Journals*, 85). In 1878 after their mother had died, Alcott wrote, "Dear Nan [Anna] is housemother now, so patient, so thoughtful and tender; I need nothing but that cherishing which only mothers can give" (*Journals*, 209).

Alcott wrote of her mother, "She was so loyal, tender and true; life was hard for her, and no one understood all she had to bear but we, her children" (*Journals*, 206). An example of Abba's hardships occurred in 1854 when her husband, after a long lecture tour, had only one dollar to show for his efforts: "I shall never forget how beautifully Mother answered him, though the dear hopeful soul had built much on his success. . . . Anna and I choked down our tears, and took a little lesson in real love which we never forgot" (*Journals,* 154). Alcott casts her sister Anna and her mother as long-suffering saints of the household throughout most of her journals.

27. This impulse reflects a cultural tendency to pathologize lesbianism. An example of this may be at work in Martha Saxton's *Louisa May: A Modern Biography of Louisa May Alcott* (Boston: Houghton Mifflin, 1977) when Saxton, despite sensitively delineating why Alcott might have feared men (187, 220), calls Alcott a "pariah" for never marrying (325). Alcott's journals and letters make frequent reference to how pressing she found her social schedule. See, for example, *Letters,* 213–16, 259; *Journals,* 235, 196–97. Members of her culture hardly seemed to view her with "fear and disgust" for never marrying, as Saxton asserts (325).

For a succinct description of how sexologists such as Richard von Krafft-Ebing and Havelock Ellis influenced the pathologization of lesbianism, see "The Spread of Medical 'Knowledge,'" in Lillian Faderman, *Surpassing the Love of Men: Romantic Friendship Between Women from the Renaissance to the Present* (New York: Morrow, 1981), 314–31.

28. Alcott, *Little Women,* 437, 203. Elizabeth Keyser, for example, describes the lesbian possibilities in *Work* in *Whispers in the Dark: The Fiction of Louisa May Alcott* (Knoxville: University of Tennessee Press, 1993), 109. So do Angela M. Estes and Kathleen Lant in "The Feminist Redeemer: Louisa Alcott's Creation of the Female Christ in *Work,*" *Christianity and Literature* 40 (1991): 245. All three critics, however, fail to note it in *Little Women.*

29. Nina Auerbach, *Communities of Women: An Idea in Fiction* (Cambridge: Harvard University Press, 1978), 200 n. 38.

30. Faderman, *Surpassing the Love of Men,* 163.

31. Smith-Rosenberg, *Disorderly Conduct,* 60.

32. Faderman, *Surpassing the Love of Men,* 157. Alcott's candid assertion of her attraction to women in her interview with Moulton supports Faderman's observation.

33. Faderman, *Surpassing the Love of Men,* 190.

34. Lisa Moore, "'Something More Tender Still than Friendship': Romantic Friendship in Early-Nineteenth-Century England," *Feminist Studies* 18 (1992): 501.

35. Martha Vicinus, "'They Wonder to Which Sex I Belong': The Historical Roots of the Modern Lesbian Identity," *Feminist Studies* 18 (1992): 471.

36. Diana Fuss, ed., *Inside/Out: Lesbian Theories, Gay Theories* (New York: Routledge, 1991), 1.

37. Bonnie Zimmerman, "Lesbians Like This and That: Some Notes on Lesbian Criticism for the Nineties," *New Lesbian Criticism: Literary and Cultural Readings,* ed. Sally Munt (New York: Columbia University Press, 1992), 9.

38. Reina Lewis, "The Death of the Author and the Resurrection of the Dyke," in Munt, *New Lesbian Criticism,* 22.

39. The temptation to conflate Alcott's and Jo's personalities has a rich tradition that can be ascribed to how the text was initially marketed in the nine-

teenth century, according to Barbara Sicherman, "Reading *Little Women:* The Many Lives of a Text," in *U.S. History as Women's History: New Feminist Essays,* ed. Linda K. Kerber, Alice Kessler-Harris, and Kathryn Kish Sklar (Chapel Hill: University of North Carolina Press, 1995), 252–53. My intention here is not to conflate the two but to focus on how the sexuality of the character is a result of the author's ambivalence on the subject.

40. Faderman, *Surpassing the Love of Men,* 173–74, 187, 218–20. Elaine Showalter also notes the "passionate female friendships in *An Old-Fashioned Girl, Work,* and *Diana and Persis*" in her introduction to Louisa May Alcott, *Alternative Alcott,* ed. Showalter (New Brunswick: Rutgers University Press, 1988), xx.

41. Faderman, *Surpassing the Love of Men,* 219.

42. Ibid., 220.

43. Showalter, introduction to *Little Women,* xiii.

44. Castle, *The Apparitional Lesbian,* 15.

45. Smith-Rosenberg, *Disorderly Conduct,* 64.

46. Bonnie Zimmerman, "What Has Never Been: An Overview of Feminist Literary Criticism," *Feminist Studies* 7 (1981): 452.

47. Smith-Rosenberg, *Disorderly Conduct,* 60. Elaine Showalter defines Alcott's relationship to her mother as informed by the type of homosociality that Smith-Rosenberg describes, but Showalter believes that that homosociality kept Alcott dependent on her mother so that she could never "forge an independent life" (introduction to *Little Women,* x).

48. Catharine R. Stimpson, "Zero Degree Deviancy: The Lesbian Novel in English," *Critical Inquiry* 8 (1981): 376–77.

49. Murphy, "The Borders," 576.

50. Ibid.

51. Murphy's analysis of Jo as entrapped in a pre-Oedipal relationship with Marmee shares resonances with Showalter's assessment of Alcott similarly trapped by her mother, as discussed above (Showalter, introduction to *Little Women,* x).

52. Murphy, "The Borders," 568, 577–79.

53. Alcott, *Little Women,* 5.

54. Ibid., 81.

55. Ibid., 79.

56. Ibid., 322.

57. Ibid.

58. Ibid., 433.

59. Ibid.

60. Ibid., 41.

61. Never using the term "lesbian" although the concept seems firmly embedded in her reading of *Little Women,* Ann Douglas, in her introduction to *Little Women* ([New York: Penguin, 1983], xxiv), notes the passion the March sisters share for one another. Douglas even describes the "couples" in the novel: Meg and Amy, Jo and Beth, and Jo and Amy (xxiv–xxv). These couples are single-gendered because boys are "almost unknown creatures" in the March girls' homosocial world (*Little Women,* 29). Douglas finds Jo and Amy's stormy relationship to be the one that mostly closely emulates the passionate nature of

lovers: "Amy and Jo are the real couple of the novel, attracted to each other in the troubled difficult way that lovers are. Louisa must marry Laurie to Amy, not to separate Laurie and Jo, but to distance Amy and her elder sister" (xxv).

62. Alcott, *Little Women*, 3.
63. Ibid.
64. Ibid.
65. Ibid.
66. Ibid., 98.
67. Ibid., 152.
68. Ibid., 226.
69. Ibid., 246.
70. Ibid., 363.
71. Ibid., 365.
72. Ibid., 434.
73. Ibid., 440.
74. Ibid., 246.
75. Ibid., 374–75.
76. Ibid., 143.
77. Ibid., 308.
78. Ibid., 329.
79. Ibid., 322.
80. Ibid., 374.
81. Ibid., 416.
82. Ibid., 325, 372.
83. Ibid., 375.
84. Castle, *The Apparitional Lesbian*, 34.
85. Ibid.
86. Alcott, *Little Women*, 372.
87. Ibid., 373.
88. Ibid., 418.
89. Ibid., 432.
90. Adrienne Rich, "Compulsory Heterosexuality and Lesbian Existence," *Signs* 5 (1980): 631–60.
91. Alcott, *Little Women*, 12, 170.
92. Ibid., 3.
93. Ibid., 26, 123, 153, 154.
94. Ibid., 21.
95. Ibid., 152.
96. Ibid., 97.
97. Ibid., 152–53.
98. Ibid., 203.
99. Ibid.
100. Ibid.
101. Ibid., 232.
102. Ibid., 233.
103. For an extended analysis of male as Other in *Little Women*, see Jan Susina, "Men in *Little Women*: Notes of a Resisting (Male) Reader," in *"Little Women" and*

the Feminist Imagination: Criticism, Controversy, Personal Essays, ed. Janice M. Alberghene and Beverly Lyon Clark (New York: Garland, 1999), 161–72.

104. Alcott, *Little Women,* 234.

105. Ibid., 232.

106. Ibid., 324.

107. Sarah Elbert denies that Laurie and Jo are androgynous, although "their individuality does not reside in specifically sexual stereotypes either" (*A Hunger for Home* [1984], 259 n. 2).

108. Alcott, *Little Women,* 27.

109. As quoted in Showalter, *Sister's Choice,* 56, and Showalter, introduction to *Little Women,* xxi–xxii.

110. Showalter, *Sister's Choice,* 6, and Showalter, introduction to *Little Women,* xxii. The textual changes in 1880 reflect the growing cultural pathologization of homosexuality and lesbianism.

111. Alcott, *Little Women,* 124, 216. For an example of how these passages appear in the revised 1880 version of the text, see Louisa May Alcott, *Little Women,* Centennial Edition (Boston: Little, Brown, 1968), 112, 194.

112. Elbert, *A Hunger for Home* (1984), 144. Angela M. Estes and Kathleen Lant, noting the presexual nature of Jo and Laurie's early friendship, call him "one of the girls" ("Dismembering the Text: The Horror of Louisa May Alcott's *Little Women,*" *Children's Literature* 17 [1989]: 105). Ann B. Murphy calls him a "brotherlover" ("The Borders," 566).

113. Saxton, *Louisa May,* 11.

114. Alcott, *Little Women,* 439.

115. Murphy, "The Borders," 578.

116. Ibid., 568.

117. Eve Kosofsky Sedgwick, *Between Men: English Literature and Male Homosocial Desire* (New York: Columbia University Press, 1985).

118. Ibid., 26. Sedgwick provides examples from Thackeray, Eliot, Dickens, and numerous others to support her thesis.

119. Alcott, *Little Women,* 452.

120. Ibid., 467–68.

121. Castle, *The Apparitional Lesbian,* 85.

122. Estes and Lant, "Dismembering," 112–16.

123. Ibid., 113–19.

124. Ibid., 115.

125. Butler, *Gender Trouble,* 139–40.

126. Alcott, *Little Women,* 438.

127. On January 22, 1869, Alcott wrote to her uncle Samuel Joseph May: "Publishers are very *perverse* & won't let authors have their way so my little women must grow up & be married off in a very stupid style" (*Letters,* 121–22).

128. For a different approach to the issue of female community in *Little Women,* see Kathryn Manson Tomasek, "A Greater Happiness: Searching for Feminist Utopia in *Little Women,*" in Alberghene and Clark, *Little Women,* 237–60.

129. *Letters,* 121.

Understood Betsy, Understood Nation

Dorothy Canfield Fisher and
Willa Cather Queer America

෧

JUNE CUMMINS

Dorothy Canfield Fisher's most well-known novel, *Understood Betsy*, published in 1917, is in many ways quintessentially American. Betsy's transformation from a timid, weak, retiring city girl to a robust, healthy, independent country girl is overtly connected to her dawning and developing consciousness of American history and values. Throughout the course of the novel, Fisher sets up clear contrasts, demonstrating two sides of many concepts—and very visibly favors the sides she aligns with Americanism. In this regard, *Understood Betsy* is characteristic of many of Fisher's novels, although all the rest were written for an adult reading audience. Critic Annika Ljung-Baruth, addressing the novels for adults, concludes that "Fisher's fiction tends to thematize a dialectic: cosmopolitanism versus country life, nihilism versus vitalism, culture versus nature. One by one, the 'superior' values are disclosed to the reader by means of simple valorization."[1] This dialecticism pervades *Understood Betsy*. A cursory reading reveals, in particular, the dichotomy between city and country, and the privileging of the country, that Fisher establishes. Betsy is nervous, self-absorbed, unhealthy, and undeveloped in the "medium-sized city in a medium-sized state in the middle of this country."[2] and becomes "a dark-eyed, red-cheeked, sturdy girl, standing straight on two strong legs, holding her head high and free" when she moves to the country.[3] Fisher makes

59

no bones about her valorization of fresh air, rural landscapes, and nature, which she aligns with health, self-sufficiency, happiness, freedom, and independence, obvious and hallowed American traits. American values are expressed physically through Betsy's body, which has grown and thrived with the liberating care of her country cousins, the Putneys.

Certainly, Fisher is not the first author to suggest that children do best in natural settings; Romantic notions of childhood go as far back as Rousseau. Other literature for children written around the time Fisher wrote *Understood Betsy* features children who thrive when allowed the opportunity to go out outside and breathe in fresh air; Mary Lennox, like Betsy, benefits from being forced to move to a rural setting when her family life is disrupted.[4] Similarly, strength and independence in female characters were in vogue for quite some time before Fisher was writing. Jo March, for example, is "perhaps the most celebrated 'tomboy' in the whole of girls' fiction."[5] What I find interesting about *Understood Betsy* is that Betsy's *transformation* is linked to her becoming an American, a trend I do not see in other literature of the period, and even more significantly, that Betsy's transformation expands rather than essentializes the definition of Americanism itself. As we will see, that expansion includes both gender and ethnic differences.

While *Understood Betsy* can be read as a clear-cut depiction and resolution of the urban/rural tension, the construction of gender in this novel troubles straightforward dichotomies. For Fisher connects the positive values of American self-sufficiency and self-determination to a character whose gender and perhaps sexual identity are anything but clear. Through her portrait of Cousin Ann, Betsy's idol and role model, Fisher complicates gender roles, and, I will argue, simultaneously complicates American identity. In short, through Cousin Ann, Fisher queers America.

Calling Cousin Ann a queer character situates this essay in a particular time and place. To queer a children's novel is an activity that could only happen in the late twentieth century or later, and in fact to use the word "queer" as a verb meaning to study a topic through a homosexually conscious critical lens is only a very recent phenomenon. But critics notice queering strategies in the work of authors who lived long ago; the terminology is new, but the activity is not. Even more recently, scholars of American fiction and culture have begun to notice the links between queerness and the formulation of American identities. Marilee Lindemann, in *Willa Cather: Queering America*, explains, "Part of the

point in conjoining the terms 'queer' and 'America' as a way of rethinking Cather is cultural and historical: both terms achieved new
salience and ideological power in the same moment, as historians of
sexuality and U.S. culture have demonstrated, and that 'moment'—
from the 1890s to the 1920s—coincides with Cather's sexual and literary coming-of-age."[6] Lindemann's goal is to demonstrate how Cather
contested the notion of America through characters marked as "queer,"
usually ethnic or sexual "others," and how America's changing definition was tied to the emerging understanding of homosexuality in the
early twentieth century. Fisher, a lifelong friend of Cather's, engages in
surprisingly similar queering in *Understood Betsy*, mostly through the
character of Cousin Ann, whom I would argue is an homage to Cather.[7]

Early in *Understood Betsy*, Fisher attempts to explain what distinguishes Cousin Ann from everyone else, and, by extension, what distinguishes *anyone* from everyone else. Focusing on individuality, Fisher,
through the voice of a gently intrusive narrator, contends that each person is unique because of *personality*, which, importantly, is not necessarily born with a person but instead develops over time. The topic
comes up on Betsy's first day with the Putneys. When Cousin Ann
peremptorily tells the horror-struck Elizabeth Ann how to get to school
by herself, the heretofore coddled, overly protected child finds she is
unable to refuse her older cousin. Writes Fisher:

> Are you wondering why Elizabeth Ann didn't turn right around,
> open the front door, walk in and say, "I can't! I won't! I can't!" to
> Cousin Ann?
>
> The answer to that question is that she didn't do it because
> Cousin Ann was Cousin Ann. There's more in that than you think! In
> fact, there is a mystery in it that nobody has ever solved, not even the
> greatest scientists and philosophers, although, like all scientists and
> philosophers, they think they have gone a long way toward explain-
> ing something they don't understand by calling it a long name. The
> long name is "personality," and what it means nobody knows, but
> for all that, it is perhaps the very most important thing in the world.
> Yet we know only one or two things about it. *We know that anybody's
> personality is made up of the sum total of all the actions and thoughts and
> desires of his life.* And we know that though there aren't any words or
> any figures in any languages to set down that sum total accurately,
> still it is one of the first things that everybody knows about anybody
> else. And that really is all we know!

So I can't tell you why Elizabeth Ann did not go back to cry and
sob and say she couldn't and she wouldn't and she couldn't.[8]

This will not be the only time Fisher has trouble articulating what it is
that distinguishes Cousin Ann, but despite her statement of inability,
she is quite assertive when she claims that personality is more a function of action and desire than of anything essential or fixed, and that
these aspects of being human may very well be beyond language, both
spoken and written. In this way, Fisher sounds presciently like the contemporary theorist Judith Butler, who also argues that one's identity
(the modern take on "personality") is not inherent, is not stable, is not
essential, and may be inexpressible by language alone.[9] For Butler,
identity is inseparable from gender:

What can be meant by "identity," then, and what grounds the pre-
sumption that identities are self-identical, persisting through time as
the same, unified and internally coherent? More importantly, how
do these assumptions inform the discourses on "gender identity"?
. . . Whereas the question of what constitutes "personal identity"
within philosophical accounts almost always centers on the question
of what internal feature of the person establishes the continuity or
self-identity of the person through time, the question here will be: To
what extent do *regulatory practices* of gender formation and division
constitute identity, the internal coherence of the subject, indeed, the
self-identical status of the person? To what extent is "identity" a normative ideal rather than a descriptive feature of experience?[10]

More politicized in this regard than Fisher, Butler nevertheless echoes
her in dismissing philosophers and the notion that anyone is "born" a
certain way. Fisher sees personality—identity—as something that develops over time and is unique to each individual, thereby implying
that everyone is different; Butler goes further and sees identity not only
as something that must develop but which is usually imposed from
without. Butler therefore believes that those with nonnormative gender
identities are those who stir up definitions and reveal the arbitrary nature of sexual assignment.

Inasmuch as "identity" is assured through the stabilizing concepts
of sex, gender, and sexuality, the very notion of "the person" is

called into question by the cultural emergence of those "incoherent" or "discontinuous" gendered beings who appear to be persons but who fail to conform to the gendered norms of cultural intelligibility by which persons are defined.[11]

In her description of personality, Fisher does not overtly mention gender, but Cousin Ann, in her refusal to behave in ways her sex demands, her "fail[ure] to conform to the gendered norms of cultural intelligibility," always quietly calls into question that which appears to be stable but which she proves, by her very existence, is not. For both Fisher and Butler, the "mystery" of identity can be questioned but perhaps never fully known, for it is through its very slipperiness that identity comes to exist.

Butler's project is to make trouble for the concept of gender in order to reveal its arbitrariness and political underpinnings. Similarly, I wish to expose not only how Fisher troubles and complicates *gender* identities in *Understood Betsy* but also how her complications expand concepts of *national* identity, particularly in terms of ethnicity, and the relationship between the two sets of identities. For recent critical discourse demonstrates that ethnic constructions are as arbitrary as gender constructions. For Butler, troubling identities is an important and necessary project. Fisher did not see herself as a troublemaker, but she believed strongly that she could participate in changing society.[12] While Fisher's interests and involvements in education, child rearing, and the shaping of middlebrow culture were well known during her day and have been studied since that time, she was not and is not seen as radical or revolutionary. Examining her and her novel *Understood Betsy*, however, alongside Willa Cather, reveals that Fisher herself "called into question" many normative values.

Dorothy Canfield and Willa Cather met in Lincoln, Nebraska, when Cather attended college there in the early 1890s. Dorothy's father, James Canfield, the chancellor of the University of Nebraska, was a very admired man, "adored by the students" and considered a "true democrat."[13] As Dorothy Canfield was six years younger than Cather, she was in high school during the years Cather attended the university. But the two became good friends. Cather biographer James Woodress describes the relationship between the two young women: "Dorothy, the member of the family that Cather was genuinely attracted to, . . . captivated everyone. . . . the students idolized Dorothy, 'a little girl . . . with lustrous brown eyes and abundant brown curls and the winning ways of a little fairy out of the storybooks'. . . . [Canfield] on her part idolized Cather as a sort of talented older sister."[14] Woodress characterizes Dorothy as Cather's "adoring younger friend" (144), and explains that Cather "loved her very, very dearly."[15] Although Canfield's family and education took her far from Nebraska—to Ohio, then Paris, then New York, then Vermont, and occasionally back to Europe—she and Cather corresponded by mail for the rest of their lives except during the sixteen years between 1905 and 1921, when Fisher did not write to Cather at all.

Scholars pondered the reasons for this gap until 1990, when Mark Madigan was able to piece together what happened to cause it. Cather had written a short story, "The Profile," that featured a female character based on a friend of Dorothy Canfield. The portrayal of this character was very unflattering, and Canfield was concerned her friend would be hurt. She begged Cather not to include the short story in a collection that was about to be published. But Cather had the story published, and Canfield did not write to her again for years.[16] Cather wrote to Fisher twice in 1916 (Canfield married John Fisher in 1907), and in March 1921, Cather wrote again, expressing her desire to reconcile.[17] Her request was apparently granted, as the correspondence resumed and continued until Cather's death. In fact, the last letter Cather wrote, one week before she died, was to Fisher.[18] Although as the years went by, both Fisher and Cather considered the six-year difference in their ages inconsequential, Fisher wrote soon after Cather's death: "My life-long admiring affection for Willa was, at first, tinctured with the respectful deference due from a younger person to a successful member of the older generation."[19] Mark Madigan explains that in the early years Fisher was Cather's "younger admirer and protégée."[20]

Cather, from a very young age, did not identify herself as feminine. According to biographer Woodress, "Before she was thirteen she had cut her hair shorter than most boys and was signing her name William Cather, Jr., or Wm. Cather, M. D. She expressed a vast contempt for skirts and dresses, wore boys' clothes, a derby, and carried a cane."[21] Cather's sexual identity has come under intense critical scrutiny since feminist critics such as Sharon O'Brien, another Cather biographer, have labeled her a lesbian. Such critics, who include Judith Butler, Eve Kosofsky Sedgwick, Walter Benn Michaels, and other scholars, accept and privilege Cather's sexual identity even though Cather herself moved in what seems the opposite direction. As a young woman,

Cather routinely dressed as a man and was open about the female objects of her affections. As she became older, she closeted her sexual identity and developed conservative political stances. So fearfully protective was she of her privacy that she destroyed most of her letters and forbade scholars and others to quote directly from any that remained. But those who knew her well could not deny that Cather was homosexual. Cather never had a romantic involvement with a man, and her letters began to reveal intense erotic attraction to women while she was in college. After living with Isabelle McClung in her family's house in Pittsburgh from 1901 to 1906,[22] Cather shared a home with Edith Lewis in Greenwich Village for almost forty years.[23]

Fisher, for her part, must have had some knowledge of Cather's choices, for she traveled with both Cather and McClung in Europe in 1902, and McClung wrote to Fisher on Cather's behalf arguing in favor of the publication of "The Profile." McClung's rhetorical tactics reveal her deep attachment to Cather and make no pretense of hiding the closeness of their relationship.

> You know as well as I the time she has spent on these stories and what they mean to her. The trouble over—The Profile—has taken away most of the pleasure, and for a few days she was sick and in bed—because of it. . . . I think it right that the story should go . . . . It seems to me that your taking away the pleasure of this first book of hers is far more cruel, more wrong even than any number of stories about any number of people—could be—you will resent my writing this to you—and I am sorry for that—but since you make it a public question.[24]

Although the rift between Fisher and Cather did not heal until 1921, Fisher knew Cather wanted to make up in 1916, the year she was writing *Understood Betsy*, because Cather wrote her two friendly letters that year, praising Fisher's novel *The Bent Twig* and demonstrating she valued and desired Fisher's friendship.[25] Whether Fisher actually intended to or not, she created a character in *Understood Betsy* that is in some ways very like Cather, perhaps a subconscious response to basing a fictional character on a living person and a way of showing Cather the proper approach to doing such a thing. Cather was a tall, "sturdy," "mannish," imposing figure.[26] In *Understood Betsy*, Cousin Ann Putney, "dark-haired . . . very tall and strong-looking,"[27] is an unmarried woman, presumably in her late thirties or early forties, who lives with her aging parents on a Vermont farm. The fact that the parents are married but Ann is not is not mentioned and certainly not explained; it is accepted as a matter of course. Both women—the real Cather and the fictional Ann—defied gender stereotypes.[28]

Fisher repeatedly refers to the Putney family as "queer," a word that in 1917 had begun to take on its connotations of sexual difference. Lindemann explains that around 1890, the word "queer" began to be used to mark "the differences between the still emerging categories of 'homosexuality' and 'heterosexuality.'"[29] Historian George Chauncey explains that in the 1910s, the word "queer" was a term "commonly used by 'queer' and 'normal' people alike to refer to 'homosexuals'" . . . and that in this time period "'queer' was not a derogatory term and that it was preferred, particularly in the middle-class culture of Greenwich Village (where Cather lived from 1906 to 1927), by men who did not see their homosexuality as connected to any abnormality in their gender persona."[30] The term was also used to designate lesbians during this time period.[31] Certainly, before the 1890s as well as during the time period during which Cather was growing up and Fisher was writing *Understood Betsy*, "queer" had or maintained the sense of "odd" or "unusual." We cannot claim with certainty that Fisher used this word fully conscious of its sexual connotations, although she was much more cosmopolitan a woman than one would suspect by reading *Understood Betsy*, having studied at the Sorbonne at the tail end of the Gay Nineties and earned her Ph.D. from Columbia University in 1904. Fisher uses the word with abandon throughout *Understood Betsy*, most often to describe the Putneys or things they own, but she also uses it to describe gender behavior of both sexes, saying at one point, "Aren't little girls queer?"[32] and at another, "How queer boys are!"[33] In both of these cases of gender designation, Fisher is describing behaviors that are actually quite typical of some children, either conflicting feelings of dependence and independence or an inability to accept praise—in fact, the behaviors are not "queer" at all. In this way, Fisher "de-queers" the word "queer," beginning to naturalize it, as it were. And indeed, almost all the things Betsy finds queer about the Putneys and the new place where she is living eventually become completely acceptable if not dear to her, a process that again naturalizes if not normalizes the queer. For example, in one significant section, Betsy actually ponders the meaning of the word "queer" (and "queer" appears in quotation marks, calling narrative attention to its meaning) when she doesn't understand a re-mark Cousin Ann makes. Interestingly, the topic of conversation is gen-der itself:

> [Ann said:] "That's Shep, our old dog. . . . Mother says, when she happens to be alone here in the evening, it's real company to hear Shep snore—as good as having a man in the house."
> Although this did not seem at all a sensible remark to Elizabeth Ann, who thought soberly to herself that she didn't see why snoring made a dog as good as a man, still she was acute enough (for she re-ally was an intelligent little girl) to feel that it belonged in the same class of remarks as one or two others she had noted as "queer" in the talk at the Putney Farm last night. This variety of talk was entirely new to her, nobody in Aunt Harriet's conscientious household ever making anything but plain statement of fact. It was one of the "queer Putney ways" which Aunt Harriet had forgotten to mention.[34]

Soon after, however, Cousin Ann says something else that at first sounds ridiculous to Betsy's ears:

> "Those Northern Spies [apples] are just getting to be good about now. When they first come off the tree in October you could shoot them through an oak plank."
> Now Elizabeth Ann knew that this was a foolish thing to say, since of course an apple could never go through a board; but some-thing that had always been sound asleep her brain woke up a little, little bit and opened one eye. For it occurred dimly to Elizabeth Ann that this was a rather funny way of saying that Northern Spies are very hard when you first pick them in autumn. She had to figure it out for herself slowly, because it was a new idea to her, and she was halfway through her tour of inspection of the house before there glimmered on her lips, in a faint smile, the first recognition of a joke in all her life.[35]

Suddenly, the "queer Putney" talk isn't so queer, is in fact understand-able, and even more, is *delightful*, bringing a smile to Betsy's lips. Queerness—whether directly related to sexuality or not—becomes a marker of that which appears to be strange but eventually becomes fa-miliar and beloved. This is exactly what happens to Betsy's perception of Cousin Ann.

Cousin Ann, who eschewed dolls when she was a child, is a hard-working, competent, direct, no-nonsense woman; the word Fisher most often uses to describe her is "firm." When Betsy first gets to know Ann, she is alarmed by her sternness and brusqueness and identifies with Shep when she sees the dog is in a "state of terror" because of Ann: "[Betsy] had a fellow-feeling about that relative of hers."[36] Over time, however, Betsy begins to like Ann and eventually idolize her, in a relationship that begins to look like the schoolgirl Dorothy Canfield's intense admiration for her older friend Willa Cather. Betsy figures out how to get out of scrapes or danger by thinking about what Ann would do in the same situation. It becomes Betsy's keen desire to *please* Cousin Ann, and when she does, she is delirious with happiness. Soon Betsy breaks through Ann's reserve by complimenting her with the admission that Ann has become her role model. "This made even Cousin Ann give a little abashed smile of pleasure."[37] "Abashed" is a very unusual word for Fisher to apply to this woman who competently strides around the farm, wearing men's clothes, presumably in order to better do men-oriented chores, although Fisher does not explain this. In fact, her description of Ann in "a very short skirt and a man's coat and high rubber boots."[38] is interestingly similar to Woodress's description of Willa Cather's attire in college: "Cather was still refusing to act and dress like a girl. She continued to cut her hair short . . . and wore starched shirts like a man instead of feminine shirtwaists; she did put on skirts, though she wore them shorter than most women, daringly short."[39] In both cases, short skirts are obviously markers not of sexy femininity but of an assertive masculinizing of female clothing.

In many respects, Cousin Ann functions in a role that Sedgwick calls "the avunculate." In her essay "Tales of the Avunculate: Queer Tutelage in *The Importance of Being Earnest*," Sedgwick defines the "avunculate" as those relatives who are not parents—and who are not heterosexual—who demonstrate to the children of the next generation—the offspring of their siblings or cousins—the possibilities *beyond* heteronormativity. Sedgwick traces the uses of the words "aunt," "uncle," and "cousin" in discourses that acknowledge the presence of the queer within the family romance. She writes, "Because aunts and uncles (in either narrow or extended meanings) are adults whose intimate access to children needn't depend on their own pairing or procreation, it's very common, of course, for some of them to have the office of representing noncomforming or nonreproductive sexualities to children."[40] Cousin Ann, I believe, not only models "noncomforming sexuality" to Betsy, but she also inspires it in Betsy herself. We see the reproduction of noncomforming sexuality in Betsy when she begins to take care of her little friend Molly, whom she rescues, protects, and sleeps with, "lying snuggled up to each other, back to front, their four legs, crooked at the same angle, fitting in together like two spoons in a drawer."[41]

But although Betsy has Molly, and at one point even seems to be interested in a boy, Betsy and Ann's relationship is the closest thing to a romance in the novel; when Betsy realizes she has "pleased" Ann, she gives "a little skip and hop of joy."[42] When either of them expresses admiration of the other, she experiences physical pleasure—their mutual compliments are a form of flirtation. Betsy spends her first few nights at Putney farm sleeping in the same bed as her warm, fat Aunt Abigail, but the hints of desire occur not during these cozy moments but when she feels Ann's approval. "Betsy's heart was singing joyfully as she trotted along, clasping Cousin Ann's strong hand."[43] The climax of Betsy's pleasure occurs when she impresses Ann by getting herself and Molly home safely from a fair where they had inadvertently been abandoned. Although almost petrified with fear when she realizes they are alone at the fair with no way to get home, Betsy figures out what to do by thinking about what Ann would do in the same situation. Once the girls are safely home, Ann "reached out her long arms and quickly, roughly, gathered Betsy up on her lap, holding her close as she listened."[44] When Ann hears the story of Betsy's triumph, she deeply compliments Betsy, who, sitting on Ann's lap for the first time, considers the event "a great, a momentous, an historic moment! . . . Betsy, enthroned on those strong knees, wondered if any little girl had ever had such a beautiful birthday."[45]

Near the end of the story, when the Putneys believe Betsy will be leaving them, each comes to her room after she is in bed for the night to give her one last hug. Betsy and Aunt Abigail share "a long embrace," while Uncle Henry gives Betsy a treasured gold watch, which leads Betsy to take "his hard, gnarled old fist in a tight grip."[46] Neither of these physical interactions, heartfelt as they are, compares to what transpires when Cousin Ann enters the room:

> Something moved in the room. Somebody leaned over her. It was Cousin Ann, who didn't make a sound, not one, but who took Betsy in her strong arms and held her close and closer, till Betsy could feel

the quick pulse of the other's heart beating all through her own body.

Then she was gone—as silently as she came.

But somehow that great embrace had taken away all the burning tightness from Betsy's eyes and heart.[47]

In this moment, Fisher describes a sensation that comes as close as possible to the pleasure that two bodies can experience together without becoming overtly sexual. As the two bodies merge, Betsy feels the peak of pleasure and then the release of tension. While the intent of the paragraph is not erotic, Fisher borrows from the rhetoric of erotica to distinguish the feelings between Betsy and Ann from those between Betsy and her other relatives.

Fisher investigates gender through Cousin Ann in nonromantic ways, as well. In one chapter, called "Betsy Starts A Sewing Society," Betsy decides that she and her friends will help out a poor, orphaned boy by sewing him a new suit of clothes so that he might be adopted. Betsy is very pleased with her plan and asks Cousin Ann for help. "She had never been afraid of Cousin Ann since the evening Molly had fallen into the Wolf Pit and Betsy had seen that pleased smile on Cousin Ann's firm lips."[48] It was Betsy who got Molly out of the pit, figuring out how to rescue the girl by imagining what Ann would have done in the same situation. Now she seeks Ann's firm, smiling lips again by asking for her help in another rescue mission.

Cousin Ann agrees and begins to supervise the sewing sessions that take place in her home. Fisher painstakingly describes the process by which the girls learn how to make the little boy's clothes:

First they made a little pair of trousers out of an old gray woolen skirt of Aunt Abigail's. This was for practice, before they cut into the piece of new blue serge. . . . Cousin Ann showed them how to pin the pattern on the goods and they each cut out one piece. Those flat, queer-shaped pieces of cloth certainly did look less like a pair of trousers to Betsy than anything she had ever seen. Then one of the girls read aloud very slowly the mysterious-sounding directions from the wrapper of the pattern about how to put the pieces together. Cousin Ann helped here a little. . . . Stashie . . . did the first basting, putting the notches together carefully, just as they read the instructions aloud, and there, all of a sudden, was a rough little sketch of a pair of knee trousers, without any hem or waistband, of

course, but just the two-legged complicated shape they ought to be!
It was like a miracle to Betsy![49]

As Cousin Ann helps the girls figure out how to make a set of boy's
clothes, she is instructing them in the construction of gender as much as
the construction of attire. For this careful attention to how clothes are
put together, how maleness must be created, must be cut, and basted,
and stitched, and does not *naturally* inhere, is an education in the artifice of gender. In this way, Cousin Ann points out what Butler would
call the *performative* nature of gender, as she shows the girls that *being* a
gender is not something that happens on its own, but has to be shaped
and stitched. By revealing this truth, Ann subtly suggests that there is
therefore no essential gender. As Butler explains, "If gender attributes
and acts, the various ways in which a body shows or produces its cultural signification, are performative, then there is no preexisting identity by which an act or attribute might be measured; there would be no
true or false, real or distorted acts of gender, and the postulation of a
true gender identity would be revealed as a regulatory fiction."[50]

Part of the way that Ann points out the constructedness of gender is
by having the girls fashion the boy's clothes out of female clothes. First,
they make the mock-up pants from Aunt Abigail's discarded skirt, as
discussed above, an act that makes Aunt Abigail exclaim, "Well, to
think of that being my old skirt!"—conveying surprise, overtly, at the
transmutability of the gender assigned to clothing and, implicitly, to the
gender assigned to people.[51] Aunt Abigail's old skirt will eventually be
replaced by blue serge purchased especially for this sewing project, but
the shirt the girls make is taken straight from Cousin Ann.

> Then they made a little blouse out of some new blue gingham.
> Cousin Ann happened to have enough left over from a dress she was
> making. This thin material was ever so much easier to manage than
> the gray flannel, and they had the little garment done in no time,
> even to the buttons and buttonholes. When it came to making the
> buttonholes, Cousin Ann sat right down with each one and super-
> vised every stitch. You may not be surprised to know that they were
> a great improvement over the first batch.[52]

While the trousers are remade with store material, the blouse is not,
demonstrating that Cousin Ann's clothes are non-gender specific. Once
again, Ann reveals that gender is a random assignment, a sort of cos-

tume, a type of performance. Through this act of revelation, Ann shows us what Butler means when she writes, "That gender reality is created through sustained social performances means that the very notions of an essential sex and a true or abiding masculinity or femininity are also constituted as part of the strategy that conceals gender's performative character and the performative possibilities for proliferating gender configurations outside the restricting frames of masculinist domination and compulsory heterosexuality."[53] In other words, as Ann shows the girls how clothing is constructed, how the gender designation of clothing is not natural but must be carefully cut and sewn, and how easily female clothing can be made into male clothing, she reveals that gender itself is a construction and hints, through her own performance as a gender-ambiguous individual, that there are other ways to cut, other ways to sew, other ways to *be*. Although Ann's performance as a mannish woman is not an act of drag, it is an act that reveals that "sex and gender [are] denaturalized by means of a performance which avows their distinctness and dramatizes the cultural mechanism of their fabricated unity."[54] Among other things, Ann demonstrates this fabrication with fabric itself.

Ultimately, Fisher connects Ann and Betsy, romantically or otherwise, by demonstrating and developing their similarities. They share a name (Betsy is actually Elizabeth Ann);[55] both of them have dark brown eyes; and Betsy's physical growth is realized when she becomes a child-sized version of her adored cousin, a "brown, muscular, upstanding child."[56] As this description aligns Betsy with Ann, it simultaneously aligns national identity with sexual identity and allows us to see that Fisher's gender interrogation is also an interrogation of who can be American. Emphasizing Betsy's new brownness, Fisher enters a tradition of authors who are concerned with the color of the skin of their white female characters. She also enters a debate in American society about who can be American. This cultural inquiry connects Fisher to two authors also concerned with the browning of their characters, Louisa May Alcott and Willa Cather, but in opposing ways.

Maude Hines, in her article "Missionary Positions: Taming the Savage Girl in Louisa May Alcott's *Jack and Jill*," sensitively analyzes how Alcott links the development of her female protagonist, "Gypsy Jill," to the whitening of her skin and the feminizing of her "tomboy" personality, both of which occur when Jill is forced to be bedridden for an extended period after a sledding accident; lying in bed, Jill becomes pale and frail. Exploring how Jill is first presented in discourses that emphasize her color and activity, Hines then demonstrates that "as Jill recovers . . . her whitening signals not only a metaphorical racial transformation but also a taming of 'savage' sexual urges, fitting her for the position of gentleman's wife."[57] Contextualizing *Jack and Jill* through late-nineteenth-century discourses of race and American identity, Hines concludes that "Jill's body is the site of violent physical transformation, and also acts as a locus of fantasies of transformation that propel the real work of the story: the creation of white, bourgeois, gender-appropriate, and heteronormative American adults, both inside and outside of the novel."[58] Betsy's transformation is remarkable in its direct opposition to Jill's; as Jill becomes passive, girlish, and pale, Betsy becomes active, physical, and dark. Hines's analysis helps us see that like Jill's, Betsy's transformation becomes part of the project of defining an American identity, although a very different one.

Comparing Betsy to other fictional characters—specifically Cather's female protagonists in *The Song of the Lark* and *My Ántonia*, Thea Kronburg and Ántonia Shimerda, respectively—helps to position Betsy in an early-twentieth-century redefinition of being American. Situating Cather's fiction of this period in the context of Progressive Era debates concerning immigration, ethnic purity, and assimilation, Lindemann demonstrates how Thea, a character of Swedish heritage, and Ántonia, a Bohemian immigrant, contravene demands of nativism. A developing opera singer, Thea needs a strong, powerful, healthy body. Thea's mother appraises her approvingly when she feels her daughter's chest and declares, "You're filling out nice."[59] While *The Song of the Lark* is not entirely progressive—Lindemann points out that Thea "fills up" on the work of other people as much as she physically "fills out"—Cather creates incidents that are critical of racism and of traditional marriages to such an extent that Lindemann can praise "the text's corporeal utopianism and its wide-ranging critique of white heteronormativity."[60] Ultimately, Lindemann describes *The Song of the Lark* as "Cather's most sustained contribution to a discourse of corporeal utopianism that is radically anti-assimilationist and queer-affirming, committed to a notion of citizenship rooted in the body rather than in flight from it."[61] Indeed, Lindemann titles this section of her book "Body-Building and Nation-Building in the Early Novels,"[62] and she demonstrates how in

Cather's novels the two processes become intertwined through characters such as Thea. In 1915, Cather's triumphant diva, Thea Kronburg, had come a long way from Alcott's weakened, whitened Jill.

Fisher may very well have read *The Song of the Lark,* despite the fact that it was published at the height of the sixteen-year breach in the Cather-Fisher friendship. Although *The Song of the Lark* and *Understood Betsy* are both stories of young girls leaving their homes and marking their development through physical growth and health, connected to the land in both cases, the two books do not have much in common in terms of plot and characters, and it's unlikely that Fisher was directly influenced by Cather when she wrote *Understood Betsy.* But at the same time Fisher was writing that novel, Cather was working on *My Ántonia;* the two novels were published within a year of each other (*Understood Betsy* was published first). Again, the two books do not have much in common on the surface, but Lindemann's analysis of Cather's "queering" project illuminates an intriguing intersection between the darkly ethnic Bohemian Ántonia Shimerda, and the robust, "brown" girl that Betsy becomes. Viewing Ántonia as a "queer" character, Lindemann establishes that her Bohemianism "emerges as a technology for the creation of racial and sexual ambiguity" that can be seen as a response to the debates concerning American identity, "the increasingly vituperative and contested discourse of Americanism."[63] While critics disagree as to whether Ántonia symbolizes American fears of foreigners disrupting white purity—because she seems to refuse to assimilate, teaching her children Bohemian and even beginning to forget English herself—or American dreams of ethnic diversity and difference—for she remains in the United States and domesticates the prairie—Ántonia undeniably remains an attractive, important character, beloved by the novel's narrator, Jim Burden.[64] And the source of Jim's love and narrative obsession (he ostensibly writes the book he determinedly titles *My Ántonia*) is a woman who is vivacious, beautiful, and *brown.* The first time they meet, as children, Jim is struck by her prettiness and her eyes: "They were big and warm and full of light, like the sun shining on brown pools in the wood. Her skin was brown, too, and in her cheeks she had a glow of rich, dark colour. Her brown hair was curly and wild-looking."[65] Later, after Ántonia starts doing heavy, outdoor farmwork, she is proud to compare herself to a man and becomes even browner and stronger. "'Oh, better I like to work out-of-doors than in a house!' she used to sing joyfully. 'I do not care that your grandmother say it makes me like a man. I like to be like a man.' She would toss her head and ask me to feel the muscles swell in her brown arm."[66] Ántonia is not a lesbian character; we do not see her desiring women. She will later have children with two different men, and at the end of the novel, she is figured as a gender-normative fountain of fecundity, a mother of ten children, a "rich mine of life, like the founders of early races."[67] But her body remains "queer," for, according to Lindemann, "'Queer' and 'Bohemian' generally function as synonyms in *My Ántonia,* but each term retains a sexual as well as an ethnic resonance."[68] Both terms are crucial for Cather's sense of Americanism, because for her, "the body that signifies the nation is a queer body indeed."[69]

Cather scholar Guy Reynolds is not concerned with Cather's sexual identity, but he strongly believes that Cather was "unusually receptive to *difference,* weaving into her novels a broad-minded acceptance of the foreign or the strange."[70] Explaining the debates within Progressivism concerning American identity, which were known as the Americanization debates, Reynolds distinguishes two arguments: the first being a conservative nativism that dictated that all immigrants learn English as quickly as possible and give up any ties to their previous countries or cultures in order to become truly American; and the second being a more tolerant liberalism that emphasized that American identities could be hyphenated, that is, that immigrants could view themselves as bicultural, maintaining ties to their former countries, and that this biculturalism was the essence of being American. The nativist side included the voice of Theodore Roosevelt, who, according to Gail Bederman, promoted "manly virtue, masculine violence, and white American racial supremacy."[71] A liberal voice was that of Randolph Bourne, who in 1916 published his article "Trans-National America" in *The Atlantic Monthly* (later he gave *My Ántonia* a positive review), in which he argued for a multicultural America. Bourne "described the encroaching uniformity of America and sought a revitalization through ethnic and cultural diversity."[72] As part of his argument, he wrote: "We have needed the new peoples—the order of the German and Scandinavian, the turbulence of the Slav and Hun—to save us from our own stagnation. . . . What we emphatically do not want is that these distinctive qualities should be washed out into a tasteless, colorless fluid of uniformity."[73] Bourne's "tasteless, colorless" fluid could easily describe the anonymous "medium-sized city in a medium-sized state in the middle of this country . . . probably very much like the place you live in yourself" that Betsy inhabits before moving to Vermont, a state where color is built right into its name.[74] Without knowing exactly which articles Fisher was reading when, we can still argue she could not have been unaware of the Americanization debates, whether she was consciously responding to them or not. We do know, however, that she approved of what Reynolds calls Cather's "[liberal attunement] to the broad currents of early twentieth-century American life—race, immigration, and multiculturalism."[75] Much later, in 1933, Fisher wrote of her friend in the *New York Herald Tribune*:

> I offer you a hypothesis about Willa Cather's work: that the only real subject of all her books is the effect a new country—our new country—has on people transplanted to it from the old traditions of a stable, complex civilization. Such a hypothesis, if true, would show her as the only American author who has concentrated on the only unique quality of our national life, on the one element which is present more or less in every American life and unknown and unguessable to Europeans or European colonials. . . . Is there any one of Miss Cather's novels which is not centered around the situation of a human being whose inherited traits come from centuries of European or English forebears, but who is set down in a new country to live a new life which is not European or English, whatever else it may be?[76]

Reynolds uses this Fisher essay as the basis of the argument of his own book, *Willa Cather in Context: Progress, Race, Empire.* He sees Fisher as the only scholar before him to have recognized Cather's liberal progressivism. "Canfield Fisher demonstrates that her friend *was* aware of the significant tendencies of her age: immigration, cultural transmission, and the 'new life.'"[77] Certainly, Fisher demonstrates sensitive awareness to the relationship between national difference and American identity, and I believe she provides her own answer to the Americanization debate through ethnicizing Betsy.

Betsy's brownness is more and more emphasized when her Midwestern Aunt Frances arrives to retrieve Betsy from the Putney farm. "Aunt Frances . . . exclaimed about her having grown so big and tall and fat—she didn't say brown too, although you could see that she was thinking that, as she looked through her veil at Betsy's tanned face and down at the contrast between her own pretty, white fingers and Betsy's leather-colored, muscular little hands."[78] "Brown" is associated with health and Americanism when Betsy is described as the "dark-eyed, red-cheeked, sturdy girl, standing straight on two strong legs, holding her head high and free, her dark eyes looking out brightly from her tanned face."[79] "High and free" are words that resonate in this book in which the Declaration of Independence is not only discussed often but made to seem vital and real. Betsy is amazed to learn that Aunt Abigail's grandmother was born the year the Declaration of Independence was signed and thinks, "Why! There were real people living when the Declaration of Independence was signed—real people, not just history people—old women teaching little girls how to do things—right in this very room, on this very floor—and the Declaration of Independence just signed!"[80] In other words, the "history" Betsy learned when living in the Midwest was meaningless to her, but when she moves to live with the Putneys and attends her Montessori-inspired one-room schoolhouse, she evolves into a girl who sees that American history is a living, breathing thing—her Aunt Abigail, whose name lightly recalls that of the second First Lady. She also sees that she herself—Betsy, whose name recalls that of Betsy Ross—is part of that unfolding history.

The first thing Betsy does in her new country school is to sing the song "America," and the first thing she reads aloud is the poem "Barbara Frietchie," by John Greenleaf Whittier. Barbara Frietchie was an old woman who insisted on hanging her American flag even though her town was full of rebel soldiers.[81] One important difference between Betsy's Midwestern aunts and her Vermont cousins is that the former own a "new and shiny" copy of *Essays of Emerson* that no one ever looks at, while Aunt Abigail reads from a "a small, worn old book" with the same title.[82] The implication is clear; the Putneys revere and live by Emerson's American principles of self-reliance and self-sufficiency, while Aunts Harriet and Frances totally ignore them.[83] When Aunt Frances arrives in Vermont, Betsy is proud to tell her that she has learned to make "apple pie and brown betty."[84] Those dishes sum up what Elizabeth Ann has become: a quintessentially American apple pie and brown Betsy.

Aunt Frances is the polar opposite of Betsy and of Cousin Ann. Nervous, fluttery, and flighty, Frances chooses to marry a man because, she explains, he "just loves to take care of people. He says that's why he's marrying me."[85] Dependent Frances, with her name that sounds so much like "France" (she even tried to teach Betsy French when they lived together in the Midwest) and her "citified," effete ways, is portrayed not only as ultrafeminine but also as un-American and a poor role model for Betsy.[86] Implicit in Fisher's critique of Frances is the hint of Frances's racism, her speechless disdain of brownness. As Fisher rejects Frances and pushes her offstage, she rejects this racism. To Fisher, Betsy, and all the Putneys, brown is beautiful.

Fisher was consciously antiracist; her biographer Ida Washington explains that Fisher's body of work "attack[s] materialism, social discrimination, religious and racial intolerance, and all forms of brutality and fraud."[87] Fisher's father believed strongly in educating immigrants and black people, and Washington explains that Fisher's parents and grandparents were abolitionists.[88] During her life, Fisher expressed sympathy for Jews and other ethnic "others" (unlike Cather, who could be grotesquely anti-Semitic), and she strongly believed in equality. By browning Betsy, Fisher does not mean to suggest that Betsy has become a different ethnicity, but she does imply that a healthy, free American is one who is indubitably not white. In this way, Fisher reveals she is like Cather in advocating an America that welcomes "immigration, cultural transmission, and the 'new life.'" Almost at the exact same moment that Cather's Ántonia became browner and more muscular as she became American, so too did Fisher's Betsy. In this sense, Betsy might be a model not just of an ideal American identity but also of an immigrant's experience of becoming American. Such an immigrant, according to this model, would maintain skin color and other ethnic ties but become strong, healthy, and *free*.[89]

Finally, we can see that for Fisher, national identity is wrapped up in gender identity after all. Washington and other critics call Fisher a feminist author based on her critique of gender roles in her novels for adults. They feel justified in using this label even though Fisher herself said, "I was never a feminist. . . . It was my older generation, my father and mother, who were. I was rather (as it often goes in generations) in reaction from their extreme zeal for 'women's rights.'"[90] But, Washington insists, "although Dorothy was not a militant, crusading advocate of women's rights, it is clear from her writings and her life that she saw no reason why women should be spared the responsibilities and rewards of meaningful work and active citizenship."[91] Washington and other critics cite novels like *The Home-Maker* (1924) in which Fisher has a husband and wife exchange traditional gender roles in order to do what they really like—which means the father stays home and cares for the children, and the mother goes to work and becomes very successful in business. Although Fisher challenges gender roles quite radically in this and in some other novels, she has not been seen as a queer author. Yet a reader can discern Fisher's difficulty in speaking about Ann, as we saw much earlier in this essay. Fisher's stumbling, self-consciously reflective use of language occurs again when she tries to explain Cousin Ann's fundamental Ann-ness. As before, she turns the question to the reader, this time by asking,

> Do you know what [Betsy] did, right off, without thinking about it? She didn't go and look up Aunt Abigail. She didn't wait until Uncle Henry came back from his round of emptying sap buckets into the big tub on his sled. As fast as her feet could carry her she flew back to Cousin Ann in the sap house. I can't tell you (except again that Cousin Ann was Cousin Ann) why it was that Betsy ran so fast to her and was so sure that everything would be all right as soon as Cousin Ann knew about it; but whatever the reason was it was a good one.[92]

Here, Fisher refers to her own utterance, the earlier quotation already explicated in this essay, where she asked the reader, "are you wondering why Elizabeth Ann" didn't say no to her cousin?[93] By deflecting the question onto the reader, Fisher hides that she herself is not sure what it is about Ann that is so compelling and attractive, or that she cannot bring herself to admit it. But when she gives her lengthy explanation of "personality," she ends the lecture with this stern warning to her reader: "But perhaps it may occur to you that it's rather a good idea to keep a sharp eye on your 'personality,' whatever that is! It might be handy, you know, to have a personality like Cousin Ann's which sent Elizabeth Ann's feet down the path; or perhaps you would prefer one like Aunt Abigail's. Well, take your choice."[94] With this directive, Fisher reveals not only that a theme of her novel is that choice is part of American identity, but that alternative sexuality—personality—is also open to choice. When she stumbles in her inability ("I can't tell you") to mark just what makes Ann so attractive—so sexy—she reveals the choice she believes Betsy should make (to be like Ann) as well as her own valorization of the choices her friend Willa Cather made (to be a lesbian).

Sedgwick focuses on the effect of avunculate queer tutelage on the Western family, which she sees functioning in a broad social context. Thus, the avunculate has the potential to transfigure not only our notions of family but of society as well. Sedgwick asks,

Can the family be redeemed? The easiest paths of argument . . . would be advocacy of a more elastic, inclusive definition of "family," beginning with the relegitimation of the avunculate: an advocacy that would appeal backward to precapitalist models of kinship organization, or the supposed early-capitalist extended family, in order to project into the future a vision of "family" elastic enough to do justice to the depth and sometimes durability of nonmarital and/or nonprocreative bonds, same-sex bonds, nondyadic bonds, bonds not defined by genitality, "step"-bonds, . . . etc.[95]

Fisher, I believe, redeemed the family in the ways Sedgwick desires over eighty years ago, and goes even further than Sedgwick by bringing racial difference together with sexual difference, in effect redefining not just the family but America itself. Cather scholar Lindemann argues that writers do not have to be homosexual to produce queer manuscripts. To queer a novel, she explains, is to "demand that the queer not be excluded from the terms and conditions of citizenship, to insist, indeed that the queer be understood to articulate and exemplify precisely those terms and conditions."[96] At the end of *Understood Betsy*, Betsy has become a bodily representation of the nation, healthy, glowing, and free. These traits are obvious. But the novel implies that part of Betsy's Americanization is her important relationship with the "dark" and manly Ann, a relationship with both homosexual and ethnic overtones. Betsy, then, embodies an America more expansive and inclusive than what we would expect from a children's book written during this time period. Fisher's American characters don't merely tolerate or accept those who are "different"; they integrate such difference within themselves, figuring through their bodies a complex and multivalent Americanism. It would not be until the end of the twentieth century that homosexuality would be addressed frankly and positively in children's books. But early in the century, Fisher quietly queered America with this beloved children's classic, opening a space for a complex and multistranded national identity and proving the possibility of the deep and important cultural contribution of children's books.

NOTES

1. Annika Ljung-Baruth, *A Steady Flameless Light: The Phenomenology of Realness in Dorothy Canfield Fisher's "The Brimming Cup," "Her Son's Wife" and "Rough-Hewn"* (Stockholm: Almqvist & Wiksell International, 2002), 156.

2. Dorothy Canfield Fisher, *Understood Betsy* (Hanover: University Press of New England, 1999), 1.

3. Ibid., 133.

4. While *Understood Betsy* can be seen as part of a Romantic tradition in its emphasis on a rural setting, it is important to realize that Fisher herself saw such rural settings, and Vermont in particular, as places where the American traits she valued could be actualized. Her biographer, Ida H. Washington, explains Fisher's rejection of the cosmopolitan life she had known in Paris and New York in favor of Vermont as influenced by her belief that Vermonters had "pride in their own traditions, self-reliance, and distrust of 'city-people'" (*Dorothy Canfield Fisher: A Biography* [Shelburne, VT: New England Press, 1982], 162). Jennifer Parchesky, in "The Business of Living and the Labor of Love: Dorothy Canfield Fisher, Feminism, and Middle-Class Redemption," *Colby Quarterly* 36.1 (2000), views Fisher as consciously rejecting the developing consumerist mentality in America at the beginning of the twentieth century and reveals how several of her novels, including *Understood Betsy*, make the argument that "it is possible to abandon the 'squirrel-cage' and still be part of a community, but only if one leaves the upwardly mobile Midwestern city behind for the acerbically tolerant Vermont village, where one is presumably allowed to be as quirky as one likes; or, more specifically, where the particular quirk of agrarian anti-consumerism is considered normal" (35). Parchesky explains that Fisher did not of course assume that all Americans would move to small towns in the country and sew their own clothing, but she did want Americans to "discover—or, if necessary, invent—new kinds of purposeful activity . . . those necessary to sustain basic life functions and those that contributed to what she called 'the work of the world,' the collective endeavor to sustain and improve society as a whole" (35). To Fisher, those living in places like rural Vermont were naturally partaking in such activities, and she advocated that all Americans adopt those Vermont values. Thus, Fisher is not interested in natural, rural settings solely for the reasons the Romantic writers and their descendants were, but because she felt that the values found in such settings were values that all Americans could and should accept, regardless of where they lived.

5. Mary Cadogan and Patricia Craig, *You're A Brick, Angela! A New Look at Girls' Fiction from 1839 to 1975* (London: Victor Gollancz, 1976), 35.

6. Marilee Lindemann, *Willa Cather: Queering America* (New York: Columbia University Press, 1999), 2.

7. I am not the first scholar to note the presence of queerness in Victorian and modernist children's literature. Claudia Nelson, for example, writes about feminized boy characters in nineteenth-century British literature. Some have seen Jo March as a prototypical lesbian (see, especially, Kent). Many scholars have noted the rise of healthy, physical, adventurous girls in the literature of both Britain and the United States during this time period (see Cadogan and Craig, Mitchell, and Tarbox). Sally Mitchell, in particular, discusses the development of the "boyish" girl character in British fiction and relates it to British national identity. As far as I know, however, no scholars have as yet seen either the positive presence of queer characters or the development of the female pro-

tagonist into a strong, independent character as related to national identity in this period of American children's literature. Works of interest: Claudia Nelson, *Boys Will Be Girls: The Feminine Ethic and British Children's Fiction, 1857–1917* (New Brunswick: Rutgers University Press, 1991); Kathryn R. Kent, *Making Girls Into Women: American Women's Writing and the Rise of Lesbian Identity* (Durham: Duke University Press, 2003); Sally Mitchell, *The New Girl: Girls' Culture in England, 1880–1915* (New York: Columbia University Press, 1995); Gwen Athene Tarbox, *The Clubwomen's Daughters: Collectivist Impulses in Progressive-era Girl's Fiction, 1890–1940* (New York: Garland Press, 2000).

8. Fisher, *Understood Betsy*, 52–53 (emphasis added).

9. In *Bodies That Matter: On the Discursive Limits of "Sex"* (New York: Routledge, 1993), Judith Butler writes, "Gender is neither a purely psychic truth, conceived as 'internal' and 'hidden,' nor is it reducible to a surface appearance; on the contrary, its undecidability is to be traced as the play *between* psyche and appearance (where the latter domain includes what appears *in words*)" (234).

10. Judith Butler, *Gender Trouble: Feminism and the Subversion of Identity* (New York: Routledge, 1990), 15.

11. Ibid., 17.

12. Parchesky provides an excellent analysis of Fisher's role in shaping American culture: "Fisher . . . although now forgotten by most historians and literary critics was in the first half of the twentieth century one of the most influential arbiters and beloved guides of mainstream American culture" ("Business of Living," 29). Fisher clearly saw herself as having an effect on influencing the public, as she wrote childcare manuals, advocated the use of the Montessori method in parenting and in schools, and perhaps most significantly, served on the Book-of-the-Month Club Board of Selection for twenty-five years. "As a member of the Book-of-the-Month Club Board of Selection from 1925 to 1950, she played an even greater role [than in publishing books and writing reviews and lectures] in shaping both what the 'average intelligent readers' of America perceived as major cultural issues and how they perceived them. . . . From her manuals on childrearing and adult education to her fictional representations of everyday family life, Canfield exerted a pervasive influence on how a variety of public discourses and reform movements would conceptualize the problem of work into the middle of the twentieth century" (Parchesky, 30).

13. James Woodress, *Willa Cather: A Literary Life* (Lincoln: University of Nebraska Press, 1987), 82–83.

14. Ibid., 83.

15. Ibid., 118.

16. The story was not included in the collection Cather published in 1905, *The Troll Garden*, her first book, but it did come out two years later in *McClure's* magazine. See Mark Madigan, "Willa Cather and Dorothy Canfield Fisher: Rift, Reconciliation, and *One of Ours*," *Cather Studies* 1 (1990): 122.

17. Madigan, " Cather and Fisher," 124.

18. Woodress, *Willa Cather*, 503.

19. Quoted in Madigan, "Cather and Fisher," 116.

20. Madigan, "Cather and Fisher," 116.

21. Woodress, *Willa Cather,* 55.

22. Sharon O'Brien, *Willa Cather: The Emerging Voice* (New York: Oxford University Press, 1987), 235.

23. Madigan, "Cather and Fisher," 124. In "Willa Cather and Others" (in *Tendencies* [Durham: Duke University Press, 1993]), Eve Kosofsky Sedgwick is frank about the relationship between Cather and McClung when she describes Cather running "back to a bedroom shared with a sumptuously beautiful young woman, Isabelle McClung, who . . . has defied her parents to the extent of bringing her imposing lover, Willa Cather, into the family home to live" ("Willa Cather and Others" 168). Sedgwick's direct disclosure of the sexual aspect of this love affair sheds a certain light on Woodress's contention that "Isabelle McClung, two years older than Dorothy but four years Cather's junior, was taking Dorothy's place as the adoring younger friend" (*Willa Cather,* 144).

24. Qtd. in Madigan, "Cather and Fisher,"121.

25. Madigan. "Cather and Fisher," 123. *Understood Betsy* first appeared in serial form in *St. Nicholas* magazine, beginning in November 1916.

26. Woodress, *Willa Cather,* 3, 69, 209.

27. Fisher, *Understood Betsy,* 23.

28. I would like to make clear that in no way am I suggesting that Fisher's novel was written as an erotic text. Although I am talking about an analysis that uses terminology based on sexual activity, and although I will be pointing out incidents in the novel that I am relating to romance and sexual behavior, I am not suggesting that Cousin Ann and Betsy are actually involved in an erotic relationship, or that Ann secretly harbors pedophilic fantasies. Rather, I am suggesting that Ann represents to Betsy and the child reader the possibility of choice in terms of a future, adult, sexual self-definition. I believe Fisher was working within what Anne Higonnet calls in *Pictures of Innocence: The History and Crisis of Ideal Childhood* (London: Thames and Hudson, 1998) the image of the "romantic child," in which innocence is assumed. Calling the romantic child the "modern definition of childhood," Higonnet explains, "To a great extent, childhood innocence was considered an attribute of the child's body, both because the child's body was supposed to be naturally innocent of adult sexuality, and because the child's mind was supposed to begin blank" (8). While Higonnet is largely concerned with visual depictions of childhood, I think her description of the romantic child more than adequately conveys Fisher's own mind-set as she developed her representation of a child in literature in 1917.

29. Lindemann, *Willa Cather,* 2.

30. Qtd. in ibid.

31. Ibid., 3.

32. Fisher, *Understood Betsy,* 34.

33. Ibid., 125. In this way, Fisher is very much like her good friend Cather, who heavily relied on this word. According to Lindemann, "The word 'queer' resonates throughout Cather's fiction with the snap, crackle, and pop of acute anxiety and ideological work. It becomes . . . [as in *The Song of the Lark*] 'a continuous repetition of sound, like the cicadas'" (*Willa Cather,* 12). "Queer" percolates through *Understood Betsy* as much as it snaps, crackles, and pops through-

out Cather's work, and I believe it does so for more than the reason that Cather and Fisher spent several developmental years in the same town together.

34. Fisher, *Understood Betsy,* 37.

35. Ibid., 39.

36. Ibid., 49.

37. Ibid., 97.

38. Ibid., 91.

39. Woodress, *Willa Cather,* 69.

40. Eve Kosofsky Sedgwick, "Tales of the Avunculate: *The Importance of Being Earnest,*" in *Tendencies,* 63.

41. Fisher, *Understood Betsy,* 112.

42. Ibid., 103.

43. Ibid.

44. Ibid., 151.

45. Ibid.

46. Ibid., 160, 161.

47. Ibid., 161.

48. Ibid., 112.

49. Ibid., 113.

50. Butler, *Gender Trouble,* 141.

51. Fisher, *Understood Betsy,* 114.

52. Ibid.

53. Butler, *Gender Trouble,* 141.

54. Ibid., 138.

55. Sedgwick might call this redundancy in names a "pun," which, she argues, alongside critic Christopher Craft, is "on the phonemic level . . . 'homoerotic because homophonic'" ("Tales of the Avunculate," 54).

56. Fisher, *Understood Betsy,* 133.

57. Maude Hines, "Missionary Positions: Taming the Savage Girl in Louisa May Alcott's *Jack and Jill,*" *The Lion and the Unicorn* 23.3 (1999): 382–83.

58. Ibid., 391.

59. Qtd. in Lindemann, *Willa Cather,* 59.

60. Lindemann, *Willa Cather,* 58.

61. Ibid., 78.

62. Ibid., 34.

63. Ibid., 68, 69.

64. See ibid., 61–69, for a discussion of this critical debate.

65. Willa Cather, *My Ántonia* (Boston: Houghton Mifflin, 1926), 23.

66. Ibid., 138. Ibid., 122. Jim notices that Ántonia is browner when he observes, "She had come to us a child, and now she was a tall, strong young girl, although her fifteenth birthday had just slipped by. . . . She wore the boots her father had so thoughtfully taken off before he shot himself, and his old fur cap. Her outgrown cotton dress switched about her calves, over the boot-tops. She kept her sleeves rolled up all day, and her arms and throat were burned as brown as a sailor's." In this description, Ántonia interestingly reflects both Cather and Cousin Ann by wearing a short skirt and men's clothing as well as

Cousin Ann and Betsy, in her sunny brownness.

67. Ibid., 353.

68. Lindemann, *Willa Cather*, 64.

69. Ibid., 61.

70. Guy Reynolds, *Willa Cather in Context: Progress, Race, Empire* (New York: St. Martin's Press, 1996), 16.

71. Gail Bederman, *Manliness & Civilization: A Cultural History of Gender and Race in the United States, 1880–1917* (Chicago: University of Chicago Press, 1995), 192–93.

72. Reynolds, *Willa Cather in Context*, 92.

73. Qtd. in ibid.

74. Cather, *Misunderstood Betsy*, 1.

75. Ibid., 11.

76. Qtd. in Reynolds, *Willa Cather in Context*, 10.

77. Reynolds, *Willa Cather in Context*, 10.

78. Fisher, *Understood Betsy*, 163.

79. Ibid., 133.

80. Ibid., 45.

81. Ibid., 59–60.

82. Ibid., 30.

83. Fisher's reference to Emerson certainly supports the principles she is expounding in *Understood Betsy*, but it also functions as a form of self-promotion, for her childcare manual, just published in 1916, is titled *Self-Reliance*. Parchesky explains that not only did Fisher endorse "purposeful activity" for children in this book, she also advocated such activity for mothers, as well as asserted, according to Parchesky, that "rural living keeps one close to the essentials of life" ("Business of Living," 32). *Understood Betsy* was in some ways a "tie-in" to *Self-Reliance*.

84. Fisher, *Understood Betsy*, 169.

85. Ibid., 164.

86. It's important to note that Fisher was not anti-French in general. During World War I, she and her family voluntarily went to France to help out the citizens of that country, and of course she herself studied at the Sorbonne and wrote her dissertation on French authors. But the French-American dichotomy does show up in places other than *Understood Betsy*. In particular, her novel *Rough-Hewn* (1922) was very concerned with explaining the differences between French and American culture. Writes Washington, in *Dorothy Canfield Fisher*:

> The problem around which the plot thread is wound is the difference between "European" (here "French") and "American." It is the same problem that Dorothy treated in *Gunhild* and in a number of her short stories. For her, "European" meant a society that places great emphasis on social distinctions, telling "necessary" lies to please others or to protect oneself, and preserving deliberately a clear distinction between the superficial image one presents to the outside world and the real person one keeps safe within a protective shell. "American" in the guise of [the

character] Neale is . . . vigorous, productive, direct, and openly ambitious. . . . In earlier narratives Dorothy had taken for granted that these
differences between European and American culture were familiar to
her readers, and she had referred to them in unconscious assumption
that the terms "European" and "American" would call to other minds
the same images that they did to hers. (113–14)

87. Washington, *Dorothy Canfield Fisher,* xi.

88. Washington explains that "there are echoes of Dorothy's abolitionist
parents and grandparents in the painful racial incident [in the novel *The Bent
Twig,* published in 1915] where [a character] appears as a fictional incarnation
of the fiery spirit of Almera Hawley Canfield [Dorothy's grandmother]. In a fit
of righteous wrath, [the character] throws picnic supplies gathered by the fifth-
grade girls into the river because they will not allow a Negro girl to join their
expeditions and then justifies her actions by saying, 'If she couldn't have a good
time—and no fault of hers—I wasn't going to let *them* have a good time either'"
(ibid., 73–74).

89. Julia Erhardt offers a different reading of Fisher's views on ethnicity in
*Writers of Conviction: The Personal Politics of Zona Gale, Dorothy Canfield Fisher,
Rose Wilder Lane, and Josephine Herbst* (Columbia: University of Missouri Press,
2004). Concentrating on Fisher's involvement with the Vermont tourist industry in the 1930s, Erhardt points to comments Fisher made that might be seen as
nativist. Acknowledging Fisher's "trademark commitment to social justice and
equality" (92) and that Fisher "tirelessly advocated for . . . racial equality" (54),
Erhardt is troubled by Fisher's involvement with the Vermont Commission on
Country Life, sections of which sought to keep French Canadians and other immigrant groups, such as Scots, out of Vermont. Erhardt marshals evidence from
some of Fisher's writings from the thirties, but she reads these selectively,
downplaying Fisher's statements and actions in favor of equality and tolerance, and she ultimately concedes that Fisher actively disassociated herself
from Vermont-style nativism in the 1940s (91). I would argue that the progressive attitudes expressed in *Understood Betsy,* a novel Erhardt does not consider,
are a truer and more enduring representation of Fisher's politics.

90. Qtd. in Washington, *Dorothy Canfield Fisher,* 115.

91. Erhardt, *Writers of Conviction,* 115.

92. Fisher, *Understood Betsy,* 96–97.

93. Ibid., 52.

94. Ibid., 53.

95. Sedgwick, "Tales of the Avunculate," 71. While this quotation makes
Sedgwick seem very optimistic about the future of the American family, her
work as a whole is not quite as sanguine. She begins her book *Tendencies,* from
which the two essays quoted in this essay are taken, by pointing out the way
that "this culture has of denying and despoiling queer energies and lives. I look
at my adult friends and colleagues doing lesbian and gay work, and I feel that
the survival of each one is a miracle" ("Tales of the Avunculate," 1).

96. Lindemann, *Willa Cather,* 83.

"There lived in the Land of Oz two queerly made men"

Queer Utopianism and Antisocial Eroticism in L. Frank Baum's Oz Series

ॐ

TISON PUGH

The film version of L. Frank Baum's *The Wonderful Wizard of Oz* serves as a pop-culture icon of twentieth-century Western gay culture.[1] With Judy Garland as the star, its exaggerated characters of good and evil, and its Technicolor wonderland of vibrant colors and outlandish costumes, the film displays a queer sensibility that countless viewers adore. Today gay bars in New Orleans, Seattle, and Sweden bear the name Oz, and the iconic polychromatic flag of the gay community pays homage to the film's theme song, "Over the Rainbow." References to the film appear in numerous other artifacts of gay culture, such as when, in *The Boys in the Band,* one character derides another's ostensible heterosexuality by declaring, "He's about as straight as the Yellow Brick Road."[2] Daniel Harris documents the "canonic" nature of references to Oz in the oft-repeated catchphrase, "Toto, I don't think we're in Kansas anymore,"[3] which, for certain T-shirt incarnations, has been campily reformulated as "Aunt Em: Hate you! Hate Kansas! Taking the dog. Dorothy."[4] Although numerous other cinematic classics—from *Mildred Pierce* to *Mommie Dearest*—display a queer sensibility that elevates them to the status of cultural touchstones in the gay community, *The Wizard of Oz* towers above the rest in terms of its iconic role in queer

87

cinema's relationship to queer culture.⁵ As Harry M. Benshoff and Sean Griffin observe, "Almost every viewer (queer or not) probably enjoys the film not for its sepia-toned representation of banal 'normality' but for its breathtaking creation of a Technicolor Oz, a land where difference and deviation from the norm *are* the norm."⁶

In this essay, however, I would like to trace the roots of Oz's queerness to its beginning as a series of children's fairy tales.⁷ As Kenneth Kidd observes, "Many classics of Anglo-American children's literature are fundamentally homosocial, or concerned with same-sex friendships and family bonds. In retrospect, some of these classics seem decidedly queer."⁸ In such a light, the *Oz* books merit a retrospective analysis to plumb their queer depths; certainly, they display an antinormative sensibility in their celebration of the unique, the eccentric, and the downright peculiar. After exploring the thematic queerness of the series in its queer-friendly messages of embracing oddness and in its construction of an antinormative utopia, I turn to the ways in which Baum's *Oz* books fundamentally reimagine procreation, heterosexuality, and erotic drives. If we see Oz as a queer utopia, as a haven from the drudgeries of heteronormative inculcation, it becomes apparent that this fairy kingdom threatens the very possibility of heterosexuality by revisioning the meaning of romance and erotic attachment. The *Oz* texts are thus particularly pertinent to contemporary queer theory, especially in regard to current debates addressing the tensions between utopianism and antisociality in the construction of queer culture and identity.⁹ As an erotically antisocial queer utopia, Oz challenges the libidinal economy of heteronormative reproduction and highlights queer alternatives to expected forms of social organization.

The Queer Utopia of Oz

In terms of Baum's portrayal of Oz as a queer utopia, numerous characters, places, and even objects in the books are passingly described as queer.¹⁰ Within the opening pages of *The Wonderful Wizard of Oz*, Dorothy meets the Munchkins, "the queerest people she had ever seen" (*WWO* 5), and she then finds the Scarecrow, who has a "queer, painted face" (*WWO* 9).¹¹ The four travelers to the Emerald City—Dorothy, the Scarecrow, the Tin Woodman, and the Cowardly Lion—comprise a "queer party" (*WWO* 18), and even Oz itself is queer: "So [Dorothy] told [the Scarecrow] all about Kansas, and how gray everything was there, and how the cyclone had carried her to this queer Land of Oz" (*WWO* 10). Of course, the queerness in these examples—and in the vast majority of other instances when "queer" is used as an adjective in the series—is decidedly asexual, and Baum typically uses the word in its connotative sense of odd, unconventional, and eccentric.

Oddness, however, can be difficult to tame, despite the ideological inflection of a given text. Steven Bruhm and Natasha Hurley argue that, in creating a piece of children's literature, authors inculcate children into an ideological system: "If writing is an act of world making, writing about the child is doubly so: not only do writers control the terms of the worlds they present, they also invent, over and over again, the very idea of inventing humanity, of training it and watching it evolve."[12] Within the genre of children's literature, oddness typically facilitates the creation of an upside-down world in which readerly expectations are tweaked but in which a return to ideological and cultural normalcy is expected, as when Alice leaves Wonderland by waking up; the oddness of much children's literature thus appears congruent with theoretical conceptions of the carnivalesque, an overturning of social structures and decorum that stimulates momentary release from the status quo yet ultimately reinforces the status quo.[13] Umberto Eco acknowledges that the return to normalcy after a carnivalesque eruption tames any revolutionary potential: "Comedy and carnival are not instances of real transgressions: on the contrary, they represent paramount examples of law reinforcement."[14] Terry Eagleton makes a similar point, declaring that "carnival, after all, is a *licensed* affair in every sense, a permissible rupture of hegemony, a contained popular blow-off as disturbing and relatively ineffectual as a revolutionary work of art. As Shakespeare's Olivia remarks, there is no slander in an allowed fool."[15]

From this perspective, it is apparent that the preponderance of odd and carnivalesque incidents in children's literature refers primarily to asexual issues and that the literature serves to interpellate children, producing heteronormative ideology; at the same time, oddness cannot always be contained within hermetically sealed and ideologically approved interpretations after being so promiscuously unleashed in a world of fantasy and wonder. For example, Kiki and Ruggedo, the primary antagonists of *The Magic of Oz*, consider mixing the shapes of several animals into a new hybrid creature. Kiki initially resists the idea, asking, "Won't that make a queer combination?" Ruggedo tersely replies, "The queerer, the better" (*MagO* 681). As with many of the other examples of queerness addressed in the ensuing analysis, these lines do not emphasize gender or sexuality, yet they highlight the fundamentally queer drive of children's literature in that it so frequently rejects the banal for the unique. "The queerer, the better" could serve as a slogan for children's literature that lionizes a topsy-turvy and carnivalesque social order. Even though such queerness in most instances appears asexual, the *Oz* series highlights the ways in which asexual oddness bleeds into queer depictions of sexuality and gender. In a world that so frequently foregrounds oddness as a delightful and amusing alternative to normativity, it is difficult, then, to hinder queerness from influencing depictions of gendered identities.[16]

In this regard, the utopian *Oz* books promote themes that embrace the odd and the unique. Eccentricity and singularity are privileged cultural values in Oz, and such messages resonate with queer meaning, as when the Scarecrow convinces Jack Pumpkinhead, who fears that his ragtag body invites ridicule, to appreciate his uniqueness: "That proves you are unusual . . . and I am convinced that the only people worthy of consideration in this world are the unusual ones. For the common folks are like the leaves of a tree, and live and die unnoticed" (*MarvO* 83). In privileging the exceptional over the everyday, the Scarecrow's exhortation resounds with metaphorical meaning, as queer readers could readily apply this moral to their own sense of separation from the dominant heterosexual culture. In a similar vein, Uncle Henry is one of the least marvelous characters in the series because he bears no magical abilities, and he declares that he and Aunt Em are unlikely citizens in a fairyland: "[It ap]pears to me . . . we won't make bang-up fairies" (*ECO* 260);[17] nonetheless, he quickly realizes that one must appreciate people as they are in Oz: "This is a queer country, and we may as well take people as we find them" (*ECO* 278). Such themes pop up throughout the *Oz* series, and the Cowardly Lion voices another paean to diversity: "To be individual, my friends, to be different from others, is the only way to become distinguished from the common herd. Let us be glad, therefore, that we differ from one another in form and in disposition" (*LPO* 587). Additionally, the Shaggy Man's words—"I think our longings are natural, and if we act as nature prompts us we can't go far wrong" (*T-TO* 447)—potentially speak to any readers whose desires clash with those of the dominant culture, assuring them that natural desires will never deceive or mislead them. As with Baum's use of the word "queer," little in these examples specifically touches on sexual queerness, but they nonetheless create a fictional world in which diversity and uniqueness are esteemed over sameness and uniformity. If readers accept these themes as the lessons to be inculcated by the books, they must be prepared for women, men, and sexuality not to appear like women, men, and sexuality ostensibly should, at least from the perspective of early twentieth-century America.[18]

Certainly, Oz is a utopia for women, where they are largely freed from traditional gender roles.[19] Even in the texts that do not feature her in the lead role, Dorothy is never forgotten, and her fame throughout Oz establishes her as the primary focus of the series. Indeed, J. L. Bell describes her as a conquering hero,[20] and Joel D. Chaston observes that she rejects the home life in Kansas that threatens to domesticate her.[21] Indeed, Dorothy regenders the typical parameters of Joseph Campbell's monomyth, as Edward Hudlin notes: "The fact that Dorothy is an orphan whose parentage and origins are obscure and mysterious is essential to the further development of the story, as it prepares the reader for Dorothy's future apotheosis."[22] Assuming the masculine narratival position of a questing hero, Dorothy queers the quest narrative from its heteronormative generic foundations.[23] The individual titles of the *Oz* series all follow the mythic structure of departure, initiation, and return, yet they do so through a focus on a predominantly feminine community rather than on the individualist quest of a lone male.

After Dorothy, the most prominent character is the fairy princess Ozma, who ascends to the throne of Oz in the second book of the series, *The Marvelous Land of Oz*, and her reign further positions Oz as a queer utopia. Gender roles and sexual morphism are topsy-turvy in this land, especially in regard to Ozma herself, who was raised as a boy named Tip before learning her true identity as a fairy queen. Tip initially resists transitioning from boy to girl ("Why, I'm no Princess Ozma—I'm not a girl! . . . I don't want to be a girl!" [*MarvO* 100]), but s/he eventually accepts his/her female identity and regal duty to rule as a queen instead of as a king: "Ozma made the loveliest Queen the Emerald City had ever known; and, although she was so young and inexperienced, she ruled her people with wisdom and justice" (*MarvO* 101). The name "Tip" connotes phallic images, and the boy must be castrated semiotically and physically to assume his position as queen of the utopian land.

Ozma's magical sex change demonstrates the ease with which sex and gender roles are swapped in Oz, and additional examples of gender switching abound. The talking chicken Billina, with her aggressive personality and forthright demeanor, prefers to be called Bill:

> "So Bill I've always been called, and Bill is my name."
> "But it's all wrong, you know," declared Dorothy, earnestly; "and, if you don't mind, I shall call you 'Billina.' Putting the 'eena' on the end makes it a girl's name, you see."
> "Oh, I don't mind it in the least," returned the yellow hen. "It doesn't matter at all what you call me, so long as I know the name means ME." (*OO* 106)

Although this encounter may be read as Dorothy's policing of gendered identities, Billina's reaction—that gendered names do not affect her sense of personal identity—shows that she remains recalcitrant in disrupting gender roles. Furthermore, the chicken cares little about the biological sex of her brood and names all of her hatchlings Dorothy in honor of her friend, regardless of their sex at birth. When she realizes that "two turned out to be horrid roosters" (*ECO* 263), she changes their names from Dorothy to Daniel, but, like Ozma, these young cocks nonetheless spent their formative period incorrectly identified in regard to their biological sex. Moreover, in a fairy kingdom such as Oz, it is within the magical abilities of many creatures to turn themselves into the other sex, as evidenced by the monstrous Phanfasm: "The First and Foremost [of the Phanfasms] slowly raised his arms, and in a twinkling his hairy skin fell from him and he appeared before the astonished Nome as a beautiful woman, clothed in a flowing gown of pink gauze" (*ECO* 275). The impermanence of gendered identities and sexual morphism in Oz, in that one's gender as well as one's sexed body can metamorphose in a moment, fundamentally subverts the ideological power of gender and sexuality to discipline subjects into traditional gender roles.

This is not to say, however, that the *Oz* books construct a protofeminist and queer utopia that is entirely free from regressive attributes in regard to gender and sexuality. Many elements of the series undermine gendered normativity, yet many other elements reinforce it. Such statements as "all girls are fond of finery" (*TWO* 622) paint females as consumerist fashion plates,[24] and similar gendered stereotypes appear frequently in the texts. At the same time that these prejudicial declarations construct women with regressively feminine characteristics, typically feminine stereotypes can also be applied to the men of Oz: If it is true that "all girls are fond of finery" in Oz, so too are many of the men portrayed as indulging in excessively stylish clothing and accessories, such as those who wear a multitude of colored ribbons in their hair (*DWO* 175, *RoadO* 207, *T-TO* 405). This tension between traditional and topsy-turvy gender roles is addressed when the men of the Emerald City must undertake the domestic responsibilities abandoned by their rebellious wives. One exhausted man thanks the Scarecrow for reinstituting order to the land:

> "I'm glad you have decided to come back and restore order, for doing housework and minding the children is wearing out the strength of every man in the Emerald City."
> "Hm!" said the Scarecrow, thoughtfully. "If it is such hard work as you say, how did the women manage it so easily?"
> "I really do not know" replied the man, with a deep sigh. "Perhaps the women are made of cast iron." (*MarvO* 80)

Here we see the ostensible return to order after a period of carnivalesque chaos, in which men will once again be men and women will once again be women, yet the passage also highlights the toughness of women who can easily handle household tasks that men find exhausting. Cast-iron women metonymically represent the difficulty of pinning down the depictions of gender in Oz, which are frequently in tension between protofeminism and traditional sexism yet nonetheless highlight the potential of women to act with strength and determination.[25]

Because the biological sex of a body bears a fluctuating correspondence to personal identity in Oz, and because stereotypes of femininity and masculinity can be applied to persons of either biological sex, it is not surprising that gender roles are frequently overturned in this queer utopia. Traditionally male activities are often performed by women, notably in the many female armies that march about the country.[26] Such gender inversions in regard to military affairs are common in Oz, and in the following dialogue between Ozma and the revolutionary Jinjur, the usurper to the throne indicates that she has already succeeded in toppling masculine authority in her household:

> "Where is your husband?" asked Ozma.
> "He is in the house, nursing a black eye," replied Jinjur, calmly.

"The foolish man would insist upon milking the red cow when I
wanted him to milk the white one; but he will know better next time,
I am sure." (*OO* 148)

Rebellious women are a recurring problem in Oz, and Ann Soforth's rebellion is linked to her rejection of female chores ("'I won't' cried Ann;
'I won't sweep the floor. It is beneath my dignity'" [*T-TO* 398]); instead,
she raises an army to seize authority from Ozma. Unfortunately, her
army is composed of milquetoast men who have been previously con-
quered by their wives:

> "Jo," said Ann, "I am going to conquer the world, and you must
> join my Army."
> "Excuse me, please," said Jo Cone. "I am a bad fighter. My good
> wife conquered me years ago, for she can fight better than I. Take
> her, Your Majesty, instead of me, and I'll bless you for the favor."
> "This must be an army of men—fierce, ferocious warriors," de-
> clared Ann, looking sternly upon the mild little man. (*T-TO* 399)

The humorous paradoxes in this passage—a female general enlisting a
timid soldier who proposes the conscription of his more powerful
wife—upend traditional constructions of masculinity and femininity.
The primary gender role valorized in this passage is that armies should
be made of men, but this concept is itself undone by the fact that Ann
functions as the leader of the army.

The regendering of armies in Oz ridicules the pretensions of masculine authority in battle, while simultaneously poking fun at women
who would replace men in these armies. At the same time that Baum
satirizes aggressive women as rebellious leaders—and it must be remembered that Jinjur's army is ultimately defeated when her soldiers
flee the sudden appearance of mice (*MarvO* 81)—he consistently depicts women as more successful soldiers than men, and female troops
appear better capable of serving militarily than male troops in many of
the *Oz* books. Ozma's male army comprises twenty-six officers and one
private, and they are all cowards: "But when it came to the twenty-six
officers and the private, their knees were so weak that they could not
walk a step" (*OO* 128). Again, the tension between subverting and reinforcing traditional gender roles obscures definitive conclusions, but the
respect some characters express for female soldiers demonstrates that

such armies should not be dismissed as unthreatening: "'Girls are the fiercest soldiers of all' declared the Frogman. 'They are more brave than men, and they have better nerves. That is probably why the magician uses them for soldiers and has sent them to oppose us'" (*LPO* 608). Female armies humorously contribute to the carnivalesque social structures of Oz, but the respect accorded these warriors cannot be entirely erased due to the comic elements of their depiction.

The queer utopia of Oz delights in inversions of gender roles, and even when these comic rebellions are quelled and the status quo is reinstated, women cannot be stripped of their impressive feats throughout the narratives. Gender roles and sexual morphism mean little in this queer utopia, and their ideological import is frequently turned upside-down to delight the reader in the unexpected zaniness of this fantastic realm. In the perfect land of Oz, oddness linked to queerness upsets the ideological impact of gender in constructions of normativity. This odd queerness also disrupts the functioning of heterosexual attachment in the propagation of this queer utopia, as this blissful paradise rejects the erotic attachments foundational to the maintenance of any civilization.

The Antisocial Eroticism of Oz

A utopia is a fundamentally social construction in which its citizens work together to create a harmonious and ideal society, but the queer utopianism of Oz is undercut by its antisocial and antireproductive edges. Scholars such as Tim Dean suggest that queerness is imbued with an antisocial bias: "Insofar as [queers] fail to reproduce the family in a recognizable form, queers fail to reproduce the social."[27] Beyond the manner in which many queers reject participating in propagation, it is also debatable to what extent queers should support normative civilizations at all. Leo Bersani adumbrates the antisocial potential of queerness with his provocative question, "Should a homosexual be a good citizen?"[28] If a given society denigrates homosexuals, it seems not unreasonable for homosexuals to reject any claims upon them to act in accordance with the defined interests of this civilization. Antisociality menaces the very core of civilization, as societies depend upon the communal interactions of their citizens if they are to continue to function, if not to flourish, most obviously in the continual necessity to reproduce.

Oz celebrates a queer diversity of identity and gender reversals, as it also foregrounds a view of sexuality incongruent with the quotidian and disciplining world of heterosexuality. Quite simply, heterosexual romantic passion is virtually absent in Oz. When questing about on their adventures, the protagonists may dine or lodge with some configuration of a nuclear family, but none of the numerous major characters in the series—including Dorothy, Scarecrow, Tin Woodman, Cowardly Lion, Ozma, Glinda, Billina, Hungry Tiger, Button-Bright, Scraps, Tik-Tok, Cap'n Bill, Trot, Betsy Bobbin, Shaggy Man, the Wizard, Toto, and Eureka—is linked in a heterosexual pairing, with the primary exception of Uncle Henry and Aunt Em, the old and childless couple who adopted Dorothy when her parents died.[29] Of course, many of these characters are children who are depicted as asexual, but it should not be overlooked that the presumed asexuality of children is itself an ideological construction. Kathryn Bond Stockton outlines the paradox of describing children's sexuality:

> Children, as children, cannot be "gay"—our culture, at least officially, presumes—a category deemed too adult since it is sexual. And yet, to forbid a child this designation uncovers contradictions in the public discourse on childhood sexual orientation: the general cultural and political tendency to officially treat *all* children as straight, while continuing to deem them asexual.[30]

Within the realm of Oz, these asexual children, who might be expected to mature into heterosexual adulthood, cannot be inculcated with the ideological imperative of heterosexuality because male/female romances are so rarely seen there. Baum sought to create with his *Oz* series "a modernized fairy tale, in which the wonderment and joy are retained and the heartaches and nightmares are left out" (*WWO* 4), and so it is surprising that he consistently refuses to end his narratives with the "and they lived happily ever" formula, which is surely intended to stimulate "wonderment and joy" from readers of fairy tales as they witness the heterosexual bliss of matrimony.

Even when it appears that a heterosexual couple may be developing, such narratival expectations are more likely to be dashed than fulfilled. For example, *Rinkitink in Oz* concludes with the handsome Prince Inga visiting the poor maiden Zella. Readers know that Inga is a valiant young man because the narrator, to erase any aspersions against this hero's heterosexuality, admonishes them "not [to] think that Inga was a molly-coddle" (*RinkO* 515).[31] A fairy-tale ending might depict their wedding so that the prince can continue his family dynasty and the maiden can escape her poverty, but no such match takes place. Perhaps the most flagrant example of unresolved heterosexual attraction in the series occurs between the Scarecrow and Scraps, the Patchwork Girl:

> "Forgive me for staring so rudely," said the Scarecrow, "but you are the most beautiful sight my eyes have ever beheld."
> "That is a high compliment from one who is himself so beautiful," murmured Scraps, casting down her suspender-button eyes by lowering her head. (*PGO* 350)

This flirtatious scene lays the groundwork for male/female romance (albeit between a straw man and a quilted woman), but Scarecrow and Scraps never develop their relationship further. Heterosexuality is merely a spectral presence in Oz: at some point in the past, men and women must have consummated relationships and produced children, but no such erotic energy drives these queer narratives in their present.

Indeed, the rejection of heterosexual romance is counterbalanced by homosocial and antireproductive intimacy, as repeatedly evidenced in the deep friendship between the Tin Woodman and the Scarecrow. If any couple in the *Oz* series models the heartfelt affection of a long-term relationship, it is these two fast friends. Their union is presented in the words of the Scarecrow as a lifelong commitment: "'I shall return with my friend the Tin Woodman,' said the stuffed one, seriously. 'We have decided never to be parted in the future'" (*MarvO* 102). Later in the series, the narrator describes the depth of their friendship: "There lived in the Land of Oz two queerly made men who were the best of friends. They were so much happier when together that they were seldom apart" (*LWS* 395). In this passage the queerness of the two men is located in their bodies constructed of tin and straw, but their relationship likewise establishes them as a unique pairing in Oz, as few other friendships are described in such singular terms. Indeed, even when the Tin Woodman searches for his long-lost fiancée, the narrator stresses the emotional bond between the two men: "But at times [the Tin Woodman and the Scarecrow] were silent, for these things had been talked over many times between them, and they found themselves contented in merely being together, speaking now and then a brief sentence to prove they were wide awake and attentive" (*TWO* 618). The simple pleasure of each other's company unites them in homosocial intimacy. The cover illustration of the first edition of *The Wonderful Wizard of Oz* captures the queer friendship of these two men, depicting them holding hands with their legs crossed, and this illustration appears to presage Baum's own portrayal of the Tin Woodman as a dandy: "[The Tin Woodman] was something of a dandy and kept his tin body brilliantly polished and his tin joints well oiled" (*PGO* 381).[32]

The queerness of Oz is part of its utopian characterization: it is a fairyland where magic brings happiness and contentment to all of its citizens, despite the peculiarities of their gendered identities in regard to constructions of heteronormativity. Yet the queerness of Oz comes at a cost, as it is also a barren land. Lush vegetation bedecks its country-side, but procreation is mostly absent. Indeed, when procreation does occur, it is decidedly asexual. For example, when Tip builds Jack Pumpkinhead and then magically brings him to life, the creature identifies Tip within a familial paradigm:

> "Why, then," said the Pumpkinhead, in a tone that expressed surprise, "you must be my creator—my parent—my father!"
> "Or your inventor," replied the boy with a laugh. "Yes, my son; I really believe I am." (*MarvO* 55)

Upon learning that the boy Tip is actually the fairy princess Ozma, Jack Pumpkinhead must reconceptualize his family: "'But—see here!' said Jack Pumpkinhead, with a gasp: 'if you become a girl, you can't be my dear father any more!'" (*MarvO* 100). Numerous other such creatures are magically brought to life in the *Oz* series, including the Scarecrow (*WWO* 10), Sawhorse (*MarvO* 87), the Gump (*MarvO* 85), Tik-Tok (*OO* 111), the Glass Cat (*PGO* 319), and Scraps (*PGO* 325). In these instances, magic facilitates the asexual creation of new life-forms, in contrast to the mostly barren populace that no longer appears interested in reproduction. New life arrives to bring companionship to the lonely and assistance to the distressed, but reproduction in Oz is firmly divorced from eroticism and sexual attraction.

It is unclear whether children could be born in Oz because the fairy magic that makes the land a queer utopia also renders it a state of eternal equilibrium, if not of endless stasis:

> From that moment [when Queen Lurline enchanted the land] no one in Oz ever died. Those who were old remained old; those who were

young and strong did not change as years passed them by; and children remained children always, and played and romped to their
hearts' content, while all the babies lived in their cradles and were
tenderly cared for and never grew up. . . . [S]o seldom was there anything to worry over that the Oz people were as happy and contented
as can be. (*TWO* 643–44)

In such a land, the asexuality ascribed to children can never metamorphose into the sexuality of adults. For example, the magic of Oz affects—or infects—Dorothy such that she can never mature into a sexually experienced woman, but must always remain a sexually innocent
girl: "She could not grow big, either, and would always remain the
same little girl who had come to Oz, unless in some way she left that
fairyland or was spirited away from it" (*GO* 718). If no child ages in Oz,
the utopia is predicated upon a rejection of heterosexual procreation: it
is unnecessary, and thus irrelevant to the formation of the social order.
The paradox of Oz is thus that it is a queer utopia predicated upon the
antisocial rejection of reproduction: its foundational utopian identity
necessitates the eternal presence of children but not their continual procreation into the future. In contrast to the fantasy of Oz that celebrates
queerness while simultaneously rejecting heterosexual eroticism, the
rejection of fertility within much of modern Western society is ideologically linked to the denigration of nonreproductive sexualities, as Lee
Edelman posits: "If, however, there is *no baby* and, in consequence, *no
future*, then the blame must fall on the fatal lure of sterile, narcissistic
enjoyments understood as inherently destructive of meaning and
therefore as responsible for the undoing of social organization, collective reality, and, inevitably, life itself."[33] In Oz, however, one can celebrate nonreproductive sexuality while simultaneously celebrating the
child; here queers are not blamed for or denigrated as a result of the
failure of heterosexual reproduction because reproduction is not a cultural goal of any relevance. This queer utopia fractures the ideological
celebration of fecund heterosexuality by reimagining the meaning and
necessity of romantic networks.

Of all of the *Oz* books, *The Tin Woodman of Oz* most abundantly exposes the antiprocreative thrust in the heart of this queer utopia. A brief
recounting of the Tin Woodman's backstory, in which a human named
Nick Chopper metamorphoses from a body of meat to one of tin, is necessary for the ensuing analysis. Prior to meeting Dorothy, as depicted in
The Wonderful Wizard of Oz, Nick Chopper was engaged to a Munchkin

girl named Nimmie Amee, whose name suggestively indicates an excessive love.[34] Nimmie Amee worked for the witch with the silver shoes,[35] and the witch opposed their marriage because she feared losing her servant. To halt their union, the witch cursed Nick Chopper's axe so that it would sever his various body parts. After each limb was cut off, the tinsmith Ku-Klip replaced the limb with tin. The Tin Woodman explains his transformation from carbon- to tin-based life-form: "'In the Land of Oz,' replied the [Tin Woodman], 'No one can ever be killed. A man with a wooden leg or a tin leg is still the same man; and, as I lost parts of my meat body by degrees, I always remained the same person as in the beginning, even though in the end I was all tin and no meat'" (*TWO* 621). One day the Tin Woodman rusted in the woods, was later rescued by Dorothy and the Scarecrow, and promptly forgot all about Nimmie Amee until the beginning of *The Tin Woodman of Oz*, when Woot the Wanderer queries him about his lost love and encourages him to find her.

The Tin Woodman of Oz thus begins with a fairly typical romantic plot: the Tin Woodman must undertake a quest to find his lost love, marry her, and live happily ever after with her.[36] But in this utopian wonderland that rejects heteronormative procreation, the unfolding narrative proves just how antisocial and antierotic a force love can be. First, the Tin Woodman does not desire to pursue his lost love. He is known as the most loving man in Oz, as the narrator emphasizes: "The wonderful Wizard of Oz had given him an excellent heart to replace his old one, and he didn't at all mind being tin. Every one loved him, he loved every one; and he was therefore as happy as the day was long" (*RoadO* 232). But when Woot reminds him of Nimmie Amee, his ability to love seems not quite as all encompassing as it initially appeared. He explains to Woot that he loves everyone with his kind heart, but he does not possess a loving heart that would impel him to pursue a romantic relationship with a woman: "'the Wizard's stock of hearts was low, and he gave me a Kind Heart instead of a Loving Heart, so that I could not love Nimmie Amee any more than I did when I was heartless'" (*TWO* 621). The Tin Woodman excuses himself from the heterosexual imperative, claiming that his heart is designed to love all living creatures but not to love one woman exclusively in marriage; he only agrees to seek out his former girlfriend because of his sense of honor and responsibility: "I believe it is my duty to set out and find her. Surely it is not the girl's fault that I no longer love her, and so, if I can make her happy, it is proper that I should do so, and in this way reward her for her faithful-ness" (*TWO* 621). In the antierotic land of Oz, heterosexuality is an ob-ligation to be bravely met, rather than a delight to be joyously sought. Indeed, in the following dialogue, Woot exhorts the Tin Woodman to find pleasure in the courtship of a beautiful woman, but the reluctant lover sees only the disciplinary force of duty:

> "It ought to be a pleasure, as well as a duty, if the girl is so beautiful," said Woot, well pleased with the idea of the adventure.
> "Beautiful things may be admired, if not loved," asserted the Tin Man. "Flowers are beautiful, for instance, but we are not inclined to marry them. Duty, on the contrary, is a bugle call to action, whether you are inclined to act, or not. In this case, I obey the bugle call of duty." (*TWO* 622)

Like flowers, women are appreciated for their aesthetic value, yet such an homage to female attractiveness is accompanied with utter reluc-tance to pursue their beauty. Only his sense of masculine honor, rather than a heteronormatively masculine sex drive, impels the Tin Wood-men on his quest to marry his long lost fiancée.

During his journey to find Nimmie Amee, the Tin Woodman dis-covers that he has a rival for her affections, and it thus appears that the narrative structure of the erotic triangle will govern this installment of the *Oz* series, in that the two tin men will compete for the hand of their mutual beloved. In her foundational work on the latent queerness of erotic triangles, Eve Sedgwick explains that "in any erotic rivalry, the bond that links the two rivals is as intense and potent as the bond that links either of the rivals to the beloved"; she further notes that "the bonds of 'rivalry' and 'love,' differently as they are experienced, are equally powerful and in many senses equivalent."[37] The Tin Wood-man's rival is a soldier named Captain Fyter, who wooed and won the Tin Woodman's beloved during his long absence. Unfortunately, the wicked witch cast the same spell on Captain Fyter, and so he too cut off his limbs one by one with his sword until nothing was left but a tin sol-dier. Having lost his heart, the Tin Soldier no longer loves Nimmie Amee ("'As for that . . . I must admit I lost my ability to love when I lost my meat heart'" [*TWO* 651]), but similar to the Tin Woodman, he also decides to find and marry her out of a sense of duty ("'Well, you see I had promised to marry her, and I am an honest man and always try to keep my promises'" [*TWO* 651]). The queerness of most erotic triangles arises in the competition between the two men for the woman, which ostensibly reveals their unresolved desire for each other, but in this instance, neither man wants to win Nimmie Amee, preferring the antieroticism of their single lives to the shared bliss of marriage:

> "If you have found such a heart, sire" said the Soldier, "I will gladly allow you to marry Nimmie Amee in my place."
> "If she loves you best, sir," answered the Woodman, "I shall not interfere with your wedding her. For, to be quite frank with you, I cannot yet love Nimmie Amee as I did before I became tin." (*TWO* 651)

The function of the typical erotic triangle is to establish a narratival structure in which a heterosexual couple is created at the narrative's conclusion, such that the groundwork for procreation is prepared (even if such procreation is not depicted in the narrative itself). In their mutual desire to avoid marrying Nimmie Amee, and thus in their concomitant desire to avoid procreating with her, the Tin Woodman and the Tin Soldier enthusiastically reject the heteronormative imperative to reproduce. The Tin Woodman and Tin Solider are indeed linked in a powerful bond, as Sedgwick posits, but this bond depends on their mutual rejection of heterosexuality rather than in its agonistic pursuit. The erotic triangle typically maps out the erotic energies of a social relationship in which two's company, three's a crowd. In this incarnation, however, one is not the loneliest number; it's the preferred solution for avoiding heterosexual intercourse.

Readers might also wonder what exactly drives Nimmie Amee's erotic energies: while the Tin Woodman and Tin Soldier reluctantly compete for her hand in marriage, what does she desire? The answer appears to be that she fetishizes tin to the extent that no meat-based man could ever make her happy; rather than a swooning young woman caught up in the delights of heterosexual attraction, she simply appreciates the aesthetic appeal of shiny metal. Captain Fyter describes how his tin body aided immeasurably in courting her:

> She told me the [Tin Woodman] was nicer than a soldier, because he was all made of tin and shone beautifully in the sun. She said a tin man appealed to her artistic instincts more than an ordinary meat

man, as I was then. . . . [F]inally Nimmie Amee permitted me to call upon her and we became friends. It was then that the Wicked Witch discovered me and became furiously angry when I said I wanted to marry the girl. She enchanted my sword, as I said, and then my troubles began. When I got my tin legs, Nimmie Amee began to take an interest in me; when I got my tin arms, she began to like me better than ever, and when I was all made of tin, she said I looked like her dear Nick Chopper and she would be willing to marry me. (*TWO* 651)

The question of why Nimme Amee finds tin such a compelling component in her beloveds is never answered beyond her declarations regarding the metal's aesthetic appeal, yet certainly procreation becomes impossible when attempted between creatures respectively composed of meat and tin. (Can a tin man ejaculate?) Sexual attraction is very rarely depicted in these children's books, but it seeps into this scene, not to advance the cause of heterosexual romance, but to make such attraction outlandish, ridiculous, and ultimately terrifying. Who would pay the price of winning a woman's love, if it necessitated the amputation of all of one's body parts? Even though the biology of meat-based life-forms is frequently derided in Oz,[38] the gruesome and horrific violence inflicted upon these men—in which they suffer every possible metaphoric castration in the loss of their limbs, as well as the actual castration of their penises—renders heterosexual attraction morbidly unattractive and antierotic.

This intriguing narrative reaches its climax when the Tin Woodman and Tin Soldier find Nimmie Amee, but they discover that, during their long absence, she married another man: Chopfyt. In yet another instance of asexual reproduction in Oz, the tinker Ku-Klip created Chopfyt out of the discarded body parts of Nick Chopper and Captain Fyter, piecing their hacked-off and leftover limbs together with Magic Glue ("First, I pieced together a body, gluing it with the Witch's Magic Glue, which worked perfectly. . . . [B]y using a piece of Captain Fyter here and a piece of Nick Chopper there, I finally got together a very decent body, with heart and all the trimmings complete" [*TWO* 655–56]). Chopfyt is thus the triunal offspring of male reproduction, necessitating the bodies of two men and the creative energies of a third. Except for the Witch's Magic Glue that binds the two male bodies together, Chopfyt is a creature corporeally and psychically constructed by (and from) men.

Indeed, in terms of Nimmie Amee's sexual attraction to tin, Chopfyt bears one limb made of tin that marks Ku-Klips's role in his genesis; he is a hybrid figure of meat and tin symbolizing the past and present identities of the Tin Woodman and Tin Soldier.

Instead of representing the "child" of the Tin Woodman and Tin Soldier, the son who should serve as the apple of their eyes, Chopfyt represents the external incarnation of their own rejected qualities. Any paternal or kindred instincts that the Tin Woodman and Tin Soldier might feel for Chopfyt are negated by the creature's surly disposition. The first vision of Chopfyt emphasizes his rude and unappealing characteristics: "A man . . . was lazily reclining in a easy chair, and he . . . turned his eyes on the visitors with a cold and indifferent stare that was almost insolent. He did not even rise from his seat to greet the strangers, but after glaring at them he looked away with a scowl, as if they were of too little importance to interest him" (*TWO* 665). After calling him such disparaging names as a "Nobody" and a "mix-up" (*TWO* 665), the Scarecrow, Woot, and the Tin Woodman discuss how much they dislike him:

> "Your old parts are not very polite, I must say," remarked the Scarecrow, when they were in the garden.
> "No," said Woot, "Chopfyt is a regular grouch. He might have wished us a pleasant journey, at the very least."
> "I beg you not to hold us responsible for that creature's actions," pleaded the Tin Woodman. "We are through with Chopfyt and shall have nothing further to do with him." (*TWO* 667)

This scene bizarrely reconfigures Jacques Lacan's description of the mirror stage in which identity formulates in response to the perceived differences between the self and the external world, in that the Tin Woodman and Tin Soldier desire to see a reflection of themselves in their offspring, yet they see only unattractive qualities instead. Lacan outlines the function of the mirror in that it "may on occasion imply the mechanisms of narcissism, and especially the diminution of destruction or aggression. . . . But it also fulfills another role, a role as limit. It is that which cannot be crossed."[39] Narcissism is negated in this encounter, as the image of Chopfyt allows no opportunity for the Tin Woodman and Tin Soldier to revel in the perfection of their own reflection; rather, Chopfyt points to the monstrous limits of heterosexuality in regard to the tin men's construction of their selves. He is the hideous reconfiguration of their bodies who must ostensibly undertake, as part of his household responsibilities, the onerous task of sexual intercourse with Nimmie Amee. Although antisocial in his interactions with his "fathers," as a husband he must participate in the sociality of marriage, which is built on a heterosexual foundation rejected by the Tin Woodman and Tin Soldier.

The extent to which the Tin Woodman and Tin Soldier reject Chopfyt is frighteningly apparent in their offer to Nimmie Amee to kill him and then to reclaim their lost body parts:

> "If you don't like him," suggested the Tin Woodman, "Captain Fyter and I can chop him up with our axe and sword, and each take such parts of the fellow as belong to him. Then we are willing for you to select one of us as your husband."
>
> "That is a good idea," approved Captain Fyter, drawing his sword.
>
> "No," said Nimmie Amee; "I think I'll keep the husband I now have. He is now trained to draw the water and carry in the wood and hoe the cabbages and weed the flower-beds and dust the furniture and perform many tasks of a like character. A new husband would have to be scolded—and gently chided—until he learns my ways." (*TWO* 666)

Nimmie Amee's unromantic view of married life dismisses heterosexual attraction and affection in favor of a husband's domestic utility. Perhaps not surprising for a woman who was formerly bound to serve a witch, she finds more benefit in a man trained to tend to her household needs than in either of the two men with whom she was romantically involved. Likewise, the Tin Woodman rejoices in his escape from domesticity and encourages the Tin Soldier to join him in his happiness free from heterosexual domestic obligations: "Be thankful. It is not our fate to hoe cabbages and draw water—and be chided—in the place of this creature Chopfyt" (*TWO* 666). A happy ending is achieved at the conclusion of this fairy tale, in that the three "lovers" in the erotic triangle each achieve their respective goals, yet no one in this triangulated affair sought the erotic attachment ostensibly at its base. In this most antisocial of erotic triangles, freedom is found in the dismissal of heterosexual attraction.

If the ending of "and they lived happily ever after" defines the heteronormative valence of the fairy tale as a genre, the *Oz* books cannot be easily construed as replicating the sexually and ideologically normative dynamics of such texts. By employing queer-friendly themes and by upsetting traditional gender roles in its construction of a fairyland utopia, and by reimagining the necessity of heterosexuality and reproduction within its antisocial critique of normativity, the oddness of the *Oz* books queers the ideological and sexual foundations of fairy tale and myth. In the final analysis, it is a bit ironic that the film version of *The Wizard of Oz* is the iconic touchstone of queer culture rather than the books, since the film ultimately depicts Dorothy's rejection of Oz and her return to Kansas. The book series, on the other hand, undermines the normatizing tendencies of the domestic sphere by celebrating infertility, asexual reproduction, and the rejection of the heterosexual imperative. Oz, your roots are showing, and they are decidedly queer.

NOTES

1. The film is titled, a bit more simply, *The Wizard of Oz* (dir. Victor Fleming, perf. Judy Garland, Ray Bolger [1939; Burbank, CA: Warner, 1999]). Baum's classic novel has been theatrically and cinematically produced numerous times; see Mark Evan Swartz, *Oz before the Rainbow: L. Frank Baum's "The Wonderful Wizard of Oz" on Stage and Screen to 1939* (Baltimore: Johns Hopkins University Press, 2000).

2. Mart Crowley, *The Boys in the Band* (New York: Farrar, Straus & Giroux, 1968), 27. The film version of the play was directed by William Friedkin and stars Frederick Combs and Cliff Gorman (1970; Farmington Hills, MI: CBS/Fox Video, 1984).

3. Daniel Harris, *The Rise and Fall of Gay Culture* (New York: Hyperion, 1997), 19. Harris also addresses Judy Garland's role in gay culture and the pivotal role her death played in the Stonewall riots (16–20).

4. See Todd S. Gilman, "'Aunt Em: Hate You! Hate Kansas! Taking the Dog. Dorothy': Conscious and Unconscious Desire in *The Wizard of Oz*," in *L. Frank Baum's World of Oz: A Classic Series at 100*, ed. Suzanne Rahn (Lanham, MD: Children's Literature Association and Scarecrow Press, 2003), 127–45.

5. Studies of Hollywood and queer cinema include Harry M. Benshoff and Sean Griffin, *Queer Images: A History of Gay and Lesbian Film in America* (Lanham, MD: Rowman & Littlefield, 2006), as well as their *Queer Cinema: The Film Reader* (New York: Routledge, 2004); Michele Aaron, *New Queer Cinema: A Critical Reader* (New Brunswick, NJ: Rutgers University Press, 2004); Martha Gever, Pratibha Parmar, and John Greyson, eds., *Queer Looks: Perspectives on Lesbian and Gay Film and Video* (New York: Routledge, 1993); Richard Barrios, *Screened Out: Playing Gay in Hollywood from Edison to Stonewall* (New York: Routledge,

2003); and Alexander Doty, *Flaming Classics: Queering the Film Canon* (New York: Routledge, 2000).

6. Benshoff and Griffin, *Queer Images,* 68.

7. For studies of Baum's *Oz* novels as an American version of the fairy tale, see Laura Barrett, "From Wonderland to Wasteland: *The Wonderful Wizard of Oz, The Great Gatsby,* and the New American Fairy Tale," *Papers on Language and Literature* 42.2 (2006): 150–80; Jack Zipes, "Oz as American Myth," *Fairy Tale as Myth, Myth as Fairy Tale* (Lexington: University Press of Kentucky, 1994), 119–38; and Jordan Brotman, "A Late Wanderer in Oz," *Chicago Review* 18.2 (1965): 63–73.

8. Kenneth Kidd, "Introduction: Lesbian/Gay Literature for Children and Young Adults," *Children's Literature Association Quarterly* 23.3 (1998): 114.

9. For an engaging example of this debate, see Robert L. Caserio, Lee Edelman, Judith Halberstam, José Esteban Munoz, and Tim Dean, "The Antisocial Thesis in Queer Theory," *PMLA* 121.3 (2006): 819–28.

10. Studies of utopias include C. S. Fern, *Narrating Utopia: Ideology, Gender, Form in Utopian Literature* (Liverpool: Liverpool University Press, 1999); Libby Falk Jones and Sarah Webster Goodwin, eds., *Feminism, Utopia, and Narrative* (Knoxville: University of Tennessee Press, 1990); and Rosemary Horrox and Sarah Rees Jones, *Pragmatic Utopias: Ideals and Communities, 1200–1630* (Cambridge: Cambridge University Press, 2001). Studies of Oz as a utopia include Andrew Karp, "Utopian Tension in L. Frank Baum's Oz," *Utopian Studies* 9.2 (1998): 103–21; Barry Bauska, "The Land of Oz and the American Dream," *Markham Review* 5 (1976): 21–24; S. J. Sackett, "The Utopia of Oz," *Georgia Review* 14 (1960): 275–91; and Edward Wagenknecht, *Utopia Americana* (Seattle: University of Washington Book Store, 1929).

11. Quotations of the *Oz* books are taken from L. Frank Baum, *Fifteen Books in One—L. Frank Baum's Original Oz Series: The Wonderful Wizard of Oz, The Marvelous Land of Oz, Ozma of Oz, Dorothy and the Wizard in Oz, The Road to Oz, The Emerald City of Oz, The Patchwork Girl of Oz, Little Wizard Stories of Oz, Tik-Tok of Oz, The Scarecrow of Oz, Rinkitink in Oz, The Lost Princess of Oz, The Tin Woodman of Oz, The Magic of Oz,* and *Glinda of Oz* (London: Shoes and Ships and Sealing Wax Ltd., 2005). Quotations are cited parenthetically, and the following abbreviations, listed to align with the above titles, are used to identify the texts: *WWO, MarvO, OO, DWO, RoadO, ECO, PGO, LWS, T-TO, SO, RinkO, LPO, TWO, MagO,* and *GO.*

12. Steven Bruhm and Natasha Hurley, eds., *Curiouser: On the Queerness of Children* (Minneapolis: University of Minnesota Press, 2004), xiii.

13. The foundational exploration of the carnivalesque is Mikhail Bakhtin, *Rabelais and His World,* trans. Hélène Iswolsky (Bloomington: Indiana University Press, 1984). Recent studies of the carnivalesque in children's literature include Susanna Davidson, "Taking 'Time Out': The Carnivalesque in Shirley Hughes's *The Trouble with Jack,* the *Tales* of Beatrix Potter, and Robert Westall's *Yaxley's Cat," Journal of Children's Literature Studies* 1.1 (2004): 1–10; Lydia Williams, "We are all in the dump with Bakhtin: Humor and the Holocaust," in *Children's Literature and the Fin de Siècle,* ed. Roderick McGillis (Westport, CT:

Praeger, 2003), 129–36; and Kathryn James, "Crossing the Boundaries: Scatology, Taboo, and the Carnivalesque in the Picture Book," *Papers: Explorations into Children's Literature* 12.3 (2002): 19–27.

14. Umberto Eco, "The Frames of Comic Freedom," in *Carnival!*, ed. Thomas A. Sebeok (Berlin: Mouton, 1984), 6.

15. Terry Eagleton, *Walter Benjamin, or Towards a Revolutionary Criticism* (London: Verso, 1981), 145–46.

16. For studies of homosexuality and queerness in children's literature, see Ellis Hanson, "Screwing with Children in Henry James," *GLQ* 9.3 (2003): 367–91; Eric L. Tribunella, "Refusing the Queer Potential: John Knowles's *A Separate Peace*," *Children's Literature* 30 (2002): 81–95; Tison Pugh and David L. Wallace, "Heteronormative Heroism and Queering the School Story in J. K. Rowling's *Harry Potter* Series," *Children's Literature Association Quarterly* 31.3 (2006): 260–81; Jody Norton, "Transchildren and the Discipline of Children's Literature," *The Lion and the Unicorn* 23 (1999): 415–36; and Kirk Fuoss, "A Portrait of the Adolescent as a Young Gay: The Politics of Male Homosexuality in Young Adult Fiction," *Queer Words, Queer Images: Communication and the Construction of Homosexuality*, ed. R. Jeffrey Ringer (New York: New York University Press, 1994), 159–74.

17. The use of "fairy" to denote homosexuality dates back to the early 1900s, and as I will show throughout this essay, Baum uses several words—including "mollycoddle" and "dandy"—that bear strong homosexual connotations. To argue that Uncle Henry is denying his homosexuality in this line exceeds the realm of Baum's likely meanings, yet it also underscores the promiscuity of words and the difficulty of curtailing their meanings from sexual implications. For the connotations of "fairy," see Richard Spears, *Slang and Euphemism* (Middle Village, NY: Jonathan David Publishers, 1981), 129.

18. For historical analyses of the *Oz* series, see Gretchen Ritter, "Silver Slippers and a Golden Cap: L. Frank Baum's *The Wonderful Wizard of Oz* and Historical Memory in American Politics," *Journal of American Studies* 31.2 (1997): 171–202; Francis MacDonnell, "'The Emerald City Was the New Deal': E. Y. Harburg and *The Wonderful Wizard of Oz*," *Journal of American Culture* 13.4 (1990): 71–75; Michael Gessel, Nancy Tystad Koupal, and Fred Erisman, "The Politics of Oz: A Symposium," *South Dakota History* 31.2 (2001): 158–68; and Henry M. Littlefield, "*The Wizard of Oz*: Parable on Populism," *American Quarterly* 16 (1964): 47–58.

19. Examinations of gender in Oz include Charles Rzepka, "'If I Can Make It There': Oz's Emerald City and the New Woman," *Studies in Popular Culture* 10.2 (1987): 54–66; Richard Tuerk, "Dorothy's Timeless Quest," *Mythlore* 17.1 (1990): 20–24; Yoshido Junko, "Uneasy Men in the Land of Oz," in *Children's Literature and the Fin de Siècle*, ed. Roderick McGillis (Westport, CT: Praeger, 2003), 157–68; and Stuart Culver, "Growing Up in Oz," *American Literary History* 4.4 (1992): 607–28.

20. J. L. Bell, "Dorothy the Conqueror," *Baum Bugle* 49.1 (2005): 13–17.

21. Joel D. Chaston, "If I Ever Go Looking for My Heart's Desire: 'Home' in Baum's *Oz* Books," *The Lion and the Unicorn* 18 (1994): 209–19. Of course, the film version of *The Wizard of Oz* depicts Dorothy's happy return to her home in

Kansas, but the books are more ambiguous in their depiction of home in the "unromantic state of Kansas" (*RoadO* 205). Dorothy, Aunt Em, and Uncle Henry relocate to Oz and leave Kansas far behind as the series unfolds.

22. Edward W. Hudlin, "The Mythology of *Oz:* An Interpretation," *Papers on Language and Literature* 25.4 (1989): 446; see also J. Scott Cochrane, "The Wizard of Oz and Other Mythic Rites of Passage," in *Image and Likeness: Religious Visions in American Film Classics,* ed. John R. May (New York: Paulist, 1992), 79–86. For Campbell's construction of the monomyth, see Joseph Campbell, *The Hero with a Thousand Faces* (Princeton, NJ: Princeton University Press, 1949).

23. Regendering the hero of a narrative often results in destabilizing the narratival expectations of a given genre. For studies of the complex interrelationship of gender and genre, see Marshall Grossman, ed., *Aemilia Lanyer: Gender, Genre, and the Canon* (Lexington: University Press of Kentucky, 1998); Karen Raber, *Dramatic Difference: Gender, Class, and Genre in the Early Modern Closet Drama* (Newark: University of Delaware Press, 2001); Philip Cox, *Gender, Genre, and the Romantic Poets* (Manchester: Manchester University Press, 1996); Rohan Amanda Maitzen, *Gender, Genre, and Victorian Historical Writing* (New York: Garland, 1998); Darby Lewes, *Dream Revisionaries: Gender and Genre in Women's Utopian Fiction, 1870–1920* (Tuscaloosa: University of Alabama Press, 1995); Franziska Gygax, *Gender and Genre in Gertrude Stein* (Westport, CT: Greenwood, 1998); Lynette Felber, *Gender and Genre in Novels without End: The British Roman-fleuve* (Gainesville: University Press of Florida, 1995); and Linda S. Kauffman, *Discourses of Desire: Gender, Genre, and Epistolary Fictions* (Ithaca, NY: Cornell University Press, 1986).

24. Stuart Culver documents that, at the same time Baum was writing *The Wonderful Wizard of Oz,* he was also writing a treatise on window dressing for stores, which in many ways illuminates the emphasis on fashion in Oz; see Culver, "What Mannikins Want: *The Wonderful Wizard of Oz* and *The Art of Decorating Dry Goods Windows,"* *Representations* 21 (1998): 97–116.

25. In regard to Baum's view of women's rights, Nancy Tystad Koupal observes that Baum "championed . . . women's suffrage" ("The Politics of Oz," 156), and Raylyn Moore points out that Baum's mother-in-law was close friends with Susan B. Anthony and Elizabeth Cady Stanton (*Wonderful Wizard, Marvelous Land* [Bowling Green, OH: Bowling Green University Press, 1974], 50–51). See also Katharine M. Rogers's biography of Baum: *L. Frank Baum: Creator of Oz* (New York: St. Martin's, 2002), esp. pp. 12, 28–29, 31–32.

26. Nancy Tystad Koupal suggests that the Aberdeen Guards of South Dakota, a group of twelve women formed as an auxiliary of the Grand Army of the Republic, inspired Baum to create the many female armies of Oz. She quotes Baum's reaction to the guard: "Much curiosity has been expended as to how well a body of young ladies can be taught to drill, but even their most confident friends were agreeably surprised at the precision of their manovuers [*sic*], the accuracy of their movements and their erect and soldier-like bearing" (L. Frank Baum and Nancy Tystad Koupal, *Our Landlady* [Lincoln: University of Nebraska Press, 1996], 72–74; see also the photograph of the guard on p. 116).

27. Tim Dean, "The Antisocial Homosexual," *PMLA* 121.3 (2006): 826.

28. Leo Bersani, *Homos* (Cambridge: Harvard University Press, 1995), 113.

29. Dorothy's parents are hardly mentioned in the *Oz* series. No explanation for her father's absence is given, and Uncle Henry's musings provide the only information about her mother: "As for Uncle Henry, he thought his little niece merely a dreamer, as her dead mother had been, for he could not quite believe all the curious stories Dorothy told them of the Land of Oz" (*ECO* 252).

30. Kathryn Bond Stockton, "Eve's Queer Child," in *Regarding Sedgwick: Essays on Queer Culture and Critical Theory,* ed. Stephen M. Barber and David L. Clark (New York: Routledge, 2002), 185.

31. As a noun, the word "mollycoddle" denotes "an effeminate male," and the prefix "molly-," as in "mollyhouse" (a male brothel) and "mollymop" (a synonym for "mollycoddle"), typically refers to male homosexuality; see Spears, *Slang and Euphemism,* 256.

32. Like "mollycoddle," "dandy" also refers to an effeminate or homosexual male, a usage that dates back to the 1800s; see Spears, *Slang and Euphemism,* 98.

33. Lee Edelman, *No Future: Queer Theory and the Death Drive* (Durham, NC: Duke University Press, 2004), 13.

34. The Latin *nimis* is an adverb meaning "very much"; "Amee" appears to be a variant of "Amy," a name derived from the Latin *amo,* to love.

35. This is the same witch that Dorothy kills with her house in the film version of *The Wizard of Oz.* The shoes were changed from silver to ruby to highlight the film's Technicolor wonders.

36. Studies of the *Oz* stories as a quest narrative include John Algeo, "Oz and Kansas: A Theosophical Quest," in *Proceedings of the Thirteenth Annual Conference of the Children's Literature Association,* ed. Susan R. Gannon and Ruth Anne Thompson (West Lafayette, IN: Purdue University, 1988), 135–39; Karla Walters, "Seeking Home: Secularizing the Quest for the Celestial City in *Little Women* and *The Wonderful Wizard of Oz,*" in *Reform and Counterreform: Dialectics of the Word in Western Christianity since Luther,* ed. John C. Hawley (Berlin: Mouton de Gruyter, 1994), 153–71; and Teresa Devroe, "Follow the Yellow Brick Road to Nirvana," *Wittenberg University East Asian Studies Journal* 16 (1991): 1–20.

37. Eve Kosofsky Sedgwick, *Between Men: English Literature and Male Homosocial Desire* (New York: Columbia University Press, 1985), 21.

38. Humans are repeatedly ridiculed as "meat people" in the *Oz* series because they must endure the many vagaries of their bodies. The Scarecrow expresses sympathy for "meat people [who must] shut their eyes and lie still during the dark hours" (*SO* 502), and the Tin Woodman describes humans as "clumsy meat people" before lauding the benefits of straw and tin bodies: "You and I do not eat meat, and so we are spared the dreadful bother of getting three meals a day" (*LPO* 616). Yet another disparaging view of the human body is voiced by the Sawhorse: "I must point out to you the fact that you are all meat creatures, who tire unless they sleep and starve unless they eat and suffer from thirst unless they drink. Such animals must be very imperfect, and imperfect creatures cannot be beautiful" (*LPO* 587).

39. Jacques Lacan, *The Seminar of Jacques Lacan, Book VII: The Ethics of Psychoanalysis, 1959–1960,* ed. Jacques-Alain Miller, trans. Dennis Porter (New York: Norton, 1997), 151.

The Queerness of *Harriet the Spy*

§

ROBIN BERNSTEIN

When Kathleen T. Horning was growing up queer in the 1960s, Harriet M. Welsch was her "role model and savior."[1] Horning recognized the heroine of Louise Fitzhugh's 1964 novel, *Harriet the Spy,* as a "kindred spirit," and she was far from alone in that assessment. Many other queer and proto-queer children saw themselves mirrored in and inspired by the brash, blunt girl who wears boys' clothes, spies on adults, and records all she sees in her notebook. Alison Bechdel, creator of the long-running comic strip "Dykes to Watch Out For" and the best-selling graphic memoir *Fun Home,* "probably read *Harriet the Spy* about 70,000 times" and considers it one of her "deepest influences."[2] A character in Elizabeth Pincus's short story, "Trouble on the Beat," says, "Harriet stole my heart when I was a kid—maybe that's what made me a dyke. Or a private eye."[3] Virginia L. Wolf, Fitzhugh's biographer, describes the book as a "milestone" for many girls "in the process by which they discovered and accepted their sexual orientation as lesbians."[4]

Readings of Harriet as a tomboy or proto-lesbian icon are common, but they attract vitriol. When *Horn Book* published Horning's essay about *Harriet the Spy* in 2005, letters to the editor accused Horning of "heavy projecting" and of writing an essay that had no purpose except to abet the censorship of children's books.[5] When a website posted Horning's essay, the guestbook recorded personal attacks such as that of "Dina Lee," who accused Horning of sexual insecurity and told her to "quit trying to find gay messages in everything and stop trying to ruin the way other people see things to suit your needs.[6]

111

The harsh critiques of lesbian readings mirror some early critical responses to the book itself. Forty years before *Horn Book* published Horning's essay, that same journal published an influential decimation of the novel by Ruth Hill Viguers, who lamented the book's "implication that New York City harbors only people who are abnormal, ill-adjusted, and egocentric."[7] Viguers assailed the characters as "merely depressing types . . . from ghoulish Janie to pathetic Sport."[8] Soon after the publication of Viguers' essay, *Harriet* became the object of widespread criticism. Librarians and book reviewers worried that Harriet's spying might inspire imitation (which it did).[9] Reviewers heaped disgust upon the characters, whom they decried as warped misrepresentations of children: One reviewer called the characters "unchildlike," while a librarian warned that "Harriet is no child."[10] Most of all, critics objected to the novel's resolution. When Harriet's classmates discover the notebook and read her unflinching observations, they ostracize and torment the girl. Harriet's governess, Ole Golly, advises Harriet to lie to preserve her friendships while remaining inwardly true to herself, and to develop her notes into fiction. Harriet follows the advice, and her two best friends, Janie and Sport, return to her side.

Arguments about Ole Golly's morality and about whether Harriet is unchildlike or proto-queer, seem unrelated to each other. This essay argues, however, that Ole Golly's final advice integrates with other aspects of the novel to trouble age as a category of analysis. This "age trouble" ultimately underwrites the novel's queer subtext. In short, the effect of queerness in *Harriet the Spy* is produced *through* Fitzhugh's construction of age.

Many readers identify genderqueerness—that is, nonnormative gender that disrupts man/woman binaries or that deconstructs the very category of gender—as constituting a queer or lesbian subtext in Fitzhugh's novel. For Horning, for example, Harriet is "the quintessential baby butch," and "her best friends, Sport and Janie, run exactly contrary to gender stereotypes."[11] Harriet does buck femininity by hollering a lot, wearing jeans and sneakers with a homemade tool belt, and slamming her notebook closed. When Janie Gibbs's mother criticizes the way Harriet moves, Harriet replies, "Fast . . . that's the way I move, fast. What's wrong with that?" Mrs. Gibbs has no answer for the question, and is temporarily struck dumb. She recovers by laughing and by telling both Harriet and Janie, "I think you have to find out you're girls."[12] For Mrs. Gibbs and many readers, then, Harriet and Janie are unfeminine.

Readings of Harriet as a tomboy or baby butch do not, however, stand up under close scrutiny. Harriet defies the image of a tomboy in many ways: she has long hair, wears dresses without complaint, has no interest in sports, and is never mistaken for a boy. And although she eschews feminine trappings such as mud packs, she does engage in some stereotypically feminine activities such as hating math, resenting other girls' beauty, and worrying about her weight.[13] Janie and Sport alternately defy and affirm gender norms as well. Sport, for example, takes care of the house and his father (Harriet once likens Sport to a "little old woman"),[14] but he aspires to be a ballplayer (or a certified public accountant). Genderqueerness is present in *Harriet the Spy*, but the rebellions against gender norms are inconsistent, and they never become the novel's most salient feature. In contrast, Fitzhugh's later novel, *Nobody's Family is Going to Change*, foregrounds genderqueerness throughout. In that novel, a child protagonist named Emma wants to be a lawyer, while her brother Willie wants to be a dancer. Emma succinctly describes the problem at the center of the novel: "Willie wants to do a girl's thing, and I want to do a boy's thing, and our father hates both of us [for that reason]."[15] That novel includes a lengthy conversation about cross-dressing (Emma even uses the word "transvestism") and a character who jokes good-naturedly about his effeminate and gay coworkers.[16] If genderqueerness were enough to provoke queer readings, then *Nobody's Family is Going to Change*, far more than *Harriet the Spy*, would be hailed as the "milestone" in proto-queer reading. But that is not the case.

Louise Fitzhugh was more consistently genderqueer than Harriet ever was. A tomboyish girl and a butch woman, Fitzhugh went by the nicknames of Sport and Willie—names that she assigned to male characters in her fiction. In 1965, soon after the publication of *Harriet the Spy*, Fitzhugh inherited significant wealth, which she used to have men's suits custom-tailored for her.[17] Fitzhugh's gender intersected and overlapped with her sexuality: according to Fitzhugh's friend, collaborator, and brief lover, Sandra Scoppettone, Fitzhugh was "always out. . . . She wore little men's suits. So there wasn't any question" about her lesbianism.[18] Fitzhugh dated some men, but she was "firmly rooted in the lesbian world," according to Marijane Meaker.[19] Meaker, herself a prolific author of children's books, lesbian pulp novels, and nonfiction (under many pen names including M. E. Kerr, Ann Aldrich, and Vin Packer), was a close friend of Fitzhugh and a source of the character of

Harriet. As a child, Meaker eavesdropped and peeked in windows (even organizing other children in the neighborhood to spy on a particular girl who captured Meaker's interest), for which she was dubbed "Marijane the Spy." In her autobiography, Meaker describes how Fitzhugh created the character of Harriet:

> I was friends with the writer Louise Fitzhugh. . . . We used to swap stories and discuss ideas, and when she wrote . . . *Harriet the Spy*, I said, "Hey, wait a minute! That's my story! I told you I was Marijane the Spy, and you stole that idea from me!" Louise said all kids are spies when they're little. She was and I was . . . and she just beat me to the punch and told the story first.[20]

Harriet is the imaginative product of one lesbian, partially based on another lesbian writer. A reading of Harriet as proto-lesbian, however, is as troublesome as a reading of her as genderqueer. Harriet has no interest in sex or romantic love. Fitzhugh did write a scene in which a character has romantic daydreams about being swept away by a stranger of the same sex—but the character is Willie, in *Nobody's Family is Going to Change*, and the stranger is a man, not a woman. The articulation of Willie's same-sex desire makes Harriet's absence of romantic feelings for any person all the more apparent. When Harriet spies, she regards women with an interest that is comparable, both in magnitude and in kind, to the interest she shows in men. Harriet considers herself, if anything, heterosexual: she draws analogies between her friendship with Sport and the love between her parents and between Ole Golly and her fiancé.[21] She also jokes that Sport is her husband and assumes she will marry him in the future.[22]

What is queerest about Harriet is not her gender or her (lack of) sexual or romantic desire, but her age. As Kenneth Kidd has shown, thinkers from Sigmund Freud to Michel Foucault have associated homosexuality with childhood, and in children's literature "the homosexual and the child are not sworn enemies but in fact a popular duo in the modern biopolitical episteme."[23] Kathryn Boyd Stockton observes that queers in literature "trail children behind them, or alongside them, as if they were wedded, one to another, in unforeseen ways"—a pairing that produces not a polarity but a mingling.[24]

The queer child and queered childhood are familiar sites at which childhood and queerness overlap, as is the psychoanalytic construction

of queerness as a form of arrested development. What has gone unana-
lyzed, however, is the ways in which age itself, as a category of analysis, can produce queer effects. Monique Wittig lays the foundation for
such analysis in her well-known essay "One is Not Born a Woman."
Wittig argues that the "refusal to become (or to remain) heterosexual always meant to refuse to become a man or a woman, consciously or
not."[25] For Wittig, lesbianism is a

> concept . . . beyond the categories of sex (woman and man), because
> the designated subject (lesbian) is *not* a woman, either economically,
> or politically, or ideologically. For what makes a woman is a specific
> social relation to a man, a relation that we have previously called
> servitude, a relation which implies personal and physical obligation
> as well as economic obligation . . . , a relation which lesbians escape
> by refusing to become or stay heterosexual.[26]

Wittig argues that women exist in binary opposition to men; lesbians refuse this opposition and therefore do not become or remain
women. What Wittig neglects to say, however, is that women also exist
in binary opposition to *girls*. Heterosexuality is crucially enacted
through a ritualistic pairing with a differently-gendered partner—in
the case of a woman, this pairing constructs a "specific social relation to
man" that entails "personal and physical obligation."[27] This opposi-
tional social relation turns females into women. However, heterosexual
pairing functions also as a punctuation mark in an evolution into maturity. Colloquially, to marry is to grow up. A lesbian who refuses to
pair heterosexually does not collect a crucial marker of adulthood. She
is therefore not a woman not only because she does not exist in binary
opposition to men, but because she refuses to locate herself in binary
opposition to *girlhood*. The "woman" that lesbianism refuses is a category equally of gender and of *age*. "Lesbian" is therefore a category that
queers age while it queers gender. If, for Wittig, lesbians are inherently
genderqueer (a term that was unavailable to her when she published
her essay in 1981), then lesbians are equally, to coin a term, agequeer. To
be queer is to trouble age fundamentally as a category of analysis.

Age is very queer in *Harriet the Spy*. Throughout the novel, Fitzhugh
destabilizes age; her inclusion of adultlike children and immature
adults disarticulates age as an identity from chronological or biological
age. For example, Harriet's classmates, Marion Hawthorne and Rachel

Hennessey, "walk like old ladies," organize an exclusive club for "the right kind of person," play bridge, and drink tea, prompting Harriet to "bet they'll be doing that the rest of their lives."[28] Marion in particular is depicted as a miniature adult: "Harriet had a sudden vision of Marion grown up, and decided she wouldn't look a bit different, just taller and more pinched."[29]

A hallmark of Fitzhugh's child characters is the seriousness with which they pursue adult professions. Janie, with her "definite mind," is a chemist focused on her goal of blowing up the world.[30] Sport manages his father's finances, maintains the apartment, and wants to be either a ball player or a CPA. Harriet assumes professionalism to be the norm among children; she considers her classmates without professions to be "JUST BATS."[31] She repeatedly insists, "I do not go out to PLAY, I go out to WORK!"[32]

As Fitzhugh's child characters professionalize, the adult characters regress. Fitzhugh's novels abound with bratty, professionless adults. Fitzhugh destabilizes age most compactly—and wittily—in her description of a sculpture purchased by a couple on which Harriet spies:

> It was an enormous, but enormous—perhaps six feet high—wooden sculpture of a fat, petulant, rather unattractive baby. The baby wore a baby cap, huge white dress, and baby booties. The head was completely round and carved out of butcher's block so that it resembled a beautifully grained newel post with a face carved in it. The baby sat on its diapered bottom, feet straight out ahead, and fat arms curving into fatter hands which held, surprisingly, a tiny mother.[33]

Critics objected, as we recall, to Fitzhugh's unchildlike children and "disagreeable"—spoiled, idle, immature, and in the case of the sculpture, overwhelmed—adults. As disturbed as critics were by the destabilized age of Fitzhugh's characters, they were even more outraged by Ole Golly's final advice to Harriet. A reviewer for the *Christian Science Monitor,* for example, decried Harriet as "a pathetic figure—too pathetic, one hopes, for young people to admire," and complained that Fitzhugh "confuses" morality: "The implication [of Ole Golly's advice] is: be true to yourself even if you can't be true to other people."[34] Fitzhugh's detractors did not view these complaints as linked. The lens of agequeerness, however, reveals the ways in which these objections intertwine.

Horning argues forcefully for a queer reading of Ole Golly's advice that Harriet lie to her classmates, "But to yourself you must always tell the truth."[35] This advice, in Horning's view, "takes on special meaning for queer kids."[36] As Horning correctly notes, the first segment of Ole Golly's advice

> aroused adult ire. . . . But for gay kids focusing equally on both sentences [the advice to lie to others and to tell the truth to one's self], the advice turned out to be a lifesaver. All those years ago, whether consciously or unconsciously, Louise Fitzhugh provided us with the tools for survival. . . . In all [Fitzhugh's] books . . . the message is inherent: *Be true to yourself. Refuse to conform. Find your own way, even if your friends and family threaten to reject you. It will be painful, but you will survive.*[37]

Horning is quite right that Ole Golly offers practical advice to enable queer and proto-queer kids to survive.[38] However, Horning neglects a different yet integral part of Ole Golly's advice: that Harriet develop her notes into fiction. Ole Golly's letter to Harriet reads in part,

> If you are ever going to be a writer it is time you got cracking. You are eleven years old and haven't written a thing but notes. Make a story out of some of those notes and send it to me. . . . Remember that writing is to put love in the world. . . . You're eleven years old which is old enough to get busy at growing up to be the person you want to be.[39]

Ole Golly advises Harriet to combine outward lies and inward honesty with, crucially, the production of fiction for public consumption: "Make a story out of some of those notes and send it to me." Ole Golly does tell Harriet to hide the truth, but she urges Harriet to hide it in plain sight—as fiction. In Horning's reading, a lesbian Fitzhugh "consciously or unconsciously" provided, through Ole Golly, the tools queer children need to stay closeted, while retaining their integrity, until it is safe for them to come out. But in fact, Ole Golly tells Harriet, equally, to go public. Ole Golly's advice incorporates two historically distinct meanings of the term "come out."[40] As George Chauncey has demonstrated, the term's meaning changed around the time of World War II. Before that war, gay people "did not speak of *coming out of* what we call the 'gay closet,' but rather of *coming out into* what they called 'homosexual society' or the 'gay world,' a world neither so small, nor so isolated, nor, often, so hidden as 'closet' implies."[41] The prewar "coming out" punned on debutante balls, society debuts. Ole Golly does advise Harriet to lie, that is, to closet herself; but she integrates this advice with a call for Harriet's literary debut. The instruction to "get cracking" at being a writer—to professionalize—for the purpose of "put[ting] love in the world" links destabilized age to nonheterosexual love. In a sense, Ole Golly tells Harriet to give birth to herself, to become her own parent by transforming herself into "the person"—the writer—"you want to be."

Following Ole Golly's advice, Harriet writes her first short story and submits it to *The New Yorker*. This action merges precocity with survival, professionalization with the simultaneous hiding and display of secrets, queer age with both closet and debut. Ole Golly's advice *is* profoundly queer—not only because it condones lying as a technique of self-preservation, but because it positions agequeerness, the destabilized age of the self-professionalizing child, as crucial to survival. Through Ole Golly, Louise Fitzhugh whispered to generations of queer children, *Sometimes you have to lie. But to yourself you must always tell the truth. Now get busy at growing up to be the person you want to be.*

NOTES

Some material in this essay appeared originally in Robin Bernstein, "'Too Realistic' and 'Too Distorted': The Attack on Louise Fitzhugh's *Harriet the Spy* and the Gaze of the Queer Child," *Critical Matrix: The Princeton Journal of Women, Gender, and Culture* 12.1–2 (2000–2001): 26–47.

1. Kathleen T. Horning, "On Spies and Purple Socks and Such," *Horn Book Magazine* 81.1 (2005): 49.

2. Trina Robbins, "Watch Out for Alison Bechdel (She has the Secret to Superhuman Strength)," *Comics Journal* 237 (2001), http://archives.tcj.com/237/i_bechdel.html; Alison Bechdel, "moose, marriage, pocket history of sex," 31 March 2009 comment on blog entry in "Dykes to Watch Out For: Life in a Box," http://dykestowatchoutfor.com/moose-marriage-pocket-history-of-sex#comment-299743.

3. Quoted in Virginia L. Wolf, *Louise Fitzhugh* (New York: Twayne, 1991), 21–22. Wolf lists many other examples of lesbians describing the novel's influence over their sexuality and their professional lives.

4. Wolf, *Louise Fitzhugh*, 21–22.

5. Marion C. Mahoney, "Letter to the Editor," and Christine Brojek, "Letter to the Editor," *Horn Book Magazine* 81.3 (2005): 244.

6. "Guestbook" to "Purple Socks: A Louise Fitzhugh Tribute Site," http://purple-socks.webmage.com/. The comment appears on the guestbook's seventh page, which must be accessed through "Purple Socks." The owner and designer of the website appears to be Horning.

7. Ruth Hill Viguers, "On Spies and Applesauce and Such," *Horn Book Magazine* 41.1 (February 1965): 74.

8. Ibid.

9. Some libraries established ad hoc committees to decide whether the book deserved space on the shelves. For an excellent overview of librarians' and critics' responses to the novel, see Jane K. Hirsch, "The Critical Reception of Three Controversial Children's Books: *Harriet the Spy* by Louise Fitzhugh, *Ring the Judas Bell* by James Forman, *Dorp Dead* [*sic*] by Julia Cunningham," MLS thesis, Catholic University, 1966, 28–34. See also Anne Commire, ed., *Something About the Author*, vol. 45 (Detroit: Gale Research Company, 1986), s.v. "Louise Fitzhugh," pp. 77–78, on the censorship of Fitzhugh's novel.

10. Qtd. in Hirsch, "Critical Reception," 29, 32.

11. Horning, "On Spies," 51.

12. Louise Fitzhugh, *Harriet the Spy* (1964; reprint, New York: Harper-Collins Children's Books, 1990), 81.

13. Ibid., 65, 139, 29–30, 53, 84; Harriet's weight is even more of an issue in the novel's sequel, *The Long Secret*).

14. Ibid., 182.

15. Louise Fitzhugh, *Nobody's Family is Going to Change* (1974; reprint, New York: Dell, 1976), 119.

16. Ibid., 114.

17. Karen Cook, "Regarding Harriet: Louise Fitzhugh Comes In from the Cold," *Voice Literary Supplement*, April 1995, 15.

18. Robin Bernstein, "Keeping Secrets: Sandra Scoppettone's Secret of Success," *Washington Blade*, September 1994, 53.

19. Cook, "Regarding Harriet," p. 13.

20. M. E. Kerr, *Me Me Me Me Me: Not a Novel* (New York: Signet, 1984), 67.

21. Fitzhugh, *Harriet the Spy*, 102, 91.

22. Ibid., 15, 46.

23. Kenneth Kidd, "Introduction: Lesbian/Gay Literature for Children and Young Adults," *Children's Literature Association Quarterly* 23.3 (1998): 116.

24. Kathryn Bond Stockton, "Growing Sideways, or Versions of the Queer Child: The Ghost, the Homosexual, the Freudian, the Innocent, and the Interval of Animal," in *Curiouser: On the Queerness of Children*, ed. Steven Bruhm and Natasha Hurley (Minneapolis: University of Minnesota Press, 2004), 278–79.

25. Monique Wittig, "One is Not Born a Woman," in *The Lesbian and Gay Studies Reader*, ed. Henry Abelove, Michele Aina Barale, and David Halperin (New York: Routledge, 1993), 105. The essay was originally published in *Feminist Issues* 1.2 (1981).

26. Ibid.

27. Ibid.

28. Fitzhugh, *Harriet the Spy*, 271, 272, 293.

29. Ibid., 148. Later, Marion is described as "the only one really *known* for pinching" (237). Fitzhugh thus connects doing (pinching) with being (looking pinched)—a connection that resonates with Harriet's conflation of profession with identity.

30. Ibid., 80.

31. Ibid., 278.

32. Ibid., 39.

33. Ibid., 157–58. J. D. Stahl demonstrated that this sculpture resembles *Baby Girl*, a sculpture by Marisol (Marisol Escobar) that Fitzhugh very likely saw at the Museum of Modern Art in 1963. Stahl suggests that Fitzhugh's text might parody Marisol's sculpture, but that more likely Fitzhugh was producing "a literary equivalent of Marisol's visual satire." J. D. Stahl, "Louise Fitzhugh, Marisol, and the Realm of Art," *Children's Literature Association Quarterly* 24.4 (1999): 160.

34. Patrice M. Daltry, "The Cold that Came in with the Spy," *Christian Science Monitor*, February 25, 1965, 7.

35. Fitzhugh, *Harriet the Spy*, 276.

36. Horning, "On Spies," 51.

37. Ibid., 51–52.

38. I made a similar argument in my article "Too Distorted."

39. Fitzhugh, *Harriet the Spy*, 276–77.

40. The term "come out" does not appear in the novel; the point is that the *idea* of coming out, in both the prewar and postwar senses, is pivotal in *Harriet the Spy*.

41. George Chauncey, *Gay New York: Gender, Urban Culture, and the Making of the Gay Male World, 1890–1940* (New York: Basic Books, 1994), 7.

Refusing the Queer Potential

John Knowles's A Separate Peace

৯

ERIC L. TRIBUNELLA

In children's literature, the boys' school story solidifies as a genre in the mid-nineteenth century. Works about boys at school, usually boarding schools, often focus on the close friendships of the boys, their hijinks and adventures, and their experience of maturation. Thomas Hughes's *Tom Brown's Schooldays* (1857) and Frederic Farrar's *Eric, or Little by Little* (1858) are two prototypical school stories that helped establish the genre.[1] Both involve boys forming intimate same-sex friendships before one of the boys is lost or nearly lost through illness or death. In the case of the former, Tom Brown is made into a better boy and ultimately a respectable man through his friendship with the sickly George Arthur, who nearly dies. In the latter novel, the protagonist, Eric, actually does die, which encourages the reader to avoid the moral decline that leads to Eric's death. Thus, through the experience of friendship and loss, the surviving boy or reader is helped along in the process of maturation, and the outcome of the boys' school story is usually the successful manhood of the protagonist, who leaves behind school and the friend he associates with childhood. John Knowles's *A Separate Peace*, first published in 1959, is a mid-twentieth-century American school story that clearly follows in this tradition. Its frequent use in schools throughout the United States points to the sense that such a narrative is useful as a guide for child readers on their own paths to proper adulthood. By the end of Knowles's novel, Gene is able to demonstrate many of the qualities that constitute maturity, and he manages to achieve this outcome through the traumatic loss of his friend and his conscious and unconscious efforts to remake himself in his friend's image.

According to Beverly Lyon Clark, school stories are "so marked by gender that it becomes vital to address questions of both the instability and potency of gender in the school story."[2] Clark recognizes that while schooling, and hence stories about schooling, are implicated in various social hierarchies, they also allow "some possibility of subversion, some possibility for giving one perspective on the marginal, on class, gender, race, ethnicity, sexuality." School is, she suggests, a site for working out contrary impulses.[3] Kathy Piehl argues for consideration of *A Separate Peace* as school story in her comparison of the novel with Hughes's own, and it is suggested elsewhere that one of the "ideal" types of contemporary adolescent fiction focuses on the burgeoning of one's sexuality, frequently in the school setting.[4] Given both the importance of gender and sexuality to the school story, a genre to which *A Separate Peace* seems clearly to belong, and the persistent use of this novel in the secondary-school classroom, an understanding of how it reinforces or potentially resists the social hierarchies of which Clark writes is crucial to deciphering its pedagogical function.

If works of fiction can be said to lead double lives, *A Separate Peace* would be the quintessential example. On the one hand, the novel is widely regarded as what some would call "homoerotic" because of the passionate or romantic friendship between the boys. The novel is sold in gay bookstores—appearing in the "queer classics" section of one chain—and it has even been featured in an advertisement for a gay nightclub in New York City that depicts a number of sexual situations involving men at a library. Several books, having been pulled from the shelves, lie strewn on the floor. The texts are ones commonly known to be available to homoerotic readings: *Leaves of Grass, Moby Dick, Billy Budd, Lord of the Flies,* and *A Separate Peace.* The advertisement assumes that an audience of gay men will recognize these works and their availability to being read as homoerotic. Thus, it is not my aim merely to confirm this quality of the text; rather, given this possibility, I am interested in how teachers have written about the text's use, in the processes that seem to underlie this homoeroticism, and in what the text might suggest about the sacrifice of the boys' queer potential as a way of constructing proper and productive adult citizenship. When I refer to queer youth or possibilities, I mean that they are marked as in some way deviant or nonnormative, in terms of either gender or sexuality, and that their expressions of desire, pleasure, or gender open up spaces or possibilities of difference from or opposition to what is considered normal. The queerness of the boys in *A Separate Peace* is constituted both by a subtle resistance to expectations of normative gender expression and, of course, by the intimate and emotionally charged friendship between Gene and Finny that is never overtly consummated or even acknowledged. Ultimately, Gene is forced to refuse his own queer potential.

While the novel is recognized as a "queer classic " on the one hand, it is widely assigned in high school English classrooms on the other, and published school curricula and teacher rationales regard the novel as useful for teaching young people about democratic values and ethical citizenship. These materials make no mention of *A Separate Peace* as a "queer classic." As with Herman Melville's *Billy Budd* (left unfinished in 1891 and published in 1924) and Oscar Wilde's *A Picture of Dorian Gray* (1891) the potential of a book like *A Separate Peace* to be read as homoerotic constitutes a kind of open secret—something a reader knows, intuits, feels vaguely, denies, rejects, or perhaps remains oblivious to— that cannot help but impinge on the experience of the reader reading it. In the age of blogs and Internet message boards, one can find pages and pages of chatter about whether *A Separate Peace* is or isn't "gay," and the energies generated by the tension between its youthful protagonists, between the novel and its readers, between the teachers who assign it and the students who read it, and between those who think it "is" and those who think it "isn't" no doubt fuel its continued popularity as a mainstay of high school reading lists *and* as a "queer classic." It provides a lesson on what alternatively might be called ambiguity or subtext, on the need to be attentive to subtlety, on the dynamics of the closet, on the possibilities of pleasure in "knowing" a sexual secret or solving its mystery, on the potential for homosexuality to be anywhere, everywhere, or nowhere. All of these acts of reading and discovery surrounding sexuality, violence, and citizenship seem particularly suited to the instruction of young people imagined to be in the process of their own sexual and civic explorations and discoveries. Indeed, the novel no doubt works to prompt precisely such explorations and discoveries without evoking the kind of hysteria that has surrounded other more explicitly sexual or gay-themed literature in schools. And although the dynamics of the closet that *A Separate Peace* seems to embody might be thought characteristic of an earlier moment in the history of sexuality, one that perhaps required more discretion, the novel that leads a double life might in fact remain especially relevant at a moment when same-sex desire can be both sanctioned as content for television sitcoms and simultaneously reason for the vehement denial of civil rights. Culturally, homosexuality itself seems to lead a double life.

The social significance of novels taught in school is manifested by the contention that surrounds many of them. *A Separate Peace* has not escaped controversy and in some cases has even been removed from classroom use. It has been the object of attempted censorship in several cases throughout the United States brought by parents who for various reasons have found its content objectionable.[5] Parents, who before the late nineteenth century "were ready to accept the most ardent degree of affection between boys [in school stories] if it involved no physical expression (except a chaste deathbed kiss)," eventually came to be horrified by the mere possibility of same-sex genitality.[6] The availability of *A Separate Peace* to a queer reading was understood by the parents of a Vernon-Verona-Sherrill (New York) School District student, who in 1980 contested the use of the novel because of its "underlying theme" of homosexuality. They claimed that the book actually encouraged homosexuality, and as a result, it was removed from classroom use.[7] Given, though, what others recognize as its literary merit and pedagogical usefulness, the attacks have been resisted by educators and librarians, resulting in the publication of rationales composed to defend its use. Educators have touted the novel as a useful tool for imparting patriotic and ethical values, but its usefulness for imparting "democratic ideals" cannot be understood without examining how the novel constructs and manages same-sex desire and friendship and how its ultimate disavowal of them might in fact constitute those democratic ideals. The book does, however, present possibilities for readings that resist such a use, as the complaint of the plaintiffs in the 1980 case attests.

In a 1983 edition of the *Connecticut English Journal* devoted to rationales for commonly challenged books used in the classroom, Diane Shugert writes that these rationales set out to explain how *A Separate Peace* "relates to the democratic ideal of the educated citizen, prepared to make her own decisions."[8] Richard Hargraves, author of a course outline entitled Values, suggests that a system of values "should encompass recognized universal but functional ethical codes and modes which provide a basis for conduct in contemporary, American society."[9] *A Separate Peace* figures as one of the primary texts in this curriculum, which seeks to foster a personal value system including positive self-images, the ability to differentiate between tolerance and intolerance, a sense of the centrality of freedom and personal independence, and the importance of truth and reconciliation. W. Michael Reed proposes that *A Separate Peace* "offers adolescents some important perspective upon the nature of human experience."[10] In Reed's view, students should value *A Separate Peace* because of its insights concerning methods by which adolescents interact with one another. Other apologists cite the novel for its "universal" lessons about moral development and the human ideal.

I would argue, however, that the rhetoric of ethics, values, and patriotism in which rationales for this book are steeped masks its *use* as a tract for inscribing the "appropriate" gender and sexuality in adolescent males and promoting their normative maturation. The novel's pedagogical guidebooks fail to acknowledge what many readers recognize as the erotic friendship between Gene and Finny, the homophobic motivation for Gene's panicked reaction to Finny's affection, the significance of the loss of the boys' passionate friendship, or the way in which Gene's social contribution and maturity are coded in gendered terms. Gene's maturation throughout the novel represents his movement away from an effete intellectualism and "adolescent" homoerotic relationship. His "moral" progression involves abandoning the queer possibility and accepting a hegemonic and necessarily heterosexual masculinity that adolescent readers of the novel are tacitly encouraged to emulate and valorize. The novel has been recruited as representative of universal adolescence in part because of its heteronormative developmental narrative, which does not simply reflect adolescent experience but contributes to the discourse compelling that experience. The themes of *A Separate Peace* do indeed represent American cultural values, including, quite significantly, heterosexuality and masculinity in men.[11]

While these rationales uphold the novel as pedagogically useful, the novel itself is far more ambiguous about what it suggests concerning Gene's development. These rationales, by incorporating *A Separate Peace* into an educational program, might significantly depart from and obscure the critique Knowles's novel potentially offers of the process by which Gene becomes a man. Indeed, the extent to which *A Separate Peace* works to promote normative maturation might be an effect more of its pedagogical applications than the qualities of the text itself, which are far more ambivalent in the way they come together to represent Gene's development. *A Separate Peace* is framed by the narration of Gene, who returns to Devon School fifteen years later to reminisce about his coming of age. By beginning and concluding the novel with the insights of an adult Gene, Knowles preestablishes the inevitable culmination of the story's movement—Gene as a man. The reader is allowed to glimpse who Gene will become, and the story told as a flashback provides the map of the course Gene follows. Hence, the process of gendering the boy to "be a man" lies at the heart of *A Separate Peace,* and the conflicts and actions it details serve to further this process as its central project. The Gene who appears at the beginning and end of the novel is one marked by nostalgia and perhaps regret, which already invokes a notion of something lost and idealized. The opening scene of the novel involves the adult Gene walking through Devon on what he describes as a cold, wet, self-pitying day in November, a decidedly melancholic description. He notes, "I felt fear's echo, and along with that I felt the unhinged joy which had been its accompaniment and opposite face, joy which had broken out sometimes in those days like Northern Lights across black sky."[12] So while his time at school is characterized by fear, it also includes great joy. The adult Gene claims that he has made his escape from fear, but that must also mean he has lost the joy that accompanies it. That joy is embodied by his friend Finny, whose loss provides the central event of the novel.

Finny and Gene's relationship is characterized by a subtle homoeroticism in which Gene eroticizes Finny's innocence, purity, and skill, and Finny eroticizes the companionship provided by Gene. With World War II serving throughout the novel as the backdrop against which the "peace" of Devon is contrasted, the boys initially engage in the ritual of taking off their clothes and jumping from a tall tree into the river below as practice for the possibility of having to jump from a sinking ship in battle. Jumping from the tree acquires special significance for Finny and Gene; it serves as a sign of loyalty and, as an act that cements their bond, can stand in for sexual play. Finny demonstrates his interest in sharing intimate moments with Gene when he encourages him to skip class and spend a day at the beach. Finny reveals in his characteristically honest way that Gene is the "proper" person with whom to share such moments as they settle down to sleep on the sand. Gene considers such a naked emotional expression to be next to suicide at Devon, and he remains unable to reciprocate Finny's admission. Gene does, however, notice Finny's physical attractiveness even if he must project this sentiment onto the anonymous passers-by: "I noticed that people were looking fixedly at him, so I took a look myself to see why. His skin radiated a reddish copper glow of tan, his brown hair had been a little bleached by the sun, and I noticed that the tan made his eyes shine with a cool blue-green fire."[13] Gene notices Finny's appearance, though Finny is the first to say about Gene, "Everybody's staring at you. It's because of that movie star tan you picked up this afternoon . . . showing off again."[14] While Gene reciprocates Finny's feelings, he cannot bring himself to admit them as Finny does. Gene's self-preserving silence allows him to resist both the possibility and the threat of consummating his platonic friendship with Finny, whereas Finny's willingness to expose his emotional vulnerabilities predicts his eventual expulsion from a context that forbids such expressions.

To describe their relationship this way is not to cite a germinal or inchoate homosexuality or to suggest that either Finny or Gene has simply failed consciously to admit an essential homosexual status. It is, however, to note, as Eve Sedgwick does, that "what goes on at football games, in fraternities, at the Bohemian Grove, and at climactic moments in war novels can look, with only a slight shift of optic, quite startlingly 'homosexual.'" It is not, she continues, "most importantly an expression of the psychic origin of these institutions in a repressed or sublimated homosexual genitality. Instead, it is the coming into visibility of the normally implicit coercive double bind."[15] The "coercive double bind" of which Sedgwick writes is the simultaneous *prescription* of intimate male homosocial bonds and *proscription* of homosexuality:[16]

> Because the paths of male entitlement, especially in the nineteenth century, required certain intense male bonds that were not readily distinguishable from the most reprobated bonds, an endemic and ineradicable state of what I am calling male homosexual panic became the normal condition of male heterosexual entitlement.[17]

The boys' very presence at a school like Devon not only underscores their access to a specifically classed and gendered entitlement, but the school itself also serves as a space in which to prepare them for claiming that entitlement. It is a space in which this double bind is particularly highlighted, since boys will make their earliest connections to other boys here, as well as perhaps their first sexual explorations. It is also a space defined by intimate relationships between boys, making it homo*social*. In order to make visible fully this double bind, it is necessary to shift the optic whereby the homoeroticism of the boys' relationship comes into view.

Gene allays the confusions that result from his affection for Finny and the tumult of emotions such forbidden feelings arouse in him by first causing the accident that forces Finny's disappearance from Devon and then incorporating Finny into himself. Following their trip to the beach, the night they spend alone there, and Finny's intimate expression of his fondness for Gene, Gene finds himself growing increasingly suspicious of Finny and attributes this reaction to the possibility that Finny plans to sabotage his grades. Finny and Gene later return to the tree where, after undressing, Finny suggests that they jump together hand-in-hand, he later recalls, an act that could substitute for a strictly forbidden sexual act between the boys.[18] They climb the tree and prepare to jump, but in a moment of panic, Gene jounces the limb and sends Finny crashing to the ground, thereby setting a series of events in motion that culminates in Finny's death. His realization that Finny's intentions are not dishonest after all, coupled with Finny's suggestion that they take the jump together, ignites the moment of homosexual panic. Gene responds to Finny's advances with an act of violent separation. Finny's attempt to jump side by side with Gene (and take Gene's hand, if Finny in fact fulfills this intention) triggers the need in Gene to conform to the heterosexual imperative that forecloses the possibility of same-sex desire by forcibly detaching himself from Finny.

As Mark Simpson writes about death scenes in war films, "Pain and death are not just a price that has to be paid [for homoeroticism]—it is as if the caress, the kiss, the embrace *were the fatal blow* itself."[19] If the jounced tree limb is read as the act that ultimately kills Finny, then it is Finny's attempt to grab Gene's hand and to jump with him—this symbolic moment of touch—that incites the homosexual panic in Gene. As Sedgwick explains, in a legal context "The 'homosexual panic' defense for a person (typically a man) accused of antigay violence implies that his responsibility for the crime was diminished by a pathological psychological condition, perhaps brought on by an unwanted sexual advance from the man whom he attacked."[20] In this case, Gene's almost reflexive movement that jounces the limb is a reaction to that moment of touch, which to Gene is too explicit a demonstration of affection, and thus constitutes a kind of unwanted advance. Or is it unwanted? As Sedgwick continues, "After all, the reason why this defense borrows the name of the (formerly rather obscure and little-diagnosed) psychiatric classification *'homosexual* panic' is that it refers to the supposed uncertainty about his own sexual identity of the perpetrator of the antigay violence."[21] This is not to suggest that Gene is somehow *really* gay, or that only a closeted gay man will commit violence against gay men. Rather, it alludes to the double bind discussed earlier in which any affection or desire of one man for another might also implicate the recipient-object himself as homosexual, requiring, so it goes, a potent demonstration of denial that cannot help but look excessive and self-implicating. Nothing but feigned or real indifference, perhaps, can extricate the recipient-object from this double bind. In any event, Gene is very clearly caught up in it. Perhaps, then, Gene's guilt, which according to the teacher rationales he must confront and overcome, is not only the violent act itself, but also the possibility of same-sex desire that act suggests.

Judith Butler suggests that we consider gender in terms of melancholia as the unfinished process of grieving a loss that cannot be acknowledged. The lost object is incorporated and preserved in the ego as a constitutive identification in order to defer suffering the loss. She proposes that this melancholic identification is central to the process by which a subject's gender is constructed. She quotes from Freud's *The Ego and the Id:*

> An object which was lost has been set up again inside the ego—that is, . . . an object-cathexis has been replaced by an identification . . . when it happens that a person has given up a sexual object, there quite often ensues an alteration of his ego which can only be described as setting up of the object inside the ego.[22]

The internalization of the object offers an alternative means of possessing the object without violating the codes that prohibit and prevent its external possession. The act of jouncing the limb, which causes Finny to fall, represents a literal acting out of Gene's rejection of Finny as an object of desire. The injuries Finny incurs ensure his separation from Gene and the loss of the prohibited homosexual attachment. The loss translates into the installation of Finny, the barred object of desire, as part of

Gene's ego. Finny is preserved by this process of internalization, which involves Gene's accessibility to penetration by Finny in such a way that avoids the repercussions of genital contact:

> I decided to put on his clothes. . . . When I looked in the mirror it was not a remote aristocrat I had become, no character out of daydreams. I was Phineas, Phineas to the life. I even had his humorous expression on my face, his sharp, optimistic awareness. I had no idea why this gave me such intense relief, but it seemed, standing there in Finny's triumphant shirt, that I would never stumble through the confusion of my own character again.[23]

When Finny does return temporarily to Devon, he attempts to aid Gene in completing the transformation. Since Finny had been a star athlete prior to the fall, he sets about attempting to train Gene to take his place and actualize the element of himself that Gene internalizes. Gene initiates the process whereby he establishes the idea of Finny at the core of a reconstituted self, and, in this instance of initiative, already demonstrates a quality originally belonging only to Finny. As Gene approaches his goal, Finny gradually fades until his death coincides with Gene's ultimate success.[24]

In Butler's view, masculinity and femininity are accomplishments that emerge in tandem with the achievement of heterosexuality.[25] Gene's homosexual panic might then be ascribed not only to the prohibition of same-sex desire but also to the related fear of being feminine or feminized. His rejection of the external possession of Finny represents not only a rejection of the homosexual attachment but also his desire to achieve a heterosexually defined masculinity by which he can bring himself into accordance with the ideal of the proper man. According to Butler, the "I never loved him, I never lost him" uttered by a man forms the core of his tenuous heterosexuality and hence his masculinity.[26] If masculinity is achieved through a heterosexuality predicated on the renunciation of the homosexual attachment, then same-sex desire serves as the necessary possibility that allows for its renunciation. A heterosexual man thus becomes the man he "never" loved and "never" grieved, and his masculinity is founded upon the refusal to acknowledge this love and its incorporation as an identification within his ego.[27] Gene becomes a man through his repudiation of the consummation of his relationship with Finny—"holding hands in a jump." This formulation makes clear the significance of renunciation to proper development.

By killing Finny, Gene assumes his own place in this "aggressive circuit of renunciation." Following Finny's first departure from Devon School and Gene's incorporation of the loss as an identification within his own ego, Gene determines along with Brinker to enlist in the war effort and, in doing so, the masculine environs of the military and battlefield. The war propels the boys forward, away from their adolescent shelter and toward the final phase of their initiation into manhood. The return of Finny forestalls Gene's entrance into the war, and the reemergence of the queer possibility effectively suspends Gene's enlistment and the verification of his masculinity. The threat posed by Finny becomes evident. His presence, in fact, his continued existence, defers indefinitely Gene's "ascension" to proper manhood. Finny must therefore die to prevent any further return and to allow Gene to claim finally his masculinity and complete the gendering process that is ongoing throughout *A Separate Peace*.

Simpson has described the buddy war film as a compilation of lessons about masculinity and how to take one's place in patriarchy.[28] Simpson's analysis of such films can be used to examine Knowles's novel, since the lingering war provides the context for Finny and Gene's homoerotic friendship. Simpson describes the intimate relationship between same-sex desire and death established in the war film as the necessary condition for any expression of same-sex desire:

> In war films of the buddy type the deadliness of war is not glossed over. But it is portrayed not in the death of the enemy, who are often faceless or even unseen, but in the death of the comrades and buddies. Classically, the moment when the buddy lies dead or dying is the moment when the full force of the love the boys/men feel for one another can be shown. And, for all the efforts of the conscientious film maker, the deadliness is thus attached not as much to war as to the queer romance of it all.[29]

Paul Fussell similarly suggests that the connection between war and love assumes a distinctly homoerotic form on the battlefield:

> Given this association between war and sex, and given the deprivation and loneliness and alienation characteristic of the soldier's ex-

perience—given, that is, his need for affection in a largely woman-less world—we will not be surprised to find both the actuality and the recall of front-line experience replete with what we can call the homoerotic.[30]

Fussell even makes the direct connection between the homoerotic desires of English officers during the Great War and their experiences at English public schools (elite boarding schools): "It was largely members of the upper and upper-middle classes who were prepared by public-school training to experience such crushes, who 'hailed with relief,' as J. B. Priestley remembers, 'a wholly masculine way of life uncomplicated by Woman.'"[31] Fussell reports finding in soldiers' recollections of frontline experiences "especially in the attitude of young officers to their men . . . something more like the 'idealistic,' passionate but non-physical 'crushes' which most of the officers had experienced at public school."[32] Gene and Finny's relationship and Gene's maturation can be understood in this context.

According to Simpson and Fussell, the battlefield is a place in which queer love can be expressed, albeit in an indirect way, because it occurs alongside of death. Desire and violence each provide conditions for the other. *A Separate Peace* implicitly likens school to the battlefields of war, and it is at the most violent or dangerous of moments that the boys are able to demonstrate their affection. Gene allows himself to admit his tender feelings for Finny only as Finny lies broken on the marble steps following Gene's trial. Seeing another student wrap a blanket around Finny, Gene recalls, "I would have liked very much to have done that myself; it would have meant a lot to me."[33] That Gene's expression of tenderness fails to find a more explicit articulation attests to that very impossibility. According to Simpson, the cathartic deadly climax satisfies the audience and allows for the homoerotic impulse of the characters while reinscribing a heterosexual economy that calls for the unattainability of the queer attachment. The desire is expressed for only an instant, and even then, it is a love that is never truly acknowledged. Its full actualization is staved off by death. In *A Separate Peace*, the possibility of consummation is canceled by Finny's death, ensuring that their "boyish love" remains eternal and unsullied by the transgression of a compulsory heterosexuality. Simpson writes: "They live by love, but one of them, the most 'sensitive' and the 'queerest', must die to save the others and the world from the practice of it, also to demonstrate the 'proper' way it should be sublimated: 'Greater love hath no man than this, that a man lay down his life for his friends.' "[34] Finny is, surely, the queerest of the Devon boys. This opens up the possibility of understanding Finny's sacrifice in Christian terms. Finny *does* in fact sacrifice himself for Gene. Instead of spiritual salvation, that sacrifice purchases Gene's heterosexual manhood.[35]

Hallman Bell Bryant calls *A Separate Peace* "an allegory about the causes of war," and so given Simpson's and Fussell's observations about the intimate connections between male-male bonding and the battlefield, perhaps it should be no surprise that this "allegory" of war cannot help but be enacted through an intensely passionate friendship between boys that is marked by same-sex desire.[36] In being *about* war, *A Separate Peace* can't help also being *about* same-sex desire. Gene's participation in the war effort is fueled by this disavowed loss of the homosexual attachment, and if Gene's development is taken to represent a collectively experienced process by which boys are made men, then it might be said that the war itself is predicated on the loss of the homosexual attachment. On the battlefield, men can place themselves in positions to be killed by the enemy such that death comes from without, and mourning one's comrades in war can stand in for mourning the homosexual attachment that was lost. The trauma of war as a purely masculine pursuit serves as a pretext for the grief that cannot be experienced at home during peacetime. One can love one's comrades and grieve their loss with the displaced love and loss "never" felt for the original same-sex object. Any resistance to the imperative that demands such an oppressive masculinity formed on the disavowal of same-sex desire can be directed toward the enemy, and any guilt suffered over one's own compliance can be transformed into a hatred of this enemy. War might be described as the only appropriate place for experiencing this grief, and the possibility of eliminating *this* motivation for war (as it certainly is not the only motivation) presents a useful rationale for refusing the loss of homosexual attachment and for changing the conditions that initially demand its loss. In other words, military life and war might be particularly appealing to some because they provide delimited contexts in which it is possible to experience intimate, same-sex bonds, just as Gene experiences same-sex bonding with Finny at Devon. The military provides not only the opportunity for those bonds to form, but also the likelihood of a marked end to the same-sex bond through the death of the friend, the cessation of the war, or the end of military service. So if we take Bryant's claim seriously that the novel is an "allegory" of war, then understanding the relationship between desire and violence in the relationship between Gene and Finny leads to these conclusions about violence and desire in the context of war.

The setting of Devon School during wartime conflates the school and the battlefield and further reinforces this allegorical reading. Seeking to act out the war, Finny invents the game of Blitzball in which the boy with the ball must run from one side of the field to the other without being tackled. At any point in the game, the player holding the ball could pass it on to another player who would then become the object of attack for the other boys. One *must* pass the ball according to Finny, who invents a game with no teams. Each player is simultaneously an adversary and an ally, so these terms effectively have no meaning in the context of Blitzball in which players fluidly shift between roles never fixed in relation to other players. One can never identify allies or enemies in Blitzball, making it a queer game resisting the fixity of identities.[37] Rather than enforcing the strict dichotomization of two competing sides, Finny rejects this fundamental attribute of competition, thereby exposing it as dispensable. Finny also adopts this resistant tactic during a snowball fight when he again begins switching sides so that "loyalties became hopelessly entangled."[38] A classmate follows suit, leading Gene to describe him as a eunuch.[39]

Finny repeatedly produces the central symbols of the novel. He initiates the practice of jumping from the tree, a practice that acquires significance as a site for both the sealing of Finny's friendship with Gene and their separation. During Finny's temporary return to Devon following his injury, he begins training Gene for the Olympics in which he himself had wished to participate. Despite the impossibility of such a goal, Finny's encouragement persists in maintaining it as a realistic possibility in their minds, again demonstrating his authority over the boys' fantasies. Finny also determines the symbolic value of the pink shirt, which he dons as an emblem ostensibly to demonstrate his pride in the Allied victories over Central Europe. Gene expresses concern that Finny's pink shirt might cause others to "mistake" him for a "fairy," a concern to which Finny responds "mildly . . . I wonder what would happen if I looked like a fairy to everyone."[40] Finny's lack of concern is itself queer in the homosocial context of a boys' school where, by the 1940s, such a label might incur a significant cost to one's social status, if not physical safety. The pink shirt, moreover, proves central to Gene's attempt to become Finny. Wearing the shirt completes Gene's incorporation of Finny into his own self following Finny's first absence from Devon. That Finny originates each of these symbols signifies a phallic authority ultimately claimed by Gene as the story's narrator. It also demonstrates Finny's queerness, both in the sense of his strangeness and in the sense of his being marked as sexually deviant.

In contrast to Gene, his schoolmate Leper fails to undergo the same process by which Gene achieves manhood. Leper is—as one might predict from his name—an outsider, never fully participating in the boys' society, never playing their games, preferring instead to wander alone in the woods. He finally leaves Devon to enlist, "escapes" from the army, and returns to school to testify in Gene's mock trial. In this narrative of gender construction, Leper represents the boy who neither refuses the loss of the homosexual attachment nor consummates a potential union. He therefore never incorporates the possible object of desire within his ego, thereby proving malformed and dysfunctional as a result of his failure to adhere to the normative developmental trajectory followed by Gene. When Finny first jumps from the tree Leper refuses to join in the ritual with the other boys. In response to Finny's insistence on Leper's participation, Gene recalls that "Leper closed his mouth as though forever. He didn't argue or refuse. He didn't back away. He became inanimate."[41] Leper simply watches, and so bears witness to the symbolic attachment created as an unrealized possibility between Finny and Gene. At the crucial moment when Gene jounces the limb and sends Finny crashing to the ground in a violent moment of homosexual panic—the refusal of the queer possibility—Leper stands by as the only witness to the event, silently observing the mechanisms by which Gene undertakes to assume his masculinity. Although the other boys work clearing snow from the railroad yard to permit trains carrying new military recruits to pass, Leper abstains from this contribution to the war effort, choosing instead to keep his distance and explore the forest trails. Ultimately Leper enlists in the army only to suffer a mental breakdown.

Leper, psychologically crippled by the army and hence by the nation, knows that Gene knocked Finny out of the tree, the way that Finny himself, crippled by Gene, knows. Finny's physical injury prevents his participation in sports and games, which the boys enact as simulations of war, and Leper's instability prevents his continued service. The novel therefore establishes an equivalency between Finny and Leper.

When Gene confronts Leper about the fact that he is home when he should be performing his military duties, Gene says that he knows "what's normal in the army."[42] Leper's being home strikes him as abnormal and as requiring an explanation, a position against which Leper reacts strongly: "Normal. . . . What a stupid-ass word that is. . . . You're thinking I'm not normal, aren't you?"[43] Leper tries to explain that he has deserted in order to escape a Section Eight discharge, and his explanation of this situation takes the form of a confession, which cannot help but look like a coming out: "But in the last few weeks . . . I admitted a hell of a lot to myself. Not about you. Don't flatter yourself. I wasn't thinking about you. Why the hell should I think about you? Did you ever think about me? I thought about myself, and Ma, and the old man, and *pleasing* them all the time."[44] His denial about having thought about Gene seems unprovoked and excessive, suggesting that he might in fact have been thinking about Gene, and he seems angry that this fact is not mutual. Although the nature of what Leper admits to himself might be nothing other than his incapacity to complete his military service, in such a sexually charged and apparently "homoerotic" novel, Leper's words assume queer implications, especially given the fact that in many ways his situation mirrors Finny's. Finny, of course, is ultimately killed for his queer desires and Leper is driven insane for his.

At the climax of the novel, when the boys try Gene for maiming Finny, Leper arrives to present the damning evidence, his testimony that Gene deliberately caused Finny's accident. Faced with this evidence, Finny flees from the truth and finally dies at the end of the sequence of events put in motion by Gene. In the context of the trial, Leper occupies the place of the witness, the one who reads through the allegory and exposes the underlying mechanisms motivating Gene's violent act. Leper stands as a figure that warns the reader to avoid reading too closely or looking too intently to uncover the reason for Gene's violence. The processes of achieving heterosexuality and masculinity cannot be completed properly in the witness if he becomes too aware of their workings. The figure of Leper functions in the story to present the potential risk of insanity to the student who might be drawn to the position of witness or bystander, who sees how the process of normative maturation works and refuses to experience it directly. The reader should not be merely a witness who observes these mechanisms of gender construction without also enacting them, since insanity looms as a possible punishment.

Leper's role as witness is not unrelated to the actions of Brinker Hadley. Brinker orchestrates a trial to expose Gene's role in Finny's accident, and he calls Leper as an eyewitness to these events. Finny might not have fled the trial had Leper not arrived to present his testimony. Leper's testimony is appropriated and used by Brinker, and the end result is to complete the process that began at the site of the tree. Brinker accuses Gene of making Finny unavailable for the war effort; he calls Finny a casualty;[45] and he suggests that Gene is postponing his enlistment because of Finny.[46] He also claims not to care about Gene's guilt;[47] however, he arranges the mock trial to expose the truth. Brinker holds a prominent position in various student organizations, and he is invested in his social and political authority at the school. He also seems concerned about Finny's well-being. He tells Gene that Gene's pity will damage Finny: "And if you don't watch out he's going to start pitying himself. Nobody ever mentions his leg to him except me. Keep that up and he'll be sloppy with self-pity any day now. What's everybody beating around the bush for? He's crippled and that's that. He's got to accept it and unless we start acting perfectly natural about it, even kid him about it once in a while, he never will."[48] Still, Brinker's desire to stage the trial cannot be accounted for fully by a concern for Finny and a respect for the truth. His motives for putting Gene on trial remain unclear unless Brinker is imagined as the successful alternative to Leper as witness and judge.

Whereas Leper is the first to enlist and is perhaps the least suited for military service, Brinker concocts "plan after plan, each more insulated from the fighting than the last."[49] He ends up settling for the Coast Guard, much to the disappointment of his stern and patriotic father, who lectures Brinker and Gene about the importance of serving their country. Brinker later apologizes for his father: "I'm enlisting. . . . I'm going to 'serve' as he puts it, I may even get killed. But I'll be damned if I'll have that Nathan Hale attitude about it. It's all that World War I malarkey that gets me. They're all children about that war. . . . It gives me a pain, personally. I'm not any kind of hero, and neither are you. And neither is the old man, and he never was."[50] Gene suggests that Mr. Hadley feels left out, to which Brinker replies, "Left out! He and his crowd are responsible for it! And *we're* going to fight it!"[51] Leper enlists without thinking through his actions because he gets caught up in the excitement of the recruitment effort. Although he comes to be critical of military life, that insight develops too late for him. Brinker provides a more successful model. He recognizes the flaws of his father's position and arranges to take part in the war effort without necessarily accepting the greatest risk. Thus, unlike Finny or Leper, Brinker can occupy the role of critic without dying or going insane. Notably, Knowles based Brinker on his Exeter classmate Gore Vidal, who is himself an essayist, social critic, and gay novelist. Brinker, like Vidal, is critical of his social context and finds ways to both live in and reimagine it.

In his report of a panel discussion held to discuss literary criticism and the teaching of *A Separate Peace*, Jack Lundy quotes panelist Betty Nelick as saying that the novel is concerned with "Gene's slow and painful dying to the world of adolescence into the world of manhood, through the outward pressures of a world at war and the inward pressure of the realization of fear and evil within himself."[52] Diane Shugert claims that books like *A Separate Peace* are taught because "the book's point of view bears upon democratic and American values," which *A Separate Peace* quite clearly accomplishes through its valorization of Gene's coming-of-age, his rejection of a possible homosexual attachment, and his ascension to proper manhood at the cost of the death of his all-too-queer best friend.[53] The lack of explicit acknowledgment by most critics of the sexual politics of the novel represents the success of Leper's warning against precisely this attention. *A Separate Peace* thus serves the education of the American ideal well—a heterosexual and "properly" gendered ideal.

When teachers take texts to be "realistic" and present them as such, they unwittingly popularize this discourse, a discourse that is generative rather than simply representational. Such texts are thought to document a psychosocial process; however, the process might instead be understood as the collective effect of those texts, an effect ensured through the perpetual repetition of their use and the insistence on their realism. The popular characterization of same-sex desire as a confusing adolescent experience at a stage that must be successfully negotiated in order to achieve a more "adult" heterosexuality lends descriptive validity to Butler's formulation in which the homosexual attachment is lost and incorporated. But this psychosocial process by which heterosexuality is achieved need not be understood as either inevitable or innate; rather, it may be understood as produced. The widespread belief that youth might experience same-sex desire during an early developmental stage that they are expected to outgrow functions as a self-fulfilling prophecy at the cultural level. Adolescents learn that they must restrict their potential object-choices by learning to understand other-sex desire as appropriate and expected, while learning to interpret any indications of same-sex desire as the product of rampant hormones, inexperience, or confusion. *A Separate Peace* encourages the understanding of this lesson. The process of gender construction allegorized in *A Separate Peace* does not fully precede the use of such texts as educational tools. Rather such texts might be said to collectively contribute to the discourse that materializes the phenomena they describe. The contribution of *A Separate Peace* to the procedure by which same-sex desire is constructed as adolescent positions the book at a crucial site of cultural production, that of the "adult" heterosexual and the "ideal" democratic citizen.

There is some evidence that readers of *A Separate Peace* have detected its regretful tone, and their responses suggest the possibility of reading it against its cultural and pedagogical application. Young readers of *A Separate Peace* have posed the question, "Why must Finny die?"[54] If the question is motivated by a desire to see Finny live, then it marks a potential impetus for the student to produce a resistant reading of the text. The question "Why does Finny have to die?" could represent the student's desire to see the homosexual attachment completed, or at least not entirely foreclosed before the possibility of consummation is realized. Finny must die precisely because he refuses to reject the possibility of loving Gene. Even when Gene attempts to confess his guilt, Finny struggles to deny Gene's need to push him away: "It was like I had all the time in world. I thought I could reach out and get hold of you." But Gene responds by flinching violently away from him: "To drag me down too!"[55] Even here when Finny speaks of his previous desire to grab hold of Gene, Gene can only recall such a wish as the desire to drag him down and prevent him from attaining a heterosexually defined manhood. Finny must die so that Gene can become a proper man, yet as Butler writes, "There is no necessary reason for identification to oppose desire, or for desire to be fueled by repudiation."[56]

These texts, if noted for the ways in which they propagate normative constructions of gender, might be employed to interact with adolescents' impulse for transgression. The excessive warning away from an overly perceptive reading symbolized by a psychotic Leper in *A Separate Peace* might provoke a desire to reveal what one is warned against revealing. The very prohibition used to enforce Gene's conformity might be eroticized in such a way that its very transgression becomes desirable. In this sense, the warning away might potentiate the desirability of the forbidden object and serve the function of drawing one closer to it. The inverted prohibition, one that attracts the subject to the prohibited object, could function to destabilize the force of the prohibition so that it ultimately loses its effect to either warn away or entice. Finny would not have to die if Gene renounced a "proper" and fixed identification. Had he rejected the need to bring about and disavow this loss, Gene might have avoided refusing the queer potential.

NOTES

1. Beverly Lyon Clark seeks to debunk the notion that *Tom Brown* was the first school story, while still crediting it as having influenced hundreds of subsequent school stories, popular culture, and mainstream literature for adults. *Regendering the School Story: Sassy Sissies and Tattling Tomboys* (New York: Garland, 1996).

2. Ibid., 11.

3. Ibid., 8.

4. Kathy Piehl, "Gene Forrester and Tom Brown: *A Separate Peace* as School Story," *Children's Literature in Education* 14.2 (1983): 67–74; Steve Roxburgh, "The Novel of Crisis: Contemporary Adolescent Fiction," *Children's Literature* 7 (1978): 249.

5. Herbert N. Foerstel, *Banned in the U.S.A.: A Reference Guide to Book Censorship in Schools and Public Libraries* (Westport, CT: Greenwood Press, 1994); Dawn B. Sova, *Banned Books: Literature Suppressed on Social Grounds* (New York: Facts on File, 1998).

6. Isabel Quigly, *The Heirs of Tom Brown: The English School Story* (Oxford: Oxford University Press, 1984), 126.

7. Sova, *Banned Books*, 213. The novel has also been challenged for containing "unsuitable language" and "negative attitudes" and for encouraging undesirable behavior, such as skipping class, breaking school rules, and trespassing (Foerstel, *Banned in the U.S.A.*, 181; Sova, *Banned Books*, 214). In spite of this occasional opposition, *A Separate Peace* has been regularly taught in high school English classrooms since the early sixties. An early apology for its use applauded it as recommending itself immediately to high school instruction. John K. Crabbe, "On the Playing Fields of Devon," *English Journal* 52 (1963): 111.

8. Diane P. Shugert, "About Rationales," *Connecticut English Journal* 15.1 (1983): 2.

9. Richard B. Hargraves, *Values: Language Arts* (Miami, FL: Dade County Public Schools, 1971), 4.

10. W. Michael Reed, "*A Separate Peace*: A Novel Worth Teaching," *Virginia English Bulletin* 36.2 (1986): 102.

11. I am not necessarily suggesting that the novel itself promotes heteronormative development or that it works in any unidirectional way. It is far too

ambiguous for that, as we will see. Moreover the interaction of reader and text, and indeed the entire cultural terrain that provides a vast array of devices for such a project, admits far too many complexities for such a simple cause-effect relationship. This essay does, however, explore the potential uses and effects of these novels, and by extension the use of the "queer" youth on whom they are centered, for the purpose of contributing to that cultural terrain. I also do not want to be understood as suggesting that the authors of these rationales are consciously motivated by an impulse to obscure the implications of these novels for the gender/sexual development of their characters or readers. The rationales are written, after all, to provide teachers with ideas for justifying the classroom use of controversial texts that some have tried to ban. This is, of course, a laudable goal. One possible explanation for this almost careful avoidance of references to gender and sexuality in these rationales is the desire on the part of their authors to avoid inciting further hostility toward this already embattled text.

12. John Knowles, *A Separate Peace* (New York: Bantam, 1959), 2.

13. Ibid., 39.

14. Ibid.

15. Eve Kosofsky Sedgwick, *Between Men: English Literature and Male Homosocial Desire* (New York: Columbia University Press, 1985), 89.

16. Ibid., 88–89; Eve Kosofsky Sedgwick, *Epistemology of the Closet* (Berkeley: University of California Press, 1990), 185–86.

17. Sedgwick, *Epistemology of the Closet*, 185.

18. Knowles, *A Separate Peace*, 163.

19. Mark Simpson, "Don't Die on Me, Buddy: Homoeroticism and Masochism in War Movies," in *Male Impersonators: Men Performing Masculinity*, ed. Mark Simpson (New York: Routledge, 1994), 214.

20. Sedgwick, *Epistemology of the Closet*, 19.

21. Ibid., 20.

22. Judith Butler, "Gender Melancholy / Refused Identification," in *Constructing Masculinity*, ed. Maurice Berger, Brian Wallis, and Simon Watson (New York: Routledge, 1995), 22.

23. Knowles, *A Separate Peace*, 54.

24. The argument I am pursuing here develops further one briefly sketched by Georges-Michel Sarotte in *Like a Brother, Like a Lover* (1978), where he notes how the relationship between Gene and Finny is characterized by an undercurrent of desire. "Their friendship changes into hatred out of fear of its changing into love," he writes, and "Gene's hatred of Finny reveals his refusal to eroticize the desire for identification with him. This frantic refusal to become Finny's masochistic partner is translated into a fatal act." Georges-Michel, *Like a Brother, Like a Lover: Male Homosexuality in the American Novel and Theater from Herman Melville to James Baldwin*, trans. Richard Miller (Garden City, NY: Achnor Press / Doubleday, 1978), 45.

25. Butler, "Gender Melancholy / Refused Identification," 24.

26. Ibid., 27.

27. Ibid., 44.

28. Simpson, "Don't Die on Me, Buddy," 214.

29. Ibid.

30. Paul Fussell, *The Great War and Modern Memory* (New York: Oxford University Press, 1975), 272.

31. Ibid., 273.

32. Ibid., 272.

33. Knowles, *A Separate Peace*, 170.

34. Simpson, "Don't Die on Me, Buddy," 227.

35. Theologians, Bible scholars, film critics, and gay lay people have commented repeatedly on the potential for seeing same-sex eroticism in Christian rituals, symbols, and texts, particularly in the relation between object and viewer created by the spectacle of Jesus' body, or in the intimate nature of his relationships with his disciples, especially John, the so-called beloved disciple. The very structure of Christian faith—which calls for the submission of men to Jesus as savior and God, love for and devotion to Jesus and to fellow Christians, meditation over Jesus' body, its consumption through the ritual of communion—suggests the kind of intense libidinal investment and carnality characteristic of eroticism. If Finny is a kind of Christ-figure, as a conventional Christian-allegorical reading might suggest, then his sacrifice for his loved friend occurs in the context of their intense and intimate bond in which the other's body has a central place.

36. Hallman Bell Bryant, *"A Separate Peace": The War Within* (Boston: Twayne, 1990), 10.

37. The term "queer" of course cannot—and should not—be reduced to some simplistic notion of fluidity. A number of scholars have taken up the possible implications of the term—not so much its "meaning," which must remain contingent if it is to be put to use in contesting normative regimes. In Michael Warner's introduction to *Fear of a Queer Planet*, he explains that "the preference for 'queer' [over gay] . . . rejects a minoritizing logic of toleration or simple political interest-representation in favor of a more thorough resistance to regimes of the normal." Judith Butler describes the term as a "discursive rallying point" for those who pursue marginalized or nonheteronormative pleasures and sexualities. Eve Kosofsky Sedgwick notes that one use of "queer" is that it can refer to "the open mesh of possibilities, gaps, overlaps, dissonances and resonances, lapses and excesses of meaning when the constituent elements of anyone's gender, of anyone's sexuality, aren't made (or *can't be* made) to signify monolithically." Judith Butler, *Bodies That Matter: On the Discursive Limits of Sex* (New York: Routledge, 1993), 230; Michael Warner, introduction to *Fear of a Queer Planet: Queer Politics and Social Theory*, ed. Michael Warner (Minneapolis: University of Minnesota Press, 1993), xxvi; Eve Kosofsky Sedgwick, *Tendences* (Durham: Duke University Press, 1993), 8.

38. Knowles, *A Separate Peace*, 146.

39. Ibid.

40. Ibid., 17.

41. Ibid., 9.

42. Ibid., 135.

43. Ibid.
44. Ibid., 137.
45. Ibid., 159.
46. Ibid., 151.
47. Ibid., 159.
48. Ibid., 152.
49. Ibid., 151.
50. Ibid., 192.
51. Ibid., 193.
52. Jack T. Lundy, "Literary Criticism and the Teaching of the Novel," *University of Kansas Bulletin of Education* 21.3 (1967): 114.
53. Shugert, "About Rationales," 4.
54. Francine G. Wacht, "The Adolescent in Literature," paper presented at the Annual Meeting of the Teachers of English, San Diego, November 1975, 7.
55. Knowles, *A Separate Peace*, 57.
56. Butler, "Gender Melancholy / Refused Identification," 35.

PART 2

After Stonewall

 IN THE EARLY MORNING HOURS OF JUNE 28, 1969, New York City police raided a gay bar named the Stonewall Inn in the Greenwich Village neighborhood of New York City. The demonstrations and protests that followed, now collectively dubbed the Stonewall Rebellion, accelerated LGBT activism and aligned such with the feminist and civil rights movements. While there's some danger to overemphasizing 1969 as a historical turning point for queer politics and visibility, it is true that the first young adult novel addressing a gay encounter was also published that year, John Donovan's *I'll Get There. It Better Be Worth the Trip.* The essays in this section take up the first wave of lesbian/gay literature for young people, published in the wake of Stonewall.

This literature tends to reflect the cultural and political success of the LGBTQ movement. For the first time, homosexuality could be openly acknowledged, with lesbian and gay (if not also yet bisexual and transgendered) young adults increasingly conceivable as subjects. Lesbian/gay characters were still marked as problems to be dealt with, but gradually the focus shifted from homosexuality to homophobia. The level of address and queer subjectivity of course varies with respect to genre; if lesbian/gay teenagers were increasingly present in young adult literature, picture books still focused on lesbian/gay adults, usually parents or uncles (respectable ones to boot). Only recently have younger children been presented as queer, even transgender, in literature for young readers, and not yet in a picture book. Moreover, for better and for worse, such "out" literature tends toward normativity, with emphasis on family life and social tolerance.

The following essays assess post-Stonewall literature in relation to LGBTQ identity politics and cultural politics more generally. Three focus on the young adult novel (Jenkins, Lee, and Crisp) and the other two on the picture book (McRuer, Ford). Jenkins's essay, which surveys young adult novels published between 1969 and 1992, has been foundational for LGBTQ studies with library science and education. Attentive to issues of race, class, and geography as well as gender and sexuality, her essay works as an introduction of sorts for the essays that follow. Jenkins takes up the (in)visibility of lesbian YA literature, the subject of Lee's piece, the politics of AIDS literature, which Ford, Crisp, and especially McRuer consider, and the pressure of homo- as well as (as a version of) heteronormativity, a central concern for Crisp.

The five essays share a penchant for taxonomy or categorical analysis, not surprising given that their challenge is to survey and analyze a quickly growing body of work. A common concern is the politics of narrative plotting, or the literary and rhetorical strategies of queer-themed storytelling in a still-homophobic culture. While all five question the ideology of child innocence in relation to sexuality, this is especially true of McRuer and Ford, who see even in the AIDS-themed picture book a vanishing of gay male selfhood. In McRuer's formulation, the gay male body functions as the "anti-body" of children's literature. Another shared emphasis is the role of consumer culture in the promotion and/or restriction of books with queer content.

More recent scholarship dealing with more contemporary "out" queer literature for children and young adults asks most of the same questions posed here: What are the politics of visibility and affirmation, especially in relation to childhood and adolescence? How does this literature function socially and pedagogically? What correspondences can we observe between social history and the literary record; can queer literature for young readers effect, as much as document, change?

Young Adult Novels with Gay/Lesbian Characters and Themes, 1969–92

A Historical Reading of Content, Gender, and Narrative Distance

ॐ

CHRISTINE A. JENKINS

The "problem novel" made its first appearance in U.S. young adult literature during the late 1960s. Although young adult novels have always centered on various life problems as experienced by young adults, critics trace the origin of the "new realism" in teen fiction to the period from 1967 through 1969, during which S. E. Hinton's *The Outsiders*, Ann Head's *Mr. and Mrs. Bo Jo Jones*, Paul Zindel's *The Pigman*, and other pivotal titles were published. These young adult novels were characterized by candor, unidealized characters and settings, colloquial and realistic language, and plots that portrayed realistic problems faced by contemporary young adults that did not necessarily find resolution in a happy ending.[1]

Homosexuality and the social prejudice against those who identify as gay or lesbian was one of the themes to emerge at this time. John Donovan's *I'll Get There. It Better Be Worth the Trip* (1969) was the first young adult novel to specifically address homosexuality. In the book, thirteen-year-old Davy describes his growing friendship with a classmate, Altschuler. One afternoon the boys wrestle and end up kissing. Davy reacts with fear and avoidance, but the two finally reconcile, agreeing that the incident won't be repeated and their friendship will continue. Although Donovan's treatment of the sexual encounter is vague and brief, some reviewers in 1969 found the book remarkable and groundbreaking. Other reviewers worried that it "might arouse in the unconcerned unnecessary interest or alarm or both."[2]

In the years from 1969 through 1992, approximately sixty young adult novels with gay/lesbian characters or themes appeared in the United States, and most reviewers are no longer so surprised—or so troubled—by them. While several studies and articles have documented the existence and content of these titles, most writing on this subject has focused on the early years of this body of literature or on a few selected titles. As yet, few researchers have examined the full range of titles published in the years from 1969 through 1992 or traced content changes over time.[3]

Although each title is an individually authored work that can, and should, be judged as such, these books, taken as a whole, may be examined as a body of literature representing choices made by writers, editors, and publishers as the appropriate portrayal of gay/lesbian characters and themes in books for a young adult audience. Young adults have many questions and much misinformation about homosexuality, and reading is one of the few private ways for adolescents to gather information about this subject. What images and messages about gays and lesbians do these books present to teenagers? Who are the gay/lesbian people and what are their lives like? What happens to teens who think (or wonder if) they are gay? What is it like to be in love with someone of the same sex? What if your friend, or your sibling, or your parent is gay? In looking at a time span of almost twenty-five years, one may gain a historical understanding of what has and has not changed in the explicit and implicit messages to several generations of young adult readers.

The following pages describe some of the information contained in the sixty young adult novels published from 1969 through 1992 that I have identified as containing significant gay/lesbian content and/or themes, using available bibliographies, lists contained in earlier studies, and reviews in *Booklist, School Library Journal,* and *VOYA (Voice of Youth Advocates)* (see the appendix). This chronological examination of the books' portrayals of gay/lesbian characters and their contexts focuses on information about gay/lesbian people, both as individuals and in relationships, and on gender representation and narrative distance. It also identifies some gender and narrative patterns that have yet to be explored in this subgenre of young adult novels.

In order to focus on novelistic presentations specifically aimed at American teen audiences, I have limited my study to books available in the United States and published and marketed as young adult novels, and thus have not included any of the many adult fiction titles read by, but not marketed to, young adults. Most are from mainstream presses, although a few small press books, including several from Canada and Great Britain, have been included if they met the above requirements.

As may be seen in the appendix, the rate of production of this body of literature has roughly doubled over the years, with approximately half (thirty-one) of the books published in the sixteen years from 1969 through 1984, and the rest (twenty-nine) published in the following eight years, from 1985 through 1992. In seeking to examine historical trends within this group of sixty novels, I have used these two chronological halves—the earlier 1969–84 group of thirty-one titles and the more recent 1985–92 group of twenty-nine titles—to describe the changes (or lack thereof) in this body of literature over time.

Demographics of Gay/Lesbian People: Race, Class, Location, Vocation

According to both the earlier and the more recent novels, most gay/lesbian people are white and middle-class. Only three of the sixty books portray people of color as gay or lesbian, all of them African-American. In Guy's *Ruby*, the female protagonist and another young woman become involved in a short-lived romantic relationship; in Woodson's *The Dear One*, a lesbian couple is part of the young female protagonist's extended family; and in Rees's *Milkman's on His Way*, a minor role is played by a black gay male with whom the white male protagonist becomes involved at the end of the book. All other gay or lesbian characters are white, including those in Childress's *Those Other People*, the only other novel besides *Ruby* and *The Dear One* written by a person of color. Gay/lesbian working-class protagonists appear in two books by and about American women (*Ruby* and Garden's *Annie on My Mind*), and three by and about British men (Rees' *In the Tent, The Milkman's on His Way*, and *The Colour of His Hair*).

Though most books take place within a white, middle-class community, the geographic location of this setting has changed somewhat over time. In the earlier group of books, rural areas and small towns were common settings, as were camps and boarding schools. Few books in the more recent group feature such settings; none are set in camps or boarding schools, and most are set in urban or suburban locations. Urban settings include New York, Phoenix, and Tucson, while the suburban settings have generic names such as Wilmont, Norwell, or Oak Grove. Like the locales for movies and television programs marketed to teens, the books' settings tend to reflect popular culture images of teen life.

An interest in some sort of creative art is commonly portrayed as a part of a gay/lesbian person's interests. Five books have a high school or summer stock theater setting, and the majority of the gay/lesbian adult characters work in creative or arts-related fields (including visual arts, interior design, writing, acting, museum work, art or antique dealing, and woodworking). Those in other fields often display a strong interest in the arts, such as a geologist who is an opera buff (Meyer's *Elliott and Win*), or a surgeon who is a gourmet cook (L'Engle's *A House Like a Lotus*). The other major occupational field is that of teaching, with one elementary and eleven secondary school teachers among the thirty-plus adults with identifiable jobs. Although gay/lesbian teachers commonly lost their jobs in the earlier books, this occurs only rarely in the more recent ones.

Gender and Appearance

One of the most noticeable patterns in the young adult novelistic portrayal of gay/lesbian people is the predominance of males, both as teens and as adults. This trend has become even more pronounced in recent years. Of the sixty books in this sample, roughly one-quarter (sixteen) portray lesbians or female teens who are concerned about their own sexual orientation, while three-quarters (forty-four) portray males. The proportion of books including females dropped from twelve out of thirty-one (39 percent) in the 1969–84 group to four out of twenty-nine (14 percent) in the 1985–92 group, while the proportion of males grew from 61 percent (nineteen) to 86 percent (twenty-five). (See figure 1.)

Physical appearance is a standard aspect of characterization in young adult novels, with most characters' looks falling somewhere on

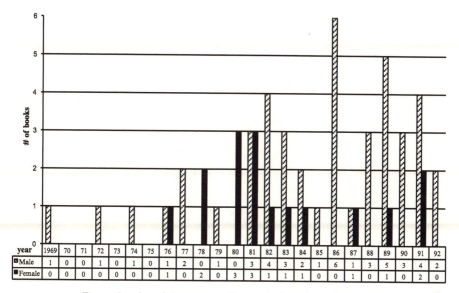

Fig. 1. Gender of character with gay/lesbian issue/identity

year	1969	70	71	72	73	74	75	76	77	78	79	80	81	82	83	84	85	86	87	88	89	90	91	92
Male	1	0	0	1	0	1	0	1	2	0	1	0	3	4	3	2	1	6	1	3	5	3	4	2
Female	0	0	0	0	0	0	0	1	0	2	0	3	3	1	1	1	0	0	1	0	1	0	2	0

a continuum between average-looking and beautiful/handsome. Young adult novels portray gay males and lesbians at various points on that continuum, but the few considered exceptionally attractive tend to differ according to gender. Beautiful lesbians, particularly those in the 1969–84 group, tend to be associated with pain, either for themselves or for those around them. Some are seductive, but lose interest once a conquest is made. Others are tragic beauties whose attractiveness seems to mark them for incurable diseases or brutal rapes. Handsome gay men, on the other hand, are neither evil nor doomed, and whatever pain they might cause others is unintentional. In remarkably similar plots, two novels (Colman's *Happily Ever After* and Rinaldi's *The Good Side of My Heart*) portray boys who are loved by the female narrators. When the boys come out, both narrators react with dismay and anger at the "injustice" of a gay male being attractive but unattainable, as when Rinaldi's female narrator laments, "All that handsomeness. All that masculinity wasted. I wanted to cry."[4] Eventually, both relationships turn into friendships, but the idea that good looks are wasted if the person possessing them isn't heterosexual is never questioned. In addition, women are shown falling for gay men, but men are never shown falling for lesbians. It appears that a man without a woman is attractive and valued, but a woman without a man is not.

Gay/Lesbian Teen Characters

Many of the novels include teenagers who have (or are contemplating) same-sex love relationships, some as protagonists and some as secondary characters. In all, the books contain forty young men and twenty young women who have same-sex attractions or concerns. Slightly over half of the young men (twenty-two) have some type of same-sex romantic encounter or relationship, and slightly less than half (eighteen) do not, through either personal choice or lack of opportunity. Almost all of the young women (nineteen) have some type of same-sex relationship in the course of the book. Portrayals have changed over time, with teen same-sex couples becoming both less common and more stable. While there are seven male and seven female couples in the 1969–84 group, the 1985–92 group contains only four male and two female couples. Of teen couples in the earlier group, half (two male, five female) separate, the five female couples because of one member's decision to end the relationship, the two male couples because of the death of one member. All of the teen couples in the more recent group (four male, two female) remain together. As noted above, almost all of single teens (eighteen or nineteen) are male. Some are content with their single status, while others are actively (or wistfully) looking for partners. It appears that young men have greater lifestyle flexibility than young women, since males may lead contented autonomous lives, while female autonomy is rarely pictured as an option.

Two contradictory social stereotypes of gay/lesbian people center on their level of sexual experience. One says that gay people are very promiscuous and think about sex constantly. This is usually applied to males. The other says that since same-sex couples are physically similar, there is little they can do together sexually. This is usually applied to females. Young adult novels in general tend to tread a fine line between general and specific when describing sexual activity, and details are often foggy beyond the first kiss. While this lack of sexual detail is evident throughout most young adult literature, fictional gays and lesbians seem to have *extremely* limited sex lives. Donovan tells the reader that Davy and Altschuler kiss, but the rest of their activity is merely alluded to as "it" and "that" when the boys talk. Charles, in Holland's *Man without a*

Face, says, "I didn't know what was happening to me until it happened."[5] In Scoppettone's *Trying Hard to Hear You,* Jeff and Phil are seen hugging once. In Scoppettone's *Happy Endings Are All Alike,* the deranged narrator Mid spies on Jaret and Peggy and exclaims, "Before I knew it, before I could believe it, they were doing IT to each other. That's right, IT. And they really acted like they dug it."[6] Even the brash teenager Neil, who begins Mosca's *All-American Boys* with "I've known I was gay since I was thirteen. Does that surprise you? It didn't me," draws the veil when he and Paul begin their affair, saying, "He touched my arm. Our kiss was gentle. As for what happened afterwards, well, there are parts of everyone's life that are not open for public inspection."[7]

These last two books are particularly interesting in matters of explicitness because they both contain detailed descriptions of violent assaults—Jaret's beating and rape fills seven pages, and Paul's bashing and Neil's kung fu revenge take five. As MPAA ratings reflect, it is thought safer for teenagers to view violence than sex, a standard that appears to hold true for young adult novels as well. Although some critics complain of "excessive violence," far more attack sexual explicitness, and any expression of homosexuality is automatically labeled "too explicit." The majority of these books contain no description of any sexual interaction—or even any physical contact—between two lovers of the same sex. The effect of this absence is to either trivialize or mystify gay sexuality. If readers are looking for sexual information, they get very little.

Gay/Lesbian Adult Characters

Twenty-five novels contain gay/lesbian adults ranging in age from early twenties to midfifties. Older adults are sometimes portrayed as aware and tolerant of others' homosexuality, but are never shown as lesbian/gay themselves. Gay and lesbian adults in more recent titles tend to be more comfortable with themselves and more likely to be in couples than those in earlier titles. A total of eighteen (twelve male, six female) adult couples appear in these books: six (two male, four female) in the 1969–84 group, and twelve (ten male, two female) in the 1985–92 group. In the earlier novels, adult male couples are infrequent and unfortunate. The two couples suffer because of their relationship, one through discriminatory job loss (in Bargar's *What Happened to Mr. Forster?*) and one through self-hate so severe that one member of the couple murders the other to avoid disclosure (in Hulse's *Just the Right Amount of Wrong*). In the more recent novels, adult male couples are more frequent and relatively more fortunate. Of a total of ten adult male couples, seven survive, while three face the death of one partner: two from AIDS and one from gay bashing. Lesbian adult relationships are less evident but fare somewhat better in these novels. All six of the adult lesbian couples survive to the end of the story, although two couples in the earlier novels have significant problems. In Garden's *Annie on My Mind*, both members of a couple experience discriminatory job loss, while in L'Engle's *A House Like a Lotus*, one member of a couple faces a terminal illness.

A small number of single gay or lesbian adults also appear in these books: four (two male, two female) in the earlier books, and seven (all male) in the more recent books. Both of the single women appear in St. George's *Call Me Margo* and are actually former lovers, one of whom is Margo's unhappy, saintly, and athletic tennis instructor, while the other is Margo's unhappy, unpleasant, and physically disabled English teacher, thus reflecting a double-sided stereotype common to many marginalized groups that depicts them as either superhumanly virtuous or subhumanly malign. The single gay men are more numerous and varied in affect. The brooding Mr. Rochester–like recluse in Holland's *The Man without a Face*, the father and children's book author in Rees's *Out of the Winter Gardens*, and the handsome art dealer uncle and verbal artiste in Koertge's *The Arizona Kid* exemplify the range of characterizations. They are, however, more likely than gay male couples to face significant misfortune; of the nine portrayed, four lead contented, though occasionally lonely, lives, while five die, face death, or are gay-bashed in the course of the book.

Gay/Lesbian Characters: Problems and Patterns

Several patterns emerge in the portrayals of teen and adult gay/lesbian characters in young adult novels. Notable, along with the ongoing and growing lack of lesbians noted earlier, is the near-absence of any single lesbians. There appears to be a continuing resistance on the part of authors and/or editors to view independent females as other than in a temporary state (if young) or other than unhappy (if adult). Males, on the other hand, appear to be capable of leading autonomous lives. Next, there is the endangered status of gay males. In the earlier books, seven die and one is gay-bashed; in the more recent books, five die or are dying, and three are gay-bashed. Many of these characters acknowledge the stress they feel in leading their lives in a potentially dangerous world, but, with a few notable exceptions, there is a great deal of attention focused on the difficulties of being a member of a minority group, with little attention paid to the strategies and skills minority group members develop in order to survive. The novels that do raise such issues tend to be those that place the gay/lesbian characters within the context of a community of friends and either biological or chosen family.

Many of the gay/lesbian characters in these books, particularly those who are young, lead isolated and lonely lives. Given the assumed (and often actual) course of gay people's lives, this may seem logical and realistic. Certainly the pressure of living in the average secondary school's atmosphere of exaggerated heterosexuality and homophobia contributes to the isolation of nonconforming students. Indeed, such pressure has been identified as one of the significant factors in the comparatively high rate of gay/lesbian teen suicide attempts.[8] In autobiographical accounts by gay and lesbian adults, authors who identified as gay or lesbian as teens often describe several stages through which they moved: first, becoming aware of their same-sex attractions; second, dealing in various ways with the difficulties arising from isolation and heterosexism; and, finally, acting to end their isolation by seeking a social milieu of gay/lesbian people and their friends as they move toward adulthood.[9] Most adult lives are sustained by a network of family and friends, and there is no reason to suppose that this would not be the case for adults who are gay or lesbian. This reality is rarely reflected in these novels. The four books by British author David Rees, Barbara Wersba's *Crazy Vanilla,* and Ron Koertge's *The Arizona Kid* are notable for their inclusion of a gay community. Most of the other novels fail even to hint at the existence of a larger community of gay/lesbian people and their friends. The message in these books is that it is important to be true to oneself and to be accepting of one's own, and others', sexual preference, but that part of what a gay/lesbian person has to accept is loneliness and the absence of a peer group, both in adolescence and in adulthood.

AIDS became an acknowledged societal concern in the early 1980s, and books for young adults containing AIDS information began to appear in 1985.[10] Several of these books have been young adult fiction, but few have included gay people.[11] The earliest novels were M. E. Kerr's *Night Kites* (1986) and Gloria Miklowitz's *Goodbye, Tomorrow* (1987). In the first, the person with AIDS is gay, and in the second, straight, but both characters suffer discrimination from nearly everyone around them. In more recent books—Koertge's *The Arizona Kid*, Levy's *Rumors and Whispers*, Rees's *The Colour of His Hair*, and Durant's *When Heroes Die*—gay people with AIDS face discrimination but are also supported by their friends. Given the difficulties that people with AIDS face, it is realistic to portray discrimination, but it is now equally realistic to portray AIDS support networks.

Gay/Lesbian YA Novels: Narrative Distance and Gender

A comparison of earlier novels with more recent novels shows that some elements have changed, while others have remained constant. One aspect of the novels' portrayals that has changed strikingly is the distance between the protagonist/narrator and the novel's gay/lesbian content. Since the mid-1980s, the trend within this body of literature has been away from homosexuality-as-main-issue, and toward treating gay issues as either a subplot or a fact about a secondary character that is stated but not commented upon at any length. Narrators have gone from dealing with their own possible gay identity to dealing with the gay/lesbian identity of their friends, siblings, relatives, or parents (see figure 2). In eighteen of the thirty-one novels published from 1969 through 1984, the issue of gay/lesbian identity is one that affects another character, commonly an adult in the role of parent, teacher, or mentor. By contrast, gay/lesbian identity is a personal concern of the protagonist/narrator in only six of twenty-nine novels published from 1985 through 1992. This trend works both to broaden and to narrow the scope of gay/lesbian YA fiction. On the one hand, more recent novels include gay and lesbian characters in a greater range of relationships to the teen protagonist than appeared in earlier years. On the other hand, most of the protagonists in the 1985–92 books are heterosexual, which may limit teen reader response by placing the gay/lesbian character consistently at a remove from the protagonist.

Of the twenty-four books dealing with the narrator/protagonist's identity, fifteen books feature male narrators (eleven from 1969–84, four from 1985–92) and nine books feature female narrators (seven from 1969–84, two from 1985–92). However, in the thirty-six books containing

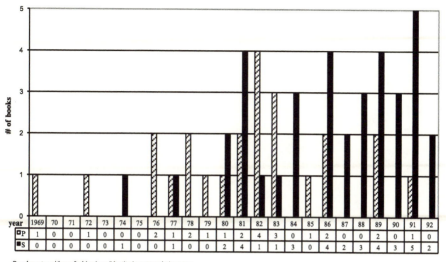

year	1969	70	71	72	73	74	75	76	77	78	79	80	81	82	83	84	85	86	87	88	89	90	91	92
▢P	1	0	0	1	0	0	0	2	1	2	1	1	2	4	3	0	1	2	0	0	2	0	1	0
▪S	0	0	0	0	0	1	0	0	1	0	0	2	4	1	1	3	0	4	2	3	4	3	5	2

P = character with gay/lesbian issue/identity is protagonist/narrator
S = character with gay/lesbian issue/identity is secondary character

Fig. 2. Role of character with gay/lesbian issue/identity

gay/lesbian nonprotagonist characters, the protagonist's gender appears to have a significant relationship to that of the gay/lesbian character. In the eighteen books with female protagonists, eleven of the gay/lesbian characters are male and seven are female; in the eighteen books with male protagonists, eighteen of the gay characters are male and none are female. The female narrators in these books have a variety of relationships with gay males, from daughter to sister to best friend to ex-girlfriend. The male narrators, on the other hand, have no relationships with lesbians, as sons, brothers, friends, or ex-boyfriends. This absence of any connection between male protagonists and lesbians is not a reflection of reality. In real life, for example, gay parents of both genders have children of both genders. In young adult novels, however, gay fathers may have sons or daughters, but lesbian mothers have daughters only. This odd and persistent omission may reflect an outdated editorial assumption as to the inherent indifference of all teenage males (as protagonists or readers) to all females—as mothers, siblings, cousins, friends, or colleagues—who are not romantically interested in males. One would hope that in the future, young adult authors and editors might give their readers—and young men—credit for a broader vision.

Still another related gender concern is that of the lack of interaction between gay male and lesbian characters. This sex segregation could reflect an actual lack of gender integration within some gay/lesbian communities, but it must be noted that none of the sixty novels in this group contain both gay male and lesbian characters except in moments so fleeting as to be nearly nonexistent, such as the passing mention of Bonny's foster parents as a female couple in Ure's *The Other Side of the Fence*, a novel featuring a young man coming to terms with his gay identity. Gender segregation plus assumptions about people with AIDS may be seen in the fact that none of the books containing lesbian characters make any mention of AIDS.

Conclusion and Future Directions

While the difficulties and isolation faced by gay/lesbian characters in these books must not be discounted, the possibility of friendship and connection between friends of different sexual orientations is also portrayed. For example, two young adult novels, both published in 1990, feature straight male protagonists who must come to terms with the gay identity of a close male friend. Although both are recent, when read together they illustrate the range of novelistic protagonist/narrator stances taken over the quarter-century discussed in this essay. In Joyce Sweeney's *Face the Dragon*, Paul comes out to his friend Eric as they walk on a deserted beach:

> "I'm different from you. . . . For a while I wasn't even sure about this, but lately, and especially after last night . . . I'm just not very interested in . . . girls."
>
> It was so sudden, Eric didn't get it. "Well, you probably . . ." Then he did get it. "What do you mean?" he asked warily.
>
> Paul wouldn't look at him now. "You *know* what I mean."
>
> "You're crazy. I've known you all your life. I'd know if you were like that."
>
> "How would you know? If I never said anything, you wouldn't know. You just said you didn't have a clue how I felt about that stuff. Well, now I'm telling you. When I think about that stuff, I think about . . . the wrong people. . . ."
>
> "Well, if I were you, I'd try to keep my options open. I'm saying it because you're talking about something that's risky and danger-

ous and makes your whole life a million times harder than it has to be. So if there is a way out, I think you should look for it."[12]

In Paul Walker's *The Method,* Mitch comes out to Albie while the two sit in a crowded gay restaurant. Albie reacts with laughter, to which Mitch responds:

> "I'm sorry that it makes you nervous, Albie. But I want you to know. I'm gay. I'm queer. I'm a faggot. I'm a homosexual. This is not a joke. This is my life."
>
> Albie . . . turned toward Mitch and asked, "Why are you telling me this?"
>
> "I need to."
>
> "How do you know? I mean, about being . . . you know . . . gay?"
>
> "I know. Believe me. Albie, there's something I want to ask you, and I want you to be completely honest. Will you do that? Are we still friends?"
>
> Albie reached out and covered Mitch's hand with his own. "You know we are."[13]

Among the most obvious differences in these two treatments of a similar event are those of setting and of language. Sweeney, unwilling to use what appears to be "the g—— word," prefers to describe Paul's sexual orientation in terms of negatives, while Walker uses a variety of standard and colloquial terms to express Mitch's message to Albie, and even allows his protagonist to show his acceptance though physical contact. One-note portrayals of gay/lesbian characters as tragic outsiders continue to appear in contemporary young adult fiction, but they are no longer hegemonic.

There are also areas as yet unexplored in YA fiction. As noted earlier, there are comparatively few books that feature lesbian characters and none that portray lesbians in any type of relationship with male teen protagonists. Portrayals of people of color as gay or lesbian are also lacking. There is also the persistent absence of settings that reflect gay/lesbian communities as they exist throughout the country. Perhaps at some future point a young adult novel will appear featuring a gay/lesbian protagonist who lives within a network of family and friends of various orientations and who faces various problems that may or may not touch upon the protagonist's sexual identity.

Gaining a historical perspective on this subgenre of young adult fiction can benefit librarians, teachers, and others who work with young people. An awareness of the strengths and weaknesses of the literature thus far can aid in the evaluation of current and future young adult novels featuring gay/lesbian characters and themes using the important criteria of realism, balance, and diversity.

APPENDIX: CHRONOLOGICAL BIBLIOGRAPHY OF SIXTY TITLES

Earlier Group: Titles Published 1969–84

1969
Donovan, John. *I'll Get There. It Better Be Worth the Trip.* New York: Harper.

1972
Holland, Isabelle. *The Man without a Face.* New York: Lippincott.

1974
Scoppettone, Sandra. *Trying Hard to Hear You.* New York: Harper.

1976
Guy, Rosa. *Ruby.* New York: Viking.
Sullivan, Mary W. *What's This About Pete?* Nashville: Thomas Nelson.

1977
Hall, Lynn. *Sticks and Stones.* Chicago: Follett.
Kerr, M. E. *I'll Love You When You're More Like Me.* New York: Harper.

1978
Hautzig, Deborah. *Hey, Dollface.* New York: Greenwillow.
Scoppettone, Sandra. *Happy Endings Are All Alike.* New York: Harper.

1979
Rees, David. *In the Tent.* Boston: Alyson.

1980
Klein, Norma. *Breaking Up.* New York: Pantheon/Random House.
Reading, J. P. *Bouquets for Brimbal.* New York: Harper.
Tolan, Stephanie. *The Last of Eden.* New York: Bantam.

1981
Bargar, Gary. *What Happened to Mr. Forster?* New York: Clarion.
Futcher, Jane. *Crush.* Boston: Alyson.
Hanlon, Emily. *The Wing and the Flame.* New York: Bradbury.
Levy, Elizabeth. *Come Out Smiling.* New York: Delacorte.
St. George, Judith. *Call Me Margo.* New York: Putnam.
Snyder, Anne, and Louis Pelletier. *The Truth about Alex* (Original title: *Counterplay*). New York: Signet. Reissued in 1987 as *The Truth about Alex*.

1982

Bunn, Scott. *Just Hold On.* New York: Delacorte.

Chambers, Aidan. *Dance on My Grave.* New York: Harper.

Garden, Nancy. *Annie on My Mind.* New York: Farrar.

Hulse, Larry. *Just the Right Amount of Wrong.* New York: Harper.

Rees, David. *The Milkman's on His Way.* London: Gay Men's Press.

1983

Ecker, B. A. *Independence Day.* New York: Avon.

Kesselman, Janice. *Flick.* New York: Harper.

Mosca, Frank. *All-American Boys.* Boston: Alyson.

Singer, Marilyn. *The Course of True Love Never Did Run Smooth.* New York: Harper.

1984

L'Engle, Madeleine. *A House Like a Lotus.* New York: Farrar.

Rees, David. *Out of the Winter Gardens.* London: Olive Press.

Ure, Jean. *You Win Some, You Lose Some.* New York: Dell.

More Recent Group: Titles Published 1985–92

1985

Bess, Clayton. *Big Man and the Burn-Out.* New York: Houghton.

1986

Colman, Hila. *Happily Ever After.* New York: Scholastic.

Kerr, M. E. *Night Kites.* New York: Harper.

Meyer, Carolyn. *Elliott and Win.* New York: McElderry.

Sakers, Don. *Act Well Your Part.* Boston: Alyson.

Ure, Jean. *The Other Side of the Fence.* New York: Delacorte.

Wersba, Barbara. *Crazy Vanilla.* New York: Harper.

1987

Klein, Norma. *My Life as a Body.* New York: Knopf.

Rinaldi, Ann. *The Good Side of My Heart.* New York: Holiday.

1988

Klein, Norma. *Now That I Know.* New York: Bantam.

Koertge, Ron. *The Arizona Kid.* Boston: Joy Street / Little, Brown.

Wersba, Barbara. *Just Be Gorgeous.* New York: Harper.

1989

Block, Francesca Lia. *Weetzie Bat.* New York: Harper.

Brett, Catherine. *S. P. Likes A. D.* Toronto: Women's Press.

Childress, Alice. *Those Other People.* New York: Putnam.

Homes, A. M. *Jack.* New York: Macmillan.

Rees, David. *The Colour of His Hair.* Exeter, UK: Third House.

Shannon, George. *Unlived Affections.* New York: Harper.

1990
Levy, Marilyn. *Rumors and Whispers*. New York: Fawcett.
Sweeney, Joyce. *Face the Dragon*. New York: Delacorte.
Walker, Paul Robert. *The Method*. New York: Gulliver/HBJ.

1991
Block, Francesca Lia. *Witch Baby*. New York: HarperCollins.
Garden, Nancy. *Lark in the Morning*. New York: Farrar.
Gleitzman, Morris. *Two Weeks with the Queen*. New York: Putnam.
Greene, Bette. *The Drowning of Stephen Jones*. New York: Bantam.
Maguire, Jesse. *Getting It Right*. New York: Ivy/Ballantine.
Woodson, Jacqueline. *The Dear One*. New York: Delacorte.

1992
Durant, Penny Raife. *When Heroes Die*. New York: Atheneum.
Wieler, Diana. *Bad Boy*. New York: Delacorte.

NOTES

1. Kenneth L. Donelson and Alleen Pace Nilsen, *Literature for Today's Young Adults*, 3rd ed. (Glenview, IL.: Scott-Foresman, 1986), 84.

2. Martha Bacon, "Review," *Atlantic Monthly* 224 (December 1969): 150.

3. Frances Hanckel and John Cunningham, "Can Young Gays Find Happiness in YA Books?" *Wilson Library Bulletin* 50 (March 1976): 528–34; Judith Mitchell, "Changes in Adolescent Literature with Homosexual Motifs, Themes, and Characters," Ph.D. diss., University of Connecticut, 1982; Jan Goodman, "Out of the Closet, But Paying the Price: Lesbian and Gay Characters in Children's Literature," *Interracial Books for Children Bulletin* 14 (1983): 13–15; David Wilson, "The Open Library: YA Books for Gay Teens," *English Journal* 73 (November 1984): 60–64; Christine Jenkins, "Heartthrobs and Heartbreaks: A Guide to Young Adult Books with Gay Themes," *Out/Look* 1 (Fall 1988): 82–92; Virginia Wolf, "The Gay Family in Literature for Young People," *Children's Literature in Education* 20 (March 1989): 51–58; Dennis Sumara, "Gay and Lesbian Voices in Literature: Making Room on the Shelf," *English Quarterly* 25 (1991): 30–34; Allan A. Cuseo, *Homosexual Characters in YA Novels: A Literary Analysis, 1969–1982* (Metuchen, NJ: Scarecrow, 1992); Laurel A. Clyde and Marjorie Lobban, *Out of the Closet and into the Classroom: Homosexuality in Books for Young People* (Port Melbourne, Australia: ALIA Thorpe, 1992).

4. Ann Rinaldi, *The Good Side of My Heart* (New York: Holiday, 1987), 222.

5. Isabelle Holland, *Man without a Face* (New York: Lippincott, 1972), 167.

6. Sandra Scoppettone, *Happy Endings Are All Alike* (New York: Harper), 122.

7. Frank Mosca, *All-American Boys* (Boston: Alyson, 1983), 7, 44.

8. Marcia R. Feinleib, ed., *Report of the Secretary's Task Force on Youth Suicide*, vol. 3, *Prevention and Interventions in Youth Suicide* (Rockville, MD: Department of Health and Human Services, 1989).

9. Elaine Laudau, *Different Drummer: Homosexuality in America* (New York: Messner, 1986); Susan Cohen and Daniel Cohen, *When Someone You Know Is Gay* (New York: M. Evans, 1989).

10. Christine Jenkins, "Books on AIDS Written for Young People," *WLW Journal* 12 (April 1988): 9.

11. Meg Tillapaugh, "AIDS: A Problem for Today's YA Problem Novel," *School Library Journal* 39 (May 1993): 22–25.

12. Joyce Sweeney, *Facing the Dragon* (New York: Delacorte, 1990), 102.

13. Paul Walker, *The Method* (New York: Gulliver/HBJ, 1990), 137–38.

"Unshelter Me"

The Emerging Fictional Adolescent Lesbian

VANESSA WAYNE LEE

Terry Castle opens the fourth chapter of *The Apparitional Lesbian: Female Homosexuality and Modern Culture* with a discussion of how fictional representations of lesbianism have progressed from inconceivability to undertheorized reality.[1] The point of contention for theorists, according to Castle, is determining what "lesbian fiction" is: who or what is represented and by whom?[2] Castle's theory of lesbian counterplotting offers a means for recognizing and evaluating adolescent lesbian fiction. This counterplot is an inversion of what Eve Kosofsky Sedgwick sees as a triangle of male homosocial desire that connects male-female-male: "the bonding 'between' two men through, around, or over the body and soul of a woman."[3] According to Castle, the lesbian counterplot successfully subverts this triangle to depict "a female-male-female triangle, in which one of the male terms from the original triangle now occupies the in between or subjugated position of the mediator."[4] The state of the counterplotting at the end of a novel determines whether it can be categorized as euphoric or dysphoric. If the female subversion maintains dominance through the end of a novel, Castle describes the counterplot as euphoric, but if the traditional male plot takes over, the novel is dysphoric.

The lesbian novel of adolescence is part of Castle's dichotomy of probable lesbian plots, the other category being "novels of postmarital experience."[5] She claims that "the lesbian novel of adolescence is almost always dysphoric in tendency."[6] The texts that she specifies are texts written for and read primarily by adults: Dorothy Strachey's *Olivia* (1949), Jeanette Winterson's *Oranges Are Not the Only Fruit* (1985), Antonia White's *Frost in May* (1933), and Christa Winsloe's *The Child Manuela* (1933). But while a close look at texts on lesbian themes written both about and for adolescents reveals plenty of dysphoric counterplots—such as Rosa Guy's *Ruby* (1976), which "depicts female homosexual desire as a finite phenomenon . . . a temporary phase in a larger pattern of heterosexual Bildung"[7]—it also reveals several euphoric counterplots that defy Castle's classification of the lesbian novel of adolescence.[8]

My analysis makes use of Castle's theories but requires a change in focus from viewing the "lesbian novel of adolescence" to viewing the adolescent novel of lesbianism. Of critical importance is how adolescent lesbian sexuality is articulated by adults for adolescents in popular literature and culture, because whether the adolescent reads for truth, experience, identification, or pleasure, she reads what the dominant culture deems publishable.[9] I propose here a critical account of how authors have textually constructed specifically adolescent lesbian sexual identities. Although Castle sees two types of counterplots in adult lesbian fiction, when the focus is shifted to adolescent lesbian fiction I find three provisional groups, in which both dysphoric and euphoric plots surface. First are texts that position lesbianism as a threat or problem. As such, they do not attend to the formation of a lesbian identity but are designed to educate audiences unfamiliar or uncomfortable with lesbianism and/or to eroticize the lesbian as a facet of male heterosexual pleasure. Texts of this sort include Deborah Hautzig's teen novel *Hey, Dollface* (1978), Elizabeth Levy's preteen novel *Come Out Smiling* (1981), and Juan Jose Campanula's made-for-cable family special *More Than Friends: The Coming Out of Heidi Lieter* (1995).

The second type of text focuses on the formation of lesbian identities.[10] The lesbian identities represented in each text vary in depth, endurance, and scope. The texts best representing this category are Sandra Scoppettone's *Happy Endings Are All Alike* (1978), Nancy Garden's *Annie On My Mind* (1982) and *Good Moon Rising* (1996), and Maria Maggenti's film *The Incredibly True Adventure of Two Girls in Love* (1995).

Texts in the third category interrogate received wisdom about lesbianism and lesbian identity. Whereas texts in the first and second categories isolate and magnify the issue of lesbianism in their plots, the texts in the final category represent lesbianism with less clarity. Stacey

Donovan's book *Dive* (1996) portrays adolescence as complicated and does not presume that this state is knowable or honestly representable. And in the film *Heavenly Creatures* (1994), writer-director Peter Jackson's interpretation of two adolescent girls' psyches turns a fact-based tale into an unnerving spectacle of adolescent lesbians whose libidos are frighteningly powerful, even murderous. Both works are less focused on sexuality than on age; they show lesbianism as part of a larger cultural landscape.

This essay's ordering of these three categories, neither definitive nor chronological, begins with texts that presuppose that their readers have something to learn from lesbian characters. Such texts can appropriately be categorized as a particular brand of "after-school special" problem novels. Hautzig's *Hey, Dollface* reads more like an informational book than like an entertaining novel. Narrator Valerie Hoffman tells the story of her intimate friendship with Chloe Fox, a classmate at New York's Garfield School for Girls. Their friendship is cemented by their exclusion from Garfield's debutante crowd and from American society's standards of normal behavior and beauty in females. Hautzig's agenda includes an acceptance of romantic friendships between adolescent girls, and her characters stand as testimony that lesbian feelings are natural and that society's reactions cause undue stress, worry, and shame. In the end, her characters turn out fine in terms of hegemonic expectations because ultimately they opt for heterosexual relationships.

Valerie's idea of homosexuality develops alongside an exaggerated notion of heterosexuality, which she associates with the threat of rape in the city streets and unwelcome advances from older men. She describes the feeling she has toward Chloe as not a "big thing, because it wasn't, not then."[11] She further explains, "I don't think I thought of it as being sexual attraction until later, or if I did I wouldn't admit it to myself. I guess I thought I wasn't capable of really having *that* sort of feeling."[12] As these passages indicate, Valerie assumes the distance of retrospective evaluation. She links her daydreaming to the retelling of the past. She does not think that her feelings for Chloe were a big deal "then," and she does not realize the sexual element of her daydreams "until later." With these techniques the narrator removes herself from the immediate story. Since these shifts occur when homoeroticism becomes more of a focus, Hautzig gives her readers the opportunity to back away from identifying with a demonstrably lesbian narrative voice, which may be uncomfortable for them.[13]

Nevertheless, although she gives them a way out, Hautzig invites readers to participate in the construction of meaning through narrative gaps, sophisticated metaphors, and intertextuality. For instance, the most sexual scene between the girls takes place at Chloe's house while Chloe's mother is out for the evening. Valerie comforts Chloe after a nightmare and unwittingly touches her breast, and Chloe does not make her move her hand. Val says to herself, "This isn't sick at all. . . . Everything I'm doing I'm doing because it's what my instinct says to do. . . . Is it wrong to feel good about doing this?"[14] When Mrs. Fox returns and witnesses the physical closeness, Val decides that she has done something wrong and leaves before anyone wakes up. But it is significant that Valerie and Chloe are uncertain what, if any, implications their feelings or actions have for their identity. These two young adults are dissatisfied with the strict dichotomy that their society offers them: "We do something like—what we did once. . . . And then there's a choice; either I'm a lesbian forever or I stop being myself with you. When I don't want either one."[15] Hey, Dollface directly challenges the dichotomy of heterosexuality/homosexuality, demanding that young adults be allowed the agency to lay their own linguistic and behavioral boundaries. The third position in Valerie and Chloe's counterplot is filled by heterosexuality, which takes the form of their families, perverted older men, male peers, and the expectation that both girls want to attract, and be attractive to, boys. Heterosexuality is the "subjugated mediator"[16] between the girls as they define sexuality for themselves. The girls gain an empowering understanding that they do not have to fit themselves into labels that are not comfortable, but the new freedom forces them to renounce a fulfilling form of closeness and stretches the counterplot to accommodate a friendship, without sex, between Valerie and Chloe and between Valerie and Chloe and their respective heterosexual partners.

Despite the narrative's dysphoric attributes, this insistence is markedly more positive than the message communicated by the next novel, Levy's *Come Out Smiling*, which narrates the story of Jenny Mandel, a confused teenager who has a crush on her riding instructor at summer camp, Peggy. Halfway through the summer, she observes Peggy and her new assistant, Ann, kissing. Putting together this open display of sexuality between females with her own attraction for Peggy, Jenny begins to think of herself as a developing sexual being. *Come Out Smiling* offers a subject position grounded in a fear of lesbianism, a position likely familiar to many preadolescent readers. The novel is ultimately about Jenny's transition from safe all-girl relationships to a desirable asexuality, because males are no more attractive to her than females. The crushes that the girls have on each other at camp are normalized by the text.[17] Jenny's age places her in the liminal space between when these crushes are acceptable and when maturing heterosexually should dominate a girl's thoughts.[18] Acting as what John Stephens terms a narrative and ideological "focalizer,"[19] Jenny directs readers to both homosocial crushes and homophobia, which situates the text tensely between lesbian and heterosexual discourses.

Come Out Smiling's subject matter, tone, vocabulary, and sentence structure identify the target audience of this novel as early adolescent. The text closes itself off from reader involvement by constructing meaning through a staccato, choppy pace that mirrors the didactic narration and reinforces the text's control over meaning. The primary sources of tension are between the sexual changes of puberty and the narrator's desire to be asexual and between the innocent first-person narration and the novel's didactic agenda. In addition, one may locate coded references to normalized lesbianism in tension with heavy-handed messages of compulsory heterosexuality. The title of the book, *Come Out Smiling*, refers both to the process of homosexual "coming out" and to Jenny's parents' method of punishment. When Jenny acts up, she is sent to her room and told not to emerge until she can "come out smiling."[20] This double entendre denies agency both for Jenny and for lesbian readings: to come out smiling from your room involves a swallowing of personal pride, a willingness to suppress feelings, and a lack of dialogue between the figures of authority and the perceived transgressor. At the closing ceremonies of the summer camp, the girls kneel down and pray to Sacajawea, the bird woman after whom their camp is named. Jenny prays, "Please, Sacajawea, don't make me turn out to be a lesbian," and "Please give me the courage to come out smiling."[21]

The text thus ends linguistically conflicted, with Jenny determined to do away with the all-female triangle of her story but also to "come out" smiling and begrudgingly accept her fate. Jenny knows that her father expects her to marry a rich man, but, after kissing a boy at the coed dance, she thinks, "I had liked dancing with Chris, but I had loved dancing with Peggy. Maybe I was queer. Chris had kissed me. If I were normal, I'd be feeling so high."[22] Jenny's father figures most prominently as the male in her counterplot with Peggy. Her father is not subjugated by the text, however, as he strongly influences Jenny and controls Peggy by labeling her a lesbian after a moment's glance. His linguistic ownership of both female elements of the triangle suggest a dysphoric counterplot, but if Jenny had her way she would separate herself from all triangles, dysphoric or euphoric.

Levy uses the metaphor of performance and masquerade to reify the concept of homosexuality in Jenny's budding sexual existence. The most influential performance, that of Peggy and Ann, is not intended to be a performance, but Jenny, arriving early for riding practice, "spies" on them "holding hands."[23] Jenny knows that "after you're ten years old, girls who hold hands are queer."[24] As she continues to watch Peggy and Ann, they kiss "lightly on the lips, not like friends—like lovers. . . . Peggy and Ann were lesbians."[25] For the rest of the book, Jenny feels "creepy" about this unwelcome sexual knowledge. Peggy and Ann represent a larger—and threatening—lesbian community.[26] Levy's narrator, in short, is fearful and distrustful of lesbianism but simultaneously loves two lesbians. In the novel, sexuality is an uncontrollable, unstoppable, and unknowable force that occupies the place that should be taken by Jenny's subjectivity and agency. Performance and masquerade are an essential part of Jenny because she does not delve beneath the surface of the issues confronting her.

In contrast to Levy's novel, one of many repressive and voyeuristic representations of adolescent lesbianism, *More Than Friends: The Coming Out of Heidi Lieter* offers didacticism from a different perspective. In the two novels I have already discussed, lesbianism is the problem. *More Than Friends* turns the tables to position society's violence against homosexuality as the cause of conflict and primes mainstream cable viewers for this developing plot structure, which, as we will see, was already in bookstores on the young adult shelves. This short film portrays two adolescent girls whose lesbian identities are developed for the most part offscreen. The story is about their demand that their community accept their relationship as equal to heterosexual relationships. As part of HBO's series *Lifestories: Families in Crisis*, *More Than Friends* makes adolescent lesbianism visible, but by the series title also pronounces it a "crisis" that families need help resolving. Even so, the film itself resists the crisis label and maintains a euphoric plot. Heidi's girlfriend, Missy, is violently attacked by a homophobic male student who does not want her to go to the prom with Heidi. The girls make a milestone of the event and move beyond it to attend the prom and tell about it on a television talk show.

After the film's completion, the real Heidi Lieter appears on the screen to tell the HBO audience why she opted for visibility. She tells proponents and opponents alike, "You may think it's strange that I've been so public about a part of my life that's private. But I didn't do it for attention. . . . This is who I am. This is who I've always been. Being gay is not a choice I made, it's not something I just decided to be. The only choice I made is not to lie about it." These comments suggest that the film's intended audience is not lesbian teenagers or even supportive adults, but families who are opposed to such visibility and pride. Nonetheless, *More Than Friends* gives adolescent lesbian viewers a central and affirmative subject position, even if it assumes the task of educating others.

The educational plots discussed above inform their audiences that lesbianism exists, whether the reader/viewer likes it or not. The "coming-out" plots I next address centralize the formation of lesbian identities in an adolescent narrator. In telling their stories, the narrators demonstrate that lesbianism does not just exist but is a valid, livable existence. Contrary to what we might expect, such texts do not represent a chronological development from the first category; in fact, the coming-out story has evolved alongside the educational stories from 1978 onward.

The coming-out plot involves movement through four steps, the middle two closely related temporally. First, one of the female protagonists experiences a feeling for another female protagonist, usually a feeling that is difficult for her to describe. Second, the feeling is shared with the other female character. Third, the feeling is manifested in physical intimacy between the girls. Fourth, there is a forced public articulation of the girls' relationship. The relationship does not always survive this public "outing" with a euphoric triangle.

Most of the female characters in these texts discover their homosexuality beginning with a "queer," unnameable feeling. As the main character, Liza, explains in *Annie on My Mind*, "I felt as if I were about to burst with I didn't quite know what."[27] *Annie* is the love story of two seventeen-year-old girls, Liza and Annie. Liza attends an exclusive private academy in Brooklyn Heights and Annie attends a crime-ridden public school in Manhattan, which results in a class tension that is also highlighted in *Heavenly Creatures* (1994). Despite their economic and ethnic differences, however, the increasing sexual awareness in the characters motivates them to identify the nature of their feelings—feelings that come as a shock to Liza if not to Annie. In *Happy Endings Are All Alike*, Peggy "had a flash of lying in Jaret's arms and realized it made her happy, warm, content. Was that love? Sexual love? Would she want to kiss Jaret on the mouth?"[28] The relationship that develops between Peggy and Jaret in *Happy Endings* is occasionally joyful, but predominantly torturous as the girls deal with judgmental family members and a violent community. Mid, the boy who rapes Jaret and threatens to tell the town about her relations with Peggy, is the male element in this counterplot and, as such, plays the role of subjugated mediator when Jaret decides that coming out about her sexuality will heal more than the scars of rape. The sexual nature of love often brings about feelings of fear and guilt, about sex in general and about the public condemnation of homosexuality in particular.[29]

Next, the girls in these novels begin to resolve the tension of identifying their queer feelings by articulating their feelings for each other, to each other. The sheer intensity of those emotions leads to verbal articulation for most of the characters discussed here.[30] In contrast, the rapport between Evie and Randy in the film *The Incredibly True Adventure of Two Girls in Love* is narrated primarily through tense and silent cinematography. One example is an awkward moment in the school bathroom with sexy backlighting as Evie silently lights her cigarette off of Randy's. Their closeness is accentuated by the way that director Maggenti positions them: each girl faces inward with her back creating the left and right edges of the frame so that what passes between their bodies is emphasized—the mock-kiss of their cigarettes. This framing technique is used throughout the film to focus on the silences and words that pass between them. During a verbal exchange, Randy explains to Evie that when two women hold hands and have feelings for each other, it is not always accepted. Evie is too caught up in the rapture of her feelings for Randy to consider the political consequences, but in fact the action of holding hands in public invites and accepts spectatorship of their love. Holding hands is used so often in lesbian fiction, specifically adolescent lesbian fiction, that it can be considered a trope of the genre.[31] Randy exclaims, "God, Evie, you are so sheltered." Evie responds, "Unshelter me."

It naturally follows that the girls in these texts begin to question their identity because the feelings they have are for another female. Experimentation with the language of sexual identity and gender, which we saw as far back as *Hey, Dollface,* appears frequently in these coming-out novels. Kerry in *Good Moon Rising* concludes, "A lover. . . . That's what we both really wanted, isn't it? Only since boys somehow didn't fit, we thought what we wanted was a friend."[32] Usually, the girls find that they have "always" had these feelings for females instead of males.[33] Sexual and gender definition are intertwined in these novels as the girls come to terms with their love for another female. In *Happy Endings,* Peggy explains that "sometimes I wish one of us was a guy," and Jaret responds, "Then we wouldn't be us. If you were a guy, I wouldn't be interested."[34] These young women do not always find empowerment in labeling themselves as gay or even in love; they avoid fitting themselves into prescribed roles and argue that labels of sexuality must be flexible, if they are to be useful at all.[35]

The girls usually engage in physical intimacy for the first time by kissing. In *Good Moon Rising* and *The Incredibly True Adventure of Two Girls in Love,* the narrators describe the girls' meeting, mutual attraction, and physical contact, from touching and kissing to genital sex. *Happy Endings Are All Alike* and *Annie on My Mind,* on the other hand, are framed texts, in the sense that one of the girls finds a reason to tell the story of meeting her lover. Roberta Seelinger Trites argues that the embedded narrative, specifically in *Annie on My Mind,* "situate[s] the text within the genre of the romance novel . . . in an act that is at once revisionary and reconciliatory," and allows the form to accent the content, since "the telling of the tale is critical to Liza's healing."[36]

The language of sexuality here is as explicit as teenage romance typically allows but tends to focus on nongenital contact.[37] *Annie on My Mind* moves from "before either of us knew what was happening, our arms were around each other and Annie's soft and gentle mouth was kissing mine," to "I remember so much about that first time with Annie that I am numb with it, and breathless."[38] In the gap between these two descriptions, the inevitable question arises: did they do it? Did they have genital sex? Precisely what Liza experienced with Annie is not shared with the reader, but as is the case in each of these coming-out stories, sexual contact is explicitly acknowledged. In *Happy Endings Are All Alike,* that Peggy and Jaret have sex is taken for granted; instead, more narrative weight is given to the various characters' reactions to the sex. And when the camera depicts Randy and Evie making love in *The Incredibly True Adventure of Two Girls in Love,* it does not eroticize their bodies for the viewer. Their bodies are shown naked, but the close-up angle of the camera emphasizes their connection rather than what one body is doing to the other.

The sex, however, is not the source of the tension in these coming-out stories. Rather, the girls' verbal and physical articulations become meaningful with the threat of public knowledge. When Jaret and Peggy's relationship in *Happy Endings Are All Alike* is forced into the public eye, it is because Mid threatens to "out" them if she tells anyone what he did to her.[39] When Jaret decides to risk the public knowledge of her sexual orientation and relationship with Peggy, they break up because Peggy cannot handle it. Peggy returns to Jaret in the end to explain how much she cares for Jaret, but she stresses that this does not necessarily mean that she wants to be in a sexual relationship with her. This ending offers a pointedly pessimistic conclusion about the future of lesbian relationships: "So what if happy endings didn't exist? Happy moments did."[40] Peggy and Jaret repair their friendship but sever the triangle as each leaves for a different college with only the memory of their "happy moment." Liza and Annie's sexual relationship in *Annie on My Mind* is discovered by a woman, Ms. Baxter, who forces Liza to make a public declaration about her sexuality. This counterplot is euphoric because there is no notable male component and because of Liza's final decision. In the expulsion hearing at her conservative school, Liza opts to lie, and she leaves for college apparently having broken off her relationship with Annie. But by the end of the novel, as an MIT freshman, Liza calls Annie to apologize and to tell her that she loves her; Annie responds that she will take the next flight to visit Liza in Boston.

Good Moon and *The Incredibly True Adventure* brave the same public outing but present endings that are more clearly optimistic than *Happy Endings Are All Alike.* In *Good Moon,* Jan and Kerry are found out because they play hooky together and rumors begin to circulate. At the cast party for their senior play, Jan plays heterosexual with Raphael, her gay male friend from summer theater stock.[41] Kent, the instigator of the rumors, publicly challenges them to admit their homosexuality. An interesting arrangement arises as heterosexual Kent and homosexual Raphael share the role of subjugated mediator when Kent makes his challenge. Jan, with Kerry's whispered approval, interrupts Raphael as he defends her heterosexuality and faces Kent, the male who threatens to offset the triangle, saying, "'You were right . . . I am gay.' With the words came a sense of relief and liberation so great that she felt she never wanted to hide again, even though she knew at the same time that she might have to. 'And so am I,' came Kerry's clear voice."[42] They find pride in admitting their sexuality *of their own agency* in public and in a highly theatrical context. They are allowed to stay together, to represent a euphoric potential for lasting lesbian relationships and euphoric plots. This potential is also suggested in *The Incredibly True Adventure of Two Girls in Love* when Randy and Evie run away together. Randy's gay male friend, Frank, completes their triangle and mediates between the runaways and their parents, but he finally succumbs and leads the parents to the hideout. When Evie and Randy decide to leave their hotel room and face their angry parents and peers, they stand in an open doorway facing and touching each other with the noisy crowd behind them. The camera shot is from inside the hotel room, so the dynamic framing has the effect of placing the viewer on the side of the girls and supporting their pledge to love each other forever.

Tellingly, the girls in each of these texts are punished once they reach a level of sexual activity. These narratives insist that the teen balance sexual identity with the rest of her identity. The ultimate punishment for transgressors is a forced coming out. Good and bad and right and wrong are knowable. In the third category of texts, however, things are not so clear for the (lesbian) characters. The works that have been discussed so far combine heteronormative adolescence and lesbianism, sharing information and representing lesbian identity through fairly static characters. Some contemporary texts do not offer such easy centerings, but instead represent fractured and less identity-bound versions of both adolescence and lesbianism. In *Heavenly Creatures* and *Dive* the lesbian characters function less as characters and more as points of narrative negotiation.

Dive narrates a few months out of the life of Virginia, including the relationship she develops with Jane, a new girl at school. The novel's narrative structure is fragmented and often abruptly stream-of-consciousness. While the book is concerned with Virginia's quest for identity, the first half is dedicated to her father's terminal illness and the hit-and-run accident that injured her dog. Virginia's self-awareness is heightened by her relationship with Jane, which helps prepare her for the loss of her father and induction of her sexuality. Lesbianism is not the central element of this text, and intimacy between adolescent girls is articulated as a negotiation, rather than a definition, of sexual identities; Virginia and Jane never identify themselves or their relationship as lesbian, but Virginia recognizes how her feelings for Jane are different from her feelings for other people. No one except the reader discovers Virginia and Jane's sexual relationship or their love for each other. *Dive* frames the process of adolescent identity formation within the complexity of social and sexual existence in general.

Virginia feels a sense of urgency to find meaningful words for her feelings for Jane: "If I can't make somebody understand what I feel, I'll disintegrate into the air."[43] Her frustration is the same as that of most of the other adolescent lesbians I have discussed and is indicative of the lesbian invisibility that results from a lack of appropriate language to signify women's desire for women.[44] Virginia's language centers on the existence of love and the need to express that love verbally without relying on labels. Expressing it physically, "how simple it is, how natural," is not as difficult as expressing emotion with effective words, "Do I love her? I mean, do I love her?"[45]

In her literary analysis of twentieth-century adult lesbian fiction, Bonnie Zimmerman identifies the heart of the lesbian novel as the search for a lesbian self.[46] *Dive* constructs a complex and mature narrative in which a female who is sexually attracted to another female does not assume a lesbian identification process, not just because of lesbianism's negative connotations in our society but because she does not give credence to a unified identity. According to Jackie Stacey, our theoretical inquiries need to "consider questions of lesbian identity and desire within the models of fragmented subjectivity."[47] True to this dogma, the book as a whole looks fragmented. Donovan does not indent her paragraphs; instead she writes them as blocks of thought and dialogue separated by a line of space. Virginia's thoughts, too, are fragmented, but in the course of the novel the fragments are held together by threads of thought, or repeating phrases. For example, "I am a stone" and "Let the wind in" appear numerous times to clarify and extend her contradictory feelings of stability and disintegration. Virginia works with all of these fragments to gain a poetic sense of self, and, in this way, notions of self and meaning constantly perform a dialogic dance, folding back on themselves as time moves forward.[48]

Virginia makes clear that a unified self is not possible as she becomes aware that many questions in life go unanswered,[49] but as soon as she sees Jane, she is able to center her attention on herself, so that the questions are no longer frayed and sensitive, but "in place."[50] Virginia is preoccupied with all that she does not understand about her life. Her confusion grows as her father's health worsens, and she realizes: "But now I need somebody. Now the world seems full of everything but magic. Except for Jane. There's Jane. But with her, there's also confusion."[51] The death of Virginia's father sends her reeling, forcing her to view a home movie in her mind of memories and experiences she does not understand, but when she sees Jane walking up to the funeral home with a bouquet of flowers, she is made "unbelievably dreamy with hopes" without having all the answers.[52] Although the connection between Jane and Virginia waxes and wanes, the final image of Jane arriving at the funeral home keeps Virginia's father in the male position of the triangle even in his death and portends reconciliation and longevity for the homosocial relationship.

Dive offers an ambitious postmodern portrayal of adolescent lesbianism. Virginia opens before us on the pages of *Dive* as an incomplete yet abundant persona. Donovan does not attempt to represent Virginia in any totality, possibly because no such totality exists. She represents complex adolescent sexuality and how it cannot be cleanly extracted from the rest of a person's identity in order to be examined or depicted. To do it right, in a postmodern sense, you have to show the whole messy picture, and it will not always fit into a nice narrative form. This may be why there are no films that succeed as well as *Dive*. Film may not be able to avoid creating a spectacle out of the observed figure on the screen.

Take, for example, *Heavenly Creatures*, a fictionalized account of the 1954 New Zealand case of the murder of Honora Parker by her sixteen-year-old daughter, Pauline, and Pauline's fifteen-year-old friend and lover, Juliet Hulme. In the well-publicized case, the judgment of the New Zealand public seemed to be that Parker came between the girls and that their unnatural lust drove them to murder her.[53] The issues raised in the film, which is told from Pauline's perspective and includes voice-overs from her diary entries, are mature and complex, and the advanced style and focus seem to target adult viewers more than adolescent viewers. Unlike the creators of the other texts discussed here, Jackson does not participate in the rhetoric of informational or identity-formation texts. To tell an informational tale about the homosocial connection between the girls would closely parallel the rhetoric of the court case, especially because it would require interrogation and invasion as motivating forces in the plot; to present a text that honored the girls' formation of lesbian identities would go against the facts, since the girls did not identify themselves as lesbian.

Jackson tries to avoid taking an explicit stance on whether the girls were "lesbian" or whether it matters to the story. For example, he stylizes their lovemaking to the point of ambiguity. At first they enact "how each saint [male actors they like] would make love in bed," with the black-and-white torsos of the men superimposed over each girl, but in the end Jackson brings the two girls into the frame to kiss as themselves. Eventually, almost every adult in the film is preoccupied with classifying and pathologizing the girls' relationship. While a diary entry makes clear that the girls had sex with one another, the film professes that their bond is more complicated than that. Jackson, who has stated in interviews that he believes the question of the girls' sexual orientations is irrelevant, implies that viewers are misled, as were the people of New Zealand, if they attempt to label the girls' sexuality. But in fact, the question is pivotal to the story. To problematize sexuality, Jackson must highlight it; lesbianism cannot function as a red herring in a plot that depends upon it elementally. For example, the most blatantly sexual scene between Pauline and Juliet occurs immediately prior to their decision to commit murder. This proximity underscores the film's association of adolescent lesbianism, family revolt, adolescent angst, and matricide.

Jackson also includes several lesbian references that substantiate a lesbian reading by the informed viewer. In French class Juliet is required to choose a French name, and since the scene takes place before the girls become friends or start writing about each other in their diaries, that Jackson has Juliet choose the name "Antoinette" suggests that Jackson believes she may already have some sort of lesbian identity. As Castle points out, "That Marie Antoinette was herself a lover of women had been rumored at least since the 1770s"; a spectator aware of this fact may identify the doomed queen, as many nineteenth-century women did, as a "secret heroine—an underground symbol of passionate love between women."[54] The association of Juliet Hulme with Marie Antoinette is suggestive, since the queen's "'crime' of homosexuality was . . . made part of the Revolutionary Tribunal's death-dealing case against her,"[55] just as Juliet's will be. The viewer who picks up on the

Antoinette reference can superimpose one lesbian martyrdom onto the other.

In short, *Heavenly Creatures* is postmodern in its subversion of "lesbian identity." Subversion is also the function that Castle gives to the essence of the lesbian counterplot. The postmodern adolescent lesbian counterplot, therefore, is right at home in a postmodern film context; with all its disturbing elements, *Heavenly Creatures* maintains a euphoric counterplot. Juliet and Pauline attend an all-girls' school and do not develop lasting male friendships. It is the all-female triangle of Pauline, Juliet, and Mrs. Parker that dominates our attention. The film, however, makes identification with the protagonists uncomfortable, problematizing not only lesbianism but even feminism; as reviewer Luisa F. Ribeiro observes, "The horror of the story lies in the unaccustomed positioning of desire and determination in the hands of two adolescent females."[56]

As *Heavenly Creatures* appears to concede, patriarchy and heterosexuality are antithetical to a woman-centered community with agency. To be sure, none of the works studied here discusses the larger lesbian community as a support network or as a possible destination. Yet the homosexual community enters many of the texts intertextually: Jaret and Peggy are initially drawn together by their common affection for Edna St. Vincent Millay, Virginia and Jane discover agency in the poetry of Arthur Rimbaud, a character in *The Incredibly True Adventure of Two Girls in Love* refers to *The Coming Out of Heidi Lieter*, Annie lends a "battered" copy of Isabel Miller's *Patience and Sarah* to Liza. These intertextual references suggest that reading lesbian texts is political because it offers a point of lesbian identification and community.[57] Indeed, readers have found identification and community in even the most negative and conflicted lesbian texts by reading against dysphoric plots and making heroes out of unfortunate characters. Kay Vandergrift, for one, claims that "engagement with story is life-affirming; it puts us in touch with the world, with one another, and with our essential selves. . . . Story helps us to shape and reshape life, to give it importance and to reflect on who we are and who we might become."[58] Similarly, Sorrel, a young lesbian interviewed in Mary Pipher's *Reviving Ophelia*, explains that "I wanted stories about girls like me that were okay. There was nothing like that. . . . I need to know that I'm not the only one. I want to read more about girls like me."[59]

Cultural representations of adolescent lesbianism in literature and film require the critical attention of future scholars, because such texts are part of "the process of coming out—a movement into a metaphysics of presence, speech, and cultural visibility. . . . Or, put another way, to be out is really to be in—inside the realm of the visible, the speakable, the culturally intelligible."[60] But the strength and potential of these texts have been weakened by their isolation from each other. Extending Castle's examination of the lesbian counterplot to include adolescent lesbian texts has revealed a large body of fiction that employs the dysphoric lesbian counterplot, as Castle notes, but we may also see that adolescent lesbian texts have progressed to include euphoric lesbian counterplots and postmodern plots that decenter, while problematizing, issues of information and identity. The power of these texts is in the changes they have made to the way stories are told and in the possibilities they continue to create for readers like Sorrel.

NOTES

1. Terry Castle, *The Apparitional Lesbian: Female Homosexuality and Modern Culture* (New York: Columbia University Press, 1993), 67.

2. Ibid.

3. Ibid., 68.

4. Ibid., 72, 74.

5. Ibid., 85.

6. Ibid.

7. Ibid.

8. Guy's *Ruby* (1976) is one of the earliest adolescent novels to include lesbianism. It is the story of a high school girl, Ruby, whose homosexual relationship with her friend Daphne is a desperate attempt to distance herself from dealing with the heterosocial world of males, dominated by her father and her ex-boyfriend, Orlando. Guy's plot thoroughly demonstrates the dysphoric counterplot because even though the female homosocial triangle represented by Ruby, her father, and Daphne dominates most of the plot, the male homosocial triangle of Ruby's father, Ruby, and Orlando is restored by the end of the novel.

9. Control by censors and publishing houses is complicated by written works "published" on the Internet.

10. In using the word "lesbian" to refer to something applicable to adolescence, I do not wholly agree with Judith Butler's quasi-nihilistic theories of gender and sexuality in "Imitation and Gender Insubordination," in *Inside/Out: Lesbian Theories, Gay Theories*, ed. Diana Fuss (New York: Routledge, 1991), 21, or with Adrienne Rich's continuum of lesbian identity as including nonsexual friendship in "Compulsory Heterosexuality and Lesbian Existence," *Signs* 5 (1980): 648. Rather, I borrow from Castle's definition of "lesbian" as "a woman

[or, better, "a female" so as to include young adults] whose primary emotional and erotic allegiance . . . is to other females" (15). Castle's definition is appropriate to a study of young adult literature because it focuses on both the emotional and the physical aspects of sexual desire. Sex is a definitive element of the adolescent lesbian text. Most literature and films for and about adolescent girls focus on girls' close friendships with other girls, a theme that began to flourish in nineteenth-century schoolgirl stories and continues in recent series fiction such as *The Babysitters' Club* or *Sweet Valley High;* contemporary lesbian texts for and about adolescents distinguish themselves from this pervasive genre by depicting varying degrees of sexual conduct between female characters.

11. Deborah Hautzig, *Hey, Dollface* (New York: Greenwillow, 1978), 76.

12. Ibid., 89.

13. John Stephens, in *Language and Ideology in Children's Fiction* (New York: Longman, 1992), argues that "part of the socialization of the child is that she learns to operate as a subject within various discourse types, each of which establishes its particular set of subject positions, which in turn act as constraints upon those who occupy them" (55). Subjectivity and agency are presented through elements of narration, such as point of view—which "has the function of constructing subject positions and inscribing ideological assumptions"—and character positions that determine sympathy (56). In other words, texts attempt to control how the actual reader, through accepting the subject position of the implied reader, responds to and sympathizes with certain characters and their actions.

14. Hautzig, *Hey, Dollface*, 127.

15. Ibid., 146.

16. Castle, *The Apparitional Lesbian*, 74.

17. Elizabeth Levy, *Come Out Smiling* (New York: Delacorte, 1981), 50.

18. Ibid., 51.

19. Ibid., 68.

20. Ibid., 140.

21. Ibid., 186.

22. Ibid., 121.

23. Ibid., 122.

24. Ibid., 123.

25. Ibid.

26. Ibid., 126.

27. Nancy Garden, *Annie on My Mind* (New York: Ariel, 1982), 65.

28. Sandra Scoppettone, *Happy Endings Are All Alike* (Boston: Alyson, 1978), 31.

29. See Garden, *Annie on My Mind,* 13, and *Good Moon Rising* (New York: Farrar, 1996), 76.

30. See Garden, *Annie on My Mind,* 85, and *Good Moon Rising,* 75. See also Scoppettone, *Happy Endings Are All Alike,* 35.

31. Consider this powerful moment from Violette Leduc's landmark adult lesbian text, *Thérèse and Isabelle,* trans. Derek Coltman (New York: Dell, 1967):

"[I] slipped my arm under hers: our intertwining fingers made love to one another" (55). The trope of political hand-holding appears most evidently in *Come Out Smiling, Hey, Dollface,* and *More Than Friends: The Coming Out of Heidi Lieter.*

32. Garden, *Good Moon Rising,* 96.

33. See Garden, *Annie on My Mind,* 94, and Scoppettone, *Happy Endings Are All Alike,* 29.

34. Scoppettone, *Happy Endings Are All Alike,* 102.

35. See Garden, *Good Moon Rising,* 152.

36. Roberta Seelinger Trites, *Waking Sleeping Beauty: Feminist Voices in Children's Novels* (Iowa City: University of Iowa Press, 1997), 93.

37. See Garden, *Good Moon Rising,* 75.

38. Garden, *Annie on My Mind,* 146.

39. Scoppettone, *Happy Endings Are All Alike,* 121.

40. Ibid., 202.

41. Randy's gay friend, Frank, and Raphael of *Good Moon Rising* function to complete Sedgwick's female homosocial triangle.

42. Garden, *Good Moon Rising,* 221.

43. Stacey Donovan, *Dive* (New York: Puffin, 1996), 188–89.

44. Bonnie Zimmerman, *The Safe Sea of Women: Lesbian Fiction 1969–1989* (Boston: Beacon, 1990), 96.

45. Donovan, *Dive,* 219, 196.

46. Zimmerman, *The Safe Sea of Women,* 31.

47. Qtd. in Martha Vicinus, "'They Wonder to Which Sex I Belong': The Historical Roots of the Modern Lesbian Identity," *Feminist Studies* 18 (1992): 468.

48. This style is very similar to that of Jeanette Winterson, author of the coming-of-age / coming-out novel *Oranges Are Not the Only Fruit,* which critics deem "postmodern." Winterson's and Donovan's broken narratives emphasize the way that communicating our own lives through storytelling demands many separate stories, which are never linear and always interwoven in our minds with other stories, thoughts, and experiences. These techniques work to involve the reader in the developing subject position of the narrator as it develops in the course of the novel. It may also function to exclude readers who are not ready or willing to participate in piecing together the fragments.

49. Donovan, *Dive,* 231.

50. Ibid., 102.

51. Ibid., 225.

52. Ibid., 240.

53. Jackson chose to glorify and revive a story involving murderous lesbians, but he is not alone. Wendy Kesselman wrote and produced the film version, *Sister My Sister* (1994), of her play, *My Sister in This House* (1983). She retells the story of the young sisters Christine and Lea, who, in France in 1932, were convicted of killing their employer and her daughter, who supposedly walked in on the sisters having sex.

54. Castle, *The Apparitional Lesbian,* 126. Marie Antoinette has also appeared

as a lesbian icon in other lesbian texts. See Radclyffe Hall's *The Well of Loneliness* (1928), Sylvia Townsend Warner's *Summer Will Show* (1936), and Winterson's *The Passion* (1987).

55. Castle, *The Apparitional Lesbian*, 131.

56. Luisa F. Ribeiro, "Movie Review: *Heavenly Creatures*," *Film Quarterly* 49.1 (1995): 33.

57. This fear of texts as cultural forces drives Lillian Hellman's play *The Children's Hour* (1934). A lesbian text, *Mademoiselle de Maupin* by Theophile Gautier (1834, trans. 1890), is located as a possible cause for a young girl's devious behavior.

58. Kay E. Vandergrift, ed., *Mosaics of Meaning: Enhancing the Intellectual Life of Young Adults through Story* (Lanham, MD: Scarecrow, 1996), ix.

59. Mary Pipher, *Reviving Ophelia: Saving the Selves of Adolescent Girls* (New York: Ballantine, 1994), 110–11.

60. Diana Fuss, ed., *Inside/Out: Lesbian Theories, Gay Theories* (New York: Routledge, 1991), 4.

Reading and Writing "Immunity"

Children and the Anti-Body

§♣

ROBERT McRUER

"Whatever else it may be," Paula Treichler writes, "AIDS is a story, or multiple stories, read to a surprising extent from a text that does not exist: the body of the male homosexual. It is a text people so want—need—to read that they have gone so far as to write it themselves."[1] Treichler's analysis of the construction of AIDS in its first decade provides a thorough account of the strategies used by science, the media, and the "general public" in their panicked attempts to locate and control the story of AIDS. In 1987, when Treichler's article was first published, the mysterious, exoticized gay male body had indeed become the site on which fears and fantasies about AIDS were inscribed. And yet, in the second decade of the epidemic, the cultural mandate to write the text of AIDS on the gay male body has been forestalled. People continue to write the story of AIDS, but that story has now moved into arenas traditionally off limits to gay and lesbian bodies.

In children's literature about AIDS, particularly, the paradox plays itself out: the story of AIDS may demand the text of the gay male body, but that body is an "anti-body" as far as children's literature is concerned. In the mid-1980s Jan Goodman noted, "As far as young children know, there's no such thing as a gay person. Lesbian and gay characters are as good as invisible in books for preschool and early elementary-age children."[2] In the late 1980s, the establishment by Alyson Publications of the Alyson Wonderland series for children remedied the situation somewhat, and yet, that a series of gay and lesbian books for children had to be produced by a lesbian and gay publishing house suggests that the exclusion of gay men and lesbians from mainstream children's literature is still an unspoken imperative. In fact, even the most domesticated representations of lesbians and gay men are heavily policed: according to the American Library Association, throughout the 1990s *Daddy' Rommate* and *Heather Has Two Mommies*, two books that do little more than depict children with gay and lesbian parents, have been among the most censored books in school and public libraries.[3] In New York City alone, five communities banned portions of a multicultural curriculum called "Children of the Rainbow" simply because the curriculum included these texts.[4] In Oregon, children's literature containing representations of gay and lesbian people was used in 1992 to rally support for initiatives designed to abolish legal protection for lesbians and gay men.[5] Apparently, to supporters of the Oregon initiative, representations of gay men and lesbians in children's books were self-evidently inappropriate. Lesbians and gay men had overstepped a boundary, and the books in question provided both evidence of the transgression and justification for measures designed to contain gay and lesbian people.

But the exclusion of gay male bodies from children's literature about AIDS in particular results from an additional, very different, paradox that emerges from shifts in AIDS discourse in the 1990s. The liberal reinscription of AIDS, from the late 1980s on, as "everyone's disease" ironically functions within the text of children's literature—as it has elsewhere—to make gay men living with AIDS invisible. This liberal discourse may no longer deny the gay man with AIDS his own voice by objectifying him as the quintessential, and stigmatized, "AIDS victim," but it silences him nonetheless. In fact, the discursive shift to understanding AIDS as everyone's disease justifies, or rationalizes, the proscription of gay male representation in children's literature. The exclusion of gay male bodies from children's literature is thus redoubled, this time under the liberal guise of not reinforcing stereotypical equations of gay men and AIDS.

Ironically, the idea that AIDS is everyone's disease emerged in the late 1980s as a result of AIDS activist successes. At that time activists, objecting to the portrayal of AIDS as only a gay disease or to the implication that AIDS and homosexuality were causally related and thus virtually synonymous, successfully argued (using posters, buttons, and the like) that "we are all living with AIDS." This mentality quickly became (and remains) hegemonic. The first-year university students in my course Reading and Writing a Crisis: Rhetoric, AIDS, and the Media, for instance, generally accept as common sense the idea that AIDS is everyone's disease. Like all common sense, this "common sense," however, serves an ideological function: If we're all basically the same, then we need not attend to the homophobia, racism, and sexism that continue to undergird the epidemic. Yet structural inequities that secure homophobia, racism, and sexism persist, and even though there is indeed a sense in which we are all living with AIDS, communities and individuals experience AIDS differently because of sexual orientation, race, gender, and class.

My students were preteens when the discursive shifts away from knee-jerk homophobia and toward a supposedly more inclusive understanding of AIDS were occurring. Consequently, many, if not most, have dutifully mastered what Cindy Patton calls the "national pedagogy" of that time period, the late 1980s and early 1990s.[6] At its most extreme, the lesson that AIDS is everyone's disease suggests for students of that national pedagogy that we should not talk about gay men with AIDS at all. And, in fact, some of my own students would read any portrayal of a gay man with AIDS as automatically reproducing the outmoded and homophobic idea that AIDS is just a gay disease.

These, then, are the complicated cultural factors working to exclude gay male bodies from children's literature during this time period. In this article, I argue that for children this exclusion is potentially lethal, since along with their bodies, the lifesaving lessons learned in gay and lesbian communities during the AIDS epidemic have been effaced. I examine here four books for young readers written in the late 1980s and early 1990s. Although the reading level is very basic in David Fassler and Kelly McQueen's *What's a Virus, Anyway? The Kids' Book about AIDS* (1990), the remaining three—Mary Kate Jordan's *Losing Uncle Tim* (1989), Sharon Schilling and Jonathan Swain's *My Name is Jonathan (and I Have AIDS)* (1989), and Neal Starkman's *Z's Gift* (1988)—would require a bit more than rudimentary reading skills (third or fourth graders would probably find all four books accessible). My position on the information presented in these books, including information on safe sexual practices, is that it should have been comprehensive.[7] I argue, however, that because of the lack of representations of gay men, frank speech is disallowed and information about AIDS is consequently not

disseminated in these books in the ways that have been most successful, over the past decade and more, in gay and lesbian communities.

Specifically, I contend that the following lifesaving lessons are not
clearly articulated in the children's books about AIDS written during
the late 1980s and early 1990s: Certain straightforward practices prevent the virus from entering the bloodstream, and the positioning of abstinence and monogamy as the only options has blocked discussion of
these safe practices; sex education can be positive and affirming and
need not be silenced (indeed, what appears to be "silence" about sexual
activity is actually management of a particular sexual ideology); a basic
understanding of communal political contexts does more to implicate
readers in the epidemic than an understanding of individual stories; individualized, decontextualized stories assume and produce in readers
only a detached, even "immunized," compassion; and finally, expertise
is diverse: doctors and others not living with AIDS are not the only ones
who should be authorized to speak (to children or anyone else) about
the AIDS epidemic.

One could certainly argue that during this time period children had
already received a disproportionate amount of attention in the media.
Jan Zita Grover asks pointedly, "What does it mean throughout the period 1985–9 that children with AIDS (1 percent of the total U.S. AIDS
cases) received more media attention than the 61 percent of diagnosed
cases among gay men?"[8] Grover's question, of course, is a legitimate
one, and her work consistently analyzes the ways in which the concerns of women, people of color, and gay men and lesbians are elided
through media representations of AIDS. Rather than calling for a mora-
torium on all considerations of AIDS and children, however, Grover's
article—and indeed, the question itself ("What does it mean?")—suggests that we look more critically at how these representations of AIDS
are made available and whose interests are served in the process. Such
an analysis could not only help to expose further the ideological forces
working to ensure the invisibility of gay men, but might also suggest
that, despite the endless representation of children with AIDS in the
media, children's best interests are hardly being served here.

Beth E. Schneider delineates the images of children and AIDS that
the media made available from the mid-1980s on. These representations
of children with AIDS still have widespread currency, and tend to inhibit the dissemination of other representations (specifically, those that
might help to protect children from HIV infection). Schneider writes:

In considerations of HIV-infection in children, there are typically two sorts of portraits: first, an infant, usually African-American, abandoned to a hospital, born to an IV drug-using mother; the second, a ten-year-old white child with HIV-infection from blood products who is refused entry into school because of the objections of parents in the local community.[9]

Schneider's description underlines what is implicit in Grover's question about why children with AIDS are so useful to the media; clearly, the child with AIDS can be constructed as the proverbial "innocent victim." I want to move beyond this by now familiar image however, by suggesting that "innocent" here actually equates with "immune."

I am using the term "immune" in the sense that Richard Goldstein employs it in his article "The Implicated and the Immune: Responses to AIDS in the Arts and Popular Culture." Goldstein explains:

> The epidemic's image in movies, popular music, comedy and television is very different—though no more accurate or inclusive—than its representation in the arts. These two images reflect quite distinct cultural responses. The first, located in the arts, is focused on people with AIDS, portraying them with a nuanced complexity intended to compensate for social stigma by "implicating" its audience in the epidemic. The other carries the perspective of the mass media; it presumes to be objective or, in terms more suited to this discussion, "immune." This mass cultural response is largely concerned with the society surrounding people with AIDS: the spouse, children, family, friends, and colleagues of the infected.[10]

Goldstein's distinction transforms a focus on positive, negative, or stereotypical images into a more complex analysis of the ways in which meanings are constructed and how audiences play a role in that construction. The immune/implicated distinction makes clear, for example, that the overrepresentation of children with AIDS in the media says more about the intended audience, which needs to read itself and its children as immune, than about actual people living with AIDS. As far as the intended audience is concerned, children with AIDS should be, by virtue of their "innocence," always already immune. Paradoxically, the representation of children with AIDS in the media works not to contest this notion, but rather to contain the equation of children with immunity. Media representations of children with AIDS are "tragedies" precisely because such children, presumably like the audience itself, should not be implicated in this epidemic (to such audiences, the stories of those who are "implicated"—namely, gay men and IV drug users—are not "tragedies"). Children with AIDS are on the wrong side of the immune/implicated binarism, but the binarism itself is left intact. Indeed, the binarism is secured through the media's overrepresentation of children with AIDS: audiences need not worry about (unsafe) actions they or their children might engage in, since AIDS is (safely) located in the tragic persona of the child with AIDS.

I want to challenge this persistent equation of children with innocence and immunity, considering more fully the ramifications for children of Goldstein's immune/implicated opposition, and to do so I need to introduce here yet another binary that complicates the issues connected to AIDS and children. The act of addressing the textual representation of AIDS for children engages and challenges assumptions about the Western binary adult/child. "Adult" and "child" are by no means innocent, descriptive categories that emerge naturally; they are categories constructed in accordance with mechanisms of power and control that would serve to keep those designated children "in their place." Knowledge and culture are assumed to belong naturally and exclusively to the category "adult," whereas ignorance and nature belong to the category "child."

Statistics related to AIDS alone, however, would point to the naïveté of always positioning children outside "adult" categories, such as knowledge and culture, or away from "adult" topics, such as sex, sexuality, drug use, or AIDS. For young women and men between the ages of thirteen and twenty-four, by the mid-1990s AIDS was the sixth and fourth leading cause of death, respectively.[11] In New York City alone, as many as 100,000 teens may be HIV positive, and the Centers for Disease Control (CDC) estimate that roughly 1 in 500 college students is HIV positive.[12] During the past two decades the age of first intercourse for children has been steadily decreasing,[13] and the Alan Gutmacher Institute now estimates that 86 percent of males and 79 percent of females become sexually active before graduating from high school.[14] Indeed, as one audience member at a Chicago conference on AIDS and adolescence, an educator in the Chicago public school system, remarked, "What all these educational efforts don't seem to take into account is that by the eighth grade kids are 'doing it.' And by the ninth grade they're doing it good." In this context, the separation of "immune" from "implicated," even when adolescents and children are the group in question, is naive. As Treichler argues, "The fact is that any separation of not-self ('AIDS victims') from self (the 'general population') is no longer possible."[15] Even as promising new treatments extend the lives of some people living with AIDS, and despite a decline in the number of new AIDS cases, the CDC reports that HIV continues to spread through the population at a steady rate—with the rate for those thirteen to twenty-four years old, in particular, "virtually unchanged in recent years."[16] Worldwide, the majority of new infections are in persons under the age of twenty-five.[17]

These statistics suggest that children and young people are already implicated in the AIDS epidemic in particular, population-specific ways. Yet the discursive construction of AIDS as everyone's disease belies this particularity and contributes to the securing of children as "immune." As Patton explains, during the late 1980s, "some attention was devoted to instilling future citizens with a sense of tolerance toward people living with AIDS. But in those crucial first years, when millions of young people were initiating sex and drug use, there was little effort to provide the tools they needed to evaluate and reduce their own risk of contracting HIV."[18]

This paradox, where AIDS is everywhere but nowhere in particular, and certainly not any particular place where children might need knowledge to protect themselves, is precisely what we will see in the texts I survey here. These texts' effacement of the lessons learned in lesbian and gay communities of resistance during the first decade of the AIDS epidemic makes them complicit with the inscription of children as always already immune.

The four children's books in question are all from the period when AIDS became everyone's disease. This is reflected not only by the books' publication dates, but also by their authorship, production, and distribution. The authors of these books are generally represented as possessing a professional identity such as teacher, minister, doctor, or medical student—identities not located within a specific community context. Quite the contrary: the authority these professional positions tend to carry in our culture suggests that AIDS at this historical juncture is no longer localizable, but has become a much more widespread societal concern. The publication and distribution of these books is delocalized as well: although the books can be obtained at gay and lesbian bookstores or through gay and lesbian book distributors, they are not published (in contrast to the Alyson Wonderland series) by predominantly gay and lesbian publishing houses.

Of the four books, only one—*Losing Uncle Tim*—has an identifiable gay male body, and even this text does not openly employ the term "gay." One might argue, however, that the exclusion in question is not homosexuality per se, but sexuality in general. The exclusion of gay male bodies from children's literature about AIDS, after all, is consistent with the more general repression of any sexualized body in children's literature. Since nonadults are constructed to be nonsexual, representations of sexuality are de-emphasized in their texts. In *What's a Virus, Anyway?* the authors make the exclusion of the sexualized body explicit in a headnote about sex education. "Understanding the sexual transmission of AIDS is clearly an important component of a comprehensive AIDS education program," they write.[19] Nonetheless, they make it clear that sex will not be spoken of in *What's a Virus, Anyway?*

> Current guidelines recommend addressing the issue of sexual transmission beginning in the sixth grade. We agree that this aspect of the disease need not be overemphasized here. We also share the concern that a child's first information about sex should not be in association with a disease. . . . The book contains minimal information regarding the sexual transmission of the disease.[20]

The dominant developmental model requires that we suppress discussion of sex and sexuality with younger children. Regardless of their cultural context, according to this universalizing model, it is only in the sixth grade that children should receive their "first information about sex."

However, the headnote to *What's a Virus, Anyway?* is probably best described not as a suppression or repression, but rather, following Michel Foucault, as "a policing of sex: that is, not the rigor of a taboo, but the necessity of regulating sex through useful and public discourse."[21] In refutation of the "repressive hypothesis" more generally, Foucault describes how these useful and public discourses operated over the past few centuries: "One had to speak of [sex] as of a thing to be not simply condemned or tolerated but managed, inserted into systems of utility, regulated for the greater good of all, made to function according to an optimum."[22] With this in mind, the discourse surrounding children, sex, and AIDS can be read less as repression than as proliferation of specific, controlled ways of knowing. For example, the incitement to discourse about sex and AIDS is evident on the cover of the December 9, 1991, *Newsweek*—an issue that effectively signals the successful shift in the mainstream media in the early 1990s to an understanding of AIDS as everyone's disease. The *Newsweek* cover announces boldly that it contains "What You and Your Children Should Know" about safe sex.

Similarly, in the children's literature about AIDS, sex is not so much repressed as it is managed in a specific way. In *My Name is Jonathan (and I Have AIDS)*, for instance, preschooler Jonathan is shown teaching his classmates about AIDS: "Maybe you know that having sex is a way that grown-ups can show their love by being very close to each other. This is one way the AIDS virus [*sic*] can go from one person to another, but only if one of them has the virus."[23] Sex for young readers is thereby defined and contained as (or even replaced by) intimacy and love. This overwriting of sex as love or intimacy is in line with many educational efforts aimed at young people during, and in the aftermath of, the Reagan-Bush years. The implicit message, conflating abstinence and monogamy, is not "engage in safe practices," but "find a safe partner," and don't have sex with anyone until you do. Rarely do educators make a distinction between abstinence as a practice and Abstinence/Monogamy as a dominant ideology for the raising of children in American culture. Even when other options are mentioned, abstinence is always presented as The Best Way. Hence, even as they attempt in *The AIDS Challenge: Prevention Education for Young People* to forge a space for being frank with young people about sex, Marcia Quackenbush and Pamela Sargent still feel compelled to concede, "We couldn't agree more on the benefits of abstinence for teenagers."[24] Under the ideology of Abstinence/Monogamy, however, sex that is not equated with love and commitment is "bad" or "wrong," whereas sex that is postponed until later in life is "good." Under such an ideology, children and teenagers may go to extreme lengths to convince others or themselves that the activity they are engaging in is not "bad," or even that it is not "sex" at all, but something else—"love," for instance.

Such a construction of sex may make those same children and teenagers less likely to practice safe sex as they grow older. After all, as Treichler argues, in agreement with many other AIDS activists and cultural theorists throughout the 1980s and 1990s, "It is not monogamy or abstention per se that protects one from AIDS infection but practices and protections that prevent the virus from entering one's bloodstream."[25] The *Newsweek* article mentioned above begins with an interview with a California teenager who reports, "We don't need no condom because he says he loves me."[26] Here monogamy is the dominant sexual ideology, but this quotation also ominously makes clear, as Douglas Crimp has argued, that in some circumstances monogamy can be a message that is "not only reactionary, [but] lethal."[27]

Jonathan's explanation in *My Name is Jonathan* is preceded by a picture of the child before a classroom of children with their hands raised. Above the picture is the acknowledgment that "some kids had heard that people can get AIDS by using drugs or having sex,"[28] which suggests that children already draw upon existing networks (relatives, peers, television) for acquiring information (however partial) about sex and drug use.[29] Hence, children's literature about AIDS might be an arena for clarifying questions and providing accurate—and comprehensive—information about the specific practices that can protect individuals from HIV infection. Instead, sex in *My Name is Jonathan* is presented to children unequivocally as a way that the disease is transmitted. *What's a Virus, Anyway?* and *Z's Gift* likewise present sex in and of itself as responsible for the transmission of HIV.[30] Apparently, the distinction between protected and unprotected sex is deemed too complex for young children. Yet both *My Name is Jonathan* and *What's a Virus, Anyway?* spend a significant amount of time explaining the complexities of viruses, T cells, and B cells.[31] Perhaps, then, the distinction between protected and unprotected sex is not too complex for children, but rather too threatening to the sexual ideology these texts construct.

Notwithstanding all this management of sex, the homosexual body is absent from these texts. AIDS is embodied for young readers by Jonathan in *My Name is Jonathan,* by a white, female elementary-school teacher in *Z's Gift,* and by various stick-figure drawings by children in *What's a Virus, Anyway?* These drawings depict people of both genders engaged in various activities, and they are positioned beside captions such as "People with AIDS are just like everybody else."[32] This caption in particular suggests that even at a very young age the artists have learned the lessons of the national pedagogy: not that they are implicated in the epidemic and should know how to protect themselves, but that they should be nice to people with AIDS since, after all, AIDS is everyone's disease. "Everyone," however, turns out to be heterosexual. The picture accompanying this particular caption is of a club or bar occupied by five crudely drawn couples engaged in conversation. Although a few of the drawings are indeterminate, each couple appears to consist of one male and one female, according to the codes children usually use to differentiate genders in their stick-figure drawings (indeed, even the most indeterminate of the drawings appears to have one member of the couple in a skirt and one in pants). A tribute to heterosexual solidarity, the couple in the foreground of the drawing serves as the representative of "everybody else." An arrow above the man's head positions him as "a person with AIDS," and an arrow above the woman's head positions her as "a friend."[33] Each figure holds a drink in one hand while they hold hands with each other.

I do not mean to suggest that every representation of AIDS in children's literature should contain a clearly identifiable gay male body. I am interested in demonstrating, though, that the erasure of sexuality in these texts actually means the erasure of homosexuality and—consequently—the erasure of the critical understanding of social stigma and of community-based protective measures that gay men and lesbians have advanced for more than a decade. The main character of *Z's Gift*, for example, has a dream that teaches him about the social stigma of living with AIDS,[34] but he learns nothing about the homophobia and racism that have fortified the stigma of AIDS for the past decade, nor does he learn anything concrete about the practices he and others might engage in to protect themselves. Rather, AIDS is constructed for children as a clear-cut moral issue; children need not worry about being implicated, but they should show compassion to the individualized (and heterosexualized) victims they may encounter. Indeed, *Z's Gift* is dedicated "to those who bestow the gift of compassion."[35] Eventually, Z (after learning that he himself is "immune") tells his teacher, Mrs. Brown, that he will eat lunch with her even if no one else will, and he thereby fulfills the altruistic imperative of the dedication.

Patton and other theorists have questioned such imperatives. Patton writes, "AIDS activists [before the mid-1980s] . . . worked with gay and heterosexual PLWAs [People Living With AIDS] in the context of community organizing rather than altruism, and understood their work in terms of political resistance rather than compassion"[36] Not surprisingly, the children's texts I am examining bear no traces of this legacy of community resistance, and this absence is quite likely related to the absence of gay male bodies in these texts. In addition, the texts discount as a matter of course the knowledge acquired in these communities during the first decade of the epidemic, deferring instead to more "qualified experts." Patton explains, "Only the 'experts' . . . are allowed to suggest policy, and then only through the proper channels and with the proper pedagogy and view of what AIDS service means."[37] One out of every ten pages of *My Name is Jonathan* contains a deferral to doctors. One of the authors of *What's a Virus, Anyway?* is a physician (the other is a medical student), and ten other doctors are thanked in the acknowledgments (v). In *Z's Gift,* as parents consider pulling their children from the school, Z asks his mother, "Can't we ask Dr. Peña about it? She would know, wouldn't she?"[38] It turns out that Dr. Peña does indeed "know," but not because she is, say, politically committed to fighting for Latina/o communities experiencing increasing incidences of HIV infection. Rather it is her position as an expert that legitimates what she has to say.

Of course, the question of the relationship of individual children to these texts is an important one. If gay and lesbian parents are indeed buying these books and reading them with their children, they may very well read these texts subversively, against the (heterosexual) grain. On the other hand, the texts themselves—particularly *Z's Gift,* with its African-American protagonist and Latina physician—suggest a broader reading arena: liberal multiculturalism. In this context, as *Z's Gift* illustrates, representation (of gender, race, ethnicity) is generally expanded without much attention to the larger systems of power that were responsible for exclusion in the first place. In many books, "difference" becomes a mere commodity—whether for children, or for those who care for them. Increased representation in and of itself is taken to be positive, and hence, in *Z's Gift,* while young readers are presented with an African-American protagonist, it doesn't matter that none of his friends is black. Likewise, in a liberal multiculturalist reading context, children might encounter a character living with AIDS, but they will not be encouraged to understand the construction of AIDS except on this simplistic, individualized level, and they will certainly not be encouraged to understand AIDS as something that affects their lives directly.

Of the four texts examined here, only *Losing Uncle Tim* depicts a character who is, presumably, a gay man living with AIDS.[39] The term is never used in the text, but several features establish Tim as gay, not the least his position as the "bachelor uncle," long a code or euphemism for homosexuality. Passages in the text construct Tim as free from the rigidity that Daniel, the young narrator of *Losing Uncle Tim*, associates with other (heterosexual) adults; for instance, one illustration has Tim and Daniel outdoors, speeding down a snow-covered hill on a sled. Daniel explains, "Uncle Tim was more fun than any other grownup I knew."[40] Daniel's own parents are only represented as instructors or compassionate listeners. Tim, on the other hand, makes Daniel's life fun. The story opens, "I used to spend a lot of time at my Uncle Tim's antique store. The store was full of neat things Uncle Tim loved. He traveled all over on treasure hunts and brought back toys and clothes and furniture for us to sell."[41] Daniel is pictured on the facing page polishing antiques, while Tim is in the background with a customer whose expression indicates that she is delighted with Tim's taste. In short, Daniel may not know that his uncle is gay, but everybody else does. The illustrations and the text position Tim's homosexuality as an open secret, one that may be kept from children according to the discretion of an adult reader.

Although Tim is never shown with other adult men, Daniel often refers to Uncle Tim's friends, and there is invariably someone at Tim's house when Daniel comes to visit, particularly during the later stages of the disease. A male friend of Tim's explains what a coma is during one of Daniel's visits, but readers only know the speaker's sex from a pronoun in the text, as the illustration only depicts Daniel's sad and confused face: "He said people who are in a coma, the special kind of sleep Uncle Tim was in, can often hear even though they can't answer."[42] Significantly, the only friend of Tim's pictured during this period is a woman who is helping the now-emaciated man walk from the bed to the bathroom. This representation of "a person with AIDS" and a "friend," however, is different from the stick-figure drawings gathered in a bar in *What's a Virus, Anyway?* There, the embrace, the drinks, and the singles bar atmosphere (hetero)sexualize the bodies. In *Losing Uncle Tim*, Tim's body at this point is evidently diseased and desexualized, while the woman's face is simply the face of concern and compassion.

Losing Uncle Tim, like the other texts I have examined, encourages young readers to understand those caring for people living with AIDS, such as this unnamed female character, as altruistic rather than political.[43] In addition, although it is one of Tim's friends who explains to Daniel what a coma is, and although these friends apparently invest much more time and energy in Tim's life, the final authority in *Losing Uncle Tim* is, once again, the doctors. Their voices are this time mediated through Daniel's father: "Mom and I asked Tim's doctor how safe it is for us to be close to him. The doctor said you can't catch AIDS just by taking care of someone."[44]

Losing Uncle Tim, in Goldstein's terms, "transforms AIDS into a crisis for the family."[45] Ironically, however, although they are given the go-ahead by Tim's physician and despite their obvious concern and distress at Tim's illness, Daniel's father and mother never visit during the course of *Losing Uncle Tim.* While Tim is actually living with AIDS, only his friends (and Daniel) are depicted as spending time with him. Still, the trajectory of the story is nonetheless focused on the family, and after Tim has died from AIDS, only the grief of his family is represented. Jeff Nunokawa's comments are relevant here: "Homophobia has seldom been more intrusive than in its current disinclination to allow the gay community to grieve its own publicly."[46]

It is certainly possible to argue that *Losing Uncle Tim* is still a significant and antihomophobic intervention, despite the displacement of Tim's homosexuality and the effacement of his friends. Tim's incidental homosexuality may in some ways prevent *Losing Uncle Tim* from furthering the homophobic insinuation that it is gay identity itself, and not certain activities, that placed him at risk. Yet Daniel (and, by extension, the young reader of *Losing Uncle Tim*) is never educated about risk activities. Although his questions to his parents indicate that he is misinformed, all Daniel learns is that he is not in any personal danger: "It's safe for you to be with Tim. . . . You can sit close to him and hug him. You can have dinner with him."[47] With this reassurance, Daniel learns nothing that he would not have learned observing the progress of almost any other serious disease. His father's vague statement that Daniel himself is not implicated in Tim's illness essentially positions the boy as already and always immune to AIDS. And since risk activities are not discussed, the stigma of AIDS is by default linked to simple identity, or at any rate to the identity of "Uncle Tim"; that is, to the identity of a man who never marries, owns an antique store, and is "more fun than any other grownup." Perhaps the homophobic insinuation is present, after all.

Ultimately, *Losing Uncle Tim* is not unlike *An Early Frost,* a 1985 television movie described by Simon Watney: "The closing shot . . . shows a 'family album' picture. . . . A traumatic episode is over. The family closes ranks, with the problem son conveniently dispatched, and life getting back to normal."[48] At Tim's funeral, Daniel mentions none of

Tim's "friends," but "everybody in the family" is present. Daniel says to his mother, "I wish dying was like sunset. . . . I wish Uncle Tim would come back in the morning."[49] Daniel and his mother sit "real close" as Daniel's father drives them to the cemetery, and Uncle Tim's life is brought to a point of closure by means of a representation of the heterosexual family.

Uncle Tim does not, of course, come back in the morning, but his face is included in one final illustration. This illustration depicts Tim's face shining in Daniel's window as the young boy gazes out. Daniel muses, "Maybe when I grow up . . . I'll own a store. Or I might do something else. I don't know yet. But I'll do something I love. Just like Uncle Tim."[50] Almost in spite of themselves, these words and the illustration indict the text that has preceded, for both might be read as an ominous rupture in the sentimental closure of the story, as well as a rupture in the ideological context that produced the children's books about AIDS written during this time period. For Daniel may well develop an identity or inhabit a body much like Uncle Tim's. Although *Losing Uncle Tim* and the other texts that I have been examining do not admit it, the children who are the intended audience here are not immune from AIDS. Gay and proto-gay (and heterosexual and proto-heterosexual) children do exist, and these children need to learn not only that they should be compassionate toward those people already living with AIDS, but rather that AIDS may affect them directly if they share needles or engage in unprotected sex. Without such interventions, educators can expect that a sequel—"Losing Uncle Daniel," perhaps?—will eventually and repeatedly need to be written.

NOTES

I would like to thank those who have provided me with helpful comments over the course of many revisions of this essay: Tom Murray, Kenneth Kidd, Lisa Duggan, Paula Treichler, Angela Hewett, Sheryl Stevenson, Thomas Dukes, and audiences in New York City and in Urbana, Illinois.

1. Paula Treichler, "AIDS, Homophobia, and Biomedical Discourse: An Epidemic of Signification," in *AIDS: Cultural Analysis/Cultural Activism,* ed. Douglas Crimp (Cambridge: MIT Press, 1987), 42.

2. Jan Goodman, "Out of the Closet, But Paying the Price: Lesbian and Gay Characters in Children's Literature," *Interracial Books for Children Bulletin* 14.3–4 (1983): 15.

3. See John Gallagher, "Censored," *The Advocate,* March 31 1998, 42–45.

4. "Alternative-Lifestyle Lessons Banned," *Gay Chicago Magazine,* July 30, 1992, 64.

5. See Timothy Egan, "Oregon Measure Asks State to Repress Homosexuality," *New York Times,* August 16, 1992, 1; and Katherine Gleason, "Not in Front of the Children," *Lambda Book Report,* November–December 1992, 8.

6. Cindy Patton, *Fatal Advice: How Safe-Sex Education Went Wrong* (Durham: Duke University Press, 1997), 7.

7. Jonathan G. Silin and other educational theorists have argued eloquently about how ill-suited the dominant developmental model is to the worlds most children inhabit. In "What AIDS Teaches Us about the Education of Children," *Educational Theory* 42 (1992), Silin writes, "While there has always been a minor but persistent commitment to viewing the child in context . . . the field's knowledge base today is dominated by traditional developmentalists. Stage theories of development tend to reinforce absolute distinctions between children and adults, and between people and their material realities" (266). I position myself with those who, like Silin, question the developmental model and who see that model as serving what Silin calls (in the subtitle to his book *Sex, Death, and the Education of Children* [New York: Teachers College Press, 1995]) "our passion for ignorance in the age of AIDS." The issues connected to teaching children about drug use are different from the issues connected to teaching them about sexual activity and would require another full-length essay. Although I do not focus directly on drug use, my position regarding it remains the same: information presented to children should be forthright, less focused on a universalized developmental model, and more focused on urban, suburban, or rural context.

8. Jan Zita Grover, "Visible Lesions: Images of the PWA in America," in *Fluid Exchanges: Artists and Critics in the AIDS Crisis,* ed. James Miller (Toronto: University of Toronto Press, 1992), 25.

9. Beth E. Schneider, "Women, Children, and AIDS: Research Suggestions," in *AIDS and the Social Sciences,* ed. Richard Ulack and William F. Skinner (Lexington: University Press of Kentucky, 1991), 144.

10. Richard Goldstein, "The Implicated and the Immune: Responses to AIDS in the Arts and Popular Culture," in *A Disease of Society: Cultural and Institutional Responses to AIDS,* ed. Dorothy Nelkin, David P. Willis, and Scott V. Parris (Cambridge: Cambridge University Press, 1991), 20. For an analysis that reads television and mass media in more complex ways than Goldstein, see Paula Treichler's "Seduced and Terrorized: AIDS and Network Television," in *A Leap in the Dark: AIDS, Art and Contemporary Cultures,* ed. Allan Klusacek and Ken Morrison (Montreal: Vehicule, 1993), 136–51.

11. PWAC: People With AIDS Coalition New York, "AIDS and Adolescents," *PWACNY Newsline,* January 1994, 23.

12. Ibid.

13. Susan L. Montauk and David M. Scoggin, "AIDS: Questions from Fifth and Sixth Grade Students," *Journal of School Health* 59.7 (1989): 291.

14. Jon Won, "Conference of Peer Educators," *PWACNY Newsline,* January 1994, 25.

15. Treichler, "AIDS, Homophobia," 66.

16. Rick Weiss, "HIV's Spread is Unchecked," *Washington Post,* April 24, 1998, A1.

17. UNAIDS and WHO, "HIV/AIDS: The Global Epidemic. December 1996," http://www.unaids.org/highband/document/epidemio/situat96 .html, accesed July 26, 1998.

18. Patton, *Fatal Advice,* 36.

19. David Fassler and Kelly McQueen, *What's a Virus, Anyway? The Kids' Book about AIDS* (Burlington, VT: Waterfront, 1990), ix.

20. Ibid.

21. Michel Foucault, *The History of Sexuality,* vol. 1, *An Introduction,* trans. Robert Hurley (New York: Random House, 1978), 25.

22. Ibid., 24.

23. Sharon Schilling and Jonathan Swain, *My Name is Jonathan (And I Have AIDS)* (Denver: Prickly Pair, 1989), 23.

24. Marcia Quackenbush and Pamela Sargent, "The Issue of Abstinence," in *The AIDS Challenge: Prevention Education for Young People,* ed. Marcia Quackenbush and Mary Nelson with Kay Clark (Santa Cruz: Network, 1988), 479.

25. Treichler, "AIDS, Homophobia," 49.

26. Jerry Adler, "Safer Sex," *Newsweek,* December 9, 1991, 52.

27. Douglas Crimp, "How to Have Promiscuity in an Epidemic," in Crimp, *AIDS,* 247.

28. Schilling and Swain, *My Name is Jonathan,* 23.

29. See Silin's discussion of a class of kindergartners in New York City processing with each other a stabbing that occurred in their playground ("What AIDS Teaches Us," 261–63). The children use information culled from peers, older siblings, and *Rescue 911.* The men involved in the fight were arguing over a woman, and the children were very much aware of the complicated relationships involved.

30. See Fassler and McQueen, *What's a Virus, Anyway?,* and Neal Starkman, *Z's Gift,* illustrated by Ellen Joy Sasaki (Seattle: Comprehensive Health Education Foundation, 1988).

31. See Schilling and Swain, *My Name is Jonathan,* 19–21; and Fassler and McQueen, *What's a Virus, Anyway?* 1–26.

32. Fassler and McQueen, *What's a Virus, Anyway?,* 42.

33. Ibid., 43.

34. See Starkman, *Z's Gift,* 32–7.

35. Ibid., 3.

36. Cindy Patton, *Inventing AIDS* (New York: Routledge, 1990), 21.

37. Ibid., 140 n. 27.

38. Starkman, *Z's Gift,* 22.

39. There are, of course, other children's books that deal with AIDS in addition to the four I examine here; the number of such books is increasing rapidly and, more importantly, diversifying somewhat as activists and theorists have looked critically at the degaying of AIDS. On such, see Edward King, *Safety in Numbers: Safer Sex and Gay Men* (New York: Routledge, 1993), 169–232. Bernard Wolf's 1997 *HIV Positive* (New York: Dutton, 1997), for instance, is a

wonderful example of the kind of text possible under different ideological conditions. Sara, a twenty-nine-year-old woman living with AIDS, speaks openly with her daughter about drug use, condoms, and the ways in which HIV is (and is not) transmitted; gay and lesbian communities are represented, and Sara receives regular bulletins from Gay Men's Health Crisis (GMHC) and participates in their annual AIDS walk. In contrast, in Niki de Saint Phalle's *AIDS: You Can't Catch It Holding Hands* (San Francisco: Lapis, 1987), gay male bodies make only a cameo appearance (the child reader is assumed to have gay friends, but is presumably not gay himself or herself). Although it continues to demonize sex per se (as opposed to unprotected sex), Saint Phalle's text—which actually mentions gay people, specific sexual practices (including anal sex), condom use, and the dangers of sharing needles—remains the best children's book I have encountered from the late 1980s. *HIV Positive*, which emerges a decade later in a discursive context in which there is at least some space for overcoming the problems I describe in this article, is the best book I have encountered from the 1980s or the 1990s.

40. Mary Kate Jordan, *Losing Uncle Tim*, illustrated by Judith Friedman (Niles, IL: Whitman, 1989), n.p.

41. Ibid.

42. Ibid.

43. Patton explains that "heterosexual white women . . . volunteered in large numbers, but not because they were depicted as at risk of HIV from their boyfriends or husbands, but because they are the traditional volunteer reservoir. Many women were personally affected by gay male friends with AIDS, but they were not encouraged to understand this experience in the social context of their participation in gay male culture" (*Inventing AIDS*, 21).

44. Jordan, *Losing Uncle Tim*, n.p.

45. Goldstein, "The Implicated and the Immune," 28.

46. Jeff Nunokawa, "'All the Sad Young Men': AIDS and the Work of Mourning," in *Inside/Out: Lesbian Theories, Gay Theories*, ed. Diana Fuss (New York: Routledge, 1991), 319.

47. Jordan, *Losing Uncle Tim*, n.p.

48. Simon Watney, *Policing Desire: Pornography, AIDS, and the Media*, 2nd ed. (Minneapolis: University of Minnesota Press, 1989), 114.

49. Jordan, *Losing Uncle Tim*, n.p.

50. Ibid.

H/Z

Why Lesléa Newman Makes
Heather into Zoe

&

ELIZABETH A. FORD

"Few changes in American mores over the past 50 years," Phillip
Lopate remarks, "have been as dramatic or as salutary as the nation's
increased acceptance of homosexuals."[1] Consider Lopate's assertion as
you read these three fragments trapped in the time capsule of a hot
month in the summer:

August 20, 1995: Denis Donoghue concludes his review of Andrew
Sullivan's *Virtually Normal: An Argument about Homosexuality* with a
personal comment. He says his interest in Sullivan's work, which as-
sesses the current politics of homosexuality, is catalyzed by his affection for his lesbian daughter "the writer Emma Donoghue,"
whose homosexuality "does not darken [his] love for her, or qualify
the joy [he] takes in her personality, her immense gifts."[2] The opening sentence of that paragraph slightly diminishes the power of his
declaration: "I am not, in my own person," Donoghue makes clear,
"directly caught in this dispute."[3]

August 25, 1995: A shopping trip to a split-down-the-middle
Carter's outlet leaves me bemused. Although department stores
have always separated boys' apparel from girls, surely baby clothing has never been so irrevocably divided, so aggressively gendered.
Marooned between two poles of certainty, the layette counter offers

the only gender-neutral option, bland infant garments sporting amorphous patterns (not flower shapes, but not airplanes either).[4] I imagine the Carter's design team heaving sighs of relief and trashing these insincere either/or ensembles, now that almost all prospective parents choose to know their babies' gender. The word "layette" (way too feminine) will vanish.

August 27, 1995: A pretty little girl grins fetchingly from the "Children's Books" page of the *New York Times Book Review.* Catherine Stock's frontpiece centers Roger Sutton's review of *Too Far Away to Touch* by Lesléa Newman.[5] Stock's watercolor still-life shows a gold-framed photo of two faces: a smiling, blonde child, eyes closed, being hugged by a tousle-haired young man whose own closed eyes are slightly shadowed. Dark background tones in this illustration foreshadow the content of Newman's text, in which the child tells about her visits with a favorite uncle, who, Sutton explains, is dying of AIDS. The descriptive phrase that Sutton applies to Newman's text could also refer to the watercolor—"poignant, but not sticky." His generally positive review of Newman's book and a similar picture book by Judith Vigna concludes with a contemplative paragraph about purpose: "What are these books for?" he asks. "Will children want to read them or hear them again?"[6]

These salvaged fragments may sound like gleanings from an Internet search generated by the terms "gay/lesbian," "children," "literature," and "clothing." But I hope to reveal the codes—Barthian and other—that connect these fragments and to use them to explore a central, unspoken anxiety that haunts the conjunction of gay/lesbian issues and children's literature. Eve Kosofy Sedgwick calls "the experience and identity of gay or proto-gay children" a "fraught space of life-or-death struggle that has been more or less abandoned by constructivist gay theory."[7] Books that present gay or lesbian themes to children may be seen as opening up that "fraught space" to their readers. Ultimately, it is the fear of what children might learn about their own sexual identities, not about the sexuality of adults around them, that makes these books controversial.

"Unsubtle, overly didactic"

Authors who chose gay themes and who write for children must also choose whether or not to be commercially viable. Those who want to sell books must learn, as Lesléa Newman seems to have learned, to maintain a "safe" distance between child and gay adult characters. More like a wall than a comfort zone, distance problematizes the treatment of gay themes in children's literature and may keep the genre from reflecting the growing cultural acceptance Lopate identifies as a contemporary reality.

Writers who hope to promote cultural acceptance would be unusual if they did not hope for readers and sales as well. The *New York Times Book Review,* itself a commodity, affects the transaction between writer and reader by dealing out praise or blame. Most importantly, it identifies writers and works worthy of review space and, consequently, of public notice. Although Roger Sutton comments on works by Vigna and Newman in the review I have cited, I focus here on Newman because she also created *Heather Has Two Mommies* (1989), which Sutton describes as "one of the first picture books to deal with a gay theme"—a book not reviewed in the *Times.*[8] Sutton's *Times* review of Newman's latest work for children provokes an important question. What makes *Too Far Away to Touch* an acceptable text for this prestigious reviewing venue, when *Heather* clearly was not? Sutton implies an answer when he labels *Heather* "unsubtle, overly didactic,"[9] suggesting that Newman's current book is less so.

Newman has noticed and reacted to lack of attention from important reviewing journals. In a 1989 interview, she comments: "my books . . . don't get reviewed in the *New York Times* or even lesser places. I assume it's because of the lesbian content."[10] Assuming that Newman's naive sounding comment—Gee whiz! The lesbianism? Really?—accurately represents her understanding of the literary market would parallel the naïveté of asserting that the *Times* stamp of approval is the single factor determining the presence of a children's book on the shelves at Barnes and Noble. Other answers from the same interview with Newman yield glimpses of a savvy young writer who is comfortable in her lesbianism but who "wonder[s] about money."[11]

The generally favorable *Times* review certainly helped *Too Far Away to Touch* (both mass-market bookstores in my suburban neighborhood could produce copies, while neither had *Heather*),[12] but it was first "helped" by its creator. A chasm separates the presentations and concepts of Newman's two picture books for children; a chasm separates their implied audiences.

A *Newsweek* blurb about *Heather Has Two Mommies* proclaims that the book is "for and about children of gays."[13] As loud as the discussion it provoked, the cover of *Heather Has Two Mommies* asks for attention coming and going. The bright red title on an equally bright yellow background trumpets the book's content. On the back cover, Heather and her mommies, who resemble composites assembled from a butch/femme stereotype clip-art file, pose happily. As do these cover illustrations, the rest of illustrator Diana Souza's drawings exude a crude energy. Although the faces of her characters morph alarmingly from page to page, the vitality of her work with its frenetic textures and decoration almost makes up for lapses of technique. The same could be said of Newman's brash text.

Verbal and visual images hug each other, their shared goal to represent an indisputably happy family. Mommies Jane and Kate do what married people who are "very much in love"[14] do: talk together, kiss, and play with their child. I agree with *Newsweek* that "tykes are unlikely to understand the pages in which a lesbian gets pregnant through artificial insemination,"[15] but I think children will notice that Mama Jane has "a baby growing inside of [her] womb"[16] and see that only a sheet separates them from Heather's delivery. Surely the third-person narrator's relentless sequential description of Jane's pregnancy, from the union of "sperm and egg" to "tender" breasts and expanding "belly," triggered some of the negative reactions to *Heather*. Must we have lesbianism, artificial insemination, and anatomical detail too?

Moreover, Newman's flexible definition of family would make Dan Quayle weep. To underscore the range of possibilities Souza incorporates drawings by real children that illustrate other "special" families with different components: a single mother and two children; two fathers and a child; a mother a father, and four adopted children—one of them in a wheelchair. But *Heather Has Two Mommies* may have another, less obvious reason than its in-your-face ideology or its lack of technical sophistication for attracting negative attention.

As the product of a "special" family, Heather must provide proof that having two mommies might be a good deal. Her image bears the weight of Newman's heavy purpose. How should she look? Although curly-headed, blonde, brown-eyed Heather looks happy, active, expressive, interested, and thoughtful, she would never be chosen as an advertisement for that "girls" half of the Carter's store. Her clothing bears little overt gender coding; neither she nor her mommies ever sport dresses, ruffles, or bows. In most of the illustrations, Heather and her mommies are fashion anachronisms. Mama Kate's "No Nukes" T-shirt recalls the 1970s, as do Kate's and Jane's shag haircuts and occasional folksy ensemble, while much of the aggressively textured and oddly shaped clothing they wear seems not to belong to any specific time or place.[17] Yet Heather's image problematizes the tale. She appears once bare-chested, and usually wears shorts, pants, and high-tops, her ensembles cut from the same dizzily patterned, highly textured cloth that garbs all Souza's characters. She also suffers from the shape-shifting endemic to the work. But in Heather's case ambiguity entails more than anachronism, more than inconsistent representation. Heather provokes the fear that gay or lesbian parents will produce gay or lesbian children because her clothing, her features, her body, signal *androgynous child*, not *boy* or *girl*.[18]

Nowhere is Heather's androgyny more apparent than on the cover. Newman's "unsubtle, overly didactic" title brashly trumpets lesbian love—the subject matter least treated in young adult novels that feature gay/lesbian characters[19]—yet Heather herself, not the title or content, may be the most controversial component of this often banned book. The image that "fronts" Newman's text, the image an adult purchaser would first see, amply demonstrates Heather's danger and her dangerousness.

Here, smiling—or grimacing—Heather runs, arms upraised, through spiky, flowered grass with, or from, a dog, or wolf, who mimics her. Her pose recalls Max's mad dance in *Where The Wild Things Are,* and the "monster" dancing behind her may or may not be under her control. Neither the situation, nor the animal's classification, nor the child's gender is static. Her flowery, feminine name (which contains, by the way, an intersection of male and female: *he* at *her*) leads the title, but Heather's image leads the imagination. Her loose-fitting garb looks archaic, rough, male in the manner that Alison Lurie describes as typical: made of "bulky material, and [designed] to emphasize angularity with rectangular shapes and sharp points."[20] Odd bends of sleeve and trouser might even mask misshapen limbs. Her hair and face resemble stylized renderings of gender-neutral putti (now reigning at mall framing shops). The book's title is a statement, but the illustration reads like a visual enactment of Roland Barthes's hermeneutic code, which encompasses "the various formal terms by which an enigma can be distinguished, suggested, formulated, held in suspense, and finally disclosed."[21] In the case of Heather's image, there is no disclosure, no coming out, only questions. Who is Heather? What is Heather? The title page of the text compounds the questioning. A black-and-white rendering of the same illustration opens the story, and here the child's shape and face are altered but still androgynous.

The Carter's Syndrome

Neither cover nor interior of *Too Far Away to Touch*, a book aimed at a wider audience, provokes questions of this sort, for Newman and illustrator Stock avoid any such flip-flop of imagery. As she moves away from *Heather*, Newman performs a transformation more telling than Souza's visual morphing. When Newman turns Heather into a new child protagonist, Zoe, she abandons danger for relative safety.

The only "unsubtle, overly didactic" thing in *Too Far Away to Touch* is Zoe's gender. The book is slicker, a more sophisticated, more marketable product. Its title evokes distance but not a specific subject, and Stock's cover, rendered more skillfully than Souza's, nicely suggests which distance. A young man in a baseball cap lifts Zoe high, her arms raised, against a background of starry sky and ocean. Subtle, coherent, and as appealing as the cover, Stock's illustrations present consistent, attractive characters in their amplification of Newman's narrative.

If you "read" by examining the pictures, the story unfolds this way: a pretty, white, blonde female child goes to a planetarium accompanied by a nice-looking young man with a shadowed, troubled face. At lunch, he lifts his baseball cap to reveal his balding head. The child appears to be worried and later talks to her mother. The man buys the child a present—glow-in-the-dark stars—and sticks them to the ceiling of her room; he then falls asleep. Later the child lunches with him and his male friend. The three walk on the beach. The child and the young man lie on a blanket, looking up at the stars. They hug; they look sad. After they see a shooting star together, the little girl closes her eyes and raises her hands towards the heavens.

Newman's text clarifies relations, and verbal nuances explain the darkness in Stock's illustrations. Zoe tells the tale in this text, and her first-person narration solves some problems introduced in *Heather* while simultaneously avoiding threatening elements. A child narrator can only offer what she sees, knows, thinks, and is told; unlike *Heather*'s narrator, who can explicate artificial insemination. Zoe identifies the young man, her Uncle Leonard. A warning from Zoe's mother that she should not "tire [her] uncle out" introduces his illness.[22] Zoe further defines it by observing that Uncle Leonard closes his eyes in the taxi, that he is losing his hair, that his voice sounds "soft and fuzzy" on the phone, and that his smile is sad.[23] Uncle Leonard speaks the word "AIDS" to Zoe near the end of the book and says that he "may die soon."[24]

Sutton found Newman's book moving. So did I, yet troubling implications lurk not far beneath the tender surface. The difference between this text and *Heather* depends on shifted focus as well as increased sophistication. Paradoxical though it may seem, disease and death—even death caused by AIDS—are safer territory for authors of children's fiction that the theme of lesbian love and commitment Newman explores in *Heather*. Here Newman does not enter new territory. Children's books that examine death or separation are an accepted genre, so *Too Far Away To Touch* has a standard generic context.[25]

Newman means the book to raise money as well as consciousness; "a portion of the proceeds," the publication page announces, will go to "AIDS organizations." Yet, like advertising campaigns that link a charitable contribution to every charge on a certain credit card, this appeal seems designed first to massage the consumer and next to elevate the product. Credit card ads blatantly seek to transform purchase into participation in a higher good, to conflate getting and giving. The announcement in *Too Far Away to Touch*, while less blatant, leaves much to interpretation. What percentage is donated per book? Which organizations will benefit? I wonder, also, how Newman would answer questions about the way her text might help cement the truism that AIDS presents a problem for the gay community only. My focus here, however, is not on the commodification of empathy or the market value of AIDS, but on the most troubling element in the tale.

Zoe, the central character, signals stereotypical femininity in every way that Heather does not; she could be an ad for Carter's clothing coded "girl," or a concrete example of Barthes's cultural code, which depends on a culture's "body of knowledge" for its reading context.[26] In the illustration facing the first page of text, Zoe sits, waiting for her Uncle, and readers absorb her head-to-toe ensemble with this first image of her. Zoe wears a jaunty rose-colored beret trimmed with little pins. Her muffler matches her hat, and a lavender warm-up jacket covers a ribbed white turtleneck. Her short, flippy green and rose patterned skirt tops green ribbed tights worn with rolled down green bobby socks and saddle shoes (her limbs are neatly formed; they suggest no Heatherian vagaries). Her blonde hair, a shiny shoulder-length pageboy, and her brown eyes recall Heather's, but she is Heather turned Skipper—Barbie's little sister. Her ensemble indicates one of her functions in the book—perhaps her primary function. She will be cute. Her cuteness will fit the accepted formula. Read her as "girl."

Of course no inherent evil resides in a little girl wearing little girls' clothing. Yet Zoe's unmistakable gender marking, the first thing the first illustration signals, recalls our drive to gender-code *everything* that surrounds a small child—wallpaper, sheets, towels, clothing, playthings. Taking no chances that gender might be hardwired, we opt for every chance to eliminate ambivalence, to signify "feminine" or "masculine." Thus Zoe's gender announces itself instantly, and if her clothing does not provide ample evidence, her passivity underscores her stereotypical femininity. Except for three illustrations that show her moving, Zoe is static. Zoe waits, she sits, she looks, she listens, and she strikes these attitudes decoratively. She lacks Heather's expressiveness and motion. Stock places the child in her color-coordinated environments—on the sofa, on the bed—as if she is accessorizing a room. When Uncle Leonard hints at his predicament, Zoe sits before a complementary vase of flowers, eyes cutely wide with concern, her hair picking up the cheery yellow of the wall behind her. The warmth and coherence of the composition and the lovable quality of her reaction, not Uncle Leonard's anxiety, are the foci. Leonard wears cool colors, deep greens and blues; he is a shadow superimposed upon the brightness of the page.

Zoe's carefully presented image updates a package that adult readers will recognize. She recalls famous little girl literary precursors after they have been processed by popular culture to emerge as pretty hair, cute face, nice dress: Alice Liddell post-Disney, Mary Lennox via Madam Alexander. Newman's text confirms Zoe's blandness. Her voice lacks the originality that raised Alice and Mary into icons of popular culture. She tries one lame joke, and she asks questions as any child of six or seven does. There is little evidence until the last page that she synthesizes information and experience. Zoe does realize then that her Uncle, like the shooting star she has just seen, will be "too far away to touch, but close enough to see." Aside from this evocative phrase, little stamps her as an individual. She is Alice without the wit, Mary Lennox without the edge. Zoe is cute, and she is average.

Mine sounds like a remicrowaved feminist drone, a ritual rejection of the traditional trappings of female childhood, and a protest that a female child is yet again dull. But the rigid construction of a female child elevated—literally elevated on the cover—in this text, by this author, worries me beyond feminism.

"I am not, in my own person, directly caught in this dispute"

Denis Donoghue prefaces his paean to his daughter with that distancing sentence, and his review of *Virtually Normal* begins with a comment that Sullivan has not included "much of [his] own story" in *Virtually Normal*. Donoghue notes that Sullivan edited out a section about his childhood, where "[Sullivan] spoke of growing up in a Catholic family . . . and of coming to realize that he was emotionally and sexually different than most of the boys in his school. That essay [in an earlier edition of the book] dealt with the anxiety and pain of that difference."[27] In any examination of the intersection between gay and lesbian themes and literature for children, the relevance of early glimmerings of difference must sooner or later surface. By editing out material that deals directly with this experience in a text for adults, Sullivan suggests that "virtual" normality may dictate narrative distance from and actual, not virtual, silence about early differences, about that "fraught space."

Narrative and visual distance help sanitize *Too Far Away to Touch* into a text that qualifies for the children's book shelves at Barnes and Noble. Newman performs a triple remove. The lesbian couple has been replaced by gay lovers, a less threatening pair.[28] Zoe's life is safely separate from that of Uncle Leonard, who is, after all, not a brother or a father. Most importantly, Zoe's culturally coded femininity places her beyond any possible contamination of the discussion of gay lovers or of AIDS. Zoe's position on the cover, where Uncle Leonard lifts her high above him, parallels her position throughout the narrative. The image of a child so traditionally feminine, so "normal," provides adult readers with a comforting, gendered little hand to hold in a slippery space—a text that includes a positive if low-key portrait of gay lovers, one an AIDS sufferer. Zoe sweetens those subjects. Remember that the *New York Times Book Review* chose to reproduce the illustration of Zoe in her Uncle's embrace, not the one in which Uncle Leonard lifts his hat to reveal those telltale tufts of hair.

In her post-*Heather* life as a lesbian writer, Newman may be trying out this postulate: you may skirt, but not approach a gay/lesbian theme in literature for children *and* sell your book if, and only if, the gender identity of your young protagonist is unambiguous. Nothing about a central child character must suggest less than a stereotypically complete construction of gender, for the child reader must always be kept too far away to touch gay/lesbian themes. Newman could have looked to young adult novels for a confirmation of this approach: "The trend within this body of literature has been away from homosexuality-as-main-issue and toward treating gay issues as a subplot or a fact about a secondary character," writes Christine Jenkins.[29] I recast Jenkins's observation about YA fiction to fit the two texts I have examined: the reviewable, marketable presentation of gay/lesbian themes in books for children rests on the narrative and visual distance between theme and child. Nothing should disturb the notion that gays or lesbians discover their sexual orientation at eighteen—or older. Consumers prefer products with recognizable logos. In children's literature the equivalent of the Carter's label is the representation of the "perfectly" male or female child for whom such clothes were designed.

The fear of leakage, of influence, appears obliquely stated in the following comment by Robert Williams, which introduces a list of "approved" young adult books presenting gay/lesbian characters: "Teachers should not fear that these books advocate a gay lifestyle."[30] Newman and Stock's creation of Zoe indicates that the perceived danger of identification increases as the age of the projected audience decreases. The younger the reader the greater the risk.

I am not advocating the creation of didactic texts in which potentially gay and lesbian children play same-sex doctor games and loudly voice their recognition of early sexual preference, and I hope that I am not attacking Lesléa Newman, whose increased visibility increases her chances of writing what she wants to write, if for adults only. By linking these fragments, I am trying to recognize pressures affecting children's literature.

"What are these books for?"

Among other questions relevant to this project, we might ask, "Who are Sutton's and Donoghue's reviews for?" Both of them arrive in a vehicle that, despite Phillip Lopate's optimism about acceptance, often clarifies the cultural recoil against the gay and lesbian community. A front-page story on August 27, 1995, the same day Sutton's review of *Too Far Away to Touch* appeared, details Bob Dole's scramble to return campaign funds from a Republican gay/lesbian group. Richard Berke sees Dole's action as proof that he is "intensifying his yearlong drive to court conservative Republican groups." I would interpret Dole's desperate rush more personally. A war hero, who carefully cultivates his manliness, Dole would surely want to shed an affiliation that did not match his persona. Although neither Sutton nor Donoghue could ever be accused of self-promoting ruthlessness, or of overtly homophobic behavior, both men do conclude their reviews by *bobbing,* by qualifying, by stepping back. Donoghue denies "direct" involvement in gay politics, but I wonder how much more directly one could be involved in the politics of homosexuality than to have a gay or lesbian child. Does "direct involvement" equal involvement of the "person" alone?

Sutton questions the literary quality, but also the purpose, of the works he reviews—"What are these books for?" He wonders who will read them. He imagines an audience composed either of children who know someone dying of AIDS, or of children who are "targets" of well-meaning adults who prescribe these texts. In the process of questioning purpose and audience, Sutton distances himself from the books he has examined by suggesting that gay books are for gay readers only. Both reviewers conclude, finally, that these works—and all such works?—are only for those *directly* (physically?) involved in the issues.

Carter's capitalizes on fear that distances difference by suggesting that coding a child unambiguously, even before birth, can pay off with the big prize later. Velcroing that bow to little Tiffany's bald head, pulling on those lacy socks, that flowered romper, might protect against the need to create anything like the garment of prose Donoghue crafts for his daughter. Newman too must clothe her child correctly, turning Heather into Zoe—imagine an *H* smashed sideways, compressed into a Z—to avoid the disruption of the text. Zoe is a normal child, just one of the multiple stories surrounding us, composed of "so many fragments of something that has already been done, seen, experienced."[31]

Although the positive cultural shift that Lopate identifies may be real, the acceptance of homosexuality he describes applies to adults thinking about adults, not to children. As rude as it is, *Heather Has Two Mommies* thrusts itself into a void. As polished as it is, *Too Far Away to Touch* stands away from the edge, defining the void nevertheless. The circle of love, fear, and commerce that connects the fragments I have assembled excludes the "fraught space" of protogay childhood sexual glimmerings. As Sedgwick says, "Advice on how to make sure your kids turn out gay . . . is less ubiquitous than you might think."[32]

NOTES

1. Philip Lopate, "Rapid Transit: How 'America's Most Despised Minority' Gained Acceptance in Record Time," *New York Times Book Review* 9 (November 1997): 12.

2. Denis Donoghue, "The Politics of Homosexuality," *New York Times Book Review* 20 (August 1995): 26. Critic, novelist, and playwright Emma Donoghue's first novel, *Stir-Fry,* was a 1995 Lambda Literary Award finalist.

3. Donoghue, "The Politics of Homosexuality," 26.

4. One pattern adorning the non-gender-specific collection I saw at the Carter's outlet resembled those overlapping pastel boomerang shapes that appeared on Formica in the 1950s. This choice seems less odd only when one tries to identify other patterns/shapes that might be gender-neutral.

5. Roger Sutton, review of Lesléa Newman, *Too Far Away to Touch, But Close Enough to See,* illustrated by Catherine Stock (New York: Clarion, 1995), and Judith Vigna, *My Two Uncles* (Morton Grove, IL: Whitman, 1995), *New York Times Book Review* 27 (August 1995): 27. Sutton has authored a young adult nonfiction book about alternative lifestyles: *Hearing Us Out: Voices from the Gay and Lesbian Community* (New York: Little, Brown, 1994).

6. Sutton, review of Newman and Vigna, 27.

7. Eve Kosofsky Sedgwick, *Epistemology of the Closet* (Berkeley: University of California Press, 1990), 42.

8. Lesléa Newman, *Heather Has Two Mommies,* illustrated by Diana Souza (Boston: Alyson, 1989). *Heather* got a boxed paragraph—it is showcased as an example of outré texts for kids—in *Newsweek,* and a brief mention in *Ms.* It was reviewed in *Belles Lettres, Bloom Review, Childhood Education,* and *Lambda Book Report.* In contrast, *Too Far Away to Touch* was reviewed in *Lambda Book Report,* but also in *The Advocate, Booklist, Children's Book Review Series, Horn Book, Publisher's Weekly, School Library Journal,* and the *New York Times.*

9. Sutton, review of Newman and Vigna, 27.

10. Gail Koplow, "Lesléa Newman: Writing from the Heart," *Sojourner: The Women's Forum* 27 (August 1995): 7a.

11. Ibid., 8a.

12. My local (Ohio, suburban) Barnes and Noble and Little Professor stores also had copies of Sullivan's *Virtually Normal* and Donoghue's *Stir-Fry.*

13. "Daddy is Out of the Closet," *Newsweek,* January 7, 1991, 60–61.

14. Newman, *Heather Has Two Mommies,* n.p.

15. "Daddy is Out of the Closet," 60.

16. Newman, *Heather Has Two Mommies,* n.p.

17. Newman's comic piece "Out of the Closet and Nothing to Wear: A Femme Shops Till Her Butch Drops," which appeared online in *The Texas Triangle: The State's Gay News* source, confirms her interest in dress. [Editor's note:

Newman's "Out of the Closet" can no longer be found online except in excerpts, at http://www.lesleanewman.com/closetex.htm.] She describes a mall
quest, a determined and joyful search for black shoes of every heel height and
strap variation to complement long and short skirts and pant suits, a paean to
variety and acquisition. Newman seems to agree with Alison Lurie that "to
choose clothes, either in a store or at home, is to define and describe ourselves"
(Lurie, *The Language of Clothes* [New York: Random House, 1981], 5). Obviously
alive to fashion's nuances, Newman must have had ideas about the mommies'
appearances and especially Heather's. She chose Souza to illustrate Heather, a
choice that implies the possibility of discussion. On this, see Tony A. Leuzzi,
"Portrait of an Artist (as a Labeled Woman): An Interview with Leslea Newman," *The Squealer* 20 (June–July 1997): 12–13, reprinted from *Gerbil* 3, "Queer
Youth Queer Families" (1995): 18–19.

18. In most illustrations for *My Two Uncles*, Vigna's child character Elly (not
too far from "elle") looks gender-neutral, but two crucial illustrations code her
femininity. Vigna describes Elly's sadness and mystification when her grandfather refuses to invite his gay son's lover (Elly's "uncle") to a golden wedding
anniversary party. For the party, Elly, who has been dressed in shorts, T-shirts,
and tennis shoes, and who resembles her gay uncle more than any other character, appears in a dress and a little wreath of flowers, unequivocal signifiers of
her gender orientation.

19. See Christine A. Jenkins, "Young Adult Novels with Gay/Lesbian Char-
acters and Themes, 1969–1992: A Historical Reading of Content, Gender, and
Narrative Distance," *Journal of Youth Services in Libraries* 7.1 (Fall 1993): 43–55.
Jenkins's essay is reprinted in this volume.

20. Lurie, *The Language of Clothes*, 215.

21. Roland Barthes, *S/Z* (New York: Hill and Wang, 1974), 19.

22. Newman, *Too Far Away to Touch*, 8.

23. Ibid., 10, 19, 24, 28.

24. Ibid., 28.

25. "Death is shown as part of life in an increasing number of books, even
for younger children," claims Zena Sutherland in the ninth edition of *Children
and Books* (New York: Addison-Wesley, 1997), 7–8. In the last ten years, violent
death has become a staple of YA literature.

26. Barthes, *S/Z*, 21.

27. Donoghue, "The Politics of Homosexuality," 3.

28. Jenkins explains that "roughly one quarter" of the sixty YA novels she
surveyed depicted lesbian characters, while "three-quarters" had gay male
characters. "Beautiful lesbians," Jenkins points out, "tend to be associated with
pain" ("Young Adult Novels," 46).

29. Ibid., 50.

30. Robert F. Williams, "Gay and Lesbian Teenagers: A Reading Ladder for
Students, Media Specialists, and Parents," *ALAN Review* 20.3 (1993): 13.

31. Barthes, *S/Z*, 5. Newman even dresses herself differently for her representations on the back covers of the two texts. In her photo for *Too Far Away to
Touch*, she looks professionally coifed and garbed; in contrast, she wears jeans

and lots of jewelry for the casual shot that is included with her bio in *Heather Has Two Mommies*. The *Heather* bio insists on the cute and the personal, including cat names and the information that Newman "lives . . . with a woman she loves named Mary." Nothing cute or personal appears in the biographical note that follows *Too Far Away*.

32. Sedgwick, *Epistemology of the Closet*, 42.

The Trouble with *Rainbow Boys*

ૐ

THOMAS CRISP

Few books for gay/lesbian/bisexual/transgender/queer or questioning (GLBTQ)[1] young adults have received the type (and quantity) of
critical, scholarly, and popular acclaim and commercial success as has
Rainbow Boys by Alex Sanchez. With the possible exception of Nancy
Garden's *Annie on My Mind, Rainbow Boys* has become as close to a
canonical work of GLBTQ fiction as any other book. Widely hailed
across publications by readers, critics, and scholars, the novel and its
sequels (*Rainbow High* and *Rainbow Road*) have joined what are only a
select number of GLBTQ pieces of literature to have found their way
into classroom and school libraries. To say that the books are beloved
almost seems an understatement: readers across a range of sexual identities and ages and from a variety of professional backgrounds (i.e., students, critics, scholars) have affirmed them as both realistic in their portrayals and positive in their content.

The popularity of the series appears to stem from several sources: it
is light in tone (a quick read for young adults) and deals quite convincingly with the angst of high school life, suggesting a reflection of reality
that strikes readers as being "honest" and "true." Furthermore, it is
nearly impossible not to admire the author himself: a quick visit to his
website[2] reveals that this professional guidance counselor and immigrant from Mexico wants nothing more than to share with readers his
own struggles with his sexual identity in ways that he hopes will simultaneously support and inspire the next generation of young people.

After acknowledging their attributes and contributions, in this essay,[3] I closely investigate the three novels in the *Rainbow Boys* series in order to demonstrate that educators may need to tread carefully when recommending these books. Like all pieces of contemporary realistic fiction, these books rely upon a representation and interpretation of reality. In her study of the depictions of girls and women in *Youth's Companion* serials, Laura Apol writes that in literature, coming of age "is characterized by a rite of passage that transforms boys into men, girls into women, often in highly stereotyped gender-specific ways."[4] She notes, "The construction of gender in literature (especially in literature for children) is profoundly important, for the images found in fiction are not only descriptive—they are normative as well."[5] In the case of the *Rainbow Boys* series, the effect of this construction is particularly seductive, as on the surface the books appear to be affirmative of homosexual young adults. Violet J. Harris claims there is a trend in literature to provide images that "uplift and inspire" as they work to educate readers about a group's history and struggles,[6] and these books have clearly appealed to progressive-minded educators and allies of GLBTQ youth who search the available literature for depictions that positively reflect this traditionally underrepresented population. While it is certainly appealing to find "affirmative" novels, it is also important to remain cognizant of the fact that in many cases, such stories rely on largely unconscious cultural associations.

In *Gender Trouble: Feminism and the Subversion of Identity*, Judith Butler theorizes that "the institution of a compulsory and naturalized heterosexuality requires and regulates gender as a binary relation in which the masculine term is differentiated from a feminine term, and this differentiation is accomplished through the practices of heterosexual desire."[7] Although the protagonists of the *Rainbow Boys* series identify as homosexual, they embody characteristics that reinforce normative conceptions of gender and, by extension, sexuality. "Western societies," Judith Lorber notes, "have only two genders, 'man' and 'woman,'"[8] and in looking beyond the surface construction of the trilogy, it seems that the books rely upon stereotypes of what it means to be "male" (i.e., aggressive and dominating) and "female" (i.e., submissive and self-sacrificing) to depict men in homosexual relationships as embodying either a "masculine" or "feminine" counterpart (perpetuating the fallacy that in gay relationships, one partner is the "man" while the other is the "woman"). While the result of this construction may make the books more appealing for readers (these tropes feel "realistic" because they are recognizable and therefore require little effort), it is precisely the familiarity with such tropes that leads to the perpetuation of myths and misconceptions.

Beyond this, the series appears to call for the gay population to become resilient to the injustices enacted upon it by homophobic heterosexuals, as the world is constructed as a frightening and dangerous place where homosexuals find solace only when isolated from the heterosexual population.[9] In *Homosexual Characters in YA Novels: A Literary Analysis 1969–1982*, Allan A. Cuseo suggests that "the literature of the young adult reflects society's impression of the homosexual as an individual it is permissible to harass,"[10] and in these books, queer characters must always be prepared to defend themselves against violent antagonists.

Finally, although well intentioned, efforts to educate and raise consciousness about the AIDS virus may actually reinforce homophobic discourse, as homosexuality is equated with AIDS in ways that imply that for gay men, contraction of the virus is an inevitability. While it is important that AIDS be present in literature for all teens, John D. Anderson warns that caution be used when depicting gay people exclusively within the context of AIDS as it is, "inadequate and dishonest, and it can easily lead heterosexual students to view this horrible disease as simply a problem for gay people."[11]

Ultimately, it would be unfair for this essay to explore only the first novel in the trilogy (*Rainbow Boys*) as the books should be considered as an artistic whole and also because much of the growth and change for the three protagonists comes in the third novel, *Rainbow Road*. However, in structuring this argument, I spend time looking at the portrayals and themes established in the first novel before moving to show how these depictions are either reinforced or complicated as one continues to read through the remainder of the series. It may feel artificial or unnecessarily extensive, but I do this for several reasons: (1) *Rainbow Boys* is a book that can (and is often asked to) stand on its own as an artistic creation—unless one is compelled to continue through the series, a reader can leave the first book with a feeling of closure. As a result, (2) more young adults are likely to pick up and read the first novel than they are to read the entire series. Additionally, (3) in academic scholarship and professional writing, it is *Rainbow Boys*—and not the other two titles—that is routinely recommended for classroom use from high school through the university. As an example, although Linda C. Salem's *Children's Literature Studies: Cases and Discussions* was published in 2006 (a year after the final book in the series was published), she asks her undergraduate preservice teacher audience only to read and consider *Rainbow Boys*. Penultimately, (4) in any classroom (even in a course devoted to the study of GLBTQ children's and adolescent literature), it is unlikely that time will be spent collectively studying the entire series of novels. Teachers who use this particular literature will mostly likely share only the first installment, leaving it up to students (if it has captured their interest) to continue reading the series on their own. Finally, (5) it is clear that Sanchez has written these books for a dual audience of both homosexual and heterosexual readers. If one of his goals is to leave "intolerant" heterosexuals (who will probably not seek out and read the remainder of the series on their own) with a depiction of homosexual characters that might positively impact how such readers subsequently view GLBTQ people, it is even more important that the representations in the first installment of the series be free of stereotypical constructions and content.

I first must acknowledge that in using words such as "masculine," "feminine," "male," and "female" (and even "gay" or "homosexual") throughout this essay, in some ways my very critique reinforces normative binaries. Judith Butler (following Monique Wittig's lead) argues such words exist *"only* within the heterosexual matrix; indeed, they are the naturalized terms that keep that matrix concealed and, hence, protected from a radical critique."[12] However, with this nod to their obvious limitations, I hope to employ these slippery constructs to examine and make explicit the ways in which the *Rainbow Boys* series operates within this dualistic frame.

The use of terms such as "authentic" and "accurate" is also complicated. The issue of "authenticity" in children's and adolescent literature has proven problematic—and often irreconcilable—for scholars, authors, and publishers. Kathy G. Short and Dana L. Fox write in their seminal *Stories Matter: The Complexity of Authenticity in Children's Literature* that "authentic" literature is presumed to include "cultural facts and values and what is considered 'truth' about a particular cultural experience."[13] However, they note that there is no standardized "authentic" insider or outsider perspective, which makes the issues surrounding cultural authenticity increasingly complex. Concrete definitions of what such depictions "look like" may not be uniformly obvious, but their importance is apparent. Short and Fox write, "All children have the right to see themselves within a book, to find within a book the truth of their own experiences instead of stereotypes and misrepresentations . . . literature is one of the significant ways that children learn about themselves and others; therefore, those literary images should not be distorted or inauthentic."[14] While authors may ultimately create depictions of their choosing, Weimin Mo and Wenju Shen write, "Authors and illustrators need to consider the implications of the cultural values they introduce in their stories."[15] Literature helps children create an understanding of the world around them, and I suggest authors have a responsibility to construct their representations with thought and care.

Arguments such as the ones made in this essay could easily be appropriated by homophobic individuals seeking to keep GLBTQ literature out of schools and the hands of the children and young adults who desperately need to see themselves represented. Therefore, it should be clarified that this essay does not call for the censorship of these novels. Its purpose is merely to raise questions around the importance of carefully selecting GLBTQ literature—especially for classroom use—because accurate depictions of GLBTQ people are profoundly important for youth of all sexual identities. Finally, it should be made clear that I am not denying the existence of gay young men who embody many (or all) of the characteristics found in protagonists Nelson, Kyle, or Jason—in fact, it is wonderful that this series provides readers with depictions of three very different gay men. However, I hope to argue that when they serve as the only representations that readers explore, these token tropes serve not to present "authentic," positive homosexual characters, but may actually work to limit readers' understandings of what it can look like (and what it means) to be gay.

"8,000 Thumbs Up!": The Success of *Rainbow Boys*

When *Rainbow Boys* hit bookstore and library shelves in 2001, there was little doubt that author Alex Sanchez had created a nearly unrivaled success in the field of GLBTQ young adult literature and over subsequent years, the accolades have continued to multiply. In 2003, the International Reading Association selected *Rainbow Boys* as "Young Adults' Choice." It's been named an American Library Association "Best Book for Young Adults," a "Gay Youth Book of the Year," a Center for Children's Books "Blue Ribbon Winner," and a New York Public Library "Books for the Teen Age" selection. In April 2006, it was listed

"Best, Notable, and Recommended" by the Young Adult Library Services Association. The success of this 2001 novel has launched author Alex Sanchez to celebrity status in the field of YA literature. In fact, on the covers of the hardback editions of his most recent novels, *Getting It* and *The God Box,* his name appears boldly and prominently, while the titles themselves are nearly lost in the background.

More than 150 readers on Amazon.com and the Barnes and Noble website have reviewed *Rainbow Boys* and in both locations, the book has earned the maximum rating, a nearly unprecedented "five stars."[16] Readers have called *Rainbow Boys,* "one of the greatest books I've ever read"[17] and give it "8,000 thumbs up."[18] They declare that "the story will inspire you to be yourself"[19] and are convinced that it "really helps break down sterotypes" [*sic*].[20] Furthermore, they recommend it "to anyone who is really narrow minded or is a gay or lesiban" [*sic*].[21] A "Top 1000 Reviewer" named T. Burger nicely sums up the overall tone of these reviews, "If you're a gay teenager, *this book should shine bright rays of hope into your life.*"[22]

These reviewers not only recommend the book for all young adult readers, they identify themselves as being from a range of sexual identities across a tremendous span of ages. A reviewer who names herself "Just Grammy's Opinion" says, "This is the definition of a page turner. Beautifully written and totally honest in tone,"[23] and a middle-school reader writes, "I love this book . . . everyone should read it!"[24] Another reviewer, who calls herself "Janell, a straight who could relate to this," says that the book made her more open to homosexuality, and, although "I know I'll never trully [*sic*] understand how I could kiss the same sex as me, but I know that to some people, it feels all right."[25] Readers refer to their anticipation of reading other books in the series and even suggest the creation of a television series based on the characters.

While it may be difficult to take some of these reviews seriously (as many of the glowing comments are at the same time speckled with phrases like "typical queer," "the sissy kid," and "faggy"), I think we must take note—these reviews tend to come from Sanchez's target audience and clearly, their opinions matter. The fact that they praise the book indicates that, on some level, it strikes them as true.

The accolades for the book continue in professional publications, where reviewers particularly praise the novel for its realism, honesty, and positive messages. Betty S. Evans writes in the *School Library Journal* that "this gutsy, in-your-face debut novel speaks the language of . . .

having what it takes to stand up and be proud of who you are . . . it can open eyes and change lives."[26] A 2003 *Kliatt* review by Paula Rohrlick declares, "YAs who are struggling with some of the same issues will appreciate this *realistic, caring portrayal* of the relationships between the three boys and their efforts to accept their sexuality in the face of intolerance."[27] A review by Kristin Kloberdanz in *Book* calls the novel "clear [and] honest" and states that "the three boys learn how to be themselves and stand up to their tormentors, who are not just ignorant students but also older predators and gay bashers.[28] A 2001 *VOYA* review by Lynn Evarts states, "This book is an important purchase for libraries serving teens."[29] Kate McDowell writes of *Rainbow Boys* in the *Bulletin of the Center for Children's Books*, "Sanchez . . . creates *believably nuanced portrayals* . . . When a work of fiction embodies such accuracy and emotional complexity, there is but one word to describe it: true."[30]

Within academic scholarship, Linda C. Salem's publication *Children's Literature Studies: Cases and Discussions* extensively uses *Rainbow Boys* in her chapter "Literature with GLBTQ Characters, Themes, and Content," where she states "[GLBTQ] fiction in the late 1990s and 2000s is characterized by authentic stories and characters,"[31] and she lists Alex Sanchez as a recommended author in the next generation of writers of GLBTQ fiction. She asks her presumed undergraduate teacher education audience to read *Rainbow Boys* as the one piece of GLBTQ fiction they examine and assumes they will recommended it to their own students. In her Braverman Prize–winning article published in *Progressive Librarian,* Jennifer Downey recommends the book because the characters are "not stereotypes whose lives revolve around sexuality or who are surrounded by violence and a lack of acceptance."[32]

An article published in the *Journal of Adolescent & Adult Literacy* by Mollie V. Blackburn and JF Buckley calls for queer-inclusive English Language Arts curricula in high schools. The authors were dismayed to find that only 8.49 percent of schools responding to their survey indicated "that they use texts, films or other materials addressing same-sex desire in their English language arts curriculum,"[33] and even these were often in a single course or through the use of a single text (many of which depicted GLBTQ people in negative ways). The authors state they want to help prepare teachers by identifying "materials that provide authentic and accurate representations of diverse LGBTQ people."[34] Although they voice concern that some heterosexual characters with stereotypically Latino names "tend to be disturbingly homophobic,"[35] they recommend teachers use *Rainbow Boys* [36] because it "disrupts the stereotypical notions of gay men."[37]

In *The Heart Has Its Reasons: Young Adult Literature with Gay/Lesbian/Queer Content, 1969–2004*, scholars Michael Cart and Christine A. Jenkins note that *Rainbow Boys* is "sometimes didactic," but even they praise the "realistic, sympathetic characters."[38] They follow in the footsteps of Rudine Sims Bishop in her groundbreaking 1982 study *Shadow and Substance: Afro-American Experience in Contemporary Children's Fiction* by naming three "phases" of GLBTQ literature. The category of *homosexual visibility* is the parallel to Sims's "social conscience" stories where homogeneity is disrupted by someone is not "one of us" and includes books that deal with characters coming out of the closet (either voluntarily or against their will). The second category of *gay assimilation* is parallel to "melting pot literature," as these books assume a "melting pot of sexual gender identity" where people "just happen" to be gay (in the same way people just happen to have red hair). The third category parallels "culturally conscious" literature, and, called *queer consciousness/community*, these books show GLBTQ characters in the context of their communities of GLBTQ people. Cart and Jenkins place *Rainbow Boys* (2001) in all three categories and *Rainbow High* (2003) in the categories of "homosexual visibility" and "queer consciousness/ community."[39]

While the sequels to *Rainbow Boys* are often recognized to be more didactic, the books are still generally lauded by readers and critics—in fact, all three books are Lambda Literary Award finalists. *Rainbow High* was named a New York Public Library "Book for the Teen Age" in 2004, the same year the Children's Book Council named it a "Notable Social Studies Trade Book for Young People." Robert Gray writes in *School Library Journal* that "Sanchez has written a respectable sequel to the noteworthy *Rainbow Boys*. . . . He has a definite feel for the thoughts, feelings and speech patterns of contemporary high school students, and his characters are believable, although perhaps not as fully developed as one would like."[40] Gray suggests "the narrative flows smoothly, with plenty of soap-opera dramatics to keep readers interested and a steamy scene or two to boot."[41] In *The Horn Book Magazine*, Roger Sutton praises the "frankness" of *Rainbow High* and ultimately refers to the novel as "a guilty pleasure—and reassuring, too."[42] Jeff Katz in the *School Library Journal* calls *Rainbow Road* "a true winner"[43] and declares the characters to be realistic, saying, "These boys are distinct personalities and genuine teens, searching for clarity and identity and acceptance, trying to make sense of themselves and a world that can be equally bright and dark."[44] He concludes that the novel is "a tender book that will likely be appreciated and embraced by young adult readers."[45] While Roger Sutton calls the book "the last and best"[46] of the *Rainbow Boys* series, Michael Cart notes in *The Booklist* that the book is highly banal until "halfway through the cross-country journey . . . the story becomes more involving as characterization finally takes the driver's seat."[47] He goes on to identify Nelson as "annoyingly predictable" but concludes "the other two boys are sympathetic charmers, and fans of Sanchez's first two Rainbow novels will certainly want to read this one."[48]

"A Bright Ray of Hope": The Appeal of Sanchez and the *Rainbow Boys* Series

Seldom are "problem novels" taken seriously as literature, so it's important to consider why the *Rainbow Boys* series has become GLBTQ literature with which to be reckoned. What has made the series popular and influential with readers of all sexual identities, both young and old? There seem to be several factors that contribute to the popularity of the series (especially the first installment) that deserve further exploration as to what they suggest about the novels' appeal.

According to his online biography, Sanchez initially set out to write a story about gay teens that reflected what he "wanted and needed to read when he was a young teenager—a book that would have told him: 'It's okay to be who you are.'"[49] Recognizing that in the history of GLBTQ literature, "there has been little focus on gays as protagonists,"[50] he decided to write a novel that worked against the trend of subjugating gays to secondary roles. It is commendable that Sanchez (unlike many authors of GLBTQ young adult fiction) is remarkably open not only about his educational, professional, and personal background, but about his own self-identification as a gay male. Clearly, he cares deeply about providing representation and voice to this population: his website includes detailed pages that guide young adults in issues ranging from "coming out" to family and friends to spirituality and censorship.

As an author, Sanchez says he is concerned that "the predominant experience for most GLBTQ youth is still one of isolation, harassment, persecution, and self-loathing"[51] and hopes that his books will help young people come to believe in themselves when those in society are telling them what they feel is wrong. In interviews, he shares excerpts of emails he receives from young adult readers of his books—all of which are deeply moving and heartfelt thanks for his work; it is work that has undoubtedly provided many gay young people an opportunity to see themselves reflected in literature for the very first time. Further, the admiration doesn't just move in one direction; Sanchez says, "Gay youth today are my heroes . . . so many of them are so willing to stand up for themselves and take risks, and I recognize the courage that takes."[52]

In the structure of his writing itself, Sanchez tackles three alternating perspectives throughout the series, something worthy of applause, as the technique often proves elusive for even the most seasoned writers. And yet, in spite of all the accolades and praise, he appears remarkably humble: in an interview for *Youth Resource: Advocates for Youth,* he states, "No one taught me to think of writing and books as agents of social change, able to inspire, empower, and change lives. That my books can do this ceaselessly amazes me."[53]

Obviously, it's not just Sanchez himself that makes the series so popular. Michael Cart has said of *Rainbow Boys* in his column "Carte Blanche" for *Booklist,* "What saves the story from problem-novel limbo are its realistic, right-on dialogue; its sympathetic characters who rise above the stereotypical; and—most important—its focus on love as the heart of homosexuality."[54]

In a genre with a history of assuming homogeneity among homosexuals, the *Rainbow Boys* series is commendable because it presents for readers different "types" of gay men. And the books are also notable because they contain both gay men and lesbian women as characters—another rarity in GLBTQ young adult fiction (certainly fitting with Cart and Jenkins's category of "queer consciousness/community"), which too often explores the lives of gay men and lesbian women in isolation of one another. The series remains important because it addresses the issue of AIDS (a subject Cart and Jenkins have noted is habitually absent from GLBTQ young adult literature) and the books appear to provide an accurate, realistic depiction of contemporary high school life: filled with cliques, heartaches and crushes, and the struggle to discover one's self-identity. But scholars, critics, and readers equally praise the book for its realistic, sympathetic characters, and that is primarily where the reading explored in this essay stands at odds with others. I suggest it is the subtext of what Sanchez has created (by depicting his themes and queer characters within a heterosexual binary) that establishes the problematic way the books work to heteronormatively construct what it means to be gay.

Alternative Viewpoints: The Stories of the Rainbow Boys

Rainbow Boys is the story of three young men struggling to successfully complete their senior year of high school. Told from alternating viewpoints, the novel introduces us to three protagonists, and the chapters alternate from Jason's perspective (described on the back of the book as "Jock. Good looks. Beautiful girlfriend. Popular. Unsatisfied"), to Kyle's (who is described as "Swim team star. Friendly. Easygoing. Intelligent. Confused"), and finally to Nelson's (described as "Independent. Opinionated. Defiant. Joker. In love") and back again in a rotating fashion as the story is told. In brief, best friends Kyle and Nelson (both identify as gay males) become involved in a complicated love triangle when classmate Jason Carrillo shows up at a gay youth meeting. Jason is not only Kyle's longtime love interest, he's also the school jock. On its surface, the story is about many of the issues teens might face in coming out (Kyle comes out to his parents and his high school and Jason comes out to himself, his family, and his girlfriend) as well as what it means to be "queer and proud" (through the character of Nelson).

Rainbow High explores the lives of the three protagonists as they move closer to the end of their senior year—for these boys, it's a period filled with the anticipation many high school seniors face, and, with the development of promising personal relationships, the "rainbow boys" look forward to their senior prom and try to iron out their individual (and collective) plans for life after graduation. As the story progresses, all three protagonists are accepted to the same college, but their plans to attend "Tech" with one another become complicated when Kyle learns he has also been accepted to Princeton. For all three boys, their personal decisions lead to a range of difficulties: Jason decides to "come out" to his coach, teammates, and the world; Nelson struggles to sustain his relationship with his HIV-positive boyfriend when those around him disapprove; and Kyle tries to weigh his relationship with Jason against the opportunity to study at a prestigious university.

In *Rainbow Road*, the final novel of the series, Jason has been invited to speak at the opening of a new high school for gay and lesbian students in California. In order to spend time with Kyle before he leaves for college, Jason opts to forgo a flight to Los Angeles and instead embarks on a cross-country driving trip with his boyfriend. The three protagonists (Nelson tags along because the road trip is his idea and involves the use of his car) travel together and encounter a range of individuals: from homophobic heterosexuals to a transgender teen, a committed gay couple, and a commune of "social misfits." As the adventure progresses, Kyle becomes increasingly unsure of his relationship with Jason, Jason tries to sort through his sexual confusion, and Nelson continues to search for Mr. Right (or at least, Mr. Right Now). By the time the journey ends, Nelson has found (what could be) love, and Kyle and Jason's relationship remains intact.

The Reflected Self: Constructing What It "Means" to Be Gay

The "Masculine" T.C.J. and "Feminine" S.U.D. Tropes as Heteronormative Couple

In this section, attention will be paid to the depiction of all three of the "rainbow boys," but while each protagonist may ultimately be individually unsettling, it is my sense that the relationship between Jason and Kyle is the most obviously troublesome. Jason, a stock character who appears in many gay young adult novels, is identified by Alex Sanchez as the "Tragic Closet Jock" (or T.C.J.), a "masculine" young man whose status as an attractive star athlete permits him to discover his sexuality at both his girlfriend's and co-protagonist Kyle's expense.

In "How to Bring Your Kids Up Gay," Eve Kosofsky Sedgwick argues that the work of revisionist psychoanalysts has served to renaturalize gender in ways that work not only to eliminate homosexuals, but claim that boys (no matter how "effeminate") can be dissuaded from homosexuality through early affirmation of their "masculinity." According to these accounts, "the reason effeminate boys turn out gay . . . is that other men don't validate them as masculine."[55] Self-identifying as a gay male, Alex Sanchez certainly should not be classified alongside homophobic psychoanalysts; however, the antiquated notions such psychologists support are implicitly reinforced throughout *Rainbow Boys* (2001). T.C.J. Jason's construction as the quintessential unemotional man comes as a result of his internalized homophobia; he desperately seeks the attention of his alcoholic father: a physically violent and verbally abusive man who consistently calls him names like "Stupid, Dummy, Fairy-Boy, Pansy."[56] Although the novel distances itself from Jason's father (as readers, we are supposed to disagree with his viewpoint), it routinely implies that if his father were more affirmative of his "masculinity" as opposed to identifying him as "feminine," Jason may not have "turned out" gay.

In all three novels, Jason's self-perceived "femininity" leads him to work constantly to embody "masculine" characteristics (i.e., he routinely wills himself not to cry, but if he must, he does so alone and privately; he is aggressive and physically violent)—as he explicitly states in *Rainbow Road*, the teasing of his peers and his father's abuse led him to "work harder to prove he wasn't gay"[57] by acting more "masculine."[58] Throughout *Rainbow Boys*, the "masculine" is routinely privileged—at even a seemingly superficial level, the "Tragic Closet Jock" Jason gets both the first and last chapter of the book, giving him both the first and last word and allowing him more opportunity for his voice to be heard (as he is given an extra chapter). When he begins seriously questioning his sexual identity, Jason continues to date his girlfriend Debra, but envisions Kyle while she is performing oral sex on him. Warren J. Blumenfeld writes in *Homophobia: How We All Pay the Price*, "Males are encouraged to be independent, competitive, goal oriented, and unemotional, to value physical courage and toughness. Females, on the other hand, are taught to be nurturing, emotional, sensitive, expressive, to be caretakers of others while disregarding their own needs."[59] If Jason is what Blumenfeld characterizes as traditionally "male," Debra fits the "female" counterpart as the sensitive nurturer who puts her own needs second to those of her boyfriend. The counterpart to the Tragic Closet Jock Jason is also played by co-protagonist Kyle in a role I've come to think of as the S.U.D.: the "Sympathetic, Understanding Doormat" who facilitates the jock's process of "self-discovery" and, in spite of bad treatment, is always willing to go back to him with little (if any) resistance.

Like the Tragic Closet Jock, the Sympathetic, Understanding Doormat Kyle is also an athlete, but the series makes clear that being a swim team star is not in the same class as the jocks who play contact sports like basketball. The sports played by "masculine" athletes (like Jason) and that carry positions of social privilege are exclusionary of those who don't identify as male, while sports like the swim team on which "feminine" Kyle participates are coeducational. Unlike the Tragic

Closet Jock, S.U.D. Kyle has "known he was different"[60] since he was little, however, he is not "Queer and Proud" as he is not "out of the closet" to everyone around him. The S.U.D. embodies many of the same stereotypical and troublesome characteristics traditionally assigned in literature to females: he is emotional, sensitive, and willing to put his own needs secondary to those of the dominant male, in this case, the T.C.J. In *Rainbow Boys*, Kyle fantasizes about Jason throughout the book and is eventually kissed by him—and then pushed away and rejected. He then loses his virginity to Jason—and is pushed away again.

The T.C.J. and S.U.D. tropes are not new. Sanchez recognizes (as evident in the fact he himself identifies Jason as the "Tragic Closet Jock" in *Rainbow Boys*) that these novels rely upon previously established gay-affirmative didacticism. In an interview with teenreads.com, he says, "I tried to depict characters that both embraced and challenged stereotypes of what gay teens are like."[61] While his acknowledgment is admirable, I believe that it comes at a tremendous cost in terms of the negative implications inherent in these depictions. In fact, I would suggest that his reliance on these constructions may actually work against the very goals he hopes to achieve: as Rosalinda B. Barrera, Olga Liguori, and Loretta Salas write, "Authenticity of content and images in children's literature is essential because inauthentic representation subverts the very cultural awareness and understanding that such literature can build."[62]

Although the surface construction of the relationship between the T.C.J. and the S.U.D. might feel new to readers (as they are both male), underneath, these are characters that have repeatedly appeared in literature and popular culture: the story of the athletic dream guy who eventually falls for the intelligent, self-conscious, introverted wallflower. As the pair walk to Jason's house to study,

> Every once in a while he glanced over at Kyle. He had never really taken a good look at him before. His eyes were hazel, and his wire-frame glasses gave him a teddy-bear face. His hair was a honey color and hung down in bangs from beneath his cap. His shoulders were broad for such a thin guy. He remembered Kyle telling him he was on the swim team. He had a body like a swimmer—long, firm, and lean.[63]

In a scene reminiscent of countless love stories, Jason looks beyond Kyle's glasses and realizes that there may be more to this guy than he originally thought: he notices his eyes—and the rest of him—for what feels like the very first time.

Early in *Rainbow High*, Kyle encourages T.C.J. Jason to come out of the closet publicly because "if you come out now, you'd be, I don't know, like, a role model—someone people would look up to."[64] After talking with his coach[65] and the school principal, Jason decides not to reveal his homosexuality because it might "screw up our chances for the [state] championship."[66] However, upon rescuing Nelson from a scuffle with one of his bully teammates in the cafeteria, Jason accidentally alludes to his own sexual identity, and it is decided that the subject can no longer be avoided. Jason comes out to his teammates, who are (to Sanchez's credit) generally accepting and supportive, and this sets in motion a series of events in which Jason is heteronormatively hailed as a hero and a role model by the media, his peers, and superiors. He is, for example, flocked by freshmen girls who yearn to take him shopping and want his opinion as to which boy band members are more attractive.

Most importantly, his status as "jock" trumps his identity as gay, and his popularity remains unquestioned: even the most homophobic students still embrace and accept him. When it is eventually revealed that Kyle and Jason are in a relationship together, "feminine" Kyle (and interestingly Jason's ex-girlfriend) becomes the focus of the verbal harassment of his peers, while Jason has positive interactions with those around him. It isn't long before Jason gets "notes shoved through the slats of my locker from people telling me I've given *them* courage"[67] and members of the local media decide to interview him as an "excellent role model"[68] for young people everywhere. Although he initially claims he is uncomfortable serving as a role model, Jason accepts this position after Kyle, his ex-girlfriend Debra, his coach, his school principal, the local media, co-protagonist (and sometimes adversary) Nelson, the faculty head of the high school's gay-straight alliance, and even complete strangers applaud "his courage for coming out."[69]

In *Rainbow High*, Jason continues to exemplify stereotypes of the "masculine" male by acting with little regard to those around him—particularly S.U.D. Kyle. As an example, he denies having a boyfriend in a television interview filmed in front of an audience of his peers. When Kyle (who was present at the interview) becomes upset, Jason wonders "since when had they become 'boyfriends.' They'd never discussed it. True, they'd had sex. But that just sort of happened . . . but did that make them *boyfriends*?"[70] In fact, "He'd never thought of Kyle and him as 'dating.'"[71] Near the end of the second novel, Jason publicly acknowledges Kyle as his boyfriend: brazenly putting his arm around him and kissing him in front of strangers and in the presence of television reporters and their cameras. As it is written, however, after the school wins the state basketball championship, the acknowledgment of Kyle comes not because Jason recognizes the role Kyle plays in his life or the importance of acknowledging his partner in meaningful, legitimizing ways, but because "high with excitement, Jason didn't think twice"[72] about answering the reporters when they ask if Kyle is his boyfriend.

It also seems the S.U.D. Kyle remains unchanged since he was first presented in *Rainbow Boys*, as he spends the bulk of *Rainbow High* swooning "at the sound of the low, husky voice"[73] of the Tragic Closet Jock. Kyle remains unfailingly self-sacrificing—buying Jason gifts and giving up his own material possessions to ensure Jason is protected and comfortable. He compromises his own emotional well-being while spending most of the book dreaming of "the image of Jason in his satin uniform, arms pumping."[74]

Kyle recognizes that his devotion to the T.C.J. forces him to silence his own voice, but resigns himself to the fact that must remain hidden even though "it was killing him to sit by invisible."[75] The dedicated "feminine" counterpart to the "masculine" jock, Kyle pines for his inattentive boyfriend:

> Kyle hugged a cushion to his chest and for the millionth time watched Jason appear on the screen. The lush curly hair, imploring brown eyes, and breathtaking lips made him look like the star of some TV teen drama. Even though Kyle wanted to hurl the remote at the tube each time Jason told the reporter he didn't have a boyfriend, he couldn't stop watching and rewatching. . . . He fell asleep on the couch, dreaming of the dark-eyed boy on the TV screen.[76]

Harboring insecurity about dating a boy who used to like girls, the S.U.D. wonders if he can really trust Jason to remain faithful if they don't attend the same college, and he begins to believe that he may have to sacrifice his own future for the sake of maintaining his relationship.

When Kyle learns he has been accepted to Princeton University's math program, he's already made plans to attend Tech to be near his boyfriend and quickly convinces himself that he and Jason "absolutely *had* to go to Tech. Once away from home, there was no way his parents—or anyone—could keep Jason and him apart."[77] Even though "masculine" Jason only "vaguely recalled"[78] his boyfriend even applying to Princeton, "feminine" Kyle suggests that he and Jason should not only attend Tech together, but if Jason instead attends community college, Kyle should do the same with the hope that the pair could transfer to Tech during their junior year (Kyle would thus be giving up his dream of attending Princeton for community college). While debating his options, S.U.D. Kyle hides his acceptance letter to Princeton "between the pages of his yearbook, opposite his favorite photo of Jason, at last year's basketball championships," and, at the height of his internal conflict, he removes the acceptance letter as "his gaze shifted back and forth between the letter and Jason's photo. How could he leave Jason? And how could he pass up Princeton?"[79]

Readers who continue through the series will find the suggestion of growth in these characters and their relationship in the final installment of the trilogy. However, in *Rainbow Road,* Jason continues to be depicted as stereotypically "masculine": practical, immature, grumbling, vulgar, and insatiable. Although he vacillates between identifying himself as "bisexual" and "gay,"[80] Jason's "masculinity" actually distances him from the other homosexuals in the book. On the road trip, he is happy to be able to take a break from Kyle and Nelson and play basketball with a group of strangers because "it felt great to be around *normal* guys again, who played by clear, established rules; guys who looked and acted like guys were supposed to look and act,"[81] and heteronormativity is reinforced when homosexual characters who aren't "masculine" are cast as deviants and outcasts.

In *Rainbow Road,* another stereotype of the "masculine" male is reinforced as Jason's eye consistently wanders outside of his current relationship. In a nightclub, he dances with a young woman he senses is attracted to him and flirts with her until "next thing he knew, her moist lips were reaching up and resting on his."[82] After attempting to hide the situation by lying about what happened, Jason eventually comes clean, and, although he "regretted having *let* [the young woman] kiss him" (distancing himself from responsibility), he doesn't understand why Kyle is upset. Jason is convinced that "Kyle was being unfair for not giving him more credit for walking away" from the situation.[83] Shortly after kissing this young woman, Jason begins to recognize that he is also sexually attracted to Kyle's best friend. He watches Nelson as he runs naked through an open field and realizes "he'd never really paid attention to Nelson's body before. Now, seeing him naked, he couldn't help notice. The guy actually had quite a nice little body."[84]

On the opening page of *Rainbow Road*, S.U.D. Kyle awakens from a sexual dream about Jason, whose "musky athletic scent"[85] and "tanned skin"[86] continue to intoxicate him throughout the novel. In this install-ment, "feminine" Kyle embodies the stereotypical myth that females are more mature than males as he acts as caregiver, protector, and the "responsible one" in the relationship (i.e., holding onto Jason's money for him, ironing his clothing, and setting his alarm), even though he rec-ognizes how it often negatively impacts him. As he tells Jason, "Part of the risk of being responsible [is that] sometimes you get hurt."[87]

Frequently (and ultimately detrimentally) ignoring his protective instincts, "feminine" Kyle is depicted as insecure for having concerns about his boyfriend's drinking and harboring suspicions about Jason's fidelity. Even co-protagonist Nelson believes Jason's indiscretions should be expected (and accepted) as an inevitable result of his "mas-culinity." He tells Kyle, "I think you're overreacting. You knew Jason liked girls when you met him. Just because he hit on some blondie doesn't mean he's dumping you."[88]

Toward the end of *Rainbow Road*, there is a dramatic shift in these two characters as Kyle begins rethinking his relationship with the T.C.J. He notes, "It felt like Jason had changed. Every day he was revealing sides of himself that Kyle had never realized were there. Although Kyle had known Jason was bi, impulsive, stubborn, and had a trigger temper, he'd never been confronted with all of who Jason was on such a daily basis."[89] Furthermore, he becomes aware of the fact that "I got caught up in this image of you . . . I know it sounds dorky, but it's like you were some sort of god . . . I felt like the luckiest guy on earth . . . I guess I kind of put you on a pedestal."[90] Jason, too, recognizes that "he was a better person because of Kyle. If it weren't for Kyle, he might never have come out to his parents or worked up the courage to keep going to the school's Gay-Straight Alliance, or come out to his coach and his team. Most im-portantly, he might never have accepted himself."[91]

Unfortunately, although these milestone recognitions indicate that these characters have grown and have a new understanding of themselves and an appreciation for one another, with approximately fifty pages remaining in the final installment of the series, they do little to counter the portrayals perpetuated across the more than 650 previous pages of text (obviously, if one fails to read past the first novel, they have no impact at all), especially when Kyle continues to "beam at [Jason] even more admiringly"[92] and the novel ends with the line: "Every time Jason smiled at him, Kyle couldn't help seeing a lifetime ahead."[93]

The *Queer* and *Proud* Homosexual as Sexually Insatiable Target

Unlike many gay young adult novels that employ the T.C.J. and the S.U.D., there is a third young man depicted in *Rainbow Boys* in the character of Nelson. While both Jason and Kyle eventually proclaim they are proud of their sexual identity,[94] it is only the character of Nelson who is widely held up as a self-aware and (to quote Michael Cart and Christine A. Jenkins) "queer and proud"[95] homosexual who is presumably supposed to show gay young adult males what it means and looks like to be openly and comfortably gay.

It should be reemphasized here that the argument I present is not intended to deny the existence of homosexual males with characteristics similar to Nelson and certainly shouldn't be read as implicitly reinforcing the ideas of revisionist pychoanalysts that "the healthy homosexual is one who . . . acts masculine."[96] The purpose of this critique is simply to raise questions about the implications inherent in hailing the depiction of Nelson as the sole embodiment of being "queer and proud" because it seems that doing so implies for readers that this is the only way one can be proudly and comfortably gay.

Following the work of Foucault, in *Gender Trouble: Feminism and the Subversion of Identity*, Judith Butler advocates "subversive" performances, such as drag shows, as they reveal the imitative structure and contingency of the (repeated) performances that construct "gender." She argues they "destabilize the very distinctions between the natural and the artificial, depth and surface, inner and outer through which discourse about genders almost always operates . . . gay and lesbian cultures often thematize 'the natural' in parodic contexts which bring into relief the performative construction of an original and true sex."[97]

Throughout the series, Nelson seems to make moves toward destabilizing notions of gender, and in some ways he certainly appears to be "queer and proud." He routinely refers to male characters as "she," "girl," and "queen" and calls himself a "diva," and at the end of *Rainbow High,* he tries on an evening gown at a postprom party. In *Rainbow Road,* he says that he "and the other femmy guys at youth group had often called each other 'girl' or 'girlfriend,' as if to champion their queenyness to the world. But . . . Nelson had never seriously desired to become a *real* girl."[98] In another scene, he shaves his legs and dresses in drag, and his "image in the mirror, with a boy's body and a girl's face, looked oddly strong and soft, vulnerable and confident" and he is "enchanted by his evolving female self."[99] Once fully transformed, he opens his eyes and "at first the girl in the mirror startled him. Then she mesmerized him. It was hard to believe she *was* him. He slowly raised a hand and the image followed. He really was her . . . if he'd been born female."[100]

However, in her essay "Imitation and Gender Insubordination," Butler warns, "Drag is not the putting on of a gender that belongs properly to some other group, i.e. an act of *ex*propriation or *ap*propriation that assumes that gender is the rightful property of sex, that 'masculine' belongs to 'male' and 'feminine' belongs to 'female.'"[101] While on the surface it may seem as if Nelson is an agent of "resignification," Butler helps us realize that in actuality, these depictions miss the ironic destabilization of gender toward which queer cultures work—the "realistic" feel that readers get from the series comes from the familiar play between "masculine" and "feminine" counterparts and reiterates (not subverts) these gender stereotypes and misconceptions about sexuality. It is because these depictions of gay men are played so "straight" (pun intended) that the books feel so inauthentic.

While he may initially seem to fit the neo-Gramscian notion of counterhegemony, working against legitimized notions of the "masculine" male, Nelson "puts on" a gender properly "belonging" to the "female" by embodying what are traditionally thought of as "feminine" qualities. In doing so, stereotypes of women are reinforced, alongside the misconception that in homosexual relationships there is one participant who plays the role of a sexually inverted "female."[102] Nelson routinely bats his eyes, pouts, cajoles physical compliments from his friends, and is overly dramatic: (as two examples) placing the back of his hand against his forehead or screeching when he finds the roots of his hair are starting to show.

What I hope to suggest here is that there is little about Nelson that reflects an image of being "proud" of who he is: he is portrayed as someone with deep-rooted self-hatred, frequently saying things like, "It's not easy being me. Imagine what I have to put up with twenty-four/seven. At least you can get away from me occasionally."[103] In the first chapter that is told from his perspective, Nelson appears chain-smoking cigarettes while he gets his hair restyled and dyed. Throughout the story, his loathing for his body eventually leads him from pinching his flesh to estimate body fat to bulimia and abusing diet pills in an attempt to slim down even though those around him insist to him that he is slender.

While many teen males are preoccupied with sex, "Queer and Proud" Nelson reinforces the portrayal that Michael S. Kimmel describes simply as "gay men as sexually insatiable";[104] virtually every scene in which he is involved deals in some way with the fact that he is "horny . . . pretty much 24/7."[105] In *Rainbow Boys*, Nelson attempts to have sex with Kyle and nearly has sex at a party with a college-aged man named Blake. While the pair shares a bottle of rum in his car, Blake is surprised to learn that Nelson is still in high school, but kisses him and "laid a hand behind Nelson's neck, gently directing his head down. A rich, musky smell wafted up."[106] Taking on the stance traditionally and stereotypically embodied by female characters, through the swirl of alcohol and lust, Nelson thinks they should use a condom, but doesn't voice his concerns as he worries he will insult "masculine" Blake. Nelson's hesitation to perform oral sex leads Blake to ask if he is a virgin—a fact Nelson tries to deny: "If he said yes, Blake might never want to have sex with him."[107] Eventually, Nelson confesses (and apologizes) that he is a virgin. Blake responds, "It's not your fault" before being overcome with a sudden wave of morality and deciding, "Look, we never should've done this. You're not even eighteen, are you?"[108] Despite Nelson's protestations, the pair does not engage in sexual activity: Blake tells him that his first time should be with someone special.

The situation takes a dramatic turn when Blake rests "a brotherly hand on Nelson's shoulder,"[109] but this sudden and complete repositioning of Blake feels unrealistic. Blake is clearly experienced in sexual activity—it is even obvious that he's well versed in the perils inherent in discreetly "hooking up" in a car (i.e., warning Nelson to avoid the horn so that it doesn't sound and draw attention from nearby partygoers)—and his knowledge that Nelson is a senior in high school does not prevent him from sharing a bottle of rum and soliciting oral sex from someone he strongly suspects is under the age of eighteen (until he discovers the young man is a virgin).

After several failed attempts to have sex with men closer to his own age, Nelson ultimately becomes seduced by an older online predator: the only portrayal of an adult gay male beyond "traditional" high school and undergraduate college-age men that we see in the novel. This character provides YA readers the only glimpse into what their lives as an adult gay male can be like. Nelson agrees to meet Brick, screen name "HotLove69"[110] at a Starbucks after chatting with him online. The pair immediately heads to Brick's quintessential predatory lair (think track lighting, glowing potted palms, a fancy stereo system, and chrome-framed prints of men in underwear) where he gives alcohol to Nelson, who he thinks is eighteen (so again, here is an adult gay male attempting to intoxicate and seduce a minor) before the pair moves into Brick's bedroom.

Brick quickly undresses Nelson and "slid on top of him, as if wanting more of him, like he was somehow trying to get inside him."[111] Nelson is unsure of Brick's intentions, but silences his urge to reveal his virgin status or request the use of protection because "if he did say something, Brick might reject him, the same as Blake, the same as Kyle. A wave of despair swept over Nelson, until it seemed he was totally lost to himself."[112] Here we have the "Queer and Proud" homosexual embodying the negative, stereotypically "feminine" stance of wishing for the use of protection during sexual activity and the subsequent abandonment of that protective instinct in order not to risk rejection and to satisfy the "masculine" male: in this case, the motorcycle-riding, muscular "HotLove69" Brick. He gives into his lust, and the two have sex, and "then just as quickly, it was over. Brick lay on top of him, head cradled in Nelson's shoulder, his breath puffing lightly across Nelson's chest. Nelson looked down at the soft blond hair and broad shoulders of the man he'd let inside of him. He'd never felt anything so incredible in his life."[113]

There is a disproportionate amount of risk involved here: Brick is the experienced male with nothing to lose and Nelson is the virgin who has everything to lose—which I suggest makes it all the more important that he stick up for himself. Nelson is not only preyed upon by Brick, he is objectified by this man who (according to the text) "depantsed" him,[114] and yet he feels romantic as he holds Brick in his arms, lovingly noticing his broad shoulders and soft blond hair as readers are told that Nelson "never felt anything so incredible in his life."[115] After this depiction of first-time anal sex, Nelson becomes fearful that he may have contracted the AIDS virus. This issue is never resolved, and at the end of *Rainbow Boys*, the reader is left with the impression that Nelson probably does have AIDS: a cautionary example for gay adolescent male readers.

If Nelson is supposed to operate as a reader's only example of what it means (and looks like) to be "Queer and Proud," it is troubling that he exists only to satisfy the needs of the "masculine" male and that he remains virtually static throughout most of the entire series: he never learns from his experiences or thinks before he acts. Of all the protagonists, it feels most important that we see him grow, and it is unfortunate that he changes little across the three books.

Although his bulimia is briefly mentioned in *Rainbow Road*, the bulk of the text in the last two novels involving Nelson revolves solely around his depiction as sexually insatiable. In *Rainbow High*, he dates Jeremy, an HIV-positive young man who serves as educator for Nelson (and readers) throughout the novel. His sexual desire for Kyle reemerges as a complication in the final installment of the trilogy: for example, Nelson notes that "he'd seen Kyle in his underwear before, but had always been curious to take things to the next level,"[116] and at one point, "Nelson gazed up into Kyle's eyes, wanting more than anything to kiss those cute thin lips."[117]

New in *Rainbow Road* is Nelson's sexual interest in Jason. At one point, he and Jason end up in a campground shower room together, and Nelson has to "fight the urge to turn and gape" at Jason's "tight pecs and ripped abs." He watches as Jason steps into a shower stall and eventually gets a quick look at his "glistening butt" before reprimanding himself for checking out his best friend's boyfriend.[118] In another scene, Nelson lies in the tent next to a sleeping Jason and it is revealed that "he'd always thought Jason's thick eyebrows were sexy, and he loved the olive color of his skin. His shoulders stuck out of the sleeping bag, broad and muscled. His lips looked so tender and inviting."[119]

It isn't only Kyle and Jason for whom Nelson harbors desire: from (as a few examples) snapping photos of an "adorable" park ranger and referring to him as "totally lickable"[120] and calling the "beefy registration guy reading a college textbook" at a campground "delicious"[121] to trying to hook up with a "total lust-magnet"[122] he meets at a dance club,

Nelson continues to live on the edge. When the "rainbow boys" visit the civil rights museum, Kyle tells Jason and Nelson (who are largely unaware of the Civil Rights Movement) the story of Rosa Parks, and Jason wonders why the museum doesn't mention the hatred toward GLBTQ people. Nelson suggests staging a "kiss-in" in order to bring attention to the issue, implying he knows something of the history of queer activism, but also reemphasizing his preoccupation with sexual acts.

Eventually, Nelson does meet a young man named Manny, a deus ex machina with similarly dyed hair and "teeth so beautifully white against his cinnamon-colored skin that it made Nelson wonder, *Why are you torturing me like this?*"[123] The two immediately fall for one another and quickly make love "as if discovering places never before experienced . . . ebbing and flowing, their ardor peaked and waned, as they kissed and touched, exploring nooks and crannies, tearing open condoms, entering one another, feeling closer than ever, and then lying quietly together, hearing only their heartbeats."[124] This connection is so powerful for Nelson that he decides to stay in Los Angeles to see where this relationship with Manny may lead.

It should be acknowledged that to Nelson's credit, he is the one character in the series who questions Jason's celebrity status upon coming out. In fact, starting in *Rainbow High*, Nelson takes issue with how Jason's standing as school jock privileges him; asking, "Why did everyone keep making such a big whoop about [Jason]? As if he was the first high school student to ever come out? So what if he was a sports champ? Did that make him superior?"[125] Unfortunately for Nelson (and for readers), no one examines this issue with him or confronts the conversation. In fact, when Nelson tells his mother that "Jason got invited to give a speech at the ceremony, since he's a jock," she adds to the sense of injustice by responding, "I should invite him to come speak to my PFLAG group"[126]—an invitation that she hasn't extended to her son.

In spite of his heightened awareness, it seems that in reality, Nelson too accepts Jason's conduct on account of his "masculine" status. As one example, he tells Kyle he's overreacting to Jason's infidelity because he knew Jason "liked girls when you met him."[127] But more revealing is the moment when Jason (in a moment of panic) attempts to convince Nelson to deliver his speech at the gay and lesbian high school on his behalf because "you're the one they should've invited."[128]

Although thrilled to have someone echo his own thinking, Nelson tells Jason, "Maybe you'll make a huge fool of yourself, but if that's what it takes for you to accept that *a lot of us look up to you*—then that's what you've got to do,"[129] suggesting that despite what he may say to the contrary, he too looks up to the T.C.J. and sets him apart from (and above) other GLBTQ young people: Even in Nelson's eyes, the T.C.J.'s "masculinity" makes him a hero and a role model.

As troubling these individual depictions of the Tragic Closet Jock, the Sympathetic, Understanding Doormat, and the "Queer and Proud" homosexual may ultimately be,[130] in the end, the series does more than just look at the story of these three boys. It moves into larger issues of gay culture through the presentation of these lives within the context of an American high school.

Resilience, Not Acceptance: Heteronormativity and Homophobia

In a series of novels that looks at three gay boys who have to navigate the tricky terrain of high school culture, predictably, things don't go easy for them. As gay adolescent "problem novels," we may expect these books to didactically work against homophobic discourse. Problem novels as a genre rely upon intrusions that are clearly written to educate and inform readers. Roberta Seelinger Trites suggests such interruptions tend to "manipulat[e] the adolescent reader"[131] toward particular ways of thinking. But I hope to suggest here that, just as the protagonists are depicted in a heteronormative binary, normativity and homophobia are also reinforced within the larger world of the novel.

Beginning with *Rainbow Boys*, readers are told that Nelson has been bullied, mocked, and tormented since middle school and is routinely told by those in positions of power that he has to learn to control his temper and put up with the abuse. When on one occasion he answers the phone and is greeted with "Hey, fag . . . Want to suck my dick?" we read, "Such calls were too commonplace to faze him."[132] Having learned to be "tough" in the face of homophobic abuse, Nelson teaches Kyle that he must be ready to defend himself (notably through physical violence) against intolerant individuals. "What good would it do?" an unconvinced Kyle asks, "For every [bully like] Jack Ransom, there's ten more. He's not the problem, homophobia's the problem."[133] On one level, this can be read as a rather contrived, predictable declaration against homophobia, but on another, it's a construction reemphasizing that because it's physically dangerous to be gay (or perceived as gay), homosexual teens need to toughen up and become resilient to intolerance. The "resilience, not acceptance" theme is further reinforced at the end of the first novel when the boys succeed in establishing a gay-straight alliance in their high school and the students who want to attend the meeting need to walk past their whispering, jeering peers.

Throughout the series, Nelson continues to be fodder for bullying and maltreatment by nearly all heterosexual characters (i.e., Kyle's father blames Nelson—not Jason or Kyle himself—when Kyle insists that he doesn't want to attend Princeton), but the focus of much of the intolerance in *Rainbow High* falls on Kyle. When a young man on his swim team expresses concern that Kyle is gay, the coach accepts Kyle's offer to shower when he returns home as opposed to in the locker room with the rest of the players. Later, when the team attends a meet requiring an overnight stay, none of the young men wants to share a hotel room with Kyle because, as one student puts it, "I'm not sleeping in the same room with no fag."[134] The coach decides that homosexual Kyle should be isolated: he will sleep by himself in her hotel room while she shares a room with some of the girls. When this arrangement leads to increased derision, instead of confronting the students who ridicule Kyle and call him a "fag" in her presence, the coach "turned to Kyle, her eyes burning with anger. 'I've had enough, Kyle. You brought this on yourself. If you hadn't started this whole coming out business, none of this would've happened.'"[135] Later, when Kyle and his father meet with the swim coach, for the first time in the series (226 pages into the middle novel) it is suggested that heterosexuals in society should adjust their misconceptions of gay people. Kyle's father says, "You're their coach. It's up to you to set the rules. But unless my son is doing something wrong, then maybe those boys and their parents are the ones who need to alter *their* behavior."[136] While we can celebrate this affirmative moment, it is still overshadowed by the predominant message across all three books that the world remains a dangerous and scary place for homosexual teens.

As the boys embark on their road trip in *Rainbow Road,* the world becomes an even more intolerant and frightening place as the protagonists are regularly confronted with prejudice. At one stop, they encounter a bus marked "FIRST EVANGELICAL CHURCH"[137] where a woman tells Nelson she has a problem with "people like you" and Jason suggests that if he didn't "dress so weird," Nelson wouldn't encounter such blatant homophobia.[138] At a gas station, they encounter two men driving a pickup truck sporting a "TERRORIST HUNTER'S PERMIT—WE NEVER FORGET" bumper sticker on its rear.[139] One man wears a cowboy hat, while the other wears a "wifebeater tank top, boots, and jeans" and spits chewing tobacco.[140] After Nelson (who is sexually attracted to one of the men) announces to the pair that the rainbow bumper sticker on his car indicates he (and by association, Jason and Kyle) is gay, the men get in their truck and menacingly attempt to force the boys' car off the road by recklessly driving and throwing beer cans at their windshield. A high-speed chase ensues on narrow, winding mountain roads before the men in the pickup truck lose control of their truck and crash.

While camping at the "Fam-E-Lee Values Campground,"[141] they meet a very young boy with a pronounced lisp named Esau. His father scoffs that Esau is "sweet like a girl! He'd better start acting like a man or he's going to get his ass kicked."[142] The father is overhead further deriding his son: "Oh, stop sounding like a girl . . . In fact, I think you *are* a girl. They must've made a mistake at the hospital. Now shut up and say your prayers. I don't want to look at you anymore."[143] Nelson declares that, regardless of how the boy will identify sexually, "with that lisp and those curls, he's going to get called queer anyway. That's what's wrong with our society—if you're in any way different, you get clobbered."[144] Nelson and Esau eventually do a facial mask together as Nelson tells him, "Life's going to get rough sometimes . . . people will call you names and try to hurt you, they'll tell you what to feel, what to think. They'll say you're a mistake. But you're not."[145] He continues, "It's okay to be you—exactly who you are, no matter what anyone says. Believe in yourself. Trust your heart. Be true to who you are."[146] A rather didactic moment, this sudden compassion and thoughtfulness is so uncharacteristic of Nelson that one cannot help but imagine author Sanchez stepping into the story and speaking directly to his reader.

Dramatically, Esau's father catches the pair together and refers to Nelson as a "faggot."[147] Although Nelson tries to reason with the father, it is only threats of physical violence from Jason (who mostly avoids the abuse of intolerant heterosexuals)[148] that convinces the man to back down. Perpetuating the idea that gays must often show resilience to injustice through physical violence, Jason (who probably sees parallels between the paternal "feminizing" of this young boy and his personal experience) tells Esau, "You grow up big and strong . . . when your day comes, you smack your dad, good and solid."[149]

In these novels, it seems gay people can only find solace from intolerance by isolating themselves from heterosexuals. In *Rainbow Road*, the boys stay the night at a "sanctuary for gay and lesbian people"[150] where "no one hassled you for being crazily queer, a place where you could totally be yourself."[151] People dress in outlandish outfits (or nothing at all), eat "roasted tofu, apple squash, apple-raisin salad, and grapes,"[152] and speak about "what's in your heart,"[153] content to be an isolated assemblage of deviant outcasts. Building on the work of Byrne R. S. Fone, Allan A. Cuseo refers to novels employing such sanctuaries as "Arcadian." He suggests that "the roots of Arcadia lie in pastoral settings, but today the homosexual community has embraced the Arcadian ideal to mean any setting which serves as a hermitage or sanctuary away from the disapproving heterosexual world . . . Arcadia represents the special place needed for the homosexual character(s) to be apart from a homophobic mainstream."[154]

The only other place we see gay people "being allowed" to be themselves in self-identifying ways is at the Los Angeles high school for gay and lesbian students. After Jason's speech, he is bombarded by students "with green hair and purple hair, with earrings and nose rings, kids he wasn't sure were boys or girls—all excited and hyper and giggling, as kids were meant to be, in a school where they could be themselves without being called names or fearing they'd get pounded."[155] The fact that Jason (himself only a couple of months out of high school) takes on this adult perspective and refers to these students as "kids" as he looks at their situation with such insightfulness suggests this is another statement directly from the author to his imagined readers, with implicit messages not only about where it is safe to be homosexual, but who can be (and what it means and how it looks to be) gay.

"When I Get It": AIDS as a Gay Inevitability

In his essay "Reading and Writing 'Immunity': Children and the Anti-Body," Robert McRuer argues that "the liberal reinscription of AIDS from the late 1980s on, as 'everyone's disease' ironically functions within the text of children's literature—as it has elsewhere—to make gay men living with AIDS invisible. . . . The discursive shift to understanding

AIDS as everyone's disease justifies, or rationalizes, the proscription of gay male representation in children's literature."[156] As if in response to this assessment, much of the *Rainbow Boys* series has been devoted to providing for its readers a source of education about the disease.

After Nelson's cautionary example in the first novel, his HIV test in *Rainbow High* provides an opportunity to make explicit the process of HIV testing (as well as to clarify how the virus is spread) through a doctor's lecture on the importance of advocating for safe sex or abstaining if your partner refuses to use protection. Later, next to his dinner plate, Nelson's mother leaves a newspaper clipping that reads: "HALF OF ALL NEW AMERICAN HIV INFECTIONS OCCUR IN YOUNG PEOPLE AGES 13–24,"[157] and, when he meets many of Jeremy's HIV-positive friends, Nelson's surprised that "none of the guys looked positive."[158]

In his 1988 book, *Policing Desire: Pornography, AIDS, and the Media*, Simon Watney claims, "From very early on in the history of the epidemic, AIDS has been mobilised to a prior agenda of issues concerning the kind of society we wish to inhabit . . . Aids is effectively being used as a pretext throughout the West to 'justify' calls for increasing legislation and regulation of those who are considered to be socially unacceptable."[159] He identifies the media's homophobic construction of AIDS as a gay disease (and subsequently those with AIDS as "the polluting person") as being implicitly suggestive of a highly problematic depiction of a "pollutive homosexual." Although Sanchez undoubtedly has the best intentions in attempting to educate young adult readers about the virus, it feels as if gay men are reduced to a stereotype through the equating of being gay with having AIDS. While there are examples of this throughout the series, this is particularly evident in the first novel: including the moment when Kyle comes out to his parents and his father immediately says, "There's one other question I need to ask, son. Since you brought all this up. Is there anything else we should know? About your health?"[160] and Kyle instinctively recognizes that his father is referring to HIV, but also believes that he had no reason "to worry about that *yet*."[161]

Although Kyle briefly worries about the fact that Jason and his ex-girlfriend Debra engaged in unprotected sex after Debra began taking birth control pills, AIDS remains a gay disease in *Rainbow High*. Jason's ex-girlfriend tells him she's "afraid something's going to happen to you"[162] now that he's self-identified as homosexual, and she identifies that "something" as being the contraction of the AIDS virus. When the second novel begins, Nelson awaits the results of his HIV test and views the contraction of the virus as inevitable, not only accepting that "he was probably going to test positive,"[163] but when he doesn't, he indicates he actually wants to contract the virus from his HIV-positive boyfriend Jeremy so he "wouldn't worry all the time about *when* I'm going to get it."[164] While readers might expect Jeremy (the character constructed as teacher) to educate Nelson that not all gay men contract HIV, he instead reminisces about when he learned he had contracted the virus: "I felt this awesome sense of relief. At least I didn't have to worry anymore if I was going to get it. . . . But take my word for it, the worrying doesn't stop. You just trade the old worries for the new ones."[165]

In contrast, with the exception of a few tangential statements, the third novel *Rainbow Road* contains virtually no reference to AIDS. Early in the novel, Nelson notes that "he was dating an HIV-positive guy,"[166] and later Jeremy makes a cameo appearance, and it is written that "Jeremy was HIV positive and Nelson was HIV negative. They'd both decided the difference in status was too big an issue between them."[167] Later, the issue of safe sex comes up when Kyle tells Nelson, "Even with a condom, he might've had some disease besides HIV. Every day the news reports some new drug-resistant STD,"[168] and at the end of the book, he asks Nelson, "Did you discuss HIV status, like you promised me?"[169] Despite this minimal content around HIV/AIDS, the book has been stamped with an HIV/AIDS awareness logo on its cover, something problematic (and heterosexist) unless every book dealing depicting teen sexual activity with any mention of HIV/AIDS is stamped with such a logo.

Depictions that Matter: The *Rainbow Boys* as Possibility

It may feel obvious that the depictions in children's literature matter. Lee Galda and Bernice Cullinan write, "Books have shaped our lives. They are . . . our means of thinking about what kind of people we are and what we value . . . Give children books and books will shape their lives."[170] One of the functions of books should be, as Michael Cart suggests, "bestow[ing] knowledge by showing us the commonalities of our human hearts."[171]

Like all children and young adults, when gay males pick up a piece of literature, they are looking for representations of themselves within the pages: who they could and should be now and what they can be like as adults. As David Levithan points out, "When we talk about the books in a library, we call them a *collection*. But to a young reader—especially a teen reader—it's really more of a *representation*."[172] He furthers the argument by Laura Apol cited at the beginning of this article when he claims that "a story doesn't have to always reflect reality; it can create reality as well."[173]

With statistics indicating that more than a third of high school students experience physical harassment and two-thirds experience verbal harassment on the basis of their sexual identity,[174] it is disheartening that 81.7 percent of students indicate they have never been taught about GLBTQ people in their school curriculum.[175] This makes the depictions in literature all the more important: gay young adults "look to literature hoping to find answers and positive role models."[176] Quality literature can provide much needed "validation for their feelings and hope for a bright future that involves self-affirmation."[177]

Rudine Sims Bishop writes that literature depicting underrepresented populations can "contribute to the development of self-esteem by holding up to its readers images of themselves,"[178] but warns that "no matter how innocent the story, and how well-meaning the author, it cannot be divorced from the sociocultural and political environment out of which it grew and the one into which it is released."[179] As Roberta Seelinger Trites notes, "All too often, gay YA literature parallels the cultural traditions of repression that have long stigmatized homosexuality."[180] Alex Sanchez himself has said that

> gay boys and girls, like any others, need positive images and affirming stories to help guide them through the often painful and confusing terrain of childhood and adolescence, to glimpse a world in which they're not bad or shameful but in which they're part of the good world. Books can provide a moral compass, a system of values, a way to understand feelings.[181]

It is utterly clear that Sanchez wants nothing more than to instill hope and inspire acceptance for future generations of gay youth and is doing his best to give voice to a population traditionally underrepresented in literature and misrepresented across popular culture and media. However, in reading the *Rainbow Boys* series, the repressive parallels against which Trites warns appear to be prevalent: from the heteronormatively "masculine" males (such as the Tragic Closet Jock and the adult Internet predator who takes advantage of young boys) and their "feminine" counterparts (like the Sympathetic, Understanding Doormat and "Queer and Proud" target of abuse and homophobia) to the depiction of a world that is a frightening and dangerous place for queer characters.

But ultimately, I would suggest it is the series' unrivaled popularity among homosexual and heterosexual teen and adult readers, critics, and scholars that makes it most problematic. The *Rainbow Boys* books are lauded because the content appears to be new, but as Kay Mussell argues of the structure of romance novels, "The shape of the narrative is predictable, even when the outline of a specific plot seems to represent an innovation."[182] It seems that readers refer to the novels as "honest" and "true" because these are stories with some heart, but they rely upon familiar tropes that have become recognizable as a result of their repeated portrayal across literature and media. This feels "realistic" because these are motifs we've seen again and again.

It could be that Sanchez's authorial decisions and depictions will provide avenues through which we as educators might explore with students many of the assumptions and constructions that undergird the novels. As Rudine Sims Bishop suggests, books with problematic constructions can often "[lend themselves] to a critical discussion of stereotyping and its consequences."[183] Vivian Yenika-Agbaw agrees: "The ability to question signs and meanings embedded in texts empowers readers with skills that enable them to construct new knowledge by subverting these signs and the dominant messages they are expected to retrieve."[184] With appropriate scaffolding, a close, critical study of the series could help students begin to identify how these pieces of contemporary realistic romance fiction depict homosexual and heterosexual people (and the context and content of their lives) in ways that rely upon and reinforce heteronormative and stereotypical constructions of gender and sexuality. Some of the difficulties explored in this article may actually supply ways to facilitate a discussion that challenges readers to reconsider previously unquestioned assumptions about how the world looks and operates—but it should be recognized that such work would require sustained, dedicated, and systematic readings of all three novels.

With this in mind, there may be books that can help facilitate these same conversations (in equally rich ways), while at the same time presenting more nuanced, "authentic," and wide-ranging depictions of GLBTQ people. As an example, I point to David Levithan's *Boy Meets Boy*. Although it may be more magical realism than contemporary realistic fiction, it is an innovative book that not only avoids didacticism, but is generally regarded to be of a higher literary quality. Although in some ways it too is normative, it's a novel that through its very construction forces readers who identify as heterosexual to step outside of the "world as we know it" in ways that reposition them as outsiders. It also provides opportunities to explore why this positioning may feel uncomfortable or unjust and subsequently to raise questions as to what it may suggest about how the "real world" positions GLBTQ people. At the same time, for insiders, the novel shows a world in which they belong as full members of society. This, coupled with the book's range of depictions of GLBTQ young adult characters from various backgrounds and identities (without the implication that the pages contain "one GLBTQ person of every flavor"), suggests for readers that there is no one way (or even three ways) to be "queer and proud."

Regardless of what we as educators end up "doing" with these novels, I once more want to caution against vilifying Alex Sanchez or the *Rainbow Boys* series by recognizing that the books have provided many gay young adults with a representation when few others (if any) were readily available to them. But it's important to remember that these aren't just depictions, these are possibilities. When these canonical texts are the only books depicting gay men used in classrooms and curriculum (or when only *Rainbow Boys* is used), they imply for readers that the only ways to "be" a gay male are to be a S.U.D., a T.C.J., or a "Queer and Proud" target. Michael Cart and Christine A. Jenkins write that GLBTQ literature "must continue to come of age *as literature*,"[185] and the ultimate goal of this analysis is merely to second that call by suggesting that the time has come to move beyond accepting any representation and begin looking for depictions that reflect for gay adolescent readers the *possibilities* of who they can become.

NOTES

1. I follow the lead of Michael Cart and Christine A. Jenkins and use the rubric "GLBTQ" as opposed to "LGBTQ" or other designations because it reflects "the fact that the human rights movement on behalf of GLBTQ people that began with the 1969 Stonewall Riots was originally referred to as the gay

rights or gay liberation movement." Michael Cart, and Christine A. Jenkins, *The Heart Has Its Reasons: Young Adult Literature with Gay/Lesbian/Queer Content, 1969–2004* (Lanham, MD: Scarecrow Press, 2006), xv.

2. http://www.alexsanchez.com.

3. A version of this argument was presented at the Seventh Biennial Modern Critical Approaches to Children's Literature conference hosted by Middle Tennessee State University on March 31, 2007. This essay would not have been possible without the generous and insightful feedback of Lawrence R. Sipe, Kenneth B. Kidd, Laura Apol, Janine Certo, Lynn Fendler, Suzanne Knezek, Jacqueline LaRose, the Children's Literature Team at Michigan State University, and two anonymous readers.

4. Laura Apol, "Taming and Ordeals: Depictions of Female and Male Coming of Age in the West in Turn-of-Century *Youth's Companion* Serials," *The Lion and the Unicorn* 24.1 (2000): 61.

5. Ibid., 76.

6. Violet J. Harris, "The Complexity of Debates about Multicultural Literature and Cultural Authenticity," in *Stories Matter: The Complexity of Cultural Authenticity in Children's Literature*, ed. Dana L. Fox and Kathy G. Short (Urbana, IL: National Council of Teachers of English, 2003), 121.

7. Judith Butler, *Gender Trouble: Feminism and the Subversion of Identity* (New York: Routledge, 1990), 22–23.

8. Judith Lorber, *Paradoxes of Gender* (New Haven: Yale University Press, 1995), 205.

9. The depictions of intolerant heterosexuals also seem to carry implications about who can be and what it looks like to be homophobic, but innumerable images exist to work against these generalizations. For readers, this series may be the only representation of GLBTQ people they have seen, which means these books carry with them a tremendous amount of power.

10. Allan A. Cuseo, *Homosexual Characters in YA Novels: A Literary Analysis 1969–1982* (Lanham, MD: Scarecrow Press, 1992), 55.

11. John D. Anderson, "School Climate for Gay and Lesbian Students and Staff Members," *Phi Delta Kappan* 76.2 (1994): 154.

12. Butler, *Gender Trouble,* 111.

13. Kathy G. Short and Dana L. Fox, "The Complexity of Cultural Authenticity in Children's Literature: Why the Debates Really Matter," in *Stories Matter: The Complexity of Cultural Authenticity in Children's Literature,* ed. Dana L. Fox and Kathy G. Short (Urbana, IL: National Council of Teachers of English, 2003), 20.

14. Ibid., 21.

15. Weimin Mo and Wenju Shen, "Accuracy Is Not Enough: The Role of Cultural Values in Authenticity of Picture Books," in Fox and Short, *Stories Matter,* 206.

16. By November 2001, *Rainbow Boys* had the distinction of being Amazon.com's top-selling book.

17. Yessy Jess, "Amazing," Amazon.com online review, May 10, 2005.

18. A reviewer, "Excellent!" Barnes and Noble online review, February 6, 2007, http://www.bn.com.

19. A reader, "A Great Book, That Everyone Should Read!" Amazon.com online review, June 18, 2003.

20. Claire, "Five Stars for the Rainbow Boys!," Amazon.com online review, June 10, 2003.

21. Megan Vickery, "The Best Book You Can Read," Amazon.com online review, July 4, 2002.

22. T. Burger, "Should Be Mandatory Reading for Gay Teens and Their Parents," Amazon.com online review, March 18, 2005; emphasis added.

23. Just Grammy's Opinion, "Honest and Open," Barnes & Noble online review, November 11, 2006, http://www.bn.com.

24. A reviewer, "Excellent!," Barnes and Noble online review.

25. Janell, a straight who could relate to this, "I Reccomend [sic] this Book!," Barnes & Noble online review, December 31, 2006, http://www.bn.com.

26. Betty S. Evans, "Rainbow Boys," *School Library Journal* 47.10 (2001): 169; emphasis added.

27. Paula Rohrlick, "Rainbow Boys," *Kliatt* (2003), http://www.findarticles.com/p/articles/mi_moPBX/is_3_37/ai_111305385; emphasis added.

28. Kristin Kloberdanz, "Recommended Young Adult Reading," *Book*, September 2001, 91.

29. Lynn Evarts, "Rainbow Boys," *VOYA* 24.5 (2001): 362.

30. Kate McDowell, "Rainbow Boys," *Bulletin of the Center for Children's Books* 55.3 (2001): 91; emphasis added.

31. Linda C. Salem, *Children's Literature Studies: Cases and Discussions* (Westport, CT: Libraries Unlimited, 2006), 103.

32. Jennifer Downey, "Braverman Prize Essay: Public Library Collection Development Issues Regarding the Information Needs of GLBT Patrons," *Progressive Librarian* 25 (Summer 2005): 86.

33. Mollie V. Blackburn and JF Buckley, "Teaching Queer-Inclusive English Language Arts," *Journal of Adolescent & Adult Literacy* 49.3 (2005): 205.

34. Ibid., 206.

35. Ibid., 207.

36. If heterosexual Latinos are uniformly depicted as homophobic, it may be enough for us to rethink the *Rainbow Boys* series because, to extend Debbie Reese's argument around depictions of Native Americans in children's literature, it is "wrong to celebrate one culture at the expense of another." Debbie Reese, "Native Americans in Children's Literature," in *Using Multiethnic Literature in the K–8 Classroom*, ed. Violet J. Harris (Norwood, MA: Christopher-Gordon Publishers, 1997), 161.

37. Blackburn and Buckley, "Teaching Queer-Inclusive," 206.

38. Michael Cart and Christine A. Jenkins, *The Heart Has Its Reasons: Young Adult Literature with Gay/Lesbian/Queer Content, 1969–2004* (Lanham, MD: Scarecrow Press, 2006), 144.

39. *The Heart Has Its Reasons* chronicles GLBTQ young adult literature through 2004 and therefore does not include the final book in the *Rainbow Boys* trilogy, *Rainbow Road* (2005).

40. Robert Gray, "Review of *Rainbow High*," *School Library Journal* (2003): 146.

41. Ibid.

42. Roger Sutton, "Boy Meets Boy/Rainbow High," *Horn Book Magazine* 80.1 (2004): 83.

43. Jeff Katz, "Rainbow Road," *School Library Journal* 51.10 (2005): 172.

44. Ibid.

45. Ibid., 173.

46. Roger Sutton, "Rainbow Road," *Horn Book Magazine* 81.6 (2005): 725.

47. Michael Cart, "Rainbow Road," *Booklist* 102.1 (September 1, 2005): 113.

48. Ibid.

49. Alex Sanchez, "Alex Sanchez—The Bio," author website, March 7, 2007, http://www.alexsanchez.com/Alex_Sanchez_bio.htm.

50. Jacqueline Dean, "Sovo Living: When You're Young and Gay," *Southern Voice Online* (November 2, 2001, http://alexsanchez.com/Rainbow_Boys/Southern_Voice_Interview.html.

51. Cynthia Leitich Smith, "Interview with Young Adult Author Alex Sanchez," author website, March 7, 2005, http://alexsanchez.com/CLSmith%20Interview.htm.

52. Mekado Murphy, "Alex Sanchez Interview—My So-Gay Life," *Dallas Voice Online,* February 15, 2002, http://alexsanchez.com/Rainbow_Boys/Dallas_Voice_Interview.htm.

53. Alana, "Our Lives: Media—Alex Sanchez," Youth Resource: A Project of Advocates for Youth (2004), http://alexsanchez.com/Youth%20resource%20Interview.htm.

54. Michael Cart, "Carte Blanche: Next!," *Booklist* 99.6 (November 15, 2002): 587.

55. Eve Kosofsky Sedgwick, "How to Bring Your Kids Up Gay," *Social Text* 29 (1991): 22.

56. Alex Sanchez, *Rainbow Boys* (New York: Simon and Schuster, 2001), 27.

57. Alex Sanchez, *Rainbow Road* (New York: Simon and Schuster, 2005), 62–63.

58. According to Sedgwick, revisionist psychoanalysts also argue that although they cannot affirm their sons' masculinity, "mothers who display any tolerance of their sons' cross-gender behavior" contribute to their potential homosexuality, a claim that is also reinforced throughout *Rainbow Boys* (Sedgwick, "How to Bring Your Kids Up Gay," 25).

59. Warren J. Blumenfeld, *Homophobia: How We All Pay the Price* (Boston: Beacon Press, 1992), 691.

60. Sanchez, *Rainbow Boys,* 12.

61. Sanchez, "Alex Sanchez—the Bio."

62. Rosalinda B. Barrera, Olga Liguori, and Loretta Salas, "Ideas a Literature Can Grow On: Key Insights for Enriching and Expanding Children's Literature about the Mexican-American Experience," in *Teaching Multicultural Literature in Grades K–8,* ed. Violet J. Harris (Norwood, MA: Christopher-Gordon, 1993), 212.

63. Sanchez, *Rainbow Boys,* 62–63.

64. Alex Sanchez, *Rainbow High* (Simon and Schuster, 2003), 27.

65. It should be noted that (after an initial misstep) Coach Cameron will eventually serve as one of the few positive portrayals of a heterosexual character in the entire series. It is clear he cares deeply for Jason and does his best to advocate and provide support.

66. Sanchez, *Rainbow High*, 101.

67. Ibid., 150.

68. Ibid., 68.

69. Ibid., 189.

70. Ibid., 62.

71. Ibid., 65.

72. Ibid., 193.

73. Ibid., 52.

74. Ibid., 83.

75. Ibid., 144.

76. Ibid., 174–75.

77. Ibid., 61.

78. Ibid., 98.

79. Ibid., 120.

80. Interestingly, Sedgwick claims revisionist psychoanalysts encourage "predominantly gay young men to 'reassure' their parents they are 'bisexual'" (Sedgwick, "How to Bring Your Kids Up Gay," 24). One way of reading this vacillation is to assume Jason is working to avoid normative labels, but its randomness across the series ultimately suggests it is accidental. It is eventually written that Jason "didn't really like to label himself as 'bi' because it made him feel like he didn't belong in either group, straight or gay" (Sanchez, *Rainbow Road*, 130).

81. Sanchez, *Rainbow Road*, 86.

82. Ibid., 131.

83. Ibid., 150; emphasis added.

84. Ibid., 153.

85. Ibid., 55.

86. Ibid., 57.

87. Ibid., 182.

88. Ibid., 136.

89. Ibid., 193.

90. Ibid., 200.

91. Ibid., 180.

92. Ibid., 224.

93. Ibid., 243.

94. In *Rainbow Boys*, Kyle writes "and proud!" underneath the word "queer" spray-painted on his locker, and on page 129 of the 2003 sequel *Rainbow High*, Jason tells his teammates he's proud to be a gay male.

95. Cart and Jenkins, *Heart Has Its Reasons*, 147.

96. Sedgwick, "How to Bring Your Kids Up Gay," 19.

97. Butler, *Gender Trouble*, viii.

98. Sanchez, *Rainbow Road*, 111.

99. Ibid., 114.

100. Ibid., 115.

101. Judith Butler, "Imitation and Gender Insubordination," in *Queer Cultures*, ed. Deborah Carlin and Jennifer DiGrazia (Upper Saddle River, NJ: Pearson / Prentice Hall, 2004), 360.

102. This is reinforced in *Rainbow High* in scenes in which heterosexual girls ask Kyle, "Which one of you is the girl?" (Sanchez, *Rainbow High*, 204), and these misconceptions go unchallenged. It is also reinforced by Nelson's boyfriend Jeremy. When he meets Nelson's mother, he is "flattering to Nelson's mom ('Those are cool earrings . . .'); and funny ('Can I borrow them sometime?')" (Sanchez, *Rainbow High*, 106).

103. Sanchez, *Rainbow Boys*, 50.

104. Michael S. Kimmel, "Masculinity as Homophobia: Fear, Shame, and Silence in the Construction of Gender Identity," in *Reconstructing Gender: A Multicultural Anthology*, 3rd ed., ed. Estelle Disch (New York: McGraw-Hill, 2004), 105.

105. Sanchez, *Rainbow Boys*, 83.

106. Ibid., 117.

107. Ibid.

108. Ibid., 118.

109. Ibid.

110. Ibid., 145.

111. Ibid., 148.

112. Ibid.

113. Ibid., 149.

114. Ibid., 148.

115. Ibid., 149.

116. Sanchez, *Rainbow Road*, 36.

117. Ibid., 76.

118. Ibid., 52.

119. Ibid., 135.

120. Ibid., 45–46.

121. Ibid., 123.

122. Ibid., 127.

123. Ibid., 207.

124. Ibid., 230–31.

125. Sanchez, *Rainbow High*, 194.

126. Sanchez, *Rainbow Road*, 18.

127. Ibid., 136.

128. Ibid., 222.

129. Ibid.; emphasis added.

130. Also included in the second installment is some explicit exposition about the cultural background of the "rainbow boys," which seems to reflect an awareness that in the field of young adult literature, there is a clear need for "more GLBTQ books featuring characters of color" (Cart and Jenkins, *Heart Has Its Reasons*, 165). Although it is implied in *Rainbow Boys* that Jason is Latino (his last name is "Carillo"), in *Rainbow High*, Jason uses token Spanish terms such as *maricon* (Sanchez, *Rainbow High*, 5) and *loco* (6). Additionally, Nelson is estab-

lished as a Jewish character—at one moment, Kyle points out, "Nelson, you're Jewish" (42) and later, Nelson uses the Yiddish term *chutzpah* (90). Nelson's identity as Jewish never reappears in the series and, although in *Rainbow Road* Nelson notes, "I've never done it with a Latino guy," to which Jason proudly responds: "Dude, we're the best!" (213), Jason never again uses Spanish terms and his identity as Latino is all but forgotten; this is troubling because it seems to reduce these characters to ethnic stereotypes.

131. Roberta Seelinger Trites, *Disturbing the Universe: Power and Repression in Adolescent Literature* (Iowa City: University of Iowa Press, 2000), x.

132. Sanchez, *Rainbow Boys*, 144.

133. Ibid., 38.

134. Sanchez, *Rainbow High*, 177.

135. Ibid., 178.

136. Ibid., 227.

137. Sanchez, *Rainbow Road*, 46.

138. Ibid., 47.

139. Ibid., 172.

140. Ibid., 171.

141. Ibid., 154.

142. Ibid., 155.

143. Ibid., 159.

144. Ibid., 16.

145. Ibid., 162.

146. Ibid., 162–63.

147. Ibid., 163.

148. Jason's intolerant high school principal encourages him to remain closeted: "'If you feel the need to jeopardize your future with this, that's one thing. But for you to risk upsetting your team as we head toward the state title . . .' He shook his head as if genuinely mystified. 'I can't believe you'd do that, Jason'" (Sanchez, *Rainbow High*, 96). Although readers are supposed to be angered by the principal's position, it becomes legitimized when Jason loses his college athletic scholarship implicitly as a result of revealing his sexual identity.

149. Sanchez, *Rainbow Road*, 164.

150. Ibid., 65.

151. Ibid., 70.

152. Ibid., 72.

153. Ibid., 73.

154. Cuseo, *Homosexual Characters*, 86–87.

155. Sanchez, *Rainbow Road*, 226.

156. Robert McRuer, "Reading and Writing 'Immunity': Children and the Anti-Body," *Children's Literature Association Quarterly* 23.3 (1998): 134 (reprinted in this volume).

157. Sanchez, *Rainbow High*, 134.

158. Ibid., 166.

159. Simon Watney, *Policing Desire: Pornography, AIDS, and the Media* (Minneapolis: University of Minnesota Press, 1988), 3.

160. Sanchez, *Rainbow Boys*, 106.

161. Ibid.; emphasis added.

162. Sanchez, *Rainbow High,* 153.

163. Ibid., 15.

164. Ibid., 168.

165. Ibid.

166. Sanchez, *Rainbow Road,* 17.

167. Ibid., 35.

168. Ibid., 83.

169. Ibid., 234.

170. Lee Galda and Bernice E. Cullinan, *Literature and the Child,* 6th ed. (New York: Wadsworth, 2006), xiv.

171. Michael Cart, "Saying "No!" to Stereotypes," *Booklist* 95.19–20 (June 1 and 15, 1999): 1811.

172. David Levithan, "Supporting Gay Teen Literature: An Advocate Speaks Out For Representation on Library Shelves," *School Library Journal* 55.10 (October 1, 2004): 44.

173. David Levithan, "Author Profile," TeenReads.com, January 25, 2006, http://www.teenreads.com/authors/au-levithan-david.asp.

174. Joseph G. Kosciw and Elizabeth M. Diaz, *The 2005 National School Climate Survey: The Experiences of Lesbian, Gay, Bisexual and Transgender Youth in Our Nation's Schools* (New York: Gay, Lesbian, and Straight Education Network, 2006), 5.

175. Ibid., 9.

176. David E. Wilson, "The Open Library: YA Books for Gay Teens," *English Journal* 73.7 (1984): 60.

177. Jan Goodman, "Out of the Closet, but Paying the Price: Lesbian and Gay Characters in Children's Literature," *Interracial Books for Children Bulletin* 14 (1983): 15.

178. Rudine Sims Bishop, "Selecting Literature for a Multicultural Curriculum," in Harris, *Using Multiethnic Literature,* 4.

179. Ibid., 9.

180. Roberta Seelinger Trites, "Queer Discourse and the Young Adult Novel: Repression and Power in Gay Male Adolescent Literature," *Children's Literature Association Quarterly* 23.3 (1998): 149.

181. Alex Sanchez, "Open Eyes and Change Lives: Narrative Sources Addressing Gay-Straight Themes," *English Journal* 94.3 (2005): 49.

182. Kay Mussell, *Fantasy and Reconciliation: Contemporary Formulas of Women's Romance Fiction* (Westport, CT: Greenwood Press, 1984), 37.

183. Bishop, "Selecting Literature," 10.

184. Vivian Yenika-Agbaw, "Images of West Africa in Children's Books: Replacing Old Stereotypes with New Ones?," in Fox and Short, *Stories Matter,* 244.

185. Cart and Jenkins, *Heart Has Its Reasons,* 16.

PART 3

Queer Readers and Writers

❧ PERHAPS NO ISSUE IS MORE DIVISIVE in the LGBTQ community than the meaning of the word "queer." The term has a long and storied history, connoting the broadly odd or unusual in the nineteenth century and now functioning as an umbrella term for nonheternormative identities. Contemporary variants on or extensions of "queer," such as "genderqueer," at once add specification and underscore the term's elasticity. Even heterosexually identified people who engage in unconventional or nontraditional sexual practices—polyamory, celibacy, BDSM (bondage, discipline, sadism, and masochism)—have been (self-)described as queer.

Mapping the parameters of queer is tricky, perhaps even counter to the antidefinitional spirit of the term. In what ways does queer function as a synonym for terms like "lesbian" or "gay," and in what ways does it connote something different? Does that something different have an essence that can be transmitted or at least communicated? Does queer offer a unifying function and thus collective power for otherwise disparate LGBT identities, or does it instead increase divisiveness? Given that heternormative sexual behavior has historically been defined as vaginal intercourse in the missionary position between one man and one woman in the privacy of their own bedroom, for procreative purposes and under the auspices of a church-recognized and state-sanctioned monogamous marriage, can't much heterosexual erotic activity be considered queer? If so, has the term itself become overdetermined? If queer can refer to almost any form of sexual conduct, does it cease to have any discrete meaning? For that matter, does the term have to signify sexuality per se?

The essays gathered in this section contemplate the perils of definition with respect to the material at hand as well as to the agents of production and consumption. Each is concerned with what it means to read queer, to write queer, and to be queer, not only in a biographical or personal sense but also as a cultural agent or player. In some respects, we all are queer readers in that we read against the grain, see what we want to see, claim personal meaning in texts that were not written expressly for us. These essays, especially the final two, attend to material that might itself seem queer—extraliterary, popular, participatory, sexually themed. What happens when queer-identified readers encounter or remake ostensibly nonqueer narratives? What does it mean, asks Wood, to choose your own erotic adventure vis-à-vis boy-love computer games, especially in a cross-cultural context? Who writes and reads slash (same-sex themed) fanfiction, and why—or is that question always already fraught, as Tosenberger suggests? Is Nancy Drew already queer, or has she been appropriated by queer readers? Are some queer texts born, others made, with still others having queerness thrust upon them? Do queer children—if we can imagine such—dream their way into new and even transgendered identities, as with *Ma Vie en Rose,* discussed in Norton's beautiful essay? Are certain genres—fantasy, perhaps?—more amenable to or constitutive of queer desire?

The Hobo, the Fairy,
and the Quarterback

§⍚

BIDDY MARTIN

Francois Roustang once disparaged the work of Lou Andreas-Salomé by arguing that she had turned psychoanalysis into a Russian novel.[1] For Salomé, childhood fantasies and Russian novels were closely associated, and she did indeed use psychoanalysis to clear a corridor back to childhood, back to the deep psychological processes that she thought of as the soul of both child and adult. One of her own childhood fantasies, one she reworked over and over, was the fantasy of the grandparent or of what she later called primary narcissism:

> We could envision it in the following way, as though we had moved from the parents' lap, from which we inevitably slip, onto the midst of the lap of God, as if onto the lap of a grandfather who spoils us much more and allows everything, who is so generous with gifts that it is as if he had all his pockets full and we could become almost as all-powerful as he, even if not nearly as "good"; he signifies both parents combined into one: maternal warmth/nurturance and paternal omnipotence. (To have to separate and distinguish them from each other, into the spheres of power and love, is already a violent break in what we might call a wishless [desireless] preworld well-being.)[2]

It is typical of Salomé that she first locates the grandparent as the compensatory fantasy, the defense against the slip off the parents' lap,

257

only to turn around and figure the grandparent as primal or original, as constituting a preworld well-being before loss, division, and sexual difference. She would have said that she was more attached to the fantasy than to the reality of her parents or of her own losses. In her excessive gratitude to Freud, Salomé repeats this fantasy over and over as she imagines him to be the being who bestows the gifts of psychoanalysis. In the folds of those pockets are surprises, but not necessarily Freud's alone. Salomé can own or acknowledge her own gifts only after projecting them onto a well-endowed grandfather, to whom she is attached, but attached at a distance. For he authorizes her independence, makes it look like dependence, and masks or pretends to mask his own indebtedness to her gifts and surprises, to what's in her pockets. Salomé's fantasy reveals something about her gendered style and the persona she created for herself. But it also says a great deal about her attachments, or her lack of attachment. That the grandparent is neither one gender nor the other seems at one level to expose Salomé's unwillingness to choose or to be one or the other herself. But that unwillingness to decide masks her resistance to the most intimate attachments, to sexual attachments. We could celebrate Salomé's refusal to occupy any fixed position, or we could lament her inability to land. She preferred to write about her idealizations rather than her relationships, even when she was thanking Freud for curing her of her childish tendency toward mystification, false syntheses, and fantasy.

Strangely, the depths of children's souls—the terrors and desires that are associated with issues of attachment and separation—seem far removed from the critical concerns of many of today's feminist and queer literary scholars, particularly those most influenced by Foucault's early work, whose theoretical evacuations of gendered cores have held out the promise of expanding our understanding of the social construction of gender cores and thereby multiplying the genders and sexualities that we imagine and that we are permitted to enact. I applaud the work that challenges assumptions of fixed gender cores of which our desires and behaviors are supposedly mere normal or abnormal expressions. But I also lament that some literary scholarship has gone too far in the direction of a sociology, concerned with mapping multiple and interwoven subject positions to the exclusion of interiority. For me, literature has also always engaged my curiosity about the complexities of interiors, the complexities of the very process by which the outside gets folded into an inside, and the distinction gets displaced.[3] Given the admittedly salutary emphasis on mobility, fluidity, and constantly reorganized surfaces, I start to wonder again at what point the infoldings of an outside become psychological processes that remain, at least to some extent, characteristics from childhood sustained over a lifetime, despite the subsequent integration and working through. And what does gender have to do with those processes? To what extent do we really want to push the argument that deconstructing gender evacuates interiority in the service of a political analysis of social regulations that masquerade as mere expressions of gender cores? Do deconstructing and expanding gender deconstruct the person? Is the project of resignifying or reconfiguring gender and sexuality really at odds with an interest in what might cohere in the psychological processes that characterize a personality, even a self?

Two friends and I sat down to talk about literature and about what we do. We got completely involved in a discussion of the books that most preoccupied us when we were growing up, favorite childhood books. All three of us described these books as the books that generated the desire to read, the books in which we most thoroughly lost ourselves or found ourselves in that process through which the losing becomes the finding, or vice versa. We all also remembered these books as producing the fantasies into which we escaped or imagined escaping the painful effects of the rules governing sexuality, gender, and maturity in the specifically racialized and class-specific immediate environments in which we grew up. Of course, what our stories reveal is how ensconced our fantasies of Neverland were in the very environments we sought to flee. They also clearly challenge the extent to which we like to imagine, even now, that the pressures we sought to manage came exclusively from the outside. Clearly, what had already folded in and become an inside exerted its own pressure on our fantasmatic positionings, even at the age of eight.

What engaged us over the course of an evening were the issues that our stories seemed both to stimulate and to manifest for each of us and the power of our attachment to these books even now, as the sort of *ur-Erlebnis* of what it can mean to lose and find oneself in a book. The boundaries between fiction and reality are so much more fragile for children than they are for adults; we were so much more capable then, at least apparently, of mixing ourselves up with the characters or with the stories: to believe ourselves into the stories and to understand extraliterary experiences in their terms. And it was clear that all three of us value the moments that offer a clear corridor back into those child-hood fantasies and the experience there of only the frailest line between fact and fiction, the experience of a kind of play without which there would be nothing interesting to say about gender or sexuality.

Afterward, it occurred to me to wonder which particular aspects of those childhood selves we were anxious to reexperience and which ones we world block; where fragile boundaries between tact and fic-tion, between self and other, between terror and desire would be plea-surable and where they would become intolerable. One way of ap-proaching those questions would be to list the literature we cannot bear to read, the literature we hate to read or that we love to hate to read, that comes too close or feels too much like rupture. But that's a task for another essay. We were into pleasure, or so we thought until we started to find one another—aspects of our personalities, our interactive styles, and even our behaviors at political meetings—in the stories we told.

For the other woman at the table, an avowed lesbian femme, *Peter Pan* had been the object of love, fantasmatic involvement, and preoccu-pation. And her most obvious identification was with Wendy. The one man's most influential, preoccupying, and to this day most vivid read-ing experience involved the story of a hobo who was shot, dropped off a steep precipice into a canyon, and left for dead. The bulk of the first part of *The Hobo of Devil's Gulch* was taken up with the day-to-day struggle of the victim to recover from the wound, survive, and ulti-mately to make it out of the canyon to the top of the cliff again to seek revenge. When he finally reached the top of the cliff, he found that the experience of struggle and longing so far outstripped what revenge could do for him that avenging the wound was no longer appealing. At the most manifest level, David had identified with the lone victim-hero, with survival.

The stories I remember living in for a great part of my youth were the stories of Chip Hilton, star athlete, whose achievements on the football field and the baseball diamond often involved injuries that threatened to remove him from a particular game, if not to end his career. But to the amazement of his worried, yet disappointed onlookers, Chip always re-turned at the last minute to help his team avoid what seemed like certain loss. At the most manifest level, I wanted to be Chip, and thus begins the story of my participation in the myth and practice of the wounded les-bian butch. But such obvious identifications—Carol's with Wendy, David's with the survivor, and mine with Chip Hilton—are not the end but the beginning of our understanding of what can never be fully understood: the twists and turns and surprises of the psyche. And perhaps I should anticipate the end and say here that the issues raised by the stories and by our analysis of them could never be aligned in any simple way with gender differences or with sexual object choice, with the differences between apparently straight and apparently queer sexualities.

Carol identified with a Wendy who wanted to be carried away by Peter Pan, carried away emotionally, but not necessarily with him. At the most obvious level, Carol remembered wanting a Peter who would take all the risks, a magical protector who would slay all the pirates and then be happy to return home to a good pot roast. Carol's Wendy assumed the domestic role, the position of the real girl in relation to her rivals Tinkerbell (the bad girl) and Tiger Lily (the exotic other). Carol's Wendy felt her superiority when she compared the diaphonous, pale nightgown in which she flew through the window to Tink's little skeleton leaves and Tiger Lily's boylike buckskin. These particular investments in Wendy are clearly class- and race-specific: whiteness and middle-classness defining what a real girl is. The real girl would make a home and be a mother to the Lost Boys, who, as Carol's fantasy had it then, needed a mother, not an activist like Tiger Lily. In fact, Peter did keep returning home to the supposedly real girl, but by the time he settled on Wendy, she was too old, so he took her daughter instead. Not an unfamiliar narrative.

But Wendy's passivity masks other levels that are more surprising— or not so surprising, given what we know of Carol. In relation to Peter, Carol's Wendy not only adores and admires Peter, but requires that Peter need her admiration. In other words, she shores up his self-sufficiency by rendering him needy, of her. Her admiration of Peter barely masks her desire to be admired herself but, as Carol put it, not too much. She would never desire so much admiration from Peter as to unsettle the distance between them. In relation to her rivals, Tinkerbell and Tiger Lily, Carol's Wendy can also begin to look a little less like the only real girl. After all, like so many butch girls, Tinkerbell and Tiger Lily, in defense of Peter, participate actively in what Judith Butler calls orthodox feminine sacrifice, while Wendy remains home alone.[4] David and I tried to make this a sign of Wendy's actual autonomy, but Carol suggested that it was more a sign of her privilege, that she got to stay home, alone, playing house and sewing pockets for the boys who had to appear to possess the gifts.

Carol's Wendy emphatically wanted to marry a boy who wouldn't be married, who wouldn't grow up, who was never played by a boy, and who lived in a neverland with other boys. She desired a boy who would leave her alone. What does it mean to want a Peter who can never be had and still be Peter—a safe object, blind to girls' desires for kisses, oblivious enough to mix up their kisses with thimbles? Perhaps Carol wanted to be Peter in her own way as much as she wanted to have him. When Carol's Wendy flies out a window to join Peter, she not only exhibits a form of attachment and a nomination of herself as mother of the Lost Boys, but also escapes her own family and then lives in a fantasy of being mother that is a reality of aloneness and play. When she flies out the window to join Peter, is she more like a mother or a lost boy? Perhaps she reveals the similarities between them.

Carol's identification with Wendy seems at one level to disown autonomy, daring, and aggression, projected as they are onto Peter. His independence is supported by her allowing him to depend on her; her apparent dependence is made possible by his never coming too close. How autonomous and powerful is Peter for Wendy? Peter appears as a lost boy, a wounded butch figure. When Wendy first sees him, he's crying because he can't get his shadow to stick to him, and his need elicits Wendy's desire not only to make a home but also to leave her own home and join, or perhaps be, him.

At this point in our discussion, Carol wondered aloud whether she had really identified with Wendy, Tinkerbell, or Peter, and she laughingly reviewed a lifetime of assuming Peter's rather than Wendy's position. The girl, Wendy or Carol, who fell in love with the girl-boy Peter seems to have fallen in love with a mother as well as a Peter. If that seems like a surprising claim, remember that Peter Pan is described as "very like Mrs. Darling's kiss,"[5] very like that inaccessible kiss in the corner of Mrs. Darling's mouth, and also as the one figure who might have been able to get that kiss. What does Carol-Wendy love, then, when she loves Peter Pan, the boy-girl who is very like Mrs. Darling's kiss?[6] She loves and identifies with the image of an inaccessible kiss. The displacement, then, from boy-girl to mother might seem like an end, of sorts, but what do mothers, fathers, or selves have to do with inaccessible kisses?

David and I were preoccupied with stories in which a boy or man operates as a lone or relatively independent survivor. But his story, on the manifest level, is far more empty of attachment than mine. His story began with victimization and isolation, with a wound and a separation from what could retroactively be imagined as a primal connection, and then became a lone struggle against incredible odds. But David remembered that his attacker had not completely disappeared from the story. As the hobo worked his way back out of the canyon, step by step, level by level, that now-paternal figure periodically peered down, creating the sense in our hobo that he was being watched. David also interrupted his account of the struggle by noting that he wasn't sure whether he was the survivor, the narrator, or the murderer. He had been aware, even as a child, of watching himself heal. Playing all the parts moves the injury and the survival around; it may also, as he pointed out, make the story safer, for he appears to be climbing without a safety net but protects himself in the way that fantasies are often protective, by playing all the parts. What would he need to be protected from if he identifies most with the healing survivor? Perhaps from the realization of the importance of the attachment and the vulnerability in that attachment, because the lone struggle masks the connection and defends against loss and connection.

David described his return to that powerful, murderous figure who had dropped him off the cliff into the canyon as a disappointment, for that figure had lost its power not only to kill, but also to satisfy. The disappointment made it unsatisfying even to take revenge. Then David added another twist. It's possible, he said, that he never got to the top of the cliff. He was interested only in the first half of the story, in the struggle, in the process, in the passion associated with healing and climbing and being on the way. The arrival was bound to be a disappointment. And that attachment to the process over the arrival seemed to mask a kind of clinging, a clinging to the fantasized original figure or relationship for which there could never be a satisfying replacement. The clinging to the desire made both attachment to and withdrawal from that original figure impossible. Now we seemed to be talking about mothers with a capital *M*—but also, of course, about fathers, and the importance of their recognition. In the story, the hobo not only reaches the top of the cliff but has a confrontation with the figure who wounded him and left him for dead. But David reported that he had a hard time remembering that part of the story and as a child had hated it for its disappointments. The actual *Vatermord* in his experience had been equally unsatisfying.

I have never met anyone who read or heard of the Chip Hilton se-

ries. Perhaps the Chip Hilton stories are a specifically southern form—
I hesitate to say art form—characteristic of the obsession in small southern towns with high school sports, and with football in particular, as a
venue for the vicarious and direct acting-out of class resentments,
racisms, misogynies, and rabid anti-intellectualisms. In Virginia high
schools and in the Chip Hilton stories, quarterbacks are supposed to be
white, blond, good-looking, gentlemanly on the surface, and manly, but
less vulgar in their manliness than the linemen or the running backs.
Being a southern quarterback requires a controlled and semi-intelligent
masculinity. Given my family's obsession with football, my mother's
brief stint as a football coach, the value of stoicism in the community,
and my favored brother's heroics on the field, it is not surprising that I
identified with Chip in my fantasies. Outside the book and the fantasies, I was forced, as a girl, to occupy the position of the adoring fan,
in particular the fan of my brother, to love rather than to be him. As it
turned out, he was an offensive tackle, not a quarterback. That disappointed me, and I felt the superiority of my fantasized quarterback position. But my secret privileging of that position of greater intelligence
over brute force also operated as a defense against my own aggression
and against my fear that I was, in fact, the offensive tackle myself.

The recurrent injuries undercut my apparent ambition, competitive-
ness, aggression, and self-sufficiency. Lesbian butchness always seems
to emerge in the form of a wound or woundedness. Like the Lost Boys,
the wounded quarterback is inhibited from making it completely alone;
he expresses a need and a longing, a loss that primarily other men—the
coach, the other players, followed then at more remove by the pom-
pom girls in the stands—can help heal, by sympathizing, admiring, and
worrying. Chip's wound accounts for his dependence on others without jeopardizing his capacity for independence and heroics. To survive
and flourish, he must, after all, return to the game and prevail—prevail
not only over his opponents but also over his own vulnerabilities and
his dependence on others. What's less apparent is the passive aggression with which he manages and prevails over other people's dependence on or attachment to him. The wound reveals butchness to be, at
times, a defense against vulnerability, which appears only in a mediated form, a form that carefully orchestrates and limits the conditions
for contact. An identification with Chip involves disowning other aspects of self, aspects that are, were, in that environment, gendered in
very predictable ways. In reality, and fantasmatically, I occupied the po-

sitions of Chip's teammates and those of his fans as well. I not only wanted to be Chip, I loved Chip. But my position as his fan included my expert knowledge of the game and my contempt for the girls whose interest in the boys on the field was what I considered to be frivolous. Here, my place among the girls in the stands is masked by my identification with Chip and then by my contempt for what got coded in that environment as femininity. In my fantasy, being in the stands at all also allowed me to disown more thoroughly, when I needed to, the desires and aggressions coded male.

As Chip, I hoped to become the object of my mother's adoration and love, the butch who desires to be the object of the mother's desire, by way of an identification with and aggression toward the brother. But what is my mother's gender, my mother the onetime football coach? And where are the fathers in Carol's and my stories? In three hours we pushed each other very hard, but we had, of course, hardly begun to uncover the ultimately endless twists and turns.

At this point we ran into a typical problem with the gendering of the stories, when masculinity and butchness got associated with defense structures and femininity with a genuine vulnerability that we found it necessary to deflect. But femininity is not the ground of victimization and limit. It, too, operates as a defense. Its association with victimization, vulnerability, loss, and death allows the masculine or butch to defend against his or her own limits and wounds. In a femme, whether gay or straight, femininity deflects and masks deeper levels of psychological processes. All our stories ultimately exposed how problematic it is to associate defense structures with masculinity and vulnerability with the feminine, even from a feminist perspective. In our stories, the butch figure, or the man, enters the scene already wounded or violated. Femmes feign a kind of dependence that masks not only their own aggressions, desires, and autonomies but also the butch's or man's dependence and limitation, facilitating a form of attachment based on a conventional distribution of gendered qualities. He is allowed on the surface to manage the presentation of his vulnerability instead of being reduced to it. And he controls his attachments, while she appears to embody them. But these are merely appearances, even if culturally prescribed ones. The oscillations between these polarities become tedious unless there is some integration of the disowned parts that becomes visible or possible. Such integration can occur only when we see that defense structures are gendered, and, further, that the deepest levels of terror and desire are both thoroughly gendered, by virtue of culture, and have nothing to do with gender. Gender, sex, and object choice do not explain or predict psychological processes at these deeper levels where we are engaged in the project of living or dying, attaching and withdrawing, though there is no way to gain any purchase on those deeper levels without going through the tight braid or weave of which gender and object choice are crucial aspects. In all our stories, gender seemed to have the status of a particular, contingent, and culturally pre-scribed stylization of psychological processes that are irreducible to gender dynamics.

These are some of the stories and fantasies in which we live as chil-dren. These are the books that got us reading and that protected us. These stories offered realms not only of freedom, passion, and expan-siveness, but also of forbiddenness and prohibition. They provided ev-idence of our isolation and queerness, however straight or queer we ended up being. In my parents' household, it was queer to read at all, forbidden to isolate ourselves in that way. Boys who read too much in-stead of playing football were sissies and eggheads; girls who read too much became bookish, became girls that boys didn't like, as my mother put it. Or, perhaps, they became girls who didn't like boys or who liked them but didn't desire them. The stories helped me stay in contact with what felt real, what remained not only concealed from others but con-cealed by my own defenses and resistances, not only to passions but also to pain and terror. The mere possibility of recalling the children we were helps us remember, or at least construct what endures. In that re-membering we know what we love, what we hate, and something of who we are.

At what point does the analysis of gender and of sexual positioning foreclose rather than open up the complexities of psychic dynamics? Here, attachment and disappearance, love and hate revolve inter-minably around a pinhead. And even the simplest story offers up lay-ers and layers of masks, with little clue to what lies at the bottom. All our efforts to find a formula, social or psychoanalytic, for the determi-nations of the folds and pleats of psychic and even social dynamics nec-essarily fail at some moment. Some of the formulas are richer than oth-ers, but virtually all of them become unsatisfying at some point, unless our desire is for easy answers. Far too much work in feminist and gay studies, including my own, prematurely puts the brakes on our atten-tion to those folds and pleats that constitute subjectivity, supplying social or formulaic psychoanalytic explanations for the links among society, psyche, and self. We pretend that we can know the determinants and the effects of the foldings-in of the outside, and we forget the surprising twists that emerge from staying with the complexities. In that, we let sexual difference defend us not only against loss and limitation but also against desire and fantasy.

The purpose of emphasizing these complexities is not to negate the political uses of putting on analytic brakes. That is, there are social and institutional constraints on gender and sexuality that are crucial to identify as determinants, rather than expressions, of embodied realities. But it is equally important not to evacuate interiority and not to let gender monopolize or exhaust that field. Gender and sexual identifications and desires are not the last word on our psychological processes; they may even operate as defenses against still deeper and more terrifying levels, against the inchoate urges and struggles out of which we identify and represent in the first place.

There are other reasons for emphasizing the forms of attachment and analysis that literature can mediate. I began by noting the more permeable boundaries in childhood between fact and fiction, between something we assume to be reality and that which we take to be fantasy. The love of literature, play, and analysis that David, Carol, and I share has to do with those boundaries, their necessities, their political implications, and their fragility. Attention to what I have been calling interiority has some potential to keep us honest about what we too quickly reduce or attribute to political positions or identities, which then block the corridors that Salomé wanted to keep open to realms that defy formulaic explanations. All our stories exposed the fundamentally race- and class-specific ways in which our fantasies appear to reduce complex struggles to simple, apparently primal structures of good and evil: the prototypical Western narrative of a white man, made vulnerable as a hobo, who fights against already existing but ultimately negligible dangers in Devil's Gulch; my always white quarterback whose teammates cannot win without him and whose vulnerability is associated with sitting (like a girl) on the sidelines; Wendy's contempt for girls who don't act like girls. Without analysis the stories simply replicate the sorry conditions of their superficial appeal. But the task for politically engaged critics has to include sustained respect for and access to the love of literature that emerges from the power it has to organize and express fantasies—fantasies that are irreducible to the effects of social and political power, however nuanced our understandings of those effects might be; fantasies hold open a gap, a space, or a gulch that cannot be covered by making subjectivity only an effect of discipline and control.

NOTES

1. Francois Roustang, *Dire Mastery: Discipleship from Freud to Lacan,* trans. Ned Lukacher (Baltimore: Johns Hopkins University Press, 1982), 11.

2. Lou Andreas-Salomé, *Lebensruckblick: Grundriß einiger Lebenserinnerungen,* ed. Ernst Pfeiffer (Frankfurt am Main: Insel, 1968), 11 (my translation).

3. I have been influenced by Gilles Deleuze's use of the metaphors of the folds and pleats of subjectivity in his analysis of Michel Foucault's late work. See, in particular, the chapter entitled "Foldings, or the Inside of Thought (Subjectivation)," in Gilles Deleuze, *Foucault,* trans. Sean Hand (Minneapolis: University of Minnesota Press, 1986), 94–123.

4. See Judith Butler's discussion of gender inversions in butch-femme interactions in "Imitation and Gender Insubordination," in *Inside/Out: Lesbian Theories, Gay Theories,* ed. Diana Fuss (New York: Routledge, 1992), 13–31.

5. J. M. Barrie, *Peter Pan* (New York: Scribner's, 1980), 11.

6. For this point, I am indebted not only to Carol Maxwell Miller's memories and analyses, but also to Judith Butler, who reminded me of the comparison between Peter Pan and Mrs. Darling's kiss during a phone conversation about Peter Pan at precisely the moment that Carol did.

Is Nancy Drew Queer?

Popular Reading Strategies for the Lesbian Reader

&

SHERRIE A. INNESS

"She is as immaculate and self-possessed as a Miss America on tour. She is as cool as Mata Hari and as sweet as Betty Crocker," says Bobbie Ann Mason of a supersleuth with whom we are all familiar: Nancy Drew.[1] No one can question her prominence as a cultural icon. Along with the eighty-million-plus Nancy Drew books (in seventeen different languages) that have been sold,[2] Nancy also has had, at various times, her own television series (twice), lunch box, cookbook, two coloring books, date book, diary, and a "Nancy Drew Mystery Game" that Parker Brothers sold from 1957 to 1959.[3] If this isn't enough Drew miscellanea to pique your interest, you might wish to hunt down the three Nancy Drew movies that Warner Brothers produced between 1938 and 1939, or join the official Nancy Drew fan club, or look up the *Playboy* story on Pamela Sue Martin that promises us "TV's Nancy Drew undraped."[4] Nancy's fame is such that the first academic conference on Nancy Drew in 1993 was featured on the front page of the *New York Times*.

Lesbians have read the Drew books, imagining that they, too, could be like Nancy or be part of her world. As evidence of lesbian fascination with Nancy, she has been the subject of a few lesbian novels and short stories. For example, Mabel Maney wrote the novel *The Case of the Not-So-Nice Nurse* (1993), a lesbian spoof on the Nancy Drew and Cherry

269

Ames stories. In this book, "Nancy Clue" is a superhuman character who manages to tie up three villains with only one short piece of rope, thanks to her Girl Scout training. Nancy Clue also reminisces about being trapped in a tunnel for three days, commenting, "Luckily I had a loaf of bread, chocolate bars, oranges, and some milk in my purse."[5] Maney's work, a parody in which the majority of characters, including Nancy, turn out to be queer, has proven very popular in the lesbian community.[6] This fascination with rewriting the life of a favorite childhood icon demonstrates Nancy's subversive potential.

To understand her subversive potential, Nancy can be compared to another omnipresent paragon of popular femininity: Barbie. Both Nancy and Barbie are names recognized even by those who have never read a Drew book or played with a Barbie doll. Both Nancy and Barbie in many ways epitomize a vision of socially acceptable and presumably desirable femininity. At first glance, Nancy, with her fashionable wardrobe, football-playing boyfriend, and lawyer daddy, and Barbie, with her long, silken tresses, Malibu beach house, and, of course, Ken the wonder boyfriend, might seem to offer little possibility for subversion of the dominant status quo, and to display little apparent homosexuality. But is this true? To borrow Lynda Hart's words from her book, *Fatal Women: Lesbian Sexuality and the Mark of Aggression* (1994), "Homosexuality is . . . most prominently represented when it is virtually under erasure."[7] Sometimes the cultural icon, such as Barbie or Nancy, that *seems* at first glance most representative of mainstream heterosexual values also offers the greatest number of possibilities for alternative homosexual readings. For instance, Erica Rand writes that Barbie "has some features particularly conducive to lesbian reappropriation: the nifty Barbie-of-the-eighties slogan 'We girls can do anything' . . . and a series of wardrobe-crafted identities to pull out of her closet."[8] Barbie has been dressed in drag, drawn as an "AIDS" Barbie, and had her computer chip replaced with one from a G.I. Joe so she yells, "Vengeance is mine."[9] All of these actions by various groups—such as one that calls itself the Barbie Liberation Organization—endlessly recreate and provide new readings of Barbie and the complex symbology that surrounds her. In a similar fashion, this essay will focus on a related destabilizing strategy: analyzing the Nancy Drew books as speaking to not only mainstream heterosexual society, but also to lesbian society. By examining the homoerotic counterplot of these books and discussing the reactions of lesbian readers to these works, this essay will explore how lesbians read texts targeted to a largely heterosexual mass society.

I must include a caveat at this point. I am not suggesting that lesbians always read differently than heterosexual women. This is not true. Despite different sexual orientations, readers might receive the very same message from reading a book, such as a volume of the Nancy Drew series, but this is not always the case. Often lesbians will read differently than heterosexual women. In this essay, I shall discuss messages that both heterosexual and homosexual women receive from the Nancy Drew books, as well as focusing on some messages that heterosexual readers most likely will not discover in the Drew novels. Such an approach, I believe, will show that many lesbian readings overlap, but are not identical to, heterosexual readings. Examining these lesbian subtexts is important because the outsider status of lesbians allows them potentially to critique heterosexual norms and to question the myth of heterosexual hegemony.

This essay is not the first feminist approach to Nancy Drew. Nancy has attracted approval as well as a plethora of criticism from feminists.[10] Eileen Goudge Zuckerman claims that the girl detective was her "first feminist role model,"[11] and Joanne Furtak argues that Nancy was "a feminist's dream before the dream became fashionable."[12] Others are more doubtful about Nancy's feminist potential, including Ellen Brown, who discusses Nancy's wasted life: "doomed forever to be eighteen, sexually frozen, unmothered and unmothering, married to the masculine world of order and reason, with avocation but no vocation, dependent on the Great White Father for economic security and permission, driving around in daddy's car."[13] Although she calls Nancy the "most independent of girl sleuths,"[14] Bobbie Ann Mason also questions Nancy's appeal for feminists: "She always has it both ways—protected and free. She is an eternal girl, a stage which is a false ideal for women in our time."[15] These critics are correct in pointing out Nancy's ambiguous character, yet it is this very ambiguity that makes the Nancy Drew books such a fruitful site for the contestation of cultural norms and gender values, as I shall show throughout this essay. The apparent "normality" of the stories calls for reading strategies that emphasize alternative approaches in order to destabilize the work's surface meaning.

I should also point out that not all lesbian readers have unambivalent responses to the Drew books. Some of the women whom I interviewed for this essay clearly feel alienated because, for them, Nancy represents mainstream heterosexual values. Elaine, for instance, comments, "I read many of the Nancy Drew books, but I preferred the Hardy Boys and the Alfred Hitchcock Adventurer series, as Nancy kept getting silly over boys." Some lesbians prefer the Hardy Boys, Frank and Joe, and their wilder adventures to Nancy's milder exploits. Another woman, Jill, writes, "My sister (who is straight) read the Nancy Drew series while *I* read the Hardy Boys series; we traded books but we each thought our series was 'better.'" Other lesbians rejected Nancy for other reasons; Laura, for example, writes: "I only read about three or four Nancy Drew books. The books I read were from the 'newer edition' where Nancy always has to have help—usually from a male counterpart. I didn't like that and so went off in search of other books." The Drew books, like so many forms of popular media, are always going to be shifting, ambiguous texts; they will never have a fixed meaning for any entire group of readers, including lesbians. But we should explore how some lesbian readers turn the Drew books into a subversive real-life experience, reading against the grain of the implied text.

How Lesbians Read

First, it is necessary to discuss how lesbians read texts that are targeted chiefly at a heterosexual market. A number of influential essays have been published on this subject.[16] One of the most astute is Danae Clark's discussion of how gays and lesbians read gayness into an advertisement that might seem to have no overt homosexual content: "Gays and lesbians can read into an ad certain subtextual elements that correspond to experiences with or representations of gay/lesbian culture."[17] This subtextual reading strategy works when lesbians read fiction, too. They look for meanings that lurk behind the text's apparently heterosexual surface, knowing that lesbian experiences, whether in fiction or reality, are rarely overt. When lesbians read, they actively disassemble the dominant heterosexual plot, demonstrating that heterosexuality does not hold its culturally prescribed central role for all readers. Clark goes on to discuss how lesbians view advertisements: "Because lesbians (as members of a heterosexist culture) have been taught to read the heterosexual possibilities of representations, the 'straight' reading is never entirely erased or replaced."[18] Although Clark is discussing advertising, her words are equally applicable to novels, including the Nancy Drew books. Lesbians are always aware that the dominant heterosexual narrative of most fiction is a myth that fails to reveal the content of lesbian lives. Thus, lesbian readers are on a search for the lesbian subtext that speaks to them and their experiences. Lesbians read and interpret aspects of a text that heterosexual readers simply might not notice in the same way (such as George's evident butchness, which I will address more fully later in this essay). Lesbian readers do far more, as Jean E. Kennard points out, than merely "substituting 'woman' wherever the word 'man' appears."[19] They are involved in altering the entire text, in ways that other lesbian readers might or might not understand. As critic Gabriele Griffin suggests, "The lesbian reader has two positions open to her in her engagement with a text: identification and dissociation. Through her reading she can impose on the text a lesbian identity simply by asserting it. Similarly, she can declare a text *'not that'*. However she argues her position, it will not inevitably be shared by others."[20] This does not suggest that the 'straight' reading is ignored by lesbian readers, but that they are reading multiple levels simultaneously.

Reading the Nancy Drew books from a lesbian perspective entails being a resistant reader who refuses to accept the book's apparent messages about society, cultural values, and gender. What exactly do I mean by a "lesbian perspective"? Julia Penelope provides an excellent explanation of this term: "The 'Lesbian Perspective' is a 'turn of mind,' a stance in the world, that asks unpopular questions, that can be comfortable only when it confronts the sources of its discomfort, a frame of mind that refuses to accept what most people believe to be 'true.'"[21] Penelope continues,

> The Lesbian Perspective makes it possible to challenge the accuracy of male consensus reality, and to create a reality that is Lesbian-defined and Lesbian sustaining. Once we learn to perceive the world from our own perspective, outside the edges of the pale male map, we'll find it not only recognizable, but familiar.[22]

By asking "unpopular questions" about a text, lesbian readers decenter the assumed "normalcy" of heterosexuality. In this way lesbians create realities that might be far more intriguing. Such an alternative reading strategy produces a text that might be unrecognizable to Carolyn Keene's implied readers (prepubescent heterosexual girls), but one that is easily recognizable to countless lesbians. (Mabel Maney made this way of reading overt and public in her novels—she brought the lesbian subtext to the foreground.)

But why bother with untangling the lesbian plot in a seemingly "straight" text? The most accurate explanation of why this approach has value appears in Marilyn R. Farwell's essay "Heterosexual Plots and Lesbian Subtexts: Toward a Theory of Lesbian Narrative Space." She writes, "Many feminist theorists, whatever their theoretical allegiances, have explored the importance of women's bonding, often termed lesbian whatever the sexuality of the women, as a powerful tool for breaking narrative codes."[23] Farwell argues that

> in opening a new narrative space the reader can forge a subtext that explores female desire while the main text does not. The subtext gives us the possibility for a transgressive narrative that can be more fully realized in other narratives or that can be part of our readings of other texts that seem to reinforce the bonding between heterosexuality and the narrative.[24]

Such a subversive approach to Nancy Drew opens up new avenues for women's desire, showing that heterosexuality, even when it seems most stable, can be undermined. Lesbianism cannot easily be separated from the text, despite the book's apparent allegiance to heterosexual values. Such a reading strategy, although applied in this essay primarily to Carolyn Keene's fiction, is a method of interpretation that also has relevance far beyond this particular series; it shows how lesbians read texts in a society that privileges the heterosexual narrative.

A Few Words about Nancy's Roots

Before turning to the series and its lesbian readers, we must first know a little about Nancy's origin. From where did this titian-haired (sometimes iris golden-haired) WASP detective spring? Many unwittingly assume that "Carolyn Keene"—the name that appears on all the books' covers—created Nancy Drew, but "Keene" is only a pseudonym that has been used by a large number of writers responsible for creating the series. Actually, Nancy was originally the creation of Edward Stratemeyer, who has been called the "Henry Ford" of the serial book business, cranking out thousands of juvenile books through an assembly-

line process.[25] The Stratemeyer syndicate was phenomenally successful; over 200,000,000 copies of Stratemeyer's serial novels have been
sold.[26] Among all the characters in these countless volumes, however,
Nancy is clearly the star, outshining a number of other girl detectives,
such as Ruth Fielding, Betty Gordon, and Nan Sherwood, who were already in the Stratemeyer lineup when Nancy appeared on the scene.
The Nancy Drew series started in 1930 with the publication of *The Secret
of the Old Clock*, which was an immediate hit, as were all the other books
in the series. Of the Stratemeyer books, the Nancy Drew and Hardy Boy
mysteries account for over half the estimated sales, with the Nancy
Drew books outselling by millions even the popular Hardy Boys.[27] And
the Drew books have continued to sell throughout the years, developing an almost cultlike following.

When Edward Stratemeyer died, his daughters took over the syndicate. One daughter in particular, Harriet S. Adams, provided the impetus for the Nancy Drew series throughout much of the twentieth century, running the company until her death. Along with her partner
Andrew Stevenson and assorted ghost writers, including Walter Karing
and Mildred Wirt Benson, who most consider the true "mother" of
Nancy, Harriet Adams wrote the Nancy Drew books until her death in
1982, when Nancy Axelrad took over. Although there is an ongoing battle about exactly what writer wrote which Drew novel, everyone acknowledges that Adams had a crucial role.[28] During her fifty years of
involvement with the Drew series, she deeply influenced the development and characterization of Nancy according to her own standards,
even referring to Nancy as her "daughter."[29]

Adams also played a crucial role in implementing the extensive revisions of the Drew series in 1959 to keep it current.[30] Some of these alterations were no doubt an improvement, like doing away with the crude
ethnic stereotypes of the earlier volumes and making Hannah Gruen almost a substitute mother for Nancy, rather than merely a servant. Other
alterations, however, were less positive. Adams thought Nancy was
"too bold and bossy," and sought to tone down her character.[31] Reflecting the cultural changes happening to women in the 1950s, Nancy lost
some of the vigor that had been associated with her in the past, which is
one reason some women readers search out the older versions.

Since Adams's death, the Drew books have continued to do well for
their new publisher, Simon & Schuster, with close to a million copies a
year sold throughout the 1980s.[32] The latter books, however, will not be

the focus of this essay for a variety of reasons. First, they have not been around long enough to analyze their impact on lesbian readers. Second, the books have actually become less interesting: recent writers have stressed girl/boy relationships ad nauseam, devoting much less space to how Nancy relates to other women, such as her crime-fighting friends Bess and George. These changes, moreover, have been made at the expense of the novels' plots, which appear far less developed than in earlier books. Third, for the sake of this essay I am primarily interested in how past lesbian readers have experienced and interpreted the older Drew stories, as well as the queer subtext that can be uncovered in these books.

Nancy Drew and Company

Nancy leads a life that any lesbian would envy.[33] The eighteen-year-old daughter (she was originally sixteen, but her age was changed so she could drive in every state) of a famous criminal lawyer, she has a remarkable amount of freedom, despite her youth. Conveniently, her mother died when she was three, leaving her with a father who is "the most elusive parent anybody ever owned,"[34] freeing his daughter to sleuth to her heart's content. Not even Nancy's schooling holds her back, since readers never actually see her in attendance at high school, although we are informed in later books that she did go to high school and did attend art school briefly. This apparent lack of education does not interfere with Nancy's intellectual accomplishments, as she speaks German, French, and Spanish and has reasoning skills that would be a match for Sherlock Holmes.

Nancy's intelligence is fortunate, because her skills are certainly put to the test in her hometown of River Heights, which must be the most crime-ridden suburban town in all the Midwest. In book after book, she encounters villains lurking in her garden, burglarizing her house, slipping away with her possessions, and hiding behind every shrub or tree. Any normal girl would know that it was time to find a new home, but Nancy is no normal girl: she glories in her crime-ridden surroundings, welcoming each new exploit. The formulaic plot of each book revolves around her being introduced to a new central mystery, which turns out to be interconnected with two or three other mysterious affairs. Trying to solve the mystery, she searches for clues, questions a variety or suspects, and travels around. While in pursuit of her goal, she is constantly menaced by evil characters. Typically, near the book's conclusion, she is locked in some confined area, which is always dark, dreary, dank, dangerous, and so excessively dirty that it is obvious her dry cleaning bills must be sky-high. Just when things look bleakest for Nancy, her father (or Ned or Bess and George or the police) appears and rescues her. The book concludes with a summary about what has happened to the central characters; the good have been rewarded, typically with wealth, while the bad have been revealed as impostors and imprisoned. The last few pages provide a glowing review of all of Nancy's skills and the thanks of those who have been aided. Not atypical is a business owner in *The Case of the Velvet Mask* (1953), who says, "I owe everything to Nancy."[35] Despite praise, however, the girl detective is always suitably modest, and only reluctantly consents to accepting a little trinket (an antique clock, an aquamarine ring, a diamond pin, and other assorted booty) from her admirers.

One of the reasons for the appeal of the Drew books to lesbian readers is that their formulaic plots suggest a possible path through a lesbian's life. The young lesbian who has yet to discover her sexual identification has a secret in her life (her lesbianism) that she must search to discover, although she will be hindered at every step of the way by individuals who would prefer that she not solve this mystery. At one point, the lesbian, although she most likely does not find herself trapped in a dark basement, does find herself trapped by society's conventions. Only when she discovers the secret of her lesbianism is the lesbian finally rewarded. On a mythical level, the books reassure lesbian readers that there is a path to lesbianism that can be negotiated, despite how dangerous it might appear at first.

Also reassuring to lesbian readers is Nancy's amazing ability to excel at anything she attempts, showing that a girl does not need to pursue only traditional feminine activities. She is an excellent swimmer, diver, and skin diver, an admirable equestrienne, a talented ballet dancer and actress, a champion golfer and ice skater, a terrific tennis player, *and* a good mechanic. Nancy seems to have little regard for what are "appropriate" activities for men and women; she simply does well at everything, making her a particularly appealing figure to young lesbians who do not want to be bound by gender conventions. Nancy also has a photographic memory, and quickly becomes an expert or near expert in the many diverse fields where her sleuthing takes her. For instance, in *The Clue of the Leaning Chimney*, Nancy learns all about rare

Chinese porcelain. In *The Hidden Window Mystery,* she finds out how to make stained glass windows.

In addition to all these traits, she is always impeccably turned out for crime fighting: "Titian-haired Nancy was a trim figure in her olive-green knit with matching shoes. Beige accessories and knitting bag completed her costume."[36] Never, never does Nancy run outside in her nightgown to chase a criminal, even though it might be three in the morning. On all occasions—including breakfast—she is always perfectly groomed, her costume carefully chosen and color coordinated. Her brains and beauty make her the match of any man, which is appealing to lesbian readers in particular because she presents an image of female empowerment. Even her careful attention to her clothing fails to conceal that she is remarkably sharp and capable.

All these abilities, and more, Nancy uses to fight the criminals who seem not only irresistibly drawn to her but also delight in threatening the girl sleuth. A not atypical description of an encounter with a villain occurs in *The Secret in the Old Attic* (1944) when Nancy is captured: "Nancy fought to escape from the man, but his clutch was like an iron vice. He whipped out a handkerchief and stuffed it into Nancy's mouth."[37] Anyone other than Nancy might be in a sticky situation, but she escapes, as she does time after time. It is all in a day's work for her to handle situations like those that confront her in *The Spider Sapphire Mystery* (1968): She is trapped in her car, knocked down, has her purse stolen, is held at gunpoint, has her suitcase and clothing burned up, hurts her hands with acid, and is locked in a dungeon. Although she is constantly being threatened or attacked, such as having her living quarters destroyed by a time bomb (*The Mystery at Lilac Inn*) or being temporarily blinded by acid *(The Ringmaster's Secret),* Nancy is not unnerved by her experiences. Even after being kidnapped and dumped into an airplane, Nancy, with hands and ankles bound, can whip a lipstick out of her pocket and scrawl a large "SOS" on a window.[38] For her, it is just a typical afternoon's work to break up a house burglary ring, crack a counterfeit ring, or restore an Indian ruler to his throne. All of these exploits establish Nancy as a nontraditional heroine, who appeals to nontraditional readers. Her life is a fantasy where, despite all perils, she always emerges unscathed, which is one of the reasons why many lesbians might be attracted to the Drew novels. Lesbian readers are able to enter a world in which a woman manages to remain unhurt, even though the society around her is filled with people who wish to do her harm. For lesbians, who frequently face persecution, this fantasy is alluring.

Nancy is also a nontraditional woman in other ways that could appeal to lesbian readers. Even her eating patterns are not typically "ladylike." Between adventures, she always makes it home for a snack, lunch, or dinner produced by Hannah, her father's trusty housekeeper. Nancy thinks nothing of consuming a meal consisting of cream of mushroom soup, tomato salad, lamb chops, French fries, peas, and chocolate pie. Chasing crooks must burn a lot of calories, because she maintains her svelte figure even when partaking of Hannah's daily gustatory excesses. Whether Nancy eats peas or pineapple might seem of little import, until one recognizes that what the consumption of food actually accomplishes in the Keene books is further developing a largely all-women community, since Nancy is most frequently found to be eating with George and Bess or Hannah. Nancy's elaborate meals work to build a sense of female community. Also, such meals show to readers, lesbian and nonlesbian alike, that consuming food is a pleasure they should relish, rather than considering such hunger not appropriate for "ladies."

No discussion of Nancy Drew would be complete without consideration of her car, a vehicle that offers the promise of endless mobility to the lesbian reader. What starts out as a battered, maroon roadster in the earliest volumes evolves into a long series of shiny brand-new cars for Nancy, culminating in the famous blue convertible. She receives more new cars than a Chrysler showroom. In *The Haunted Showboat* (1957), she receives a new yellow convertible. In *The Password to Larkspur Lane* (1966), her father gives her a "powerful black and green roadster."[39] But Nancy's cars have short life-spans. They are frequently stolen (*The Witch Tree Symbol, The Haunted Showboat, The Moonstone Castle Mystery*) or smashed up (*The Clue of the Dancing Puppet* and *The Clue of the Whistling Bagpipes*). Every crook in town seems to desire nothing more than destroying Nancy's latest prize, but she is never left without a car for long because the car represents freedom and autonomy; with it, she is able to travel anywhere.[40] As Carol Billman points out,

> The lasting effect of Nancy Drew's all-encompassing independence is that she can be supremely active and mobile, free-wheeling in a word. Always on the go, she merely stops in at home to refuel. . . . Then she is off again in her car, or her motorboat, or her plane.[41]

Nancy creates a fantasy of endless mobility for any reader, particularly young readers who might not yet have access to a vehicle. Readers also learn, however, that driving a car is not supposed to make a woman less feminine; Nancy always maintains her feminine appearance. Even after a high-speed car chase in *The Sign of the Twisted Candles* (1933), she has not a hair "out of place or a pleat wrinkled." Clearly, these novels send ambivalent messages to their readers about desirable gender behavior, which is one of the reasons why the lesbian reader does not just read the text, but redesigns it, paying little attention to messages that she might consider irrelevant to her own experiences.

Nancy's attention to presenting a feminine appearance, however, should not lull one into assuming that she is more interested in her image than in crime-solving. Crime always comes first for the ace detective, and she is endlessly on the lookout for codes and clues. She cannot even walk to the corner store without finding one or more clues on the way. In her world, everything is a clue that must be uncovered, sometimes with the aid of her magnifying glass, which she uses obsessively, often finding clues that others have missed. She glories in clues, telling one woman who complains that she would have no patience with Nancy's work, "That's the fun of being a detective. You look and keep on looking. And suddenly, when you least expect it, you find a clue."[42] It is a rare house that doesn't have a secret passage, room, or compartment for Nancy to discover. Codes, too, pose little difficulty for her; she breaks them with ease in *The Secret of the Red Gate Farm* (1931), *The Clue of the Velvet Mask* (1953), and other volumes. Nancy even manages to create her own clues, such as in *The Clue of the Tapping Heels* (1939), in which she learns how to tap dance in Morse code in order to send secret messages. Her obsession with codes and clues shows readers that the world is an understandable, logical place, but only for those who look closely. Girls are also shown that they, just like Nancy, can figure out puzzles that leave grown-ups baffled. Additionally, we can look at the search for clues as being metaphorically the search for homosexuality that any lesbian must conduct when reading the Nancy Drew novels or other literature. Lesbianism is a "clue," a "secret," a "mystery" that must be detangled from the surface narrative. This is the quest and search that the lesbian reader must pursue, because mainstream fiction and life are typically so inimical to lesbian representation.

Lesbians also read the Drew books for the release they provide from the conventions of the real world. Clearly, the novels fail to provide a mimetic replication of reality. Instead, these books create a fantasy world in which none of society's conventions about correct behavior for young women ever appear to hinder Nancy in the least. The serial stories also provide a sense of order in a seemingly random world, as Lee Zacharias writes: "Each volume contains several mysteries which eventually come together in one solution; this common solution reassures the reader . . . that the seemingly random events of her life and the confusion she perceives in the world do have a pattern."[43] This fantasy world, which is so much more orderly than the real world, is alluring to any leader, heterosexual or homosexual. Lesbian readers, in particular, might find an escape into the ordered world of Nancy Drew appealing, because their own world is often chaotic and frightening. One woman recalls:

> The books must have definitely been an escape/fantasy for me because I grew up in a very sheltered and overprotective environment. I loved Nancy's self-confidence, persistence. independence, and leadership. She was everything I wasn't and did everything I couldn't. She had her own car, had her own business, and engaged in all sorts of interesting, challenging, and scary activities.

Another lesbian, Sarah, thinks back to reading the books:

> I was simply delighted to read about another girl. I think. I would stop in the middle of a sentence and literally hug the book. I think I was proud to be a girl, like her. I always envied the fellas in books who got to go fishing and camping and got to play detective and have clubhouses. So I guess Nancy Drew and friends gave me a character with whom to identify.

A third lesbian, Kate, remarks, "I loved Nancy Drew! I enjoyed the action and the fact that she had to think so much. My mom said that I read every Nancy Drew book the library had. When I was sick, she would offer to go out and get me books. She said I would list off all the ones not to get." Another woman, Sue, remembers as a young girl pretending to be like Nancy and her friends, and "sleuthing around, finding mysteries to solve." All of these women point out the escape that Nancy offered them from society's conventions about how girls should behave. These readers used Nancy's experiences to explain their own lives, and perhaps to serve as a role model for their own behavior. Nancy might have served as an example to some of these lesbian readers, showing that women do not have to follow society's dictates about desirable behavior. Readers could also see in the Drew books that male companionship is sometimes far less absorbing than the friendship and company of other women. Certainly, at least until the most recent books, Nancy appeared far more interested in George and Bess than in Ned. Ned has a difficult time even wheedling a date out of her, whereas George and Bess seem to spend most of their waking hours with Nancy.

Other reasons exist for Nancy's appeal to lesbians. She shows herself to be remarkably free from the dictates of men, and is able to twist any man around her little finger. Only Nancy would have the nerve to ask her father if he would fly to London with her "right away."[44] Without blinking an eye, Carson Drew agrees to leave that very day (why couldn't my father take a lesson from Nancy's dad?). Nor does he ever complain when his daughter sends him the bill for her extensive wardrobe and her trips to such exotic locales as Belgium, Greece, France, Turkey, Hong Kong, Mexico City, Peru, Scotland, and Africa. It takes Nancy to make grown men gush, "Miss Drew, you're the most ingenious girl I've ever met!"[45] or "you certainly have the best ordered mind . . . of any person I ever met."[46] Instead of men controlling Nancy, she controls them, and they are eager to do her bidding. She is a model of feminine strength that would appeal to many lesbians (as well as nonlesbians).

The most tractable man of all is Ned Nickerson, star football player of Emerson College, who is Nancy's "special friend" through many volumes. Ned isn't even rewarded with a kiss until some of the later books, and he must always recognize that sleuthing is far more important to Nancy than a date with him. In one book, he even begs, "Nancy, how about taking your mind off mysteries for a while and thinking of me instead."[47] Nancy only laughs, paying little heed to his words. Although his physical strength sometimes helps Nancy to escape from a difficult situation, she doesn't even always need Ned as backup; when he pleads to be taken along one time, she leaves him behind, remarking blithely that if Ned is not around, she will "depend on George and her judo to take care of troublemakers."[48] Poor Ned.

Like Nancy, lesbian readers tend to minimize Ned's role. One lesbian, Marilyn, looks back and remembers "Nancy's strength and self-sufficiency" and recalls little about the assistance provided from the boys in her life. Megan, another lesbian who read the Nancy Drew books in the late 1960s, explains: "I loved the books because Nancy was smart and she was doing something, not just watching boys doing something. She was the protagonist, George and Bess secondary characters, and Ned merely tertiary, or less. Ned seemed an okay guy, but who needed him? It did get irritating that he had to rescue Nancy so often." Another lesbian, Winifred, wrote about Ned, "I have a vague recollection of some boyfriends, but I never paid much attention to them. I actively disliked Nancy's boyfriend. I remember that pretty clearly." Other lesbian readers reported similar feelings about Ned and Burt Eddleton and Dave Evans, George's and Bess's respective boyfriends.[49] For these readers, the book's apparent plot is malleable. Individuals can perceive Ned as either crucial or completely dispensable to the narrative. In this way, lesbians refashion a text that is superficially heterosexual into a homosexual work. Ned is perceived as being merely camouflage for Nancy; she seems heterosexual by having him around, despite her far greater interest in bonds with other women. Thus, just as Danae Clark argues, lesbians create a vision of the world that is more in line with their own experiences. They also call into question the assumed import of the heterosexual romance by showing that it is an insignificant part of the text, at least for them. Such a perspective recrafts canonical and noncanonical texts, revealing the lesbian subtexts.

George and Bess: Butch and Femme?

Looking beyond the heterosexual-oriented surface plot, the lesbian reader finds extensive support for seeing the Nancy Drew books as having a lesbian subtext. Particularly revealing is the relationship between Nancy and George and Bess. The three young women form a cohesive community that not even Ned can disrupt. In fact, one can argue that the Keene novels revolve around women's community. One has only to think of the women who help Nancy—like Hannah Gruen, Helen Corning, and Nancy's Aunt Eloise—or the women whom Nancy helps—like Nancy and Allison Hoover in *The Secret of the Old Clock* or Manda Kreutz in *The Witch Tree Symbol* or Millie Burd in *The Secret of Red Gate Farm*—in order to recognize that men play a minor role in these novels. Nancy's father is frequently away on business trips, and the only male characters are typically crooks, or relatively superfluous figures like the police or Ned.

Bess and George, who are easy to slight in favor of the more glamorous Nancy, must be studied in order to understand the Drew books' strong lesbian subtext. George Fayne and Bess Marvin, who are cousins, are introduced in the fifth volume of the series, replacing Nancy's original crime-solving friend, Helen Corning (who always seemed a trifle lackluster). The two cousins are opposites, with George being an enthusiastic supporter of Nancy and her pursuit of mysteries, while Bess quails at the thought of adventure:

> Bess and George were cousins, but there any likeness ended. Bess, blond and pretty, had a penchant for second desserts and frilly dresses. She shared Nancy's adventures out of deep loyalty to her but was constantly fearful of the dangers involved. George was as boyish as her name. Her hair was dark, her face handsomely pert. George wore simple clothes and craved adventure.[50]

Bess is all that is feminine, while George is all that is masculine. Curiously enough, the writers of the early Nancy Drew novels frequently tried to build up George's masculinity rather than downplay it. The books commonly mention George's short haircut: in 1932, "George had cropped her straight dark hair as short as the style would permit, and combed and brushed it as infrequently as possible."[51] In *The Secret in the Old Attic* (1944), Nancy tells George, "If you have much more hair cut off people will think you're a boy."[52] George's masculine name is stressed: in 1932, she was described as "proud of her masculine name, and dressed the part. Woe to the person who called her Georgette or even Georgie, let alone Georgiana or any other feminization of her real name!"[53] George is also proud of her athletic form, boasting in 1932 to Bess, "Look at my brawn! I assure you I haven't wasted all the time I spent in the gym."[54]

George is truly butch. Even today, going back to read the older Nancy Drew books, I find myself surprised at George's masculinity. It is difficult to *avoid* seeing her as a butch lesbian. She fits neatly into the category of the mannish lesbian, which was described by late nineteenth-century sexologists, such as Richard von Krafft-Ebing, who discussed in the 1880s what he named the "female urning" who ignored "girlish occupations," neglected her toilet, and affected "rough boyish manners,"[55] or Havelock Ellis, who wrote that "the commonest characteristic of the sexually inverted woman is a certain degree of masculinity or boyishness."[56] Sigmund Freud, too, emphasized the masculinity of the "true" lesbian. Since the supposed linkage between lesbianism and masculinity was already apparent to a general audience by the 1920s and has been assumed to be true throughout this century, it is surprising from our historical perspective that George was depicted as so butch.

Some critics have sought to downplay George's (and Bess's) apparent lesbianism. In 1964 Arthur Daigon claimed that George "introduces a suggestion of sexual ambivalence."[57] He does not elaborate on his ideas. A few years later, Russel Nye wrote about George that she is "a masculine girl who cuts her hair short and wears mannish clothes (facts which are absolutely not to be misconstrued in this context)."[58] In 1976 Lee Zacharias was more outspoken: "The extremes of possibility for female characters push Bess and George into stereotyped sex roles. To conclude that the girls are lesbians, however, is a camp but erroneous interpretation."[59] I would have to concur with Nye and Zacharias that the writers of the Nancy Drew series probably did not intentionally sit down to make George and Bess seem like the stereotype of a butch and femme couple; Nye and Zacharias overlook, however, that the text created by homosexual readers is as "real" as the text heterosexual readers construct.

Lesbian readers quickly spot Bess and George as lesbians, seeing these unusually close cousins as a butch and femme couple, a duo that has existed in the lesbian community since at least the 1920s.[60] Few lesbian readers could avoid thinking about George as butch, showing why she is frequently their favorite character in these books. One lesbian, Megan, writes, "I preferred George to Bess because she was the tomboy like me." Another comments, "I always thought that George and Bess were a couple." Sarah, who read the Drew books in the late 1970s, writes, "George was my favorite character, probably just due to her male name and her short haircut. God was I a tomboy. Anyhow, I hated Bess. All I can remember about her was her boyfriend." Other lesbians also comment favorably on George's name and her general appeal as a character. In order to increase their reading pleasure, these readers are consciously manipulating the text's codes. By reading the narrative as lesbian, the readers also question the idea that the dominant heterosexual text is "naturally" right.

George, unfortunately, was too openly lesbian to last. In the later books from the 1950s until the present day, George has undergone some disconcerting changes. In *The Legend of Miner's Creek* (1992), she is described as "tall and athletic. Her short, curly, dark-brown hair was full of bounce and seemed to reflect her energetic personality."[61] Although modern-day George has developed a talent for judo, she has simultaneously become less apparently masculine. No longer is she boyish. No longer does she have a boy's haircut. No longer does she strive to wear the most masculine style clothing possible. In 1932, George had been "too blunt and boyish to captivate the young men."[62] When *The Haunted Showboat* was written in 1957, George is already being described as an "attractive brunette"[63] with a boyfriend. There is an evident uneasiness that George could be interpreted as anything other than an all-American girl. The books' writers struggle with the anxiety-provoking fact that creating women characters who appear adventuresome and courageous imbues them with some of the traits that also supposedly identify lesbians in our culture.

Although they are one of the most obvious lesbian signs in the Drew books, Bess and George should not make readers lose track of the many other ways in which these books are queer. As I have already mentioned, Nancy's independence and her allegiance to Bess and George and the women's community that is emphasized throughout the novels points out a lesbian-centered universe. Nancy, her aunt, Bess, and George might not be lesbians if one narrowly defines lesbians as women who have sex with other women, but they certainly are if one uses a broader definition, such as Adrienne Rich's philosophy of a lesbian continuum in which many women can be identified as lesbian, even women who never have sex with other women. According to Rich, "We can see ourselves as moving in and out of this continuum, whether we identify ourselves as lesbian or not."[64] Although I feel it is important to recognize the unique problems faced by lesbians who self-identify as lesbian and, thus, face the dominant society's wrath, I believe Rich's continuum can help us to understand the lesbian subtexts that exist in the Drew novels. Nancy, Bess, and George in their women's community are part of the lesbian continuum.

Nancy Today

In their attempts to make the modern Nancy Drew books appear non-threatening to heterosexual girls, the current publisher and writers have de-emphasized the all-female community and included new boys wherever possible.[65] The girls' boyfriends gain a new prominence, and Bess always seems to be ogling a new male rock star or movie star. Nancy is far more concerned about Ned (and the other men she dates) than she ever was in earlier volumes. Critic Jackie Vivelo remarks that the new Nancy is evolving into a "Barbie doll detective,"[66] and it does appear that Nancy is more one-dimensional these days, more interested in rock and roll and boys than in learning yet another foreign language or translating Middle English (which she actually does in an earlier volume). Yet are Nancy's changes truly that drastic? In popular culture, everything changes—even Nancy. In former years, Nancy quoted Shakespeare and learned foreign languages; now she studies karate and frequents shopping malls. In past years, Nancy relied on her trusty magnifying glass; now she also has the help of computers, fax machines, video cameras, and cell phones. Even today, she is primarily absorbed with crime-solving, but usually on a larger scale, such as tracking down the culprits in a million-dollar jewel heist (*The Case of the Disappearing Diamonds*, 1987) or ferreting out who is stealing top secret government information (*The Ghost of Craven Cove*, 1989). No matter what activities engage Nancy's time, there always exists room for subversion of the dominant story lines. Readers will still receive messages radically different from those that the publisher intended. Examining the Nancy Drew novels has shown that popular texts, even though aimed at a heterosexual audience, can be interpreted in a queer fashion, a reading that is no less significant because it probably is *not* what the writers intended.

Such an approach to popular reading and popular culture studies in general is empowering to lesbian readers. So many texts that seem closed off to lesbians or at least distanced from their experiences open up and become more relevant when the lesbian subtext(s) lurking beneath many dominantly heterosexual texts is recognized. Watching the 1960s television show *Bewitched*, viewing the film *Thelma and Louise*, reading Nancy Drew books or Harlequin romances—one finds a textual universe that is filled with lesbian interpretations and lesbian meanings. Studying this universe starts a person along the long and laborious path of decentering heterosexuality as the "norm." In addition, such lesbian-centered interpretations of popular culture—whether the subject is a Barbie doll or Nancy Drew mystery—allow critics better to understand the multiplicity and complexity of popular culture. Popular culture has as much to say about nondominant groups and forms of cultural resistance as it has to say about the white, heterosexual middle-class public.[67]

NOTES

1. Bobbie Ann Mason, *The Girl Sleuth: A Feminist Guide* (New York: Feminists, 1975), 50.

2. Bruce Watson, "Tom Swift, Nancy Drew and Pals All Had the Same Dad," *Smithsonian* 22.7 (1991): 60.

3. Bernadine Chapman, "The Quest for Nancy Drew," *Antiques and Collecting Hobbies* 98.6 (1993): 31.

4. Betsy Caprio, *The Mystery of Nancy Drew: Girl Sleuth on the Couch* (Tabuco Caynon, CA: Source Books, 1992), 181.

5. Mabel Maney, *The Case of the Not-so-Nice Nurse* (San Fransisco: Cleis, 1993), 142.

6. The popularity of Maney's work has even led her to write a sequel, *The Case of the Good-For-Nothing Girlfriend* (San Francisco: Cleis, 1994).

7. Lynda Hart, *Fatal Women: Lesbian Sexuality and the Mark of Aggression* (Princeton: Princeton University Press, 1994), 66.

8. Erica Rand, "We Girls Can Do Anything, Right Barbie? Lesbian Consumption in Postmodern Circulation," in *The Lesbian Postmodern*, ed. Laura Doan (New York: Columbia University Press, 1994), 190.

9. See "Barbie: Vengeance is Mine,'" *Off Our Backs* 24.2 (1994): 4.

10. For a thought-provoking feminist view of Nancy Drew, read Ellen Brown, "In Search of Nancy Drew, the Snow Queen, and Room Nineteen: Cruising for Feminine Discourse," *Frontiers* 13.2 (1992): 1–25. Another feminist approach to Nancy Drew is found in Jackie Vivelo, "The Mystery of Nancy Drew," *Mrs.* 3.3 (1992): 76–77. A feminist fictional retelling of Nancy Drew's life is Zana's "Nancy Drew and the Serial Rapist," *Common Lives / Lesbian Lives* 24 (1987): 4–19.

11. Eilen Goudge Zuckerman, "Nancy Drew vs. Serious Fiction," *Publishers Weekly* 229.22 (May 30, 1986), 74.

12. Joanne Furtak, "Of Clues, Kisses, and Childhood Memories: Nancy Drew Revisited," *Seventeen*, May 1984, 90.

13. Brown, "In Search of Nancy Drew," 10.

14. Mason, *The Girl Sleuth*, 49.

15. Ibid., 75.

16. Some of the best-known essays about lesbian reading are Marilyn Farwell, "Homosexual Plots and Lesbian Subtexts: Towards a Theory of Lesbian Narrative Space," in *Lesbian Texts and Contexts: Radical Revisions*. ed. Karla Jav and Joanne Glasgow (New York: New York University Press, 1990), 91–103; Jean F. Kennard, "Ourself Beyond Ourself: A Theory of Lesbian Readers," *Signs* 9.4 (1984): 647–62; and Catherine R. Stimpson, "Zero Degree Deviancy: The Lesbian Novel in English," *Critical Inquiry* 8.2 (1981): 363–79. Also see Terry Cas-

tle's related work in *The Apparitional Lesbian: Female Homosexuality and Modern Culture* (New York: Columbia University Press, 1993).

17. Danae Clark, "Commodity Lesbianism," *Camera Obscura* 25–26 (1991): 183.

18. Ibid., 187.

19. Kennard, "Ourself Beyond Ourself," 651.

20. Gabriele Griffin, *Heavenly Love? Lesbian Images in Twentieth-Century Women's Writings* (Manchester: Manchester University Press, 1993), 7.

21. Julia Penelope, "The Lesbian Perspective," in *Lesbian Philosophies and Cultures*, ed. Jeffner Allen (New York: State University of New York Press), 90.

22. Ibid., 107.

23. Farwell, "Homosexual Plots," 93.

24. Ibid., 102.

25. Russel Nye, *The Unembarrassed Muse: The Popular Arts in America* (New York: Dial, 1970), 78. For more information about the Stratemeyer Syndicate, see Carol Billman, *The Secret of the Stratemeyer Syndicate: Nancy Drew, the Hardy Boys and the Million Dollar Fiction Factory* (New York: Ungar, 1986); Deidre Johnson, *Edward Stratemeyer and the Stratemeyer Syndicate* (New York: Twayne, 1993); Karen Plunkett-Powell, *The Nancy Drew Scrapbook* (New York: St. Martin's, 1993); Peter A. Soderbergh, "The Stratemeyer Strain: Educators and the Juvenile Series Book, 1900–1973," *Journal of Popular Culture* 7 (1974): 864–72; and Watson, "Tom Swift."

26. Johnson, *Edward Stratemeyer*, ix.

27. Ibid., 142. The Nancy Drew series was not unique as a girls' series that focused on a girl sleuth. There are dozens of other series about girl detectives, including the Beverly Gray College Mystery Series (Grosset, 1934–55), the Blythe Girls (Grosset, 1925–1932), the Connie Blair Mysteries (Grosset, 1948–58). the Dana Girls Mystery Series (Grosset, 1931–76), the Judy Bolton stories (Grosset, 1932–67), the Kay Tracey Mystery Stories (Cupples, 1934–42), and the Penny Parker Mystery Stories (Cupples 1941–18). These series, however, never achieved the same huge sales as did Nancy Drew.

For an article on the success (or lack of success) of some of these stories, see Anne Scott MacLeod, "Nancy Drew and Her Rivals: No Contest," *Horn Book* 63 (May–June 1987): 314–22.

28. For an article on the difficulties of assigning authorship to the Nancy Drew books, see Geoffrey S. Lapin, "The Ghost of Nancy Drew," *Books at Iowa* 50 (April 1981): 8–27, in which the author argues that Mildred Win Benson is the true mother of Drew.

29. Caprio, *Mystery of Nancy Drew*, 157.

30. Johnson, *Edward Stratemeyer*, 145.

31. Qtd. in Caprio, *Mystery of Nancy Drew*, 22.

32. Johnson, *Edward Stratemeyer*, 147.

33. Background information can be found in Billman, *Secret of the Stratemeyer Syndicate*, 99–120; Patricia Craig and Mary Cadogan, "The Sweet Girl Slueth: The Teenage Detective in America," in *The Ladies Investigate: Women Detectives and Spies in Fiction* (New York: St. Martins, 1981), 149–63; Caprio, *Mys-*

tery of Nancy Drew; Arthur Daigon, "The Strange Case of Nancy Drew," *English Journal* 53 (1964): 666–69; Caroline Stewart Dyer and Nancy Tillman Romalov, eds., *Rediscovering Nancy Drew* (Iowa City: University of Iowa Press, 1995); John F. Enright, "Harriet Adams: The Secret of the Old Clock," *Dime Novel Roundup* 58.4 (1959): 52; Deborah Felder, "Nancy Drew: Then and Now," *Publishers Weekly* 229.22 (May 30 1986): 30–34; James P. Jones, "Nancy Drew: WASP Super Girl of the 1930s," *Journal of Popular Culture* 6.4 (1973): 707–17; Mason, *The Girl Sleuth,* 18–75; Plunkett-Powell, *The Nancy Drew Scrapbook;* Vivelo, "Mystery of Nancy Drew"; Lee Zacharias, "Nancy Drew: Ballbuster," *Journal of Popular Culture* 9 (1976): 1027–38. The children's literature journal *The Lion and the Unicorn* also devoted an entire issue to Nancy; see *The Lion and the Unicorn* 18.1 (1994).

34. *Nancy's Mysterious Letter* (New York: Grosset, 1932), 178.

35. Caroline Keene [pseud.], *The Case of the Velvet Mask* (New York: Grosset, 1969), 176.

36. Caroline Keene [pseud.], *The Secret of Shadow Ranch* (New York: Grosset, 1965), 2.

37. Caroline Keene [pseud.], *The Secret in the Old Attic* (New York: Grosset, 1944), 197.

38. Caroline Keene [pseud.], *The Mystery of the Fire Dragon* (New York: Grosset, 1961), 144–45.

39. Caroline Keene [pseud.], *The Password to Larkspur Lane* (New York: Grosset, 1966), 122.

40. The Nancy Drew series is not the first girls' series to focus on cars. Earlier serials that gave an important role to the automobile are listed in *Girls Series Books: A Checklist of Hardback Books Published 1900–1975* (Minneapolis: University of Minnesota, Children's Literature Research Collections, 1978) and includes the Motor Girls (1910–17), the Automobile Girls (1910–13), and the Motor Maids (1911–17). In numerous serials in the first half of the century, the automobile provided serial characters with "mobility, speed, protection, and often the opportunity to demonstrate exceptional physical coordination" (David K. Vaughan, "On the Road to Adventure: The Automobile and the American Juvenile Series Fiction, 1900–1940," in *Roadside America: The Automobile in Design and Culture,* ed. Jan Jennings. [Ames: Iowa State University Press, 1990], 78). It is Nancy, however, who has been most identified with the car she drives.

For more information on cars in earlier serial novels see Sherrie Inness, "On the Road and In the Air: Gender and Technology in Girls' Automobile and Airplane Serials, 1909–1932," *Journal of Popular Culture* 30 (Fall 1996): 47–60; and Vaughan, "Road to Adventure," 74–78.

41. Billman, *Secret of the Stratemeyer Syndicate,* 113.

42. Caroline Keene [pseud.], *The Clue of the Black Keys* (New York: Grosset, 1968), 137.

43. Zacharias, "Nancy Drew: Ballbuster," 1027.

44. Caroline Keene [pseud.], *The Ringmaster's Secret* (New York: Grosset, 1953), 164.

45. Caroline Keene [pseud.], *The Bungalow Mystery* (New York: Grosset, 1960), 140.

46. Caroline Keene [pseud.], *The Sign of the Twisted Candles* (New York: Grosset, 1933), 160.

47. Caroline Keene [pseud.], *The Quest for the Missing Map* (New York: Grosset, 1943), 178.

48. Caroline Keene [pseud.], *The Clue in the Crossword Cipher* (New York: Grosset, 1967), 16–17.

49. Penelope J. Engelbrecht, for instance, writes, "Like many budding lesbians, I was once perplexed at clever Nancy Drew's retention of that tag-along boyfriend." Penelope J. Engelbrecht, "Lifting Belly is a Language: The Postmodern Lesbian Subject," *Feminist Studies* 16.1 (1990): 85.

50. Caroline Keene [pseud.], *The Secret of the Wooden Lady* (New York: Grosset, 1967), 20.

51. Caroline Keene [pseud.], *The Clue in the Diary* (New York: Grosset, 1932), 2.

52. Keene [pseud.], *Secret in the Old Attic*, 10.

53. Keene [pseud.], *Nancy's Mysterious Letter*, 95.

54. Keene [pseud.], *The Clue in the Diary*, 174.

55. Richard von Krafft-Ebing, *Psychopathia Sexualities: A Medico-Forensic Study* (New York: Stein and Day, 1965), 418.

56. Havelock Ellis, *Studies in the Psychology of Sex*, 1897, vol. 1 (New York: Random House, 1936), 244.

57. Daigon, "The Strange Case of Nancy Drew," 668.

58. Nye, *The Unembarrassed Muse*, 86–87.

59. Zacharias, "Nancy Drew: Ballbuster," 1032.

60. Further accounts of the role of butch/femme couple can be found in Vern Bullough and Bonnie Bullough, "Lesbianism in the 1920s and 1930s: A Newfound Study," *Signs* 2 (1977): 895–904; Shelia Jeffreys, "Butch & Femme: Now and Then," in *Not a Passing Phase: Reclaiming Lesbians in History 1840–1995*, ed. Lesbian History Group (London: Women's Press, 1989), 158–87; Elizabeth Lapovsky Kennedy and Madeline Davis, "The Reproduction of Butch-Fem Roles: A Social Constructionist Approach," in *Passion and Power: Sexuality in History*, ed. Kathy Peiss and Christina Simmons (Philadelphia: Temple University Press, 1989), 241–56; and Joan Nestle, ed., *The Persistent Desire: A Femme-Butch Reader* (Boston: Alyson, 1992).

61. Caroline Keene [pseud.], *The Legend of Miner's Creek* (New York: Simon and Schuster, 1992). 2.

62. Keene [pseud.], *The Clue in the Diary*, 118.

63. Caroline Keene [pseud.], *The Haunted Showboat* (New York: Grosset, 1937), 1.

64. Adrienne Rich, "Compulsory Heterosexuality and Lesbian Experience," in *Adrienne Rich's Poetry and Prose*, ed. Barbara G. Gelpi and Albert Gelpi (New York: Columbia University Press, 1994), 219.

65. Studies that address the new image of Nancy Drew include Kathleen

Chamberlain, "The Secrets of Nancy Drew: Having Their Cake and Eating It Too," *The Lion and the Unicorn* 18.1 (1994): 1–12; Frances Fitzgerald, "Women, Success, and Nancy Drew," *Vogue,* May 1980, 323–24; James Hirsch, "Nancy Drew Gets Real," *New York Times Book Review,* October 9, 1988, 47; Connie Richards, "Nancy Drew: Gothic or Romance?," *Feminisms* 3.5 (1990): 18–21; and Nancy Wartik, "Nancy Drew, Yuppie Detective," *Mrs.* 3.3 (1992): 76–77.

66. Vivelo, "Mystery of Nancy Drew," 76.

67. I wish to thank Ruth Ebelke, Julie Inness, Michele Lloyd, and the anonymous readers from *Women's Studies* for their comments on this essay. I would also like to thank all the lesbian readers who talked to me about their youthful experiences with the Nancy Drew books.

Transchildren and the Discipline
of Children's Literature

❧

JODY NORTON

Oh, if you were a little boy,
And I was a little girl—
Why you would have some whiskers grow
And then my hair would curl.
Ah! If I could have whiskers grow,
I'd let you have my curls;
But what's the use of wishing it—
Boys never can be girls.

—KATE GREENAWAY, "WISHES"

In 1992 a delegation from the Colombia Human Rights
Committee of Washington, D. C. and the Lawyers Committee
for Human Rights interviewed a group of transvestite sex
workers. One of their complaints was that the police would
round up people like them and take them to a site known as
the "road to Choachi," a winding road with sharp precipices,
from which they were thrown to their death.

—JUAN PABLO ORDONEZ

"Children's literature" is a deceptively simple term. In the United
States, among other things, it names a commodified, politically charged
body of texts created, produced, and selected for use with children.
Children's literature also describes a field of academic endeavor that is
in part complicitous in the discipline (regulation, constraint) both of the

corpus of children's texts and of the ideological body of the child within those texts, and in part committed to the critical interrogation of the multiple political investitures in and around "the child" as cultural construction. My concern in this essay is, first, to analyze the multiple relations between children's literature and a particular gender minority, transchildren; that is, children whose experience and sense of their gender does not allow them to fit their sexed bodies into seamless accord with a congruent, conventional gender identity. The disciplinarity (in both senses) of these relations, I will argue, has permitted us, as readers, occasionally to play among such children, but almost never to recognize them.[1] Second, I want to illuminate the liberatory role that children's literature, conceived as a matrix of creative texts and critical inquiries, can play in creating interpretive strategies, curricular revisions, and pedagogical interventions that will contribute substantially to the amelioration of the condition of cultural, institutional, and political neglect through which transchildren have been denied their reality, and their worth. Finally, I will suggest a theoretical reconceptualization of gender that would make possible an aesthetic transumption of romantic and realist impulses in children's literature into what I will call *sublime realism*. Such a transumption could occur either as a reading of existent texts or a writing of new ones.

The historical desire to deny, by one means or another, the reality of alternative forms of sex and gender vividly reflects the intrapsychic as well as the institutional stakes involved in the maintenance of the false binary male ("adult," dominant) / nonmale ("child," subordinate).[2] The threat of the loss, through contamination or degeneration, of the a priori symbolic value of masculinity creates unprocessed anxiety, and unexamined, or rationalized, antipathy—the necessary conditions for the efflorescence of gynephobia or transphobia. According to the hysterical logic of transphobia, insofar as transgendered persons do not accommodate themselves to a heterocentric ideology of gender that interprets reproductive functions as the naturalized basis of differential power relations, they must be made to do so. They must, that is, be institutionally and discursively disciplined, since masculinity is not a matter of anatomy but of meaning.

In *Gender Shock,* her exposé of the institutional maltreatment of transchildren, Phyllis Burke writes:

> If a doctor believes that there is a link between gender nonconformity and adult homosexuality, something that has never been

proven, and further believes that adult homosexuality is a mental ill-ness, [a gender-nonconforming child] will be aggressively treated with behaviorism, psychiatric drugs and counseling. This is known as "reparative" or "conversion" therapy, and the American Psychi-atric Association has yet to forbid the practice. . . . As a result, hun-dreds of adolescents, either suspected of being gay because of gen-der nonconformity or self-declared as gay, are involuntarily locked into psychiatric hospitals.[3]

It is partially for the sake of such children—that their moral and mater-ial existence not be denied—and partially for the sake of our other chil-dren's education toward joyful acceptance and compassionate inclu-sion of their trans sisters and brothers that we must both create and acknowledge their presence in children's literature.[4]

He acts like a sissy. He has expressed the wish to be a girl. He doesn't play with boys. He's afraid of boys, because he's afraid to play boys' games. He used to dress in girls' clothing. He would still like to, only we have absolutely put our foot down.[5]

As a discipline and as a body of texts, children's literature continues to operate on the basis of an outmoded binary paradigm of gender, in part because psychiatry, the social sciences, legal theory, education, and the humanities continue to function, for the most part, as though it had not already been clearly demonstrated that there are neither two sexes and two genders, nor two sex/genders.[6] Psychiatrist Richard Green's work on nontraditionally gendered boys exemplifies the extent to which academic research continues to be constrained by conservative assumptions that inhibit more complex, and more realistic, theoriza-tions of gender. In *The "Sissy Boy Syndrome" and the Development of Ho-mosexuality*—still the authoritative work on the subject—Green sets out to determine the gender characteristics and developmental patterns of sixty-six "feminine boys." While Green notes that "the 'feminine' boys had few behavioral problems other than sexual identity conflict," he implies that the majority of the boys in his study meet the criteria for a diagnosis of "Gender Identity Disorder of Childhood" in the American Psychiatric Association's *Diagnostic and Statistical Manual of Mental Dis-orders*, III.[7]

But why should atypical gender expression be understood as a be-havioral problem at all—that is, something unhealthy or destructive to the individual or those around hir?[8] Isn't it likely that feminine boy behavior is most likely to be a "problem" either because parents feel embarrassed (in a male-dominant society, their boy is acting like a member of the "weaker sex"), or because the child's peers torment hir? And in each of these cases, isn't the problem accurately diagnosed as the parents' or the peers', not the feminine boy's? Rather than "treating" transchildren, shouldn't we provide counseling for adults and children whose speech and behavior clearly shows them to be transphobic—that is, irrationally anxious and fearful in the presence of gender diversity?

Again, why should transgender behavior be assumed to connote "sexual identity conflict"? The children in Green's study seem, for the most part, remarkably *un*conflicted. They gravitate to dolls or mommy play as "naturally" as most other anatomical males gravitate to ball games and roughhousing. The conflict, in fact, is a matter of definitional categories. Hence, it is a conflict that should be attributed mutually to culture and to science, not to the transchild.

Green and his associates are both the consequents of their own constructed assumptions about gender, and contributors, in their turn, to the oppression of alternatively gendered children both directly, in their therapeutic practices, and indirectly, in that the gender ideology structuring their research perpetuates parental and societal conservatism with respect to gender. Together, physician and socioculture absorb and promote the notion that nurturing, or even permitting, alternative sexes and genders subjects a child to unnecessary hardship and discomfort. That suppression of a subject's "deviant" gendering might itself cause profound suffering is seldom acknowledged.[9]

In Green's study, while a minority of feminine boys were entered into formal treatment to attempt to eradicate their transbehaviors, the only choices that seem to have occurred to either Green or the study members' parents were professional intervention or informal attempts "gently to discourage the [feminine] behaviors as they occurred."[10] No one speaks of affirming a child's developing identity, except as that identity is (mis)understood to be truly masculine, beneath a veneer of affectation or deviance constituted as effeminacy. To the extent that this kind of attitude, filtered through multiple professional (medical, psychiatric, psychological), academic, and popular discourses, comes to shape and color the social understanding of gender, it creates massive pressure on authors, producers, and marketers of designated children's texts to stigmatize, and thus in practice largely to avoid, allusion to, or representation of, transchildren.

Among the specific obstacles to more inclusive representations of gender in books for children are the vexed relations between author, publisher, and consumer. In "H/Z: Why Lesléa Newman Makes Heather into Zoe," reprinted in this volume, Elizabeth A. Ford describes the market pressures that appear to have motivated Lesléa Newman to move from Heather, the tomboyish protagonist of *Heather Has Two Mommies,* to Zoe, the flawlessly feminine heroine of *Too Far Away to Touch.* Arguing that "Heather provokes the fear that gay or lesbian parents will produce gay or lesbian children because her clothing, her features, her body, signal *androgynous child,* not *boy* or *girl,*"[11] whereas Zoe, "a pretty, white, blonde female child,"[12] "signals stereotyped femininity in every way that Heather does not,"[13] Ford concludes that "you may skirt, but not approach a gay/lesbian theme in literature for children *and* sell your book if, and only if, the gender identity of your young protagonist is unambiguous."[14] In the contemporary American world of children's literature, author reacts to publisher, who reacts to school, library, and bookstore constituencies, which react to their fear of "trouble" (read parents). One parent/constituent indignantly accusing a school board or library commission of condoning the dissemination of immoral or inappropriate materials will usually send everyone involved into crisis control mode—which all too often has the effective result of the despised work being removed from circulation.

Another important factor contributing to the effacement of transchildren from the accessible corpus of children's literature is the way in which the subject of gender is approached in textbooks designed for training teachers of children's literature—persons who clearly play a significant role in mediating the purchasing relations between publisher and adult/child consumer. In most of these, gender is assumed to be a clear, commonsense notion; but, in fact, it amounts to a confused version of the medically approved sex/gender binary: gender denotes sex, and/or sexed identity, and/or sexed social role, as needed. In a chart in her textbook on children's literature, *Through the Eyes of a Child: An Introduction to Children's Literature,* Donna E. Norton asserts that ten-to twelve-year-old children "have developed strong associations with gender-typed expectations: Girls may fail in 'masculine' tasks, boys in 'feminine' tasks."[15] She suggests that teachers "provide books and discussions that avoid sex-stereotyped roles," and "emphasize that both sexes can succeed in many roles."[16] This, of course, is unexceptionable in its intent to avoid the tracking of children into narrow models of sex-appropriate behavior. But through her conflation of the categories of sex and gender ("gender-typed," "sex-stereotyped"), and her assumption that there are only two ("both") sexes/genders, Norton creates a conceptual dead end: it is impossible for her to envision strategies for accessing the gendered complexity—which is the gendered reality—of polymorphous or alternatively gendered children, since she understands all children as either pregender or, in effect, as conventionally sexed/gendered adults.[17]

Clearly, the educators must be reeducated, and this is a task that must begin from the top, with informed, enlightened faculty in a variety of academic disciplines, including psychology, biology, history, English, education, communications, theater arts, anthropology, and sociology. Most crucially, this reeducative process must be fostered within the field of children's literature, simply because stories, whether literary, oral, or audiovisual, are the cultural medium through which the largest number of people are molded, moved, and inspired to value and accept the diverse ways of being human.

> Realism is nothing more and nothing less than the truthful treatment of material.
> —WILLIAM DEAN HOWELLS

If, in the interests of an ethical as well as an aesthetic realism, we seek explicit representations of transchildren in children's literature itself, we will, as we might expect, seek largely in vain—for the taboos of the adult operate, as a crucial political determinant of the adult/child distinction, to define and circumscribe the culture of the child. The first order of business, then, in the reconstruction of sex and gender in and for children, is to jettison the outdated dimorphic notions of sex and gender, and start talking, teaching, and writing about intersexed people, masculine girls (and not just the domestic tomboy who falls in line at puberty), feminine boys, male-bodied and female-bodied two-spirit children (recall the boygirl character in the Dustin Hoffman film *Little Big Man*), and so on.[18]

In *The Case of Peter Pan, or the Impossibility of Children's Fiction,* Jacqueline Rose quotes, at some length, an anonymous critic in the

Times Literary Supplement addressing the question of aesthetic value and its durability, on the occasion of J. M. Barrie's death in 1937. Among other universalist claims, the critic asserts that "the test of validity in any work of art is its realism on its own plane."[19] Rose poses, obliquely, the obvious poststructural reservations about the critic's "Concept of the *literary* as truth":[20] that it is essentialist; ahistorical; oblivious to its own conflation of ideology, textuality, and reason; and so on. Yet, granting Rose the need to scrutinize truth claims, especially in their always political relation to symbolic systems, it seems to me that the *TLS* critic is right, if we understand his statement as a philosophically nominalist one. The test of a successful children's text would then become, not its adherence, beneath the whimsy and invention, to a founding set of realist or idealist assumptions, but its capacity to reflect its characters' phenomenological and psychosocial reality with an intensity that could facilitate the engagement of the child reader's or child auditor's own perceptions, fantasies, and desires.

A realism of this contingent sort, that recognizes the materiality of the individual and the psychostructural force of desire, colored by experience, is arguably the most effective in delineating the individualities of transchildren. As a kind of textual practice, *sublime realism* would dedicate itself to the production of as fully knowledgeable and efficacious a representation of the subject, and hir/his world as might be viable within the imaginative and conceptual range of the intended audience.

Pending the creation of a substantial body of specifically transchildren's literature, we can intervene in the reproductive cycle of transphobia through strategies of transreading: intuiting/interpreting the gender of child characters as not necessarily perfectly aligned with their anatomies. Transreading may involve as simple a move as locating a male identity in a female body (for example, the practice of casting female actresses in the role of Peter Pan). Or it may constitute itself as a much subtler imaginative enactment of a much wider range of identities. For if there is no such thing as "the opposite sex" (unless we restrict the corporeality and signification of sex to the radically limited sphere of species reproduction), there is assuredly no such thing as an "opposite gender."[21] Often, we are given considerable interpretive leeway in reading character by the text itself—and for that matter, who is to deny us—after postmodernism, after intertextuality and hypertextuality—the right to play a bit beyond the bounds of interpretive legitimacy if we so choose?

In a section of *Through the Eyes of a Child* titled "Guidelines for Selecting Controversial Fiction," Donna E. Norton quotes Dorothy Butler
at length, to the effect that those who would tamper with the canon of
children's literature to advance their antiracist, antisexist, etc., agendas
reveal "an arrogance which may be excused as ignorance, but must not
be tolerated."[22] But suppose one is less interested in removing "Cinderella" from children's reading lists or in marketing a PC knock-off,
than in offering a way of reading Perrault's version as a kaleidoscope of
fantasies of transformation that might include a boy dressing up as a
girl, or *becoming* a girl, for the duration of the story (or at least until
"midnight")? After all, we tacitly expect child readers (most often girls)
to (cross)identify with the male protagonists of the vast majority of children's stories, from Peter Rabbit to Winnie the Pooh, to Peter Pan, to
Bartholomew Cubbins. If this form of gender transitivity is acceptable,
why not also encourage further flights of the gendered imagination: for
example, reading Cinderella as a male-bodied character, or Robin Hood
(like Peter Pan) as a female-bodied one, and explaining that some children (and adults) identify fundamentally (not just transiently) across
sex/gender lines; or drawing attention to alternatively gendered beings like fairies, who are not always represented as clearly either masculine or feminine?

One response might be not "Why not?" but "Why?" A cogent answer to this question, I believe, is the same that I would provide to Norton's question, "Are children harmed by the male and female stereotypes developed in traditional literature?"[23] Children *are* harmed by the
male and female stereotypes developed in traditional literature. First, if
the stereotypes are uncorrected, they contribute to the construction and
validation of retrograde, politically unequal meanings for males and females. Further, the hegemony of the binary model of sex/gender ef-
faces the indefinite range of variant genderings, enforces that effacement with taboo: Gender "deviance," if it is visible at all, is sick,
disgusting, and immoral. The big feet, graceless carriage, physical un-
attractiveness, and aggressive attitude of Cinderella's stepsisters mark
them simultaneously as masculine and bad, their "inappropriate" masculinity a semiotics of their moral character. Rather than capitulate to
the demeaning, phobia-inducing conventions of gender representation,
then, we should act on Dayann K. McClenathan's suggestion, as para-
phrased by Norton, that "problems in books can provide some children
with opportunities for identification and allow other children opportunities to empathize with their peers."[24]

Despite pervasive political investments in the maintenance of binary models of gender, legible in the practice of child psychiatry, the education of teachers, and the marketing of literature for children, some texts that either are, or could easily be, considered children's literature or film exist that present characters who are clearly transgendered, or fantasizing transgendering, in one way or another. Mark Twain's eponymous "Hellfire Hotchkiss," for example, is a stalwart young fantasy figure of female masculinity, when we meet him, but one who, with his opposite number, the feminine boy Oscar (Thug) Carpenter, is ultimately destined to a narrative limbo.[25] The beginning of the fragment in which they appear is promising. Seventeen-year-old Thug is described as flighty, "a creature of enthusiasms" of short duration,[26] and in need of encouragement, of which his father observes, "The boy that needs much of it is a girl in disguise. He ought to put on petticoats."[27] Hellfire, on the other hand, is "a hardy and determined fighter,"[28] more competent in the "masculine arts . . . than any boy of her age in the town."[29] The common wisdom is that "Hellfire Hotchkiss is the only genuwyne male man in this town and Thug Carpenter's the only genuwyne female girl, if you leave out sex and just consider the business facts."[30]

However, once past the novelty of his conception, Twain seems to have been unable to get a real purchase on his characters. He is finally unable to engage imaginatively with Thug to any significant extent (that is to say, he resists, or is incapable of, identification with Thug), so s/he stops speaking to him and drops out of the narrative after hir rescue from drowning by Hellfire. Twain's problem maintaining the latter character is the classic heteronormative one: what do you do with a tomboy once she's too old to be a tomboy? Permanent gender transitivity and lesbian sexuality are equally "impossible," and after a few lingering years of fighting fires and beating up town bullies, Hellfire is finally confronted by his Aunt Betsy, and informed that he is the subject of sexual (ironically heterosexual) gossip. At this point, Hellfire vows to bring himself into accord with the mores for one of his bodily (female) sex, and the narrative breaks off, but not before Hellfire soliloquizes as follows:

> Thug Carpenter is out of his sphere, I am out of mine. Neither of us can arrive at any success in life, we shall always be hampered and fretted and kept back by our misplaced sexes, and in the end defeated by them, whereas if we could change we should stand as good a chance as any of the young people in the town.[31]

That there is no closure to this tale can be pedagogically useful, if frustrating for young readers. A little historical background may make it possible to elicit the recognition, in adolescent readers, that a life without resolution, in various senses, has been precisely the fate of numberless nontraditionally gendered and/or nontraditionally sexually oriented Americans in the last two centuries.[32]

It will continue to be difficult for contemporary authors and filmmakers, as it was for Twain, to conceive and create realistic representations of alternative gender while the available theoretical and pedagogical models of gender remain so limited and inadequate. Jessica Benjamin's work, in conjunction with the object relations theory of D. W. Winnicott, offers a way of thinking about gender that can help to break down the anachronistic paradigm of dimorphism and to integrate the abstractions of theory into the lives of historical subjects. Benjamin begins *Like Subjects, Love Objects: Essays on Recognition and Sexual Difference* by pointing out that the intrapsychic (psychoanalytic) and intersubjective (object relations) models of personality development are nonexclusive even though they are incongruent. Using the separate lenses of each theoretical matrix allows us, Benjamin argues, to foreground the subject's structuration through layerings of identification and to recognize the definitive difference between the subject and the other-as-subject that is crucial to a genuine engagement with another human being. This balancing of theoretical perspectives in fact mimes the internal psychic balance that is necessary for optimal development of the individual as an interrelational, rather than dominant (or subordinate), being.

One of the critical implications of this model of accommodation is that the terms of competing theories need to be conceptualized less rigidly. Thus, Benjamin suggests reconceiving identity as identification: "In giving up the notion of identity, reified as thing, one need not (and should not) throw out the notion of identification, as internal psychic process."[33] "Correspondingly, the categories of gender need to become more fluid: The idea that the child renounces the other's prerogatives in the oedipal phase seems to misconstrue gender identity as a final achievement, a cohesive, stable system. . . . A gendered self-representation is continually destabilized by conflicting mandates and identifications, requiring a capacity for living with contradiction that is in no way culturally supported."[34] There is thus a need "to decenter the notion of gender identification, so that it refers to the plurality of developmental positions rather than to a unilinear line of development, which is ultimately referable to . . . anatomical difference."[35]

Implicit in Benjamin's conception of gender as identificatory rather than identical is the potential for variable (trans)gender subjectivities, and even coincident multiple gender identifications. Such a theory licenses transreading as a specifically literary practice, I would argue, in that the capacity for (re)memory, fantasy, and imaginative identification that constructs the subject (through the mediation of culture) is the same that actualizes the identification of the reading subject with the literary character (through the mediation of the text). Hans Robert Jauss, Wolfgang Iser, and other reader reception theorists, furthermore, have made it abundantly clear that readers (which of course we all are, as we become enculturated) are always in at least two places at once: we retain a strategic sense of self and world against which to understand and evaluate the textual world with whose characters we simultaneously identify.[36]

D. W. Winnicott's model of play as a practice crucial to the child in her evolving sense of self-in-social-relation combined, in turn, with Hans-Georg Gadamer's theorization of play and the hermeneutic consciousness seems to me to offer a richly suggestive model for the social negotiation of gender in childhood, through the flexible process of provisional (transitioning) identification that Benjamin delineates. For Winnicott, play is a crucial, creative practice that enables the child to include, gradually, experimentally, and safely, external objects within the sphere of her ego-consciousness as subjects themselves. The process begins by a taking of inanimate objects (toys, etc.) into the isolated fantasy world of the child: "In playing, the child manipulates external phenomena in the service of the dream and invests chosen external phenomena with dream meaning and feeling."[37]

Play, as such, is not possible if its content is dictated from outside. It comprises a proactive, creative articulation of the subject with her environment: "The precariousness of play belongs to the fact that it is always on the theoretical line between the subjective and that which is objectively perceived."[38] With practice and confidence the child can move from insular fantasy play toward the eventual sharing of cultural roles and relations with other subjects. Winnicott writes: "There is a direct development from transitional phenomena to playing, and from playing to shared playing, and from this to cultural experiences."[39]

Gadamer provides a more philosophically oriented vision of play. For Gadamer, play is a mediatory, indefinitely repetitive "movement backwards and forwards"[40] that, like the physical environment in which we exist, takes us up into itself so that we *become* our play: "Play fulfills its purpose only if the player loses himself in his play."[41] "All playing," then, "is a being-played."[42] Being-played, in turn, is necessarily a condition of transformation and exchange. Thus, while one's play need not necessarily involve another person, "There is an ultimate sense in which you cannot have a game by yourself":[43] In, and as, the to-and-fro of play, the subject is perpetually in relation to an Other. If we think Gadamer's notion of play as repetition and exchange in the context of Winnicott's analysis of child development, specifically as elucidating the fantasmatics and dialogics of gender formation, we can conceptualize gendering as absorption *into* a play that is *for* both self and Other.[44]

Let us see how this works in Kate Greenaway's "Wishes," first published in 1885 in *Marigold Garden,* a kind of Mother Goose assemblage of brief, whimsical, vaguely moral poems and illustrations that "depicts the day-to-day life of children and their mothers."[45] "Play is always representation," Gadamer asserts,[46] and in "Wishes" we see a boy fantasizing his own transformation into "girl," and that of his playmate into "boy." Gadamer shows us where this leads:

> In spending oneself on the task of the game, one is, in fact, playing oneself out. The self-representation of the game involves the player's achieving, as it were, his own self-representation by playing, i.e., representing something.[47]

In this case, of course (as in many others), what is represented is the self—or more precisely, the desire of the subject for the achievement of his own self-representation. This is why "it becomes finally meaningless to distinguish in this sphere [of play] between literal and metaphorical usage,"[48] since gender, in particular, is as much the metaphorization of the literal as it is the literalization of the metaphoric. The game, however (as always), is also one of exchange (whiskers for "boy," curls for "girl")—a game in which the girl is offered a parallel part that she must accept if this particular fantasy of inversion is to be played.

In Greenaway's poem, the boy initiates the fantasy of exchange. The girl responds by entering into this play-within-a-play of gender, and acceding with apparent enthusiasm to the proposed terms. She then quickly retreats from the game on the grounds of efficacy ("what's the use of wishing it") and reason ("Boys never can be girls"—note, however, that she does not explicitly deny herself the potential to be a boy). For a moment, both children have been absorbed. Then, the poem, and the play, are over. Gadamer writes that "the game itself is a risk for the player,"[49] and here the risk for one player has felt too great—for after all, as Gadamer notes, "One can only play with serious possibilities."[50]

One of the delights of the poem, it seems to me, is that it represents the "boy" as the dreamer (who perhaps continues to play, in fantastic silence, beyond the "end" of the game), and the "girl" as the practical one, so that the gender roles of the two are already transposed before the possibility of such a transposition is raised. As is the case with Hellfire Hotchkiss and Thug Carpenter, the "business facts" of sexual difference in this play couple may be more importantly matters of gender than of sex—and, moreover, of a gender that is not necessarily congruent with the bodily sex of either subject.

French director Alain Berliner's 1997 film *Ma Vie en Rose* represents a far more intense experience of the play of gender. Ludovic, a seven-year-old with three older siblings (a girl and two boys) and suburban middle-class parents who had hoped for a girl, believes (or hopes) the s/he is a girl. S/he cross-dresses whenever possible and gravitates to girls and women and their activities (dolls, dance, romantic fantasies and rituals). "It's a scientific matter," Ludo announces, explaining hir very out transgender behavior (an ongoing source of embarrassment to hir would-be upwardly mobile parents) as the result of hir other X chromosome's having accidentally fallen into the trash on its way down from heaven. And indeed, Ludo may turn out to be a true transsexual. In the meanwhile, as Ludo instructs Jerome, the boy next door, s/he is "a girlboy." The film evolves into a bitter struggle by Ludo to keep "playing" (a French Barbie lookalike is Ludo's fairy godmother) while hir family, and the people of the neighborhood marshal their combined social, political, and cultural resources to force Ludo to stop.

Trouble starts when Ludo announces that s/he and Jerome are "going to marry when I'm not a boy." Ludo subsequently stages a mock wedding (dressed in a pink satin dress that once belonged to Jerome's deceased sister), which is interrupted by Jerome's mother just as Ludo is informing Jerome that he may kiss hir. Ludo's high femme gender causes hir to be misread by Jerome's father and others as gay, which, in a Catholic society, is understood as the next thing to damnation. A harrowing series of violent and transphobic confrontations (including some with hir parents) drives Ludo to attempt to kill hirself by going to sleep in a freezer. Ludo's father (who works for Jerome's dad) loses his job, and the family is hounded from the neighborhood, with many recriminations inside the family and out.

In the new neighborhood Ludo is approached by a transboy named Christine. The two make friends, and at the latter's birthday party exchange clothes: Christine's dress for Ludo's cavalier outfit. After a final burst of hysteria from Ludo's mother, hir parents finally decide to leave hir to hir own devices. The film ends with Ludo, in Christine's satin dress, chain-dancing with the other children.

Ludo's heavily constructed sense of what "girl" means instantiates Gadamer's contention that a child at play (specifically, in *Truth and Method*, a child engaged in what Gadamer calls "dressing-up") desires to represent hirself in such a way that only what is represented exists. The child does not want at any cost to be discovered behind his disguise. He intends that what he represents should exist, and if something is to be guessed, then this is it. What it "is" should be recognized.[51] But if our first response is to deplore Ludo's somewhat commodified sense of gender (as cultural feminists have often deplored male-to-female transsexuals), we should perhaps interrogate our own need to discipline gender variance into more and less correct forms.[52]

In any case, the film is (utterly irrationally) rated R, and hence could not be taught, in public schools, at least as a children's text. But it *is*, certainly, a children's story, in the sense that it focuses on a child in a social world composed of other children and adults, engaged in a moral drama, mediated through a fantasy life in which the protagonist's lack of social power is compensated for by hir imaginative ability to transform hirself freely, through hir own agency (like Alice in Wonderland), and to fly away, escaping the constraints of hir condition, to a marvelous alternative world (like Peter Pan, Dorothy, and many others). But Ludo is free, also, to return, and to continue growing, the stronger for hir experience.

The boy is mother of the woman.

—U. C. KNOEPFLMACHER

I want to close with a brief speculation on the origins of transgender in children that I intend as a suggestive vision rather than as a thoroughly supportable claim. The first step toward this vision is mundane in the extreme, but it also represents a counterreformation against the decaying, but still reigning orthodoxy of an unreconstructed poststructuralism: it may be that children like Ludo are moved—as, indeed, are all children—to pursue the directions of gender that they do partially as the result of genetic and other biological factors. Ludo's speculation about hir "lost" X chromosome ("c'est une matiere scientifique") may be more than a child's fantasy (even if the fantasy itself is as significant a formative element of hir gender as the somatic elements involved).

We must acknowledge that historically, we have been disproportionately interested in the reproductive anatomy and physiology of the body, as a determinant of sex differences. We are beginning to understand that the female body is, in fact, much less different from the male than post-Renaissance male discourse on the subject had led us to believe. Furthermore, we know that many humans are neither "male" nor "female," at least according to strict biological definitions of those terms. At the same time, we also know that there is evidence (albeit inconclusive) for statistically significant differences in male and female developmental rates, predilections for certain kinds of large and small motor activities, patterns of conscious and unconscious identification, and patterns of social cohesion or lack of cohesion, among other characteristics. We should therefore be willing to think of sex, and of genes, and of gender as perhaps being related, but in much more subtle, complex, and negotiable ways than have generally been conceived.

The question is whether it really is senseless to say, not necessarily that a male-to-female transchild is a girl in a boy's body, but that s/he is not a boy. This, in turn, leads not necessarily to Judith Butler's point that male and female are constructed categories, but perhaps to a way of understanding the relation between the biochemistry of the body and the formation of embodied consciousness (and consciousness of the body) as a dynamic potentiation. Ludo, then, may not *feel* like a boy (gender) because s/he may not *be becoming*, psychosomatically and eco-biologically, a boy (sex/gender) in the way that most boys (sex) do.

Genes are only and always elements of extremely complex bio-chemical psychodevelopmental processes that do not take place either entirely predictably, nor in a vacuum (environmental factors affect child development at every step, prenatally as well as postnatally). However, it may be that genetic, endocrinological, bioenvironmental (ecological and biosocial) factors make possible or potentiate the development, through the dynamics of play theorized above, within a child whose reproductive anatomy is male, of an *affinity* for females, female connections, and female communities, or for specifically transcommunities, if these exist in the child's world. Affinity, in turn, might shape itself as *affiliation*—the sense that I belong with, and am comfortable with, the kind of people my society calls "women" (or xaniths or hijras or mahus) and/or with the behaviors, styles of self-presentation, and activities that such people engage in, in my field of perception (as well as, perhaps, a disaffiliation with men).

For example, Ludo dances, with women and by hirself. Ludo's fondness for expressive dance, as a form of play, may be part of hir affinity for women (in hir case, though not as a theorem, since many boys dance, for many reasons). Ludo's pattern of group dancing with women reminds one of Margaret Mead's anecdote of the Omaha Indian adolescent repeated by Walter L. Williams in his book on Native American two-spirit people, *The Spirit and the Flesh: Sexual Diversity in American Indian Culture*:

> At dances in which the sexes danced separately, he would begin the evening dressed as a man and dancing with the men, and then, as if acting under some irresistible compulsion, he would begin to move closer and closer to the women, as he did so putting on one piece of jewelry after another. Finally a shawl would appear, and at the end of the evening he would be dressed as a berdache, a transvestite. The people were just beginning to speak of him as "she."[53]

There is already much evidence that femaleness is not a condition of being that begins with a beginning (two chromosomes, say), but rather a becoming that, as embryo/infant and environment interact, may take an indefinite number of modal shapes, some of which are more common than others. The femaleness, or transness, if one prefers, of a child like Ludo, or the Omaha Indian youth, may be a rich, genetically and biochemically influenced strand in the tapestry of what might, with another genetic, psychobiological, and biosocial history, have become actualized as a "male."

Let us hold the speculative space of gender open until we know more, and let us open, in the meanwhile, the sociopolitical and aesthetic question of the representation of (trans)gender in children's literature. If it is manifestly untrue, in life and, as we have seen, in literature and film, that children come in only two genders, can we, should we, continue to deny reality, fantasy, moral standing, and political rights to those who are alternatively gendered? Children in contemporary American children's literature come in all shapes, sizes, races, religions, and economic conditions. When it comes to the semiotics of gender, there are almost more girls pictured in pants than in skirts. Why not a boy in a dress? Who is it, finally, that is going to be upset by such a depiction (and it is important not to assume that anyone is): children or fearful adults? And if that fear is phobic and discriminatory, ought we to capitulate to it, under the pretense of objectivity?

Let us commit ourselves to an unabashed romanticism of imagination, in the creation and interpretation of texts for children—but to a romanticism redefined to include a range of child subjectivities so broad, and at the same time so individually distinct, as to constitute what I have called a sublime realism. For it is my contention that the child does not only long, in some transient way, for the transformation of the real into the imaginary, but that, in fact, the most profound desire of the child is precisely to transform the romantic (the fantastic, the fantasmatic) into the real. This, it seems to me, is the project both of the Wordsworthian and the Lacanian child.

Let us strive, in particular, for a sublime realism of subjectivity—the kind of life-affirming, child-affirming psychosocial realism that not only recognizes, but celebrates, diversities of gender, sexuality, race, and culture on the multiple intersecting planes of the polymorphous carnival of wonders we call childhood.

NOTES

1. I refer to the academic discipline of children's literature, the pedagogy and curriculum of which are largely governed by the binary model of gender reflected in Donna E. Norton's work below; and to the more insidious, because less conscious and systematic, gender policing of the content of children's literature in the United States by teachers, parents, libraries, publishers, authors, agents, bookstores, trade groups, churches, and community organizations.

2. In this hierarchy, "child" includes women; children; transpeople; inter-sexed persons; "sissies," or homosexuals; and even, contingently, men of color, and "common," or working-class, white men

3. Phyllis Burke, *Gender Shock: Exploding the Myths of Male and Female* (New York: Doubleday-Anchor, 1996), 85.

4. That transchildren exist in significant numbers is not open to question. The very existence of the diagnostic category "Gender Identity Disorder in Children," according to which discrimination passes for science in the current edition of the *Diagnostic and Statistical Manual of Mental Disorders,* published by the American Psychiatric Association (DSM-IV), testifies to the existence of a population of transgendered children large enough to warrant its existence.

5. Richard Green, *The "Sissy Boy Syndrome" and the Development of Homosex-uality* (New Haven: Yale University Press, 1987), 2.

6. See, for example, Judith Butler, *Gender Trouble: Feminism and the Subver-sion of Identity* (New York: Routledge, 1990); R. W. Connell, *Masculinities* (Berke-ley: University of California Press, 1995); Julia Epstein, *Altered Conditions: Dis-ease, Medicine, and Storytelling* (New York: Routledge, 1995); Julia Epstein and Kristina Straub, eds., *Body Guards: The Cultural Politics of Gender Ambiguity* (New York: Routledge, 1991); Anne Fausto-Sterling, "The Five Sexes: Why Male and Female Are Not Enough," *The Sciences,* March–April 1993, 20–25; Anne Fausto-Sterling, *Myths of Gender: Biological Theories About Women and Men,* 2nd ed. (New York: HarperCollins–BasicBooks, 1992); Leslie Feinberg, *Transgender Warriors: Making History from Joan of Arc to RuPaul* (Boston: Beacon, 1996); Ju-dith Halberstam, *Female Masculinity* (Durham: Duke University Press, 1998); Gilbert Herdt, ed., *Third Sex, Third Gender: Beyond Sexual Dimorphism in Culture and History* (New York: Zone, 1994); Ruth Hubbard, "Gender and Genitals: Constructs of Sex and Gender," *Social Text* 46–47 (1996): 157–65; Suzanne J. Kessler, *Lessons from the Intersexed* (New Brunswick: Rutgers University Press, 1998); Suzanne J. Kessler and Wendy McKenna, *Gender: An Ethnomethodological Approach* (Chicago: University of Chicago Press, 1985); and Walter L. Williams, *The Spirit and the Flesh: Sexual Diversity in American Indian Culture* (Boston: Bea-con, 1988).

7. Green, *Sissy Boy Syndrome,* 13. Note that the DSM-III used a slightly dif-ferent diagnostic name than the DSM-IV uses, above.

8. Transgender pronouns are in flux at the moment. Here I use male pro-nouns for female-to-male transpeople, to emphasize that masculinity is not a born privilege. I use "hir," "hir," and "s/he" for male-to-female transpeople, to respect the history of negative—and positive—difference that belongs to born-female human beings.

9. See Eve Kosofsky Sedgwick, "How to Bring Your Kids Up Gay: The War on Effeminate Boys," in *Tendencies* (Durham: Duke Univeristy Press, 1993), 162–63, for a critique of Green. It is worth noting that in a work, *The Transsexual Experiment* (London: Hogarth, 1975), that is in some ways quite harsh, Robert Stoller writes, "We see the terrible pain and sadness in these little boys as we force them to resolve their bisexuality. . . . They are like refugees driven from a beloved homeland. . . . Compelled by neighbors, companions, siblings, teach-

ers, and finally 'the police'—us therapists—to leave this lovely homeland, they cannot help but fight against us, and as our power begins to show its full strength, their fight to return home goes underground into fantasy" (92). Toward the end of the book, Stoller reflects, "I wonder how much anguish we have a right to bring to them. I would not ask, were our success in getting them to create masculinity deep and true. But core gender identity is so fixed so early, and to try to remove it and replace it with its opposite—masculinity, the most alien identity the boy could create—is a cruel process. . . . one begins to wonder: might it not be no worse, and perhaps a bit better, if one encouraged the feminization process. So far neither we nor anyone else—probably—has dared" (273–75). Cross-cultural anthropological knowledge would allow Stoller to recognize that in fact many other societies, and some in our own country—Native American peoples with two-spirit traditions, contemporary urban drag families—have dared to give freedom and support to feminine boys in following their own gender direction. See Williams, *Spirit and Flesh,* and the film *Paris Is Burning,* directed by Jeanie Livingston.

10. Green, *Sissy Boy Syndrome,* 260.

11. Elizabeth A. Ford, "H/Z: Why Lesléa Newman Makes Heather into Zoe," in "Lesbian/Gay Literature for Children and Young Adults," ed. Kenneth Kidd, special issue of *Children's Literature Association Quarterly* 23 (1998): 129.

12. Ibid., 130.

13. Ibid., 131.

14. Ibid., 132. Ford notes that the commercial viability of such a book also depends on maintaining "a 'safe' distance between child and gay adult characters" (128).

15. Donna E. Norton, *Through the Eyes of a Child: An Introduction to Children's Literature,* 4th ed. (Englewood Cliffs, NJ: Prentice-Hall, 1995), 33.

16. Ibid.

17. Donna E. Norton also uses the phrase "the opposite sex" (33), which of course transparently binarizes sex as a conceptual category. Other children's literature textbooks make similar assumptions about gender. In *Children's Books in Children's Hands* (Needham Heights, MA: Allyn & Bacon, 1998), Charles Temple and his colleagues (including Miriam Martinez, Junko Yokota, and Alice Naylor) claim that "well-written gender-sensitive literature fights stereotypes by depicting the diversity and multidimensionality of men and women, girls and boys" (110). They recommend *Max,* by Rachel Isadora, which they describe as about a boy who "defies the stereotype that 'boys don't dance' when he finds that dance lessons are a good warm-up to his afternoon baseball games" (110), and *William's Doll,* by Charlotte Zolotow, in which Grandmother "gets William a doll so that he can prepare for when he will be a father" (130). In each case, mildly transgressive gender behaviors are quickly recuperated into traditionally masculine, heterosexual contexts and outcomes. Where is the "diversity" in this? I would suggest that finding out that each boy is really utterly appropriately masculine accomplishes nothing but the insidious reinforcement of the disciplinary norms that are ostensibly being challenged.

18. For critical reviews of twenty-six of the most important works on trans-

gender, see Jody Norton, "Transsexualism/Transgenderism: Theoretical, Psychological, and Medical Accounts," and "Transsexualism/Transgenderism: History, Politics, and Cultural Formations," in the *Reader's Guide to Lesbian and Gay Studies*, ed. Timothy F. Murphy (Chicago: Fitzroy Dearborn, 2000).

19. "Barrie as Dramatist: A Divided Mind," *Times Literary Supplement* 26 (June 1937): 469.

20. Jacqueline Rose, *The Case of Peter Pan, or The Impossibility of Children's Fiction* (Philadelphia: University of Pennyslvania Press, 1984), 112.

21. See Butler, *Gender Trouble*; also see Fausto-Sterling, "The Five Sexes," and *Myths of Gender*.

22. Dorothy Butler, "From Books to Buttons: Reflections from the Thirties to the Eighties," in *The Arbuthnot Lectures: 1980–1989* (Chicago: American Library Association, 1990), 37, quoted in Norton, *Eyes of a Child*, 447.

23. Norton, *Eyes of a Child*, 281.

24. Ibid., 447.

25. See Susan Gillman, *Dark Twins: Imposture and Identity in Mark Twain's America* (Chicago: University of Chicago Press, 1989), 108–10, for a brief critical discussion of "Hellfire Hotchkiss."

26. Mark Twain, "Hellfire Hotchkiss," in *Mark Twain's Satires and Burlesques*, ed. Franklin R. Rogers (Berkeley: University of California Press, 1968), 177.

27. Ibid., 178.

28. Ibid., 194.

29. Ibid., 195.

30. Ibid., 187.

31. Ibid., 199.

32. Resources for such a discussion include George Chauncey, *Gay New York: Gender, Urban Culture, and the Making of the Gay Male World, 1890–1940* (New York: HarperCollins–BasicBooks, 1994); Martin Duberman, *Stonewall* (New York: Dutton, 1993); David F. Greenburg, *The Construction of Homosexuality* (Chicago: University of Chicago Press, 1988); and Jonathan Ned Katz, *Gay American History: Lesbians and Gay Men in the U.S.A.*, rev. ed. (New York: Penguin-Meridian, 1992) and *Gay/Lesbian Almanac: A New Documentary* (New York: Richard Gallen, 1994).

33. Jessica Benjamin, *Like Subjects, Love Objects: Essays on Recognition and Sexual Difference* (New Haven: Yale University Press, 1995), 51.

34. Ibid., 70.

35. Ibid., 126.

36. See Wolfgang Iser, *The Implied Reader: Patterns of Communication in Prose Fiction from Bunyan to Beckett* (Baltimore: Johns Hopkins University Press, 1974); Hans Robert Jauss, *Aesthetic Experience and Literary Hermeneutics*, trans. Michael Shaw (Minneapolis: University of Minnesota Press, 1982) and *Toward an Aesthetic of Reception*, trans. Timothy Bahti (Minneapolis: University of Minnesota Press, 1982). See also Jody Norton, "History, Rememory, Transformation: Actualizing Literary Value," *Centennial Review* 38 (1994): 589–602.

37. D. W. Winnicott, *Playing and Reality* (New York: Routledge, 1982), 51.

38. Ibid., 50.

39. Ibid., 51.

40. Hans-Georg Gadamer, *Truth and Method* (New York: Continuum, 1975), 93.

41. Ibid., 92.

42. Ibid., 95.

43. Ibid.

44. See Judith Butler's theory of the performativity of gender, in *Gender Trouble,* and Lacan's notion of the mutually reflective logic of representation, most readily accessible in *Ecrits: A Selection,* trans. Alan Sheridan (New York: Norton, 1977) and *The Four Fundamental Concepts of Psycho-Analysis,* ed. Jacques-Alain Miller, trans. Alan Sheridan (New York: Norton, 1981).

45. The first epigraph to this essay.

46. Gadamer, *Truth and Method,* 97.

47. Ibid.

48. Ibid., 94.

49. Ibid., 95.

50. Ibid.

51. Ibid., 102.

52. There are few truly balanced perspectives yet available on the ethics of transsexuality and transgenderism. See Halberstam's *Female Masculinity* and Jay Prosser's *Second Skins: The Body Narratives of Transsexuality* (New York: Columbia University Press, 1998) for two interesting analyses of forms of female-to-male transitioning and their ethical implications.

53. Margaret Mead, *Sex and Temperament in Three Primitive Societies* (New York: Morrow-Quill, 1963), 294–95.

Trans Magic

The Radical Performance of the Young Wizard in YA Literature

ف

JES BATTIS

> We tacitly expect child readers (most often girls) to
> (cross)identify with the male protagonists of the vast majority
> of children's stories, from Peter Rabbit to Winnie the Pooh . . .
> if this form of gender transitivity is acceptable, why not also
> encourage . . . reading Cinderella as a male-bodied character,
> or Robin Hood (like Peter Pan) as a female-bodied one?
>
> —JODY NORTON

This essay will focus on various performances of magic in YA fantasy literature, paying special attention to how magic and gender—as radical and transformative powers—are often linked. Both magic and gender are sites of pedagogy, spaces of learning (where "correct" learning is rewarded, and "incorrect" learning or performance has a variety of social consequences), and wizardry schools like Hogwarts tend to impart gender regulations just as much as magical instruction. For the purposes of this discussion, I will be treating various instances of gendered magical performance, occurring either in wizardry schools, remote villages, alternate dimensions, or contemporary urban landscapes. I will not be talking about the wizardry school tradition as such, since a great deal of work on writers like J. K. Rowling and Ursula K. LeGuin—whose writing deals with such institutions—has already been done, and done well. I instead want to focus on magic itself as a transformative site for the politics of gender.

The production codes of children's and YA fantasy literature can invite transgressive readings, while simultaneously trying to prevent them. Even when magic seems constrained by gender and class assumptions, it can still deconstruct and derail those assumptions through imaginative readings and rereadings. And, as Deborah Thacker suggests, it is just this sort of flexible reading process often evidenced by child readers—a process commonly disavowed by academic opponents of children's literature as a genre—that allows for such imaginative revision to take place. "Re-reading," she states, "can also be conceived of as an exercise in re-writing, or taking possession of a text . . . [and the] need for children to re-read, sometimes at the expense of parental sanity . . . may proceed from the notion of re-enacting the play of desire."[1] Children, then, become in some sense the readers most capable of discovering gender transgression, just as they are the readers most stridently protected against such transgression by concerned adults.

Critics of fantasy literature in general have been debating articulations of the uncanny, the marvelous, and the fantastic since Freud first proposed the idea of the *unheimlich* ("uncanny") in his 1925 essay of the same name. Tolkien applied the idea to secondary worlds in his lectures on fairy stories (1939) at the University of Leeds, and Tzvetan Todorov drew complex structural distinctions between "the uncanny" and "the marvelous" in his benchmark text "The Literature of the Fantastic" (1973). These distinctions have been variously taken up, extended, and critiqued by later theorists of the fantastic, such as Rosemary Jackson and Anne Swinfin, who offer revisions of Todorov's work that are inflected by feminist and Marxist principles (since Todorov himself writes in a weirdly apolitical mode at times). Although I will not be significantly debating fantasy as a genre within this discussion—since there is already plentiful critical debate around that topic—I would like to align Todorov's notion of the fantastic as "a hesitation between genres" with similar presentations of magic in children's fantasy texts.[2] Magic is also a "hesitation" of sorts, a momentary gap in time/space, in narrative progression, that allows for radical gender insubordination (even in instances where it is designed expressly to contain such insubordination).

J. K. Rowling's Harry Potter series, for instance, hinges on the distinction between magic and "normal," wizard and muggle, but there is also a sort of transparent gender binary of male/female at work throughout the texts. There seem to be two critical poles of magic in Rowling's world: there is learned or competent magic, as embodied by Hermione Granger, and then there is intuitive or creative magic, which Harry himself demonstrates on several occasions. Hermione is clearly the most competent wizard at Hogwarts, having read everything from *Hogwarts, A History* to *Quidditch Through the Ages*. It is her logical deductive abilities that allow her, in *The Philosopher's Stone,* to solve most of the magical puzzles directed at Harry, including a nefarious potion puzzle at the end of the book.

Over the course of five novels, she manages to alter time, fend off all manner of monsters with her defensive magic, freeze people in stasis, obliterate door locks, and patiently explain matters of history and philosophy to the clueless Ron and Harry. Yet Hermione declares Harry to be "a great wizard."[3] When he protests, citing her various contributions to their adventures, Hermione completely elides her own skills as a talented wizard by dismissing them as "books! And cleverness! There are more important things—friendship, and bravery, and—oh Harry, be careful."[4] Harry thus becomes emblematic of friendship and bravery, while Hermione's "oh Harry!" utterance repositions her as a frightened girl rather than a powerful wizard in her own right.

Harry is often frightened, in fact, but he rarely expresses it, since that would violate the masculine codes of Hogwarts, Rowling's fantastic British boarding school. Beverly Lyon Clark reminds us that Rowling's depiction of such a school is itself exotic, given that Harry seems surrounded by cultural oddities that "nobody younger than 80" in Britain would even recognize.[5] Harry's imagined vulnerability as a child always in danger—he is, after all, locked in a cupboard under the stairs—is a crucial component in selling Harry's "everyboy" identity to both child and adult readers. Suman Gupta interprets Harry at the beginning of *Harry Potter and the Philosopher's Stone* as "a sort of boy Cinderella in the Dursley's home . . . he lives in a cupboard under the stairs, a space that serves as both bedroom and punishment chamber."[6] But this vulnerability gradually becomes an artificial one, a construct similar to the masochistic sign of the wounded white male—a figure who can appropriate historical trauma while still cohering as powerful, masculine, and privileged (the character of Spike on *Buffy the Vampire Slayer* comes to mind). Harry's masculinity may seem conflicted, but he is always being reinstated as a masculine character through Hermione's exaggerated "feminine" drama and Ron's feminized antics (moaning, complaining, pulling faces, tripping over himself, and other Stooges-like strategies of establishing his own ineptitude).

Let us turn from Hermione Granger to a very different young wizard, Dairine Callahan, a central character in Diane Duane's Young Wizards series (*So You Want To Be a Wizard, Deep Wizardry, High Wizardry, A Wizard Abroad*). Like Hermione, much of Dairine's agency comes from her "excessive" speech, which she uses to defy and critique forms of patriarchy. Unlike Hermione, Dairine is perfectly aware that she is one of the most powerful wizards in the world, and—with the charming hubris of an eleven-year-old—she has no qualms about reordering space and time, meddling with the cosmos, and battling the incarnation of death and entropy itself in order to prove her powers.

Unlike her sister Nita's wizardry, which is grounded in research and textuality, Dairine's wizardry fuses technology with magic. Her "spell-book" is actually a computer, and its arrival seems to coincide with Dairine's own conviction that she is "beating her fists against the walls of life, knowing there's more, more, but she can't figure out what it is, then finding out that someone knows the secret. Wizardry. And it doesn't come fast enough, it never comes fast enough, nothing ever does."[7] This quote is actually taken out of context, for it occurs near the end of the book, not at the beginning. Dairine imagines that "[nothing] ever comes fast enough" later in the text as she is pouring her essence into the race of sentient computer-beings that she has created, attempting to make them understand what "slowlife" (humanity) is.

This desperation at the slowness of knowledge, this anxiety of an eleven-year-old "stick of a thing" who wishes angrily, immediately for what she construes to be the logical and ordering powers of an adult, becomes a site of repetition throughout High Wizardry. Dairine, who has always thirsted for the fantastic powers of Luke Skywalker—who wants to rewrite her own life in an epic, even intergalactic, vein—is the prototypical young hero wishing for agency through adulthood. But she also defies this formula, and it is ultimately her emotion, her brashness, and her irresponsibility—all stereotypical markers of childhood behavior—that allow her to save the Mobiles (her newly created race of beings) from corruption and eventual extinction at the hands of the Lone One. Her role in the literal, almost parthogenetic (from silicon rather than clay) production of the Mobiles becomes, in *High Wizardry,* a reenactment of the wizard's role in capitalist production. Only, in this case, she's not just casting a spell: she's making a species.

Magic is the circulating capital of epic fantasy, and, like capital, it enacts a contradiction: producing something called "labor power" out of nothing, or nearly nothing. Magical production has to be linked to capitalist production, not only because magic requires raw materials—reagents, liquids, powders, parchment, and sometimes electricity—but because wizards in epic and urban fantasy operate as capitalist agents, using their mystical skill-set in order to survive in a financially hostile environment. Whether it's Middle Earth or Los Angeles, a wizard has to eat. So the ability to fashion a proper spell becomes identical to any accomplished craft or trade. Wizards have guilds and schools, just like medieval crafts communities. And learning to weave speech-acts together to form a coherent meme, a "spell," is structurally similar to learning a musical instrument. David Hawkes, in his article on *Faust*, discusses the contractual and fiduciary elements of demonic magic, which becomes essentially "the ability to appropriate and direct supernatural labor."[8] But what happens when young people are thrown into the financial ring of the working wizard? Do systems of magic, as extensions of late capitalism, have the perverse ability to suppress and regulate desire within kids? Do they often succeed?

By becoming an expert programmer and cyberwizard, Dairine is choosing to work, choosing to *produce*. She refuses what she sees as the vacuous, timeworn princess-role that young female characters are often forced to inhabit in children's fantasy. But being a princess can simply require different tactics of production and labor. Princess Eilonwy, from Lloyd Alexander's Prydain series, remains an ambiguous and overlooked character within the children's fantasy canon. After rescuing Taran from the perilous castle of the witch Achron (her dubious guardian and instructor in the arts of magic), Eilonwy fades into the background while Taran evolves as a heroic character. Yet Eilonwy, despite Taran's many attempts to silence her, remains a verbose presence throughout the Prydain books, establishing her agency precisely through her excessive speech. It is Eilonwy who explains to Taran the crucial difference between "Pig-Boy" and "Assistant Pig-Keeper," telling him (quite stridently) that "you're an Assistant Pig-Keeper! That's honor in itself!"[9] Much of Eilonwy's dialogue seems invested in educating Taran, and the entire Prydain series can in fact be read as a sort of medieval boy's conduct manual—a grand adventure whose extravagance serves to cloak Taran's own moral evolution from boyhood to manhood.

Yet Taran's adolescence is highly inflected by Eilonwy's comments and advice, her many interruptions and criticisms, and her penchant for saying precisely what Taran doesn't want to hear about himself. Alexander's language when describing Eilonwy's magic—especially her "magic bauble," a small golden orb which glows brightly—is always coy without being too suggestive, although it takes very little imagination to make the leap from magic to sex (a conflation often evident in adolescent fantasy, where magic stand in for sex, and/or sex emerges from intensely magical situations). The many scenes in which Taran has to gingerly hold Eilonwy's bauble, punctuated by her exasperated responses, such as "Oh, you'll never learn how to use my bauble,"[10] suggest that magic is being substituted for sexuality here, as in the scene in which Taran asks Eilonwy to "gird" his sword for him, saying nervously, "I want you to be the one to do it," while Eilonwy blushes.[11]

In addition to creating the possibility of sexual tension, these scenes also reinforce Eilonwy's character as an inexperienced girl, a princess who must ultimately be saved by Taran, who is a hero-in-training. The ambiguity emerges when we realize that Eilonwy is, in a sense, the one who is training Taran to be a hero, and not by merely establishing herself as an object of lack, a princess waiting to be saved. Eilonwy provides the majority of Taran's moral instruction, and has no fear of contradicting or even publicly insulting him. While the distinct "femininity" of Eilonwy's magic, its mysterious, organic, and circular qualities, is meant to enforce her femininity as a character, she manages to exceed the constraints of this characterization through her brazen speeches and pointed interruptions of masculine dialogue. While it seems more likely that Alexander meant to present her as a slightly updated version of the archetypal shrewish maiden, Eilonwy—somewhat like Chaucer's Wife of Bath—becomes a character whose sheer verbosity actually explodes the boundaries of her textual construction and confinement.

One of the characters who actually seems most like Harry Potter (and also the character who has been given the least amount of critical attention) in contemporary children's fantasy is Alanna, the female knight of Tamora Pierce's Lioness series (*Alanna: The First Adventure, In the Hand of the Goddess, The Woman Who Rides Like a Man, Lioness Ram-*

pant). In order to attain knighthood, Alanna dresses like a man and becomes "Alan," thereby reinventing herself as a male squire. The two characters are quite different, but both have a sort of greatness and nobility thrust upon them by adults; both are trying to outdistance some essential "flaw" that they see in their own lives (Harry wants to escape from his unwanted fame, and Alanna wants to escape from the social constraints of her gender); both are incredibly powerful and insubordinate, often stumbling into dangerous situations precisely because they have chosen to flaunt adult authority. Yet Pierce's novels tend to ask tougher questions than Rowling's, dealing with the trials of an adolescent female character—including physical development, menstruation, pregnancy, and sex—that the Harry Potter series would never touch.

Near the beginning of *Alanna: The First Adventure*, Alanna asks, "Why couldn't [I] have been a boy?"[12] which produces an even more complicated question that runs throughout the series—is Alanna a boy? Furthermore, how does one "be" a boy or a girl in children's fantasy literature? Alanna seems to have a subjective understanding of herself as a girl, a feminine embodiment, but that embodiment is constantly being threatened by her interest in the masculine arena of knighthood. By the end of the second novel in the series, Alanna still doesn't have any female friends (aside from the mother of her love interest, the thief Roger), and seems to actually despise courtly ladies for what she perceives as their seductive qualities and intellectual vacuity. Like Eilonwy, Alanna has several lines that may or may not be read as coy authorial humor, such as when she advises Prince Jonathan (another love interest), "My sword—it's humming."[13] Alanna's sword, the mythical weapon called Lightning, becomes the representation of her phallic power, the most important piece of artifice in her performance as a male knight.

The fascinating thing about this "performance" is that it seems to entirely undermine Pierce's knightly code itself, a code based on masculine ethics of camaraderie, honesty, and honor. Alanna is able to fulfill the code in every aspect without actually being honest about her "real" gender. She does what a woman is not supposed to be able to do, and does it "better" than any of her male counterparts, which suggests that Alanna is actually more masculine than any biological male within the knightly institution. In *Female Masculinity*, Judith Halberstam notes that masculinity as a characteristic has emerged just as often from female bodies as from male, and that "manliness is built partly on the

vigorous disavowal of female masculinity and partly on a simultaneous reconstruction of male masculinity in imitation of the female masculinity it claims to have rejected."[14] In comparison to Thom, her feminized brother who rejects knighthood in order to become a wizard,
Jonathan, whom she must save from a fatal illness, and Roger, who has
no magical or knightly abilities at all, Alanna herself stands out as the
most visibly masculine character in the series. What remains odd, however, is that she is never read as queer by any of her (much larger, much
more physically developed) male friends. Nobody ever seems to suspect that Alanna, rather than being a "real" boy, or a girl passing as a
boy, might actually be a queer boy instead. Pierce is unwilling to confront this possibility, and so Alanna must constantly be reaffirmed as
being a "girl on the inside."

On the opposite side of the chivalric spectrum is Sabriel, the heroine
of Garth Nix's *Abhorsen* trilogy (*Sabriel, Lirael, Abhorsen*), who has little
interest in combat, knighthood, or masculine ethics of any sort. Sabriel
is a necromancer, the daughter of the powerful Abhorsen, and her control over the life/death boundary makes her profoundly interesting as
a female character. Forced to attend Wyverly, a school for girl's eti-
quette that also teaches "safe" magic, Sabriel flouts adult authority by
continuing to learn the secrets of necromancy. Rather than a sword,
Sabriel is given "her father's instruments . . . the tools of a necromancer,"[15] which are actually bells that can summon and bind different
spirits. Sabriel doesn't simply blur the boundary between life and
death—she actually penetrates the boundary, entering the metaphysi-
cal realm of death in order to converse with spirits (or to abjure them).

Sabriel's instructor in the art of necromancy is Mogget, a malevolent
and dangerous force imprisoned in the form of a cat. His sarcastic asides
have much the same purpose as Eilonwy's interruptions, allowing
Sabriel to see past her own adolescent understanding of the world—although, whereas much of Eilonwy's speeches are hopeful and optimistic, Mogget seems bent on transforming Sabriel into a cynic. There is
also a touch of sexual mentorship to his instruction, especially given the
inscrutable qualities of his "true" form. When Mogget first meets
Sabriel, he says, "I have a variety of names . . . as to what I am, I was once
many things, but now I am only several."[16] There is something incredibly coy about this description, the tantalizing suggestion that Mogget's
"variety" includes a much older, much more experienced male being.
When he is freed from his magical collar (itself reminiscent of a fetish ob-

ject), Mogget becomes a ravenous and decidedly evil creature, a tower of white flame capable of destroying Sabriel in an instant. This radical transformation—from a sleek, sensual feline to a destructive force whose sarcasm has now become deadly—suggests a similar transition from teasing boy to threatening man, from innocence to experience.

Later in the first novel, it is Sabriel's power as an Abhorsen that allows her to deal with the "problem" of Touchstone, an illegitimate male heir who has been magically preserved as a statue. At first, when she gazes at the statue of Touchstone and notices that "the details [of the statue] even extended to a circumcised penis, which [she] glanced at in an embarrassed way,"[17] Sabriel seems to freeze. Her necromantic logic has not prepared her for this bit of anatomy in excess, this circumcised penis. Alanna never has to contend with such descriptive narrative techniques, and her sexual activities with Jonathan always become tutorials in "love" that politely fade out into the next chapter. But Sabriel, here, has to deal with the fleshy counterpart to her own phallic authority. Rather than blushing, she "carefully [examines] him from every angle," deciding that "the man's body was an intellectual problem now."[18] It is her power as a necromancer, her removal from any recognizable feminine sphere within the novel's world, that allows her to "intellectualize" this male body hanging before her, reversing the parameters of the male gaze and studying Touchstone with a rigorous gaze of her own.

In the textual examples that I have provided thus far, magic operates as both an indicator of gender and a transgression against gender, marking both male and female characters even as it creates imaginative possibilities for breaking gender codes. Eilonwy's grasp of magic may seem, at first, to be childish, with her half-remembered spells and glowing golden bauble, but her agency as a character actually emerges from her ability to speak freely. Her rhetorical strategies become magical, interrupting Taran's own selfish logic and forcing him to carefully consider what "manhood" means to him. Although Alexander's notion of manhood is more than likely in line with heroic stereotypes, the very fact that Eilonwy's speech has in part shaped Taran's manhood makes him, in a sense, a bit queer. It is a female character who has taught him how to "be" a man, and how manhood actually emerges from, as well as incorporates, principles that might at first be read as stereotypically feminine. In Sabriel's case, it is a masculine spirit who instructs her in the process of adulthood, teaching her how to "be" a woman (despite the fact that Mogget isn't human at all, and seems to have no definitive grasp of gender).

In the case of Alanna, her magic focuses on healing, but her martial skills tend to destabilize any stereotypical notion of "feminine" healing magic. In fact, there are plenty of male healers in Pierce's world, although there are no female knights save for Alanna herself. It is Alanna's multiplicity of abilities, in fact, that makes her the subject of criticism among many teenage readers. In *Presenting Young Adult Fantasy Fiction*, her participant analysis of adolescent fantasy writing, Cathi McCrae notes that several readers found Alanna to be too powerful, and that a common criticism of Pierce's work was that it left very little room for Alanna to actually grow as a character.

Jennifer Dowe, a sixteen-year-old respondent, described the Lioness series as "stale and stereotypical,"[19] and a reviewer in *Hornbook* points out that "the reader must feel that the odds run very heavily in favor of Alanna—not only is she hard-working, sensible, and modest, but she is blessed with beauty, intelligence, apparently invincible martial skills, and possesses supernatural abilities."[20] There should be nothing wrong with a powerful young female character, yet both critics and young readers notice that there does seem to be something wrong. Alanna is lacking the vulnerability that makes characters engaging, and that allows for readers to make a personal connection with them. Alanna's sheer invincibility at times becomes an invisibility, rendering her so heroic and unassailable (even Beowulf could be selfish, after all) that she ceases to have human appeal. Thus, it is possible for a character to have "too much agency" through magic; yet we cannot uncritically say that Alanna is "too powerful" when she remains a heroic figure for many of her teenage (and adult) readers. In part, it is this desire to dismiss "too powerful" female characters (Pierce's Alanna, Buffy, Xena, among others) as being somehow "unreal," somehow "not women," that allows feminist resistance in literature and popular culture to be contained by hegemonic and patriarchal forces of production.

Another character similar to Alanna is Vanyel, the hero of Mercedes Lackey's Last Herald Mage trilogy, who is also given a tremendous amount of power to deal with at a relatively young age. Vanyel is, as the name of the series suggests, the last wizard with the ability to combine the protective powers of the Heralds with the combative spell-casting of the Mages (hence, a Herald-Mage); although, it has been so long since anyone in Valdemar has seen a Herald-Mage that we might as well call Vanyel the first, just as Alanna is the first female knight. At six-teen (during the first novel, *Magic's Pawn;* the others in the series are *Magic's Promise* and *Magic's Price*), Vanyel is possibly the youngest openly queer character in fantasy-fiction history, and his coming-out process is narrated in exquisite and often painful detail by Lackey, who has never shied away from controversial storylines in her work. Mc-Crae notes that though her work is "inconsistent in quality, Lackey writes her best novels with intense compassion for her teenaged pro-tagonists. Lackey's YA characters, some of whom are abused or gay and many of whom are misunderstood, are authentic."[21]

What "authentic" means is a mystery, but Vanyel's experience of coming out, as well as first sexual experience, is given a surprising amount of narrative focus within the books. DAW Books, which pub-lished the Last Herald Mage series (as well as several other Lackey ti-tles), has never again—to my knowledge—published anything more sexually controversial than this series, aimed at a teen audience, which focuses on a queer teen trying to negotiate a hostile medieval world (al-though they have also published Fiona Patton's excellent Branion se-ries, which has many bisexual/queer protagonists). While fantasy liter-ature itself is often dismissed by literary and poststructuralist critics as being an inferior genre of writing (much like children's literature), Lackey in particular is dismissed even by critics of fantasy literature as being a "romantic" writer, or being "inconsistent in quality." The fact that Lackey is committed to a grueling publication schedule, which de-mands that she complete a new book every three months, is more than likely the primary reason for this inconsistency. But it remains fascinat-ing that her characters, often completely absorbed by their own dra-matic emotional worlds, are often shunted by critics into the realm of formulaic romance.

Vanyel's sexual awakening is literally elemental, since he feels as if he is surrounded by ice. The ice is "all around me," Vanyel says. "I'm trapped . . . then I cut myself, and I start to turn into ice . . . [and] I'm all alone. So totally alone."[22] Tylendel, his doomed love interest, is the first person who attempts to melt this ice, and their first physical encounter together grows conflated with Vanyel's own magical power, his own development as a Herald-Mage (similar to the conflation of sex/witch-craft in the relationship between Tara and Willow, two queer witches in *Buffy*). When Tylendel kills himself, Vanyel tries to follow suit, demon-strating the very real and upsetting incidence of attempted (and completed) suicide among gay teens beyond the limits of the text. One of the most explosive scenes in the text occurs when Vanyel's aunt, Savil, confronts his homophobic father, who accuses her of "turning my son into a perverted little catamite."[23]

Savil's reply is worth quoting in full:

"All *you* can think of is that he did something that your back-country prejudices don't approve of . . . a *man*!" She laughed, a harsh cawing sound that clawed its way up out of her throat. "My *gods*—what the hell did you think he was? Tell me, Withen, what kind of a *man* would send his son into strange hands just because the poor thing didn't happen to fit his image of masculinity?"[24]

This scene, I would argue, recapitulates a very particular psychic landscape within queer life—the defiance of the queer youth against his or her unresponsive parents—but it is also the resistance of the exiled wizard, the magical subaltern who wants to make a claim for social rights in a world that rejects him, even if such a claim seems impossible. Vanyel is making a claim here, and his ability to make that claim emerges precisely from two relations—his magic and his queerness—that should prohibit his attempt in the first place. He is even able to read his father's mind, and he finally erupts: "'Lendel *loved* me, an' I loved *him* an' you can *stop* thinkin' those—god—damned—*rotten—things.*"[25] Years later, in *Magic's Promise,* Vanyel observes that "magic seemed to offer solutions to everything when I was nineteen . . . for a while—for a little while—I thought I held the world . . . but magic couldn't force my father to tell me I'd done well in his eyes . . . it couldn't make being *shay'a'chern* any easier."[26] In many ways, the power to alter the physical world—the same power demonstrated by global labor—becomes useless for him, since it can produce nothing but chains of powerful events, but it can't change his emotional or psychic life.

In my attempts, throughout this discussion, to link magical agency to gender and sexuality, I have possibly (probably) come no nearer to answering the question "What role does the use of magic play in the construction of gender?" The most coherent answer I can offer is that magic is always gendered, sometimes transgendered, and that different authors gender their magical characters in different ways. Harry Potter's magical successes are part of what make him a visibly masculine character, even though he is constantly being undermined by the knowledge and prowess of Hermione. Alanna's magic, as well as her knightly skills, is what makes her difficult to visualize as a female character, and so Pierce is always having to compensate for this transgendered characterization by reinforcing Alanna's very heterosexual attachments to Jonathan and Roger. Vanyel's magic is fed, in part, by his frustrated queer desires, and despite his impressive storehouse of magical power (much like Harry's and Alanna's broad and legendary abilities) he never arrives at any coherent definition of what it means to be masculine. It is Aunt Savil, in fact, who names him as "a man," although her enunciation of it seems profoundly critical and ironic.

In Madeline L'Engle's *Time Quartet,* the character of Charles Wallace is read as frail, underdeveloped, and even a bit queer, precisely because of his uncanny perceptive abilities. It is his older sister Meg, ultimately, who must grow out of the magic that she experienced as a teenager, which is why she reappears in *A Swiftly Tilting Planet* as an anxious mother-to-be who can barely remember what it was like to be an awkward teenager. Magic, for her, seems like a regression, and yet it is Charles Wallace, working in tandem with Meg, who manages to save the world from nuclear annihilation. In L'Engle's work, as well as in the work of many other children's fantasy authors, magic is the province of childhood and adolescence—a power that emerges from deep uncertainty, emotion, and confusion. Magic, like gender, is a site of perplexity and often trauma, something that is supposed to come from "within" but often seems to attack us from the outside world, and a bizarre tradition that we are supposed to intimately understand even as we struggle to figure out what it means to have a body, what it means to desire someone else, what it means to desire incorrectly (and how can we know the difference?).

Gender and sexuality are inseparable from magic in children's fantasy fiction, since they all seem to emerge from the same organic drives, the same spaces of wonderment and confusion, and the same uncertain borderlands between body and mind, male and female, queer and straight. Magic is, after all, a queer force—a force that makes one "not normal" (if you happen to live outside of Hogwarts), but which can also paradoxically make you fit in (if all of your friends are wizards). Like gender, magic seems wholly unverifiable, a collection of disparate influences and physiological coincidences—since magical ability is often passed on genetically—that adults often pretend to understand even when they haven't the faintest clue what they're looking at. Like gender, magic is a power that confuses children, a power that they are supposed to ascertain clearly but often don't, and a power that they would often like to be rid of. And to be a child who embraces fantasy literature, a child who skips out of gym class to read *The Hobbit*, who walks around the school field dreaming up new adventures for Harry and Hermione, is also to be a sort of queer child, an exiled child, a person who doesn't fit in among her peers precisely because, through the fantasy tradition, she is critically questioning what it means to be a boy or a girl, what it means to be a child, what it means to be human at all.

Any young girl who has thrilled along/alone with Bastian Balthazar Bux as he rides Falkor the luck dragon, any young boy who has hummed with excitement as he discovers the secret garden with Mary Lennox, or wished that he might be as clever as Hermione Granger, any straight teenager who has sympathized with Vanyel and thought, I know how it feels to be alone like that, to be surrounded by ice and alone with nowhere to turn, has experienced the ways in which magic can cross gender lines and allow us to escape (or extend) the signature of our own bodies.

The most enduringly powerful thing about children's fantasy texts is their openness, their willingness to invite multiple readings, and their desire to queer what Jan Jagodzinski calls "the capitalist construction of 'youth' since its inception in the eighteenth century . . . [as] a fetishized substance"[27] with the ability of young readers to surpass, adapt, and rewrite what is also the capitalist construction of gender as it delimits what they should feel, desire, and understand. These imaginative expeditions into new gender territory are as possible, as plentiful, as the many luck dragons, boy wizards, and lady knights waiting patiently in the children's section of the library—knowing that, as Clark contends, "canonical works are always, in some sense, children's literature,"[28] since they are the works that we try to pass onto children, and so the "children's section" of the library is actually the entire library. Accordingly, gender and sexuality, as the intimate matter of children's literature, are required by and belong to child readers, just as the entire library belongs to them.

NOTES

Jody Norton, "Transchildren and the Discipline of Children's Literature," *The Lion and the Unicorn* 24.3 (1999): 420.

1. Deborah Thacker, "Disdain or Ignorance? Literary Theory and the Absence of Children's Literature," *The Lion and the Unicorn* 24.1 (2000): 4.

2. Tzvetan Todorov, *The Fantastic: A Structural Approach to a Literary Genre,* trans. Richard Howard (Cleveland: Press of Case Western Reserve University, 1973).

3. J. K. Rowling, *Harry Potter and the Philosopher's Stone* (Vancouver: Raincoast, 2000), 208.

4. Ibid.

5. Beverly Lyon Clark, *Kiddie Lit: The Cultural Construction of Children's Literature in America* (Baltimore: Johns Hopkins University Press, 2003), 164.

6. Suman Gupta, *Re-Reading Harry Potter* (New York: Palgrave, 2003), 111.

7. Diane Duane, *So You Want To Be a Wizard* (New York: Harcourt, 2003), 456.

8. David Hawkes, "Faust Among the Witches," *Early Modern Culture* 1.4 (2004): 17.

9. Lloyd Alexander, *The Black Cauldron* (New York: Dell, 1985), 199.

10. Ibid., 49.

11. Ibid., 26.

12. Tamora Pierce, *Alanna: The First Adventure* (New York: Simon Pulse, 2005), 15.

13. Ibid., 248.

14. Judith Halberstam, *Female Masculinity* (Durham, NC: Duke University Press, 1998), 49.

15. Garth Nix, *Sabriel* (New York: Eos, 1997), 28.

16. Ibid., 121.

17. Ibid., 204.

18. Ibid., 205.

19. Cathi D. MacRae, *Presenting Young Adult Fantasy Fiction* (New York: Twayne, 1998), 133.

20. *Hornbook,* quoted in ibid., 333.

21. Ibid., xxi.

22. Mercedes Lackey, *Magic's Pawn* (New York: Daw, 1994), 117.

23. Ibid., 249.

24. Ibid.

25. Ibid., 252.

26. Mercedes Lackey, *Magic's Promise* (New York: Daw, 1990), 79.

27. Jan Jagodzinski, *Youth Fantasies: The Perverse Landscape of the Media* (New York: Palgrave, 2004), 233.

28. Clark, *Kiddie Lit,* 53.

Homosexuality at the Online Hogwarts

Harry Potter Slash Fanfiction

ఈ

CATHERINE TOSENBERGER

Many of the most devoted aficionados of J. K. Rowling's Harry Potter series have not merely contented themselves with the just-completed septilogy, but have gone online in droves to create and publish new Potter stories. These new narratives are called "fanfiction"—fiction that utilizes preexisting characters and settings from a literary or media text. Fanfiction ("fanfic" or "fic," for short) differs from other forms of "recursive" fiction[1]—such as Tom Stoppard's *Rosencrantz and Guildenstern are Dead*, Geraldine Brooks's Pulitzer Prize–winning *March*, and every Sherlock Holmes pastiche ever created—by its unofficial methods of distribution.[2] The legal status of fanfiction based on in-copyright texts, such as the Potter books, is uncertain, though in the United States it is likely defensible under transformative fair-use laws.[3] Fanfiction is, by preference or necessity, not formally published; it initially was circulated by way of self-published "zines," and, these days, on the Internet. While fan writers are unable to capitalize on their work in terms of money or official recognition, they are compensated by not being restricted to institutionalized discourses. Fan writers are often characterized as refusing merely to consume media, but rather to engage actively with texts; fandom as a space of engagement is especially valuable for young fans, who constitute a significant portion of Potter fandom. In our era of what Henry Jenkins calls "convergence culture,"[4] fan-produced writing provides a means for studying the impact of the Potter books on creative, motivated readers. One of the most interesting and fruitful areas of study is "slash" fanfiction—fan writing concerned with same-sex romance.[5]

Internet fanfiction, especially in the Potter fandom, gives younger writers access to a wider audience than ever before. As Ernest Bond and Nancy Michelson observe:

> It is not a new phenomenon for young readers to occasionally extend a literary creation by becoming authors of new versions, sequels, or spin-offs of the story. However, the advent of Harry Potter has generated an unprecedented number of voluntary literary responses by adolescent readers.[6]

Jenkins has expanded upon this theme, arguing forcefully that adolescent Potter fans who participate in the online fandom benefit enormously, in the form of greatly increased literacy (both traditional and media), from access to this egalitarian, cross-generational space "outside the classroom and beyond any direct adult control."[7] Jenkins believes, and I agree, that "we should not assume that someone possesses media literacy if they can consume but not express themselves."[8] Moreover, the production and distribution of fanfiction "demystifi[es] . . . the creative process," and allows young writers to take on the mantle of "author," a role that traditional publishing reserves for a cultural elite.[9]

Jenkins is not the only scholar to praise the possible pedagogical benefits of participating in fandom; Bond and Michelson, Kelly Chandler-Olcott and Donna Mahar, and Chris Ebert Flench have all discussed fan communities as spaces where adolescents can hone their writing skills.[10] However, fandom is more than a space to simply acquire technical expertise at writing. One avenue that has yet to be explored, with specific regard to adolescent fans, is the potential to encounter and experiment with alternative modes of sexual discourse, particularly queer discourse. Potter fandom, due in part to its sheer size, but also to the great diversity of ages and sexual orientations of its members, is ideal ground for exploring many varieties of nonheteronormative discourses in fandom. Slash is therefore one of the most popular genres of Potter fanfiction.

The term "slash" arose in *Star Trek* fandom in the 1970s, referring to the punctuation mark separating the characters' names (Kirk/Spock).[11] The "X/Y" model indicated that the major romantic pairing was homosexual; stories of heterosexual *Star Trek* romance were labeled "ST" or "adult ST."[12] Although later fandoms adopted the slash punctuation mark for all romantic pairings (i.e., Hermione/Ron), the term "slash" stuck, retaining its original meaning of homoerotic romance. I have chosen to concentrate in this article on male/male slash, as these pairings constitute the majority of Potter slash fanfiction, but female/female slash—often marked as "femslash," "femmeslash," or even "saffic" (a portmanteau of "Sapphic fic")—certainly exists and deserves critical attention; the most popular Potter femslash pairing is Hermione/Ginny.

Some fans and academics wish to narrow the definition of slash, and claim that the same-gender relationship must be noncanonical—that is, not present in the source text, in this case the Harry Potter books. However, this qualification poses several problems. First, it does not reflect common usage within fandom. The term "slash" generally functions in fandom as the binary opposite of "het" (heterosexual) fic, which features romantic and sexual relationships between characters of different genders. As no one places a similar limitation on het fics—stories that concern canonical heterosexual pairings, such as Molly/Arthur, are still labeled "het"—most fans reason that it doesn't make sense to apply the restriction to slash. Second, no one has ever come up with a satisfactory term for fanfic that concerns canonical same-sex relationships; in the fandoms for television programs such as *Queer as Folk* and *Xena: Warrior Princess*, fan stories about the canonical homosexual relationships are still usually called "slash."

Third, and perhaps most importantly, is that what constitutes "canon" is never a clear-cut issue: as Mafalda Stasi points out, "Beyond the bare factual minimum, canon constitution and interpretation are a highly debated and controversial critical activity in the fannish milieu."[13] A number of slash stories and pairings build upon on a reading of subtext that fans claim is present in the canon. In the case of the relationship between the young Albus Dumbledore and his boyhood friend turned enemy Gellert Grindelwald, Rowling would agree. Three months after the release of *Deathly Hallows,* she confirmed the speculations of many slash fans, and announced, in response to a fan's question, that Dumbledore was gay and had loved Grindelwald.[14] She commented, "I think a child will see a friendship and I think a sensitive adult may well understand that it was an infatuation."[15] Slash fans, who constitute many of these "sensitive adults," are often accused of "distorting" or "misreading" texts, so this public validation of their method of reading is a somewhat rare pleasure. Though Rowling has never made any explicit statements on the topic, many fans defend, passionately, the pairing of Remus Lupin / Sirius Black as canon, a reading that many other fans just as passionately oppose; I will discuss these issues in greater detail below.

In short, the insistence that slash must transgress the existing canon rather troublingly assigns to the canon a heteronormativity it may not necessarily possess. Moreover, it reinforces the assumption that queer readings are always readings "imposed" from the outside.[16] This is not to say that slash lacks transgressive or subversive potential: in a homophobic culture that attempts to police or censor expressions of nonheteronormativity, any depiction of queerness, especially a positive, sympathetic depiction, qualifies as such. However, for the reasons outlined above, I believe it is a mistake to claim that slash is intrinsically more transgressive/subversive of a given text than other forms of fanfiction.[17]

Regarding transgression, how do depictions of adolescent sexuality in Potter fanfiction differ from those of published literature for adolescents? The cultural construct of adolescence and its literature does, albeit grudgingly, allow a space for sexuality, and the discourse shifts from blanket condemnation to strategies for containment. Our culture's relationship with adolescent sexuality is complex and contradictory: on the one hand, we valorize their youth and beauty, their erotic appeal, and often wink at the sexual escapades of "horny teenagers" on television and film; on the other, we are anxious to contain adolescent sexuality within parameters acceptable to adult sensibilities. The literature aimed at teenage audiences reflects this tension. Roberta Seelinger Trites argues that "adolescent literature is as often an ideological tool used to curb teenagers' libido as it is some sort of depiction of what adolescents' sexuality actually is."[18] While YA literature has gradually allowed itself to become more sexually explicit, there is still a strong imperative toward pedagogy—inculcating "correct" attitudes about sexuality to an audience deemed in need of education. Trites expresses frustration at the overwhelming emphasis in our discourses concerning sexuality in general, and adolescent sexuality in particular, upon "repression" rather than "jouissance."[19]

So where does Potter fanfiction fit into all this? First and foremost, it operates outside of the institutional paradigms that control children's and YA literature; unlike the Potter books themselves, it is not bound by publishing conventions that obligate it to contain sexuality within parameters of age (of both characters and readers) or of pedagogy. What makes Potter fanfic different is that teens have unprecedented license not only to read stories that might not meet with adult approval, but also to write and distribute them.

Slash, like other forms of fanfiction in the modern era, initially circulated by way of self-published zines. Because of the controversial nature of the stories, slash was available only to those who knew the right people in order to be put on mailing lists, and who had the financial resources to order zines and attend conventions—in other words, adults. Equally important, those who wished to write and distribute slash were subject to the whims, preferences, and limited resources of zine editors; writers of unpopular pairings or scenarios had a more difficult time getting their stories published and therefore finding an audience. The Internet cut out the middlemen; anyone, of any age, with a computer and a modem could obtain access. The rise of Potter coincided with the mainstreaming of the Internet, and this combination of a source text aimed at young readers with advanced communications technology enabled young fans not only to access slash, but also to write and distribute their own.[20]

Many of the most influential academic studies of slash—Henry Jenkins's *Textual Poachers,* Camille Bacon-Smith's *Enterprising Women,* and Constance Penley's "Brownian Motion,"[21] in particular—date from the pre-Internet period, and many academic theories reflect this. All of these scholars report that slash (like most fanfiction in general) is written primarily by women, and discuss the feminist implications of this in great detail. The existence of slash complicated conventional notions about women's interest in erotica in general, and the types of erotic material women were supposed to be interested in (i.e., heterosexual romance novels). It is unsurprising that most fandom scholarship presents slash as a potential site for women to resist the dominant ideologies of patriarchal, heteronormative culture. Penley draws upon the work of Joanna Russ, as well as that of Patricia Frazer Lamb and Diana L. Veith, and discusses slash as a subversive act, wherein women can articulate a fantasy of equality between romantic partners that is difficult to achieve in heterosexual relationships.[22]

The focus in slash scholarship on these adult female writers—and their engagement with media oriented toward adults, such as *Blake's 7, Starsky and Hutch,* and especially *Star Trek*—had a noticeable effect on removing some of the adolescent stigma of fannishness. The popular image of the fan was marked by immaturity: the teenage girl able to express her sexuality only by screaming and crying for pop stars,[23] and the adult man who lives in his parents' basement and has never kissed a girl, are the standard gender stereotypes.[24] The concept of "adolescence," whether actual or inappropriately retained, is a key component of the stereotypical fan.[25] The work of scholars writing not just about fandom, but slash fandom in particular, changed that: They recast slash fandom as a space for savvy, subversive women, engaging in creative—and very adult—ways with media texts.

The advent of the Internet and the popularity of the Potter books, which allowed for an influx of actual teenagers into participatory fandom, as reported by Jenkins[26] and Bond and Michelson, are forcing a reassessment not just of fandom in general, but of slash in particular—and expansion of the potential liberatory benefits of slash fandom to young people. Michael Cart and Christine Jenkins have spoken of the importance of queer-positive YA lit, the "community on the page," for young people exploring their sexual orientation.[27] But fandom, especially Harry Potter fandom, offers young people the opportunity not simply to passively absorb queer-positive (and adult-approved) messages, but to actively engage with a supportive artistic community as readers, writers, and critics. Moreover, the identity-bending, pseudonymous nature of online fannish discourse affords fans a certain measure of concealment, which proves especially valuable for young fans who fear the consequences of expressing nonheteronormative desires. Julad, a fan, proposes a theory of slash as a space:

> Slash is not so much queer in the act as it is queer in the space. . . . Slash is a sandbox where women come to be strange and unusual, or to do strange and unusual things, or to play with strange and unusual sand. The women may be queer or not, strange or not, unusual or not. The many different acts and behaviors of slash may be queer or not, strange or not, unusual or not. The queerness may be sexualized or it may not, and what is sexual for one woman may not be for another. The space is simply that: a space, where women can be strange and unusual and/or do strange and unusual things.[28]

This conception of slash as a space is, I believe, the most useful way of understanding it; what slash writers have done is to carve out a space for themselves where they are free to tell the narratives they wish, linked only by the common thread of queerness. Julad speaks of a space where "women come to be strange and unusual." In the Potter fandom, it is not just adult women, but young people as well who have a safe space in which to be "strange and unusual."

Harry Potter Slash: The Beast in the Plumbing

Potter fandom particularly resists "univocal"[29] theories of slash. Since the Potter fandom was born and bred on the Internet, its members never experienced the top-down editorial control of zine-based fandoms. Fan communities develop their own cultural norms for what is or is not acceptable in fanfiction; in small fandoms where everyone knows one another, those rules can extend over the entire group. But the sheer size of the Potter fandom makes this impossible. The result is very much a fandom of subgroups, and each subgroup can churn out its own stories for its own audience with impunity.[30] The enormous number of people participating in the online fandom almost guarantees that however outré your fanfictional desires, someone will share them—and will have written a story, or be willing to read yours. Moreover, while slash has always been far less isolated from the general fannish landscape than many academic accounts would have readers believe—just as fanfiction in general has been treated as if isolated from literary discourse as a whole [31]—fans sometimes perceive it as a dominant mode within the Potter fandom. A panel at a recent Potter conference was entitled "Heterosexuality and Feminism in a Male/Male Slashcentric Fandom."[32] The size of the fandom, and the variety of material on offer, means that Potter fans are spoiled for choice when it comes to fanfiction; with so many subgroups, they can without too much effort find themselves a comfortable niche where they can explore their interests in a more or less nonjudgmental environment. This is especially important for young fans, whose desires, and the expressions of those desires, are policed more heavily than are those of adults.

The fragmentation of the fannish landscape means that in Potter fandom, there is no dominant "One True Pairing" (abbreviated "OTP"), like *Star Trek*'s Kirk/Spock. Unlike classic slash fandoms (*Star Trek*, *Starsky and Hutch*, *The Professionals*), which were built around television series with, in Bacon-Smith's term, a "hero dyad,"[33] the Potter books contain an enormous cast of intriguing characters, in a wide variety of emotional relationships to one another, all of whom have been slashed at some point. But in a landscape where most available slash stories explored romance between men who were best friends and/or professional partners (Kirk/Spock, Starsky/Hutch, Bodie/Doyle), the equality theory, based on what fan Dira Sudis calls the "buddyslash" model, made a great deal of sense.[34] Market forces and the limitations of technology meant that those fans who preferred narratives other than "friends become lovers" had fewer opportunities to publish their stories, at least in spaces where academics would see them. However, the Internet changed all that. Among those other narratives made more visible by the Internet are what Dira Sudis identifies as "enemy-slash" (slash between characters who are foes or foils) and "powerslash" (slash between characters who have differing levels of personal, social, or cultural agency), neither of which have tended to receive quite as much attention in scholarship.[35] Buddyslash, enemyslash, and powerslash are all highly visible in Potter fandom. The most popular Potter slash pairing—indeed, one of the most popular pairings in general—is Harry/Draco, followed by Sirius/Remus and Snape/Harry. A number of the early stories in the Potter fandom were Harry/Draco; after the release of *Goblet of Fire,* Potter fandom grew to gargantuan proportions, and Harry/Draco grew accordingly, helped along by the "Big Name Fan" (abbreviated "BNF") status of many of the early writers—Aja's "Love Under Will" and Rhysenn's "Irresistible Poison" were among the most influential early stories.[36] Eventually, such a glut of Harry/Draco stories appeared that older fans who felt the possibilities of the pairing had been exhausted, and fans who had no interest in it at all, produced reams of stories about other characters. The nature of Internet technology meant that the popularity of Harry/Draco did not limit the existence of other pairings, but rather enabled them to flourish—market forces were not pressuring writers to keep churning out Harry/Draco, and fans who didn't like the pairing had equal access to the means of publication. Perhaps most importantly, the sheer number of Harry/Draco stories meant that fan readers—including teenagers—who had never heard the term "slash" were likely to encounter it, and thus more likely to become slash writers themselves.

Slash about Harry and Draco, who are enemies in canon, complicates academic theories of slash that are predicated upon the Kirk/Spock buddyslash model. Jenkins, referencing Eve Kosofsky Sedgwick's articulation of homosocial desire, argues that slash throws conventional notions of masculinity into crisis by removing the barriers blocking the realization of homosocial desire. Slash unmasks the erotics of male friendship, confronting the fears keeping men from achieving intimacy.[37]

While this is an excellent model for talking about Kirk/Spock, Starsky/Hutch, or in the Potter fandom, Harry/Ron (among many others), it clearly cannot currently function as a global assessment of slash, if indeed it ever could. Jenkins, always nuanced, discusses other, nonbuddy forms of slash (such as the classic *Blake's 7* enemyslash pairing Blake/Avon), but other writers have often tended to treat slash as if it were synonymous with buddyslash. Happily, this is changing, though there is still overall a somewhat disproportionate emphasis on the buddyslash model, which is most amenable to the equality theory. But Harry/Draco, as an enemyslash pairing, must negotiate a rather different "semiotics of masculinity" than theories predicated upon a buddyslash model will allow.[38] And powerslash, such as Harry/Snape, contradicts outright the premises of the equality theory.[39]

The joy of an enemyslash pairing is in watching antagonists overcome their differences, at least long enough to have sex. Dislike is recast as sexual tension, and when the characters are both men, part of the pleasure is in seeing their negotiation of expectations of male aggression (rather than friendship) in terms of desire. A scene in Aja's "Pop Quiz" captures this tension nicely:

> Whenever they pass in the hallways, Malfoy does his best to jostle Harry. He is scrawny and bony, so if Harry doesn't feel like moving that day, their sides scrape together, and Harry's hip might bruise a little. If that happens, he has the satisfaction of knowing that Malfoy's is bruised a little, too. When he reaches his palm up, his hand connects briefly with the flat plane of Malfoy's hip. He can only do this once, on the excuse of shoving Malfoy away—but it's not bad, really. Just stupid, like the whole thing is to begin with.[40]

Harry is careful to articulate his consideration of Malfoy as a combination of violence and disinterest ("if Harry doesn't feel like moving that day, their sides scrape together"), which underlines both the depth of his attraction and his denial of same. He then denigrates their enmity, and expressions of that enmity, as "stupid"—a disavowal that foreshadows their later romantic connection.

Fear of a homophobic response, or a struggle with internalized homophobia is, as Jenkins notes,[41] an effective way of creating tension in a buddyslash story, and there are a number of Potter stories that treat homophobia, internal or external, as an obstacle to the lovers' happiness. In Mireille's "Falling," Oliver Wood finally musters his courage to tell Percy Weasley how much he loves him, and how happy he is in their secret relationship, but his heart is broken when he discovers that Percy is dating Penelope Clearwater in order to keep suspicions at bay:

> I could have seen this coming if I'd been willing to look. Too many secrets, too many nights when Percy went off by himself, too many times when he couldn't look me in the eye. But all I had to do was hear "I need you, Oliver," and I was willing to forget them. To close my eyes and wait to hit the ground.[42]

Enemyslash pairings such as Harry/Draco, however, generate an enormous amount of tension on their own; while a number of Harry/Draco stories deal with homophobia, lingering upon the issue may come across as overkill. Indeed, many Potter slash stories completely ignore the issue of homophobia, or articulate it in different ways. One factor is the more widespread (Muggle-world) societal acceptance of gays and lesbians, so both authors and characters may feel less of a need to have characters confront homophobia in themselves and others than in earlier fanfiction. The "We're not gay, we just love each other" trope that featured in so much pre-Internet slash is fairly rare in Potter slash. Again, the more widespread acceptance of gays and lesbians has had an effect, as neither authors nor characters feel the need to distance themselves from the term. The sometime corollary, "I've never been with another man before," tends not to be loaded with the homophobic overtones sometimes present in earlier slash, where the implication was often that macho Kirk is assuredly not the sort of man attracted to other men, but his connection with Spock is simply too transcendent to ignore. In Potter slash, given the ages of many of the characters, it's quite likely that a character's first sexual encounter with the same gender is also his/her first sexual encounter with anyone. That so many of the characters are teenagers—in a British boarding school, no less—carries its own powerful discourse as well. This will be discussed in more detail later, but for now, that the characters are "horny teenagers" is often treated as good enough justification for any variety of sexual activity: hetero, homo, or interspecies.

Another key feature of the Kirk/Spock model is that the characters will embark upon a committed, monogamous relationship—buddyslash as a genre tends to argue that the characters are soul mates, and understand one another better than anyone else ever could. While a number of Potter slash stories do, in fact, move toward this end, "romance ending in committed relationship" is far from the only story told by slash writers. PWPs ("Plot? What Plot?" or "Porn Without Plot") stories abound, as they always have, but Potter fans are by no means limited to these models.

The buddyslash, enemyslash, and powerslash models will be familiar to readers of heterosexual genre romance novels; indeed, Catherine Driscoll argues that "the most consistent conventions of [fanfiction] remain that of formulaic romance."[43] Likewise, Sarah Gwenllian Jones and Catherine Salmon and Donald Symons argue that romance novels are the primary influence upon slash narratives.[44] This is not necessarily incorrect—slash is concerned with love and desire, and it makes sense that the literary genre most visibly dedicated to those themes should bear a strong relationship to slash fanfiction. However, what scholar and romance novelist Jennifer Crusie Smith names the overriding theme of genre romance—belief in "an emotionally just universe,"[45] where good people are rewarded with love—is common, but not universal, in romantic fanfic, both het and slash.[46] The presence or absence of this theme as an organizing principle depends on the fandom, the characters, the pairing, the author, and the story. Insisting too strongly that genre romance is the primary influence upon slash is just as troublesome as a sole focus on buddyslash narratives, in that it ignores the intense specificity of slash fiction. There really is no such thing as a typical Potter slash story: with such a variety of characters available, the tropes in Potter slash are highly dependent upon the pairing.

For example, the buddyslash pairing Remus/Sirius can never, post-*Order of the Phoenix*,[47] fit unproblematically within the discourse of the genre romance, as their relationship trajectory in the books is one of mistrust, betrayal, despair, and Sirius's senseless and preventable death. In the face of that, it is difficult to construct a believable narrative of an "emotionally just universe." And yet, Remus/Sirius is one of the most popular pairings; fan writers relish both the opportunity to explore the dark, painful aspects of love and loss, and the challenge of creating a hopeful narrative under such sad conditions.

One of the most haunting Remus/Sirius stories is "That the Science of Cartography is Limited," by Rave. Remus, living alone in Grimmauld Place after Sirius's death, drifts between the present and the past, preferring to dwell on happier moments at Hogwarts when he and Sirius first fell in love. As they work on the Marauders' Map, Remus solves the puzzle of how to account for the fact that Hogwarts is essentially a sentient organism whose walls move about at will. However, in the empty, silent Black house, Remus's discovery of a way to track the lives of that which is not living takes on a bitterly ironic cast in the face of Sirius's death, and his own inability to keep track of the traces of Sirius that are left: "Remus has heard of haunted houses being full of the dead; he thinks it is strange that anyone could find this terrible."[48] Remus's attempts at precision—all of his skill with words, with understanding—break down in the face of crushing loss:

> But none of them, he realizes now, ever really got round to explaining the everyday weirdness of loss: the way things get quiet, and bright, and far away, and how everything is slightly out of focus, mis-timed—except when they aren't, sometimes, some things that make no sense.[49]

The story is intensely romantic, but bears little resemblance to what is commonly understood as genre romance. Even happy Remus/Sirius, such as Victoria P.'s "The Love There That's Sleeping"—a sweet schoolboy love story, set to the soundtrack of the Beatles albums Remus smuggles into Hogwarts—can never fully escape the shadow of the coming tragedy.

Prior to Rowling's announcement of Dumbledore's homosexuality, fans most often articulated the pairing of Sirius/Remus as (possibly) canon, and it is therefore a good segue into a more detailed discussion of how Potter slash comments upon the books themselves.[50]

Queering the Canon

Whether slash fans view their pairings as supported or unsupported by canon, and how important that is, varies from pairing to pairing, and from fan to fan. The Potter books invoke a number of cultural and literary narratives, gleefully seized upon by fans, that leave the text open to a slash reading. Some fans argue vehemently that their favored pairing is canon; as mentioned earlier, Rowling announced that in her view Dumbledore was in love with Grindelwald, which pleased fans of that pairing and many slash fans in general. However, Internet debates sprang up immediately over the canonicity of Rowling's outing of Dumbledore, coming as it did after the publication of the books. Jeffrey Weiss expressed the views of some fans when he said, "If you didn't put it in the books, please don't tell us now."[51] Rebecca Traister elaborated further when she argued, "[Rowling's] pronouncements are robbing us of the chance to let our imagination take over where she left off, one of the great treats of engaging with fictional narrative."[52] (Neither Weiss nor Traister seems willing to read Dumbledore's love for Grindelwald as actually present in the books, which some fans have claimed, and which Rowling appears to believe.) However, fans have always been perfectly content to "let [their] imagination take over where she left off," and ignore Rowling's commentary on the books, or even elements that are indisputably canon, if it conflicts with the stories they want to tell. Rowling has insisted for years that Draco and Snape are unattractive, unappealing characters, but the effect her views have had on the Draco and Snape segments of the fandom is negligible. Likewise, Rowling's lack of explicit commentary upon Remus/Sirius has certainly not altered some fans' willingness to read the pairing as canonical.

Even Lupin's marriage to Tonks hasn't stopped the widespread fandom perception that Sirius was his one true love.[53] At Nimbus 2003, a Potter conference that took place shortly after the release of *Order of the Phoenix,* a speaker shouted, "Joint Christmas presents!"—a reference to Sirius and Remus giving a present to Harry from both of them,[54] as couples often will—which earned a resounding cheer from the audience. Fans also cite the coding of Remus's werewolfism as a terminal illness analogous to AIDS: victims, while posing a genuine danger to others, are subject to fear and discrimination far out of proportion to their likelihood of infecting anyone.[55] One of the most interesting Remus/Sirius stories, "The Most Ridiculous First Name I've Ever Heard," by Mousapelli, takes this argument to a terrifying conclusion, and argues that the lycanthropy "virus" becomes, when transmitted to Muggles, HIV—and Gaetan Dugas, HIV's "Patient Zero," was the name Remus had chosen for himself on his travels.[56] Lending further credence to the

Remus/Sirius reading of the text, fans point out that of all the Animagi (wizards who can change into animals) depicted in the series, Remus and Sirius are the only two characters who are physically compatible in both human and animal forms. And last but not least, Sirius's character trajectory in *Order of the Phoenix* follows the trope in early gay-themed YA literature that homosexual characters must be lonely, tormented, and then die—though he is dispatched by a fall through a veil rather than a car crash.[57]

Remus/Sirius slash stories explore all these themes and more, especially concentrating upon the characters' school days in the 1970s—for fans who want a happy ending, Hogwarts is the last chance for Remus and Sirius. (Compare Victoria P.'s previously mentioned "The Love There That's Sleeping" to her post-Hogwarts "All the Sinners, Saints"[58] or the flashbacks in Rave's "That the Science of Cartography is Limited.") Alfonso Cuaron's 2004 film of *Prisoner of Azkaban* strengthened the Remus/ Sirius reading even further. Actor David Thewlis, who plays Lupin, confirmed that both he and Cuaron read Lupin as gay.[59] The film contains a number of lines—not found in the book—that support this: Snape accuses Sirius and Remus of arguing like an "old married couple"; when Remus begins his (in the book, involuntary) change to wolf form, Sirius makes a non-book-supported appeal to Remus's humanity, embracing him and shouting, "This is not the man you are inside!"; and finally, Remus explains his resignation by saying that "parents will not want a, um, . . . someone like me teaching their children."[60] In the book, he simply says "werewolf."[61] All of these additions lend support to the Remus/Sirius reading of the text.

Other fans couldn't care less about the canonicity, or lack thereof, of their favorite pairing, but may still argue for subtext, and scour the text for details that can be spun into a story. And fans take the nature of such support with varying degrees of seriousness: when Ron declared that going out with Lavender Brown was "like going out with the giant squid,"[62] some fans jokingly declared Ron/squid canon—how would he know what dating the giant squid was like unless. . . ? Also, the sexual attitudes of the Potterverse are, in Rowling's text, unclear. Fans have a great deal of freedom to imagine the discourse of homosexuality in the wizarding world, and may actively construct or passively assume a more tolerant culture than that of the Muggles. A current topic of debate within the fandom is whether Dumbledore was out or not, as the text and Rowling give few clues in either direction.

New canon invariably inspires a great deal of fanfiction, and not only about whatever new characters are introduced. Canon is able to dramatically invigorate little known or stagnating slash pairings. *Order of the Phoenix* featured Harry and Snape (a powerslash pairing par excellence) forced to become uncomfortably intimate with each other: Snape is teaching Harry how to prevent Voldemort from reading his thoughts by . . . reading Harry's thoughts; Harry, angry and frustrated, does the wizarding equivalent of reading Snape's diary, and peeks at his most secret, humiliating memory. Snape/Harry fans rejoiced, and many fans who had never been interested in the pairing before were inspired to write it. And *Half-Blood Prince* gave Harry/Draco fans their previously elusive holy grail: a Harry fixated upon Draco. Before this book, the chief narrative problem for Harry/Draco writers was that while Draco is canonically obsessed with Harry, Harry had never seen Draco as anything more than a passing nuisance. To overcome this, fans devised a number of ingenious schemes, often involving magical accidents, to force the two together: for example, Rhysenn's "Irresistible Poison" had Harry and Draco accidentally ingest a love potion. In *Order of the Phoenix*, Draco barely registered in the book at all, which effectively slowed down production in the already saturated Harry/Draco portion of the fandom. Snape/Draco writers, though fewer in number and a bit drowned out by the cheers of the Harry/Draco crowd, were also immensely pleased with *Half-Blood Prince*, and immediately started work on stories about Snape and Draco, on the run from Death Eaters and the Ministry alike, comforting each other sexually (or having angry resentful sex). Harry slashers cheered the number of times Harry described a male character (usually Tom Riddle) as "handsome." Little things, perhaps, especially when compared with the overt Harry/Ginny romance plot, but more than enough to construct a story around—and in fandom, that's all one needs.

And of course, *Deathly Hallows* introduced the pairing of Dumbledore/Grindelwald; while fans began writing this pairing the day after *Deathly Hallows* was released, Rowling's announcement has kindled even more interest, and new stories are appearing daily. Like Remus/Sirius, Dumbledore/Grindelwald ends in tragedy: there is an even darker cast to their narrative trajectory, as Grindelwald actually turns out to be as evil as pre-*Azkaban* Remus believes Sirius to be.

The construction of the Potterverse itself, as well as its characters, is conducive to slash readings. Fans long anticipated the argument put forth by Tison Pugh and David A. Wallace[63] that Harry's discovery of his wizard nature is akin to a coming-out narrative—he escapes from a literal closet, and his relatives' horrified reactions bear a striking resemblance to the language of homophobia, especially in the way they hurl about words like "abnormality"[64] as weapons. Thus, one can, from the perspective of the Muggle realm, read the entire wizarding world in terms of Julad's "queer space." Even more telling is Harry's destination: Hogwarts is a British boarding school, an institution that is so consistently coded as queer space that it's practically shorthand for homosexuality, British-style.[65] The "school story" has a long pedigree in children's literature, most famously in Thomas Hughes's 1857 novel *Tom Brown's Schooldays*. While Hughes's novel was not the first school story, it was the most influential; although the bulk of the text exalts the boarding school as the ideal place to form manly Christian servants of the empire, a curious passage, emphasized by a footnote, troubles its complacent uprightness:

> He was one of the miserable little pretty white-handed curly-headed boys, petted and pampered by some of the big fellows, who wrote their verses for them, taught them to drink and use bad language, and did all they could to spoil them for everything in this world and the next.[66]

The footnote coyly claims, "There were many noble friendships between big and little boys, but I can't strike out the passage; many boys will know why it was left in."[67] The adult version of the genre dispenses with the coyness; Stephen Fry's *The Liar,* and pornographic novels like the works of Chris Kent—including, appropriately enough, *The Real Tom Brown's School Days*—among many others, depict boarding school as a locus for homoerotic encounters.[68]

Although Hogwarts is coeducational, which neutralizes some of the queer coding, students are still somewhat isolated from the other gender, and living with almost no privacy among students of the same gender, which affords ample temptation and opportunity. Stories in which the characters share a dormitory—Harry and Ron, Percy and Oliver, Crabbe and Goyle—frequently use this lack of privacy as the catalyst for slash; there are dozens of stories in which one character walks in on or overhears another character calling out in his sleep or masturbating. Oliver and Percy also have the advantage of being the only two named characters of their year in Gryffindor, which has led some fans to posit that they have the dormitory to themselves (Mireille's "Falling" makes use of this trope). Quidditch players have postgame showers, prefects have a special bathroom, and of course all students have access to the Astronomy Tower, sundry abandoned classrooms and broom closets, dark corners of the library, the Room of Requirement (which features in enough stories to qualify as a character in its own right), and Snape's desk.

While other highly structured sex-segregated communities, such as the military, are coded as homoerotic, the cocktail of teenage hormones lends boarding school narratives a special potency. Teenage characters' newfound overwhelming desires can, to a certain extent, function as a get-out-of-jail-free card for all manner of sexual behavior; our culture often winks at homosexual activity among teenagers, reading it as "experimentation." Not that most fan writers dismiss the plight of GLBTQ teenagers or construct homosexuality as something that characters will grow out of, but the narrative of "horny teenagers experimenting," in addition to the unspecified general sexual mores of the wizarding world, means that slashers do not have to depict characters going through a lot of soul searching about their attraction to the same gender, unless they want it to be a major issue. (Aja, in the author's note for her story "Monsoon Season," remarks, "The idea for the story arose out of a discussion . . . regarding under what circumstances touching would be appropriate for two teenage boys.")[69]

Fanfiction writers are not bound to a pedagogical imperative, which means they are free to concentrate on eroticism rather than on social issues. Published YA novels, a category to which the later Potter books belong, do not have this luxury. Trites observes that the majority of YA novels about gay and lesbian teens "are very Foucaultian in their tendency to privilege the discourse of homosexuality over the physical sexual acts of gay men, defining homosexuality more rhetorically than physically."[70] She later states, "Denying the corporeality of homosexuality too easily divorces it from pleasure, which potentially disempowers gay sexuality."[71] Published YA novels, hemmed in as they are by institutional discourses of teenage and queer sexuality—not to mention that of bibliotherapy—have until fairly recently shied away from graphic depictions of gay sex, and even nonexplicit gay and lesbian novels for teens suffer localized repression in the form of censorship and book burnings. But slash, like all fanfiction, is subject to no such constraints; while it is important to note that not all slash is overtly erotic, the point is that it can be. Slash fans can be as graphic or as circumspect as they wish, but on the whole, the balance tips toward the corporeal. Potter slash readers and writers have access to a space where queer sexuality, whether teen or adult, can be depicted in its full, messy, exuberant glory, and the emphasis is on *jouissance*.

As an exemplar of these issues, V's "True But Not Nice"[72] is one of the finest depictions of adolescent boarding school culture in Potter slash, and makes full use of the Potter fandom's freedom to tell a charmingly foul-mouthed and unapologetically erotic story about an affair between two teenage boys. The pairing is Oliver Wood / Marcus Flint, the Gryffindor and Slytherin Quidditch captains,[73] and the story features a funny portrait of teenage whispering campaigns and the paranoia they can induce; the characters' responses to gossip are both individual and believable. Marcus wants to make it very clear that, whatever gossip has been floating around, he certainly does not like Oliver. After threatening violence upon those responsible for the rumors, Marcus hunts Oliver down to tell him so. This, of course, ends in sex in an abandoned classroom. Oliver makes the first move, and pride compels him to follow through, even though Marcus insists, unconvincingly, that he does not have feelings for the other boy:

> "I fucking told you," [Marcus] started, but the words seemed to die on his tongue. "Just don't," he said, but Oliver couldn't not do it, because there'd be talk, more talk about how he couldn't even land the fucking worst catch in the whole school.[74]

Oliver, tellingly, frames his actions not in terms of desire (which both he and Marcus are too embarrassed to admit to—out of fear of rejection, not homophobia), but in terms of what others will say. V has a terrific ear for hilariously profane teenage dialogue, especially when it comes to the rumor-mongering that kicks off the story. While the boys are enemies, which provides the apparent obstacle to their relationship (Adrian Pucey assures Marcus, "It's fine, no one thinks you're a traitor"), the real obstacle is their inability to express themselves. Marcus and Oliver are both rather stupid adolescent boys, and while their incoherence provides much of the humor of the story, it also causes them genuine frustration and anxiety, and V never condescends to them. They are athletes, physical creatures, and V makes their experience of the sex act a way of delineating their less-than-articulate characters—Marcus and Oliver are completely lost when it comes to negotiating the skillful speech of those around them, but this they can do. The story is a romance, but a cockeyed, antiromantic one; funny as it is, there is far too much of an undercurrent of anxiety (on Oliver's part) and rage (on Marcus's) to make this an unequivocal romp, though it ends on a hopeful note. Their desire, and, at the end, their budding regard for one another, are, as the title says, "true but not nice."

Jenkins argues that the Potter books, because of their championing of "children's rights over institutional constraints" and their enormous success among reluctant readers, are an ideal road into considerations of the ways in which literacy—especially young people's freedoms to read and write—is policed and curtailed.[75] Potter fanfiction—a form of literacy that is not subject to the usual constraints on young people's reading and writing—offers a safe space for them not only to improve their writing skills, but also to explore discourses of sexuality, especially queerness, outside of the various culturally official stances marketed to them, and with the support of a community of like-minded readers and writers. In an era when representations of adolescent sexuality are both exploited and policed, Potter fandom is an arena in which fans of all ages, genders, and sexual orientations can tell stories to satisfy their own desires; this freedom is especially valuable for younger fans, whose self-expressions are heavily monitored in institutional settings. Fans are able to tell narratives of sexuality in a space not directly controlled by adults, and do not have to shape their stories to adult sensibilities and comfort levels. Potter fandom is a lively, intellectually stimulating, and tolerant interpretive community, and fans reap great rewards not only in the form of increased literacy, but also by exposure to discourses outside of culturally mandated heteronormativity.

Though the series is now complete, it is highly unlikely that Potter fans will stop producing new fanfiction, if not necessarily in the same volume as before; completion of the canon has certainly not stopped fans of *Buffy the Vampire Slayer*, *The Lord of the Rings*, or even Jane Austen's novels from churning out new stories. Rowling has left an enormous amount of room for speculation; the famous epilogue of *Deathly Hallows* only discusses certain aspects of the fates of a few major characters, nineteen years after the events of the main narrative—and for those readers dissatisfied with the epilogue, "correcting" the text has long been a motivating factor for many fan writers. While I do not wish to speculate too fervently about directions Potter slash will take at this early stage, I predict that Harry/Draco will continue to thrive, Remus/Sirius will acquire even more emotional urgency, and, of course, there will be an explosion of Dumbledore/Grindelwald. For those who wish to assess the overall impact of the Potter books, especially regarding issues of sexuality and same-sex relationships, Potter slash will provide an invaluable record of the creative responses of some of the series' most dedicated and engaged readers.

NOTES

I am indebted to the many fans who not only allowed me to quote and reference them, but who also gave me helpful suggestions throughout the writing of this essay. I would also like to thank Kenneth Kidd, Anastasia Ulanowicz, Anne Kustritz, Tim Smith, Hallie Tibbets, and Kristina Busse for reading and commenting upon drafts, and Michelle Abate for discussing citation issues.

1. David Langford, "Recursive Fantasy," in *The Encyclopedia of Fantasy,* ed. John Clute and John Grant (New York: St. Martin's Griffin, 1997), 805.

2. Abigail Derecho argues the need for a replacement for the more usual terms "derivative" or "appropriative" fiction, which, as she rightly points out, contain an implied value judgment on the quality of the work. She proposes the term "archontic," but I prefer the breakdowns put forth by Langford and Clute in *The Encyclopedia of Fantasy,* in part because their terms allow for a more nuanced distinction between folk and literary sources. Abigail Derecho, "Archontic Literature: A Definition, a History, and Several Theories of Fan Fiction," in *Fan Fiction and Fan Communities in the Age of the Internet: New Essays,* ed. Karen Hellekson and Kristina Busse (Jefferson, NC: McFarland, 2006), 63–64; Langford, "Recursive Fantasy," 805–6; John Clute, "Twice-Told," in Clute and Grant, *The Encyclopedia of Fantasy,* 968.

3. See Henry Jenkins, *Convergence Culture: Where Old and New Media Collide* (New York: New York University Press, 2006), 185–91, for a discussion of legal issues and Potter fanfiction. There has never been a case of amateur, not-for-profit fiction making it to court for copyright infringement. The legal dispute over the print publication of Steve Vander Ark's Harry Potter lexicon is due to the fact that it will be published for profit—Rowling has repeatedly stated that she has no problems with fan material available on the Web for free. "Warner Brothers, J. K. Rowling Sue over School Librarian's Potter Project," *American Libraries: Weblog of the American Library Association. ALA.org,* November 21, 2007, http://www.ala.org/ala/alonline/currentnews/newsarchive/2007/november2007/rowlingsues.cfm (accessed December 14, 2007).

4. Jenkins, *Convergence Culture.*

5. Will Brooker has attempted to define "slash" as "any romantic/erotic pairing," but this is incorrect; fans, and the vast majority of scholars, reserve "slash" for same-sex pairings only. Brooker admitted that fans resisted his at-

tempt to push the definition of "slash" beyond same-sex pairings: Will Brooker, *Using the Force: Creativity, Community and "Star Wars" Fans* (New York: Continuum, 2002), 144. For orthodox definitions of slash: Henry Jenkins, *Textual Poachers: Television Fans and Participatory Culture* (New York: Routledge, Chapman and Hall, 1992), 185–222; Patricia Frazer Lamb and Diana L. Veith, "Romantic Myth, Transcendence, and *Star Trek* Zines," in *Erotic Universe: Sexuality and Fantastic Literature,* ed. Donald Palumbo (New York: Greenwood Press, 1986), 235–56; Joanna Russ, "Pornography by Women, for Women, with Love," in *Magic Mommas, Trembling Sisters, Puritans and Perverts: Feminist Essays* (Trumansburg, NY: Crossing Press, 1985), 79–99; Camille Bacon-Smith, *Enterprising Women: Television Fandom and the Creation of Popular Myth* (Philadelphia: University of Pennsylvania Press, 1992), 228–54; Shoshanna Green, Cynthia Jenkins, and Henry Jenkins, "Normal Female Interest in Men Bonking: Selections from the *Terra Nostra Underground* and *Strange Bedfellows,*" in *Theorizing Fandom: Fans, Subculture, and Identity,* ed. Cheryl Harris and Alison Alexander (Cresskill, NJ: Hampton Press, 1998), 9–40; Catherine Salmon and Donald Symons, *Warrior Lovers: Erotic Fiction, Evolution and Female Sexuality* (New Haven: Yale University Press, 2003), 70–80; Anne Kustritz, "Slashing the Romance Narrative," *Journal of American Culture* 26.3 (2003): 371–84; Mafalda Stasi, "The Toy Soldiers from Leeds: The Slash Palimpsest," in Hellekson and Busse, *Fan Fiction,* 115–33; and Sara Gwenllian Jones, "The Sex Lives of Cult Television Characters," *Screen* 43 (2002): 79–90, among many others.

6. Ernest Bond and Nancy Michelson, "Writing Harry's World: Children Coauthoring Hogwarts," in *Harry Potter's World: Multidisciplinary Critical Perspectives,* ed. Elizabeth E. Heilman (New York: RoutledgeFalmer, 2003), 111.

7. Jenkins, *Convergence Culture,* 177.

8. Ibid., 170.

9. Ibid., 179.

10. Bond and Michelson, "Writing Harry's World"; Kelly Chandler-Olcott and Donna Mahar, "Adolescents' Anime-Inspired 'Fan Fictions': An Exploration of Multiliteracies," *Journal of Adolescent and Adult Literacy* 46.7 (2003): 556–66; Chris Ebert Flench, "Young Adult Authors on the Internet," *Book Report* 17.4 (1999): 44–46.

11. *Star Trek* is widely considered to be the first "modern" fandom, and the majority of studies of participatory media fandom begin their history with Trek fans. However, activities that could be called "fannish" go back much further, and include eighteenth-century unauthorized sequels of works such as *Gulliver's Travels,* the aforementioned Sherlock Holmes pastiches, and the entire body of literary and folk "retellings." See Derecho, "Archontic Literature"; Stasi, "Toy Soldiers from Leeds"; David Brewer, *The Afterlife of Character: 1726–1825* (Philadelphia: University of Pennsylvania Press, 2005); and Pat Pflieger, "Too Good to be True: 150 years of Mary Sue," 2001, http://www.merrycoz.org/papers/MARYSUE.HTM (accessed December 14, 2007).

12. Constance Penley, *NASA/TREK: Popular Science and Sex in America* (New York: Verso, 1997), 102.

13. Stasi, "Toy Soldiers from Leeds," 120.

14. Hillel Italie, "J. K. Rowling Outs Hogwarts Character," *SFGate.com*, October 20, 2007, http://www.sfgate.com/cgi-bin/article.cgi?f=/n/a/2007/10/19/entertainment/e190351D69.DTL (accessed December 14, 2007).

15. Victoria Ahearn, "Rowling knew early on Dumbledore was Gay," *Toronto Star: TheStar.com*, October 23, 2007, http://www.thestar.com/entertainment/article/ 269527 (accessed December 14, 2007).

16. Ika Willis, "Keeping Promises to Queer Children: Making Space (for Mary Sue) at Hogwarts," in Hellekson and Busse, *Fan Fiction*, 154; see also Jones, "Sex Lives."

17. For detailed critiques of the "incorporation/resistance" paradigm: Jones, "Sex Lives"; and Willis, "Keeping Promises," 153–70.

18. Roberta Seelinger Trites, *Disturbing the Universe: Power and Repression in Adolescent Literature* (Iowa City: University of Iowa Press, 2000), 85.

19. Ibid., 95.

20. Of course, the Internet was not entirely a free-for-all: access to the technology was, and is, still a privilege of those in the middle and upper socioeconomic tiers. However, investing in a computer and Internet access is not the same thing as laying aside comparable amounts of money for strictly fannish activities, such as attendance at fan conventions; Internet users who bought (or received from their parents) their computers for school and work usage were able to find and participate in fandom. For an overview of the history of modern fandom: Francesca Coppa, "A Brief History of Media Fandom," in Hellekson and Busse, *Fan Fiction*, 41–60.

21. Constance Penley, "Brownian Motion: Women, Tactics and Technology," in *Technoculture*, ed. Constance Penley and Andrew Ross (Minneapolis: University of Minnesota Press, 1991), 135–61.

22. Ibid., 155–57; and Penley, *NASA/TREK*, 127–30.

23. See, for example, Barbara Ehrenreich, Elizabeth Hess, and Gloria Jacobs, "Beatlemania: Girls Just Want to Have Fun," in *The Adoring Audience: Fan Culture and Popular Media*, ed. Lisa A. Lewis (New York: Routledge, 1992), 84–106.

24. It comes as no surprise that the titular *40-Year-Old Virgin* of the 2005 film engaged in stereotypical fannish activities like toy collecting.

25. See Joli Jenson, "Fandom as Pathology: The Consequences of Characterization," in Lewis, *The Adoring Audience*, 12; and Lisa Lewis, "'Something More Than Love': Fan Stories on Film," in Lewis, *The Adoring Audience*, 157–58.

26. Jenkins, *Convergence Culture*; also, Jenkins, "Why Heather Can Write," *Technology Review: An MIT Enterprise*, February 6, 2004, http://www.technologyreview.com/read_article.aspx?id=13473&ch=biztech (accessed December 14, 2007).

27. Michael Cart and Christine A. Jenkins, *The Heart Has Its Reasons: Young Adult Literature with Gay/Lesbian/Queer Content, 1969–2004* (Lanham, MD: Scarecrow, 2006), xvii.

28. Julad, comment on Aerye's post "Strange and Unusual" (April 3, 2003), *Livejournal*, comment posted April 4, 2003, www.livejournal.com (accessed December 14, 2007). All quotation of and reference to specific online fan materials is with the permission of the authors.

29. Green, Jenkins, and Jenkins, "Normal Female Interest," 11.

30. According to Francesca Coppa, the Internet enabled "an increasingly customizable fannish experience." As a result, "Arguably, this may be fandom's postmodern moment, where the rules are 'there ain't no rules' and traditions are made to be broken." This is especially observable in a fandom the size of Potter. Coppa, "Brief History," 54, 57.

31. For critiques of this academic attitude: Green, Jenkins, and Jenkins, "Normal Female Interest," 11; Derecho, "Archontic Literature"; Stasi, "Toy Soldiers from Leeds"; and Elizabeth Woledge, "Intimatopia: Genre Intersections Between Slash and the Mainstream," in Hellekson and Busse, *Fan Fiction,* 97–114.

32. Julie M. Holmes (moderator), Meg Cook, and Vicki Dolenga, "Heterosexuality and Feminism in a Male/Male Slash-Centric Fandom," panel presented at "The Witching Hour: A Harry Potter Symposium," Salem, MA, October 6–10, 2005.

33. Bacon-Smith, *Enterprising Women,* 145.

34. Dira Sudis, "Nothing to See Here, Move along," *Livejournal,* December 16, 2007, http://www.livejournal.com (accessed December 17, 2007).

35. Ibid.

36. Aja, "Love Under Will," *Topgallant,* 2002–6, http://www.notquiteroyal .net/topgallant/ (accessed December 14, 2007); Rhysenn, "Irresistible Poison," *Magical Intrigue,* 2001–3, http://rhysenn.morethanart.org/ (accessed December 14, 2007).

37. Jenkins, *Textual Poachers,* 205. He is referencing Eve Kosofsky Sedgwick, *Between Men: English Literature and Male Homosocial Desire* (New York: Columbia University Press, 1985).

38. Tania Modleski, quoted in Jenkins, *Textual Poachers,* 207.

39. See Willis, "Keeping Promises," for a discussion of Harry/Snape fic, an excellent example of slash scholarship moving beyond the buddyslash model.

40. Aja, "Pop Quiz," *Topgallant,* 2004, http://www.notquiteroyal.net/top gallant/ (accessed December 14 2007).

41. Jenkins, *Textual Poachers,* 205.

42. Mireille, "Falling," *Fan Fiction by Mireille,* 2000–2003, http://mireille.af ternoonsandcoffeespoons.org/index.html (accessed December 14, 2007).

43. Catherine Driscoll, "One True Pairing: The Romance of Pornography and the Pornography of Romance," in Hellekson and Busse, *Fan Fiction,* 84.

44. Jones, "Sex Lives"; Salmon and Symons, *Warrior Lovers.*

45. Jennifer Crusie Smith, "This is Not Your Mother's Cinderella: The Romance Novel as Feminist Fairy Tale," in *Romantic Conventions,* ed. Anne K. Kaler and Rosemary E. Johnson Kurek (Bowling Green, OH: Bowling Green State University Popular Press, 1999), 56.

46. Woledge rightly questions the privileging of genre romance in considerations of slash, arguing that it is unnecessary to "recast homoeroticism into heterosexuality." Woledge's reading of the fantasy world of what is here called "buddyslash" as an "intimatopia" (in contrast to Salmon and Symons's "romantopia"), where the "central defining feature is exploration of intimacy," is an interesting take upon the model. Woledge, "Intimatopia," 98, 99.

47. J. K. Rowling, *Harry Potter and the Order of the Phoenix* (New York: Scholastic, 2003).

48. Rave, "That the Science of Cartography is Limited," *Livejournal,* June 28, 2004, http://www.livejournal.com (accessed December 14, 2007).

49. Ibid.

50. Victoria P., "The Love There That's Sleeping," *Achromatic,* July 15, 2007, http://www.unfitforsociety.net/musesfool/index.htm (accessed December 14, 2007).

51. Jeffrey Weiss, "Harry Potter and the Author Who Wouldn't Shut Up," *Dallasnews.com,* October 24, 2007, http://www.dallasnews.com/sharedcon tent/dws/ent/stories/DN-rowlingcolumn_1024gl.State.Edition1.2292bdc .html (accessed December 14, 2007).

52. Rebecca Traister, "Dumbledore? Gay. J. K. Rowling? Chatty," *Salon.com,* October 23, 2007, http://www.salon.com/books/feature/2007/10/23/dumb ledore/ (accessed December 14, 2007).

53. Tonks, a Metamorphagus (a wizard who can change her appearance at will), is often read as queer herself. The Remus/Tonks marriage, which takes place more than a year after Sirius's death, does not necessarily negate Remus's love for Sirius; he could very well be bisexual. Moreover, Remus seems rather ambivalent about the entire process—he resists Tonks's advances throughout *Half-Blood Prince,* and has to be practically ordered by Harry to go back to his wife and child in *Deathly Hallows.* (Harry also links Tonks with Sirius in *Prince* when he assumes that her grief is over his death.) And finally, when Harry goes to what he believes is his death in *Hallows,* he is accompanied not only by his parents, but by Sirius and Remus together. J. K. Rowling, *Harry Potter and the Half-Blood Prince* (New York: Scholastic, 2005); J. K. Rowling, *Harry Potter and the Deathly Hallows* (New York: Scholastic, 2007).

54. Rowling, *Order of the Phoenix,* 501.

55. Philip Nel reports that Rowling specifically designed the response to Lupin's werewolfism to be "a metaphor for people's reactions to illness and disability"; as fans realized, the discourse of AIDS seems to be a primary influence. Pugh and Wallace (2006) also note the correspondences, but, I feel, stretch the metaphor beyond its breaking point when they argue that werewolfism equals queerness in general. Fan readings do not bear this out, especially given that Sirius, Remus's usual partner in slash, is not similarly "diseased." Philip Nel, *J. K. Rowling's Harry Potter Novels: A Reader's Guide* (New York: Continuum, 2001), 15–16; Tison Pugh and David A. Wallace, "Heteronormative Heroism and Queering the School Story in J. K. Rowling's Harry Potter Series," *Children's Literature Association Quarterly* 31.3 (2006): 260–81.

56. Mousapelli, "The Most Ridiculous First Name I've Ever Heard," *The Rat Box,* no date, http://www.theratbox.com/potter.html (accessed December 14, 2007).

57. See Michael Cart, *From Romance to Realism: Fifty Years of Growth and Change in Young Adult Literature* (New York: HarperCollins, 1996), 225–26; and Cart and Jenkins, *The Heart Has Its Reasons.* Dumbledore also arguably fits into the category of the "safely contained" homosexual, as he is both elderly (and

therefore presumably celibate) and dead. However, fans have seized upon the textual glimpses of a young, handsome Dumbledore, and have found them adequate for their purposes.

58. Victoria P., "All the Sinners, Saints," *Achromatic*, September 24, 2003, http://www.unfitforsociety.net/musesfool/index.htm (accessed December 14, 2007).

59. *CityNews.ca* Staff, "David Thewlis on Potter's Lupin: I always thought he was the gay character," *Citynews.ca*, October 24, 2007, http://www.citynews .ca/news/ news_16092.aspx (accessed December 14, 2007).

60. *Harry Potter and the Prisoner of Azkaban*, DVD, directed by Alfonso Cuaron (Burbank, CA: Warner Home Video, 2004).

61. J. K. Rowling, *Harry Potter and the Prisoner of Azkaban* (New York: Scholastic, 1999), 423.

62. Rowling, *Half-Blood Prince*, 450.

63. Pugh and Wallace, "Heternormative Heroism," 264–65.

64. J. K. Rowling, *Harry Potter and the Chamber of Secrets* (New York: Scholastic, 1998), 2.

65. For a thorough discussion of the history of homosexuality in the British boarding school: Alsidare Hickson, *The Poisoned Bowl: Sex, Repression, and the Public School System* (London: Constable, 1995).

66. Thomas Hughes, *Tom Brown's Schooldays*, ed. Andrew Sanders (Oxford: Oxford University Press, 1989), 233.

67. Ibid.

68. Stephen Fry, *The Liar* (London: Soho Press, 1994); Chris Kent, *The Real Tom Brown's School Days: An English School Boy Parody* (New York: GLB Publishers, 2002).

69. Aja, "Monsoon Season," *Topgallant*, 2002, http://www.notquiteroyal .net/topgallant/ (accessed December 14, 2007).

70. Trites, *Disturbing the Universe*, 102–3.

71. Ibid., 114.

72. V, "True But Not Nice," *Hoping is Out of Style*, 2002, http:// v.twin ners.org/ (accessed December 14, 2007).

73. Marcus/Oliver became popular after the release of the 2001 film version of *Sorcerer's Stone*. The pairing has been characterized as "Harry/Draco light": it contains some of the same tensions as Harry/Draco, but without all the canon and fandom baggage. Another appealing element of the pairing is its potential for goofiness, as neither Oliver nor Marcus is, in fannish readings, overblessed with intelligence. Also, while movie-Oliver (Sean Biggerstaff) is exceptionally handsome, Marcus is described by Rowling as "trollish," and movie-Marcus (Jamie Yeates) was fitted with hideous teeth for the role. Many stories treat the pairing as a skewed Beauty and the Beast. J. K. Rowling, *Harry Potter and the Sorcerer's Stone* (New York: Scholastic, 1997), 185; *Harry Potter and the Sorcerer's Stone*, DVD, directed by Chris Columbus (Burbank, CA: Warner Home Video, 2002).

74. V, "True But Not Nice."

75. Jenkins, *Convergence Culture*, 171.

Choose Your Own
Queer Erotic Adventure

Young Adults, Boys' Love *Computer Games,
and the Sexual Politics of Visual Play*

ANDREA WOOD

When it comes to video games, many people in the West are already familiar with popular Japanese franchises such as *Mario Bros., Pokémon,* and *Final Fantasy* that are geared toward children and teenagers.[1] Far less well known, however, is a genre of erotic Japanese computer games[2] often referred to in Japan on the Internet as *eroge.*[3] Alternately called "dating-sims" (short for dating simulation) or "H-games"[4] in the West, these sexually explicit computer games typically operate like visual "Choose Your Own Adventure" novels. Players have minimal interactive engagement with the game apart from reading through scripted dialogue and narrative text, viewing static anime-style CG images, and listening to accompanying audio dialogue. The only input players have revolves around making choices throughout the game, in a fashion similar to a "Choose Your Own Adventure" novel, to make the story progress. Not surprisingly, the objective of these games is sexual in nature—in other words, *eroge* function as erotic adventure quests.

Although the majority of *eroge* in Japan are geared toward heterosexual teenage boys, developing plotlines in which a male protagonist must successfully seduce beautiful young women, there is a vibrant subgenre of erotic computer games that are aimed specifically at girls and young women. These games are part of a queer subgenre known in Japan as *yaoi* or *Boys' Love*.[5] As Mark McLelland explains:

> *Boys' Love,* also commonly known as *yaoi,* is a literary genre (comprising manga, that is, graphic novels, as well as illustrated stories and poetry) dedicated to highly romanticized depictions of *bishōnen* or "beautiful boys" which first arose in Japan in the 1970s. . . . [They involve] detailed romantic, erotic, and sexual relationships between boys and young men.[6]

In more recent years, this transmedia genre has expanded into the realm of computer games as fans have demonstrated their desire to access *Boys' Love* texts across multiple media platforms. As one might imagine from McLelland's definition, the primary objective of *Boys' Love* games is radically different from other *eroge* in that the lead male character does not attempt to seduce gorgeous young women, but rather an array of beautiful young *men*.

In Japan, *Boys' Love* narratives are produced primarily by and for teenage girls and young women, although the expanding transnational circulation of *Boys' Love* media has brought a more diverse array of fans to the genre.[7] I have argued elsewhere[8] that the genre has given rise to a global queer counterpublic that engages with and enjoys these texts precisely because they trouble monolithic understandings of gender and sexuality. My previous research, and that of most scholars in the West, has focused on *Boys' Love* manga and anime, but we also need to consider how computer games intersect with this discourse. Fans of *Boys' Love* games are often participants in other areas of the genre's fandom, and in fact, many *Boys' Love* games derive from or generate related manga and anime texts.[9] Despite the obvious transmedia dimensions of many popular *Boys' Love* franchises, very little research in English has been done on these games and none thus far that deals with English translations of *Boys' Love* games being sold in the North American market.

I seek to remedy this gap by analyzing how *Boys' Love* computer games, as erotic gaming media aimed at adolescent girls, continue to transgress and queer the bounds of normative sexual ideologies marking acceptable erotic desires, fantasies, and modes of representation in ways particular to their gaming context. Specifically, I examine how conceptualizing "play" in relation to these computer games intersects the polemic sexual politics of visual media, adolescent consumption of erotic media, and the decision-making model of *Boys' Love* games. Such an analysis can be a complicated endeavor, however, because actual game play, in the sense of user interaction, is quite minimal by current standards. Therefore, I will be limiting my scope to encompass the one fundamental feature of interactivity that these games do offer players—decision making—and assessing how this works to develop and sustain a player's erotic investment and ludic pleasure in the game. Drawing connections with the young adult "Choose Your Own Adventure" fiction model, in which the choices one makes often fulfill a didactic or moralizing function, I show how *Boys' Love* computer games queer this model by encouraging players to make choices that will take them on the quickest path to unlocking the myriad sexual vignettes, complete with explicit CG visuals and titillating audio tracks, hidden in the games. My analysis focuses on two specific *Boys' Love* games that have been released in North America, *Zettai Fukuju Meirei: Absolute Obedience* and *Enzai: Falsely Accused,* which are translated and sold by the company JAST USA.[10]

Young Adults, Access to Erotic Media, and Camp Sensibilities in *Boys' Love* Computer Games

Given the queer themes and sexually explicit content of most *Boys' Love* texts—whether they are manga, anime, or games—one might assume the primary audience is adults. However, as Mark McLelland explains, in Japan *"Boys' Love* comics are openly sold in designated sections of large bookstores . . . and their primary readerships are young women and schoolgirls." McLelland claims that in the United States, in contrast, *Boys' Love* media are "restricted to an adult audience." [11] I would like to complicate McLelland's latter claim and distinguish more clearly between "audience" as intended consumer market, and the counterpublic of fans who do not necessarily access *Boys' Love* media through sanctioned commercial channels. Therefore, while it is true that *Boys' Love* media sold in the United States tend to feature warning labels and "mature content" disclaimers indicating that the material is adult in nature, publishers are also keenly aware of the fact that young adults comprise a substantial segment of *Boys' Love* fandom and court that demographic.[12] At the same time, when many Western young adult fans of the genre cannot or do not wish to obtain certain *Boys' Love* texts through traditional commercial avenues, they instead turn to the Internet for access.[13]

Adolescents are therefore more reliant upon and often prefer the immediacy of noncommercial modes of peer-to-peer filesharing in order to obtain *Boys' Love* manga, anime, and computer games. As I have discussed before, there are myriad online fan groups that translate and provide English-language scanlations[14] of manga and anime titles that have not yet been licensed for publication in the United States. Scanlators and fansubbers do this work, free of charge, in order to share these texts with other readers around the world.[15] Similar projects have been undertaken to translate and provide English-language "patches" for *Boys' Love* computer games, a more recent expansion of the genre, that have not yet reached the same level of circulation and popularity as their manga counterparts in the United States. For instance, *Boys' Love Game Headquarters*[16] is one of the most frequented English-language websites that hosts downloads to commercial and *dōjinshi*[17] *Boys' Love* computer games. The site also provides a detailed Japanese game installation guide so that fans can learn how to load and play untranslated games on their computers even if they do not read Japanese—a point to which I will return later. What is critical here is the way in which fansubbers and scanlators facilitate the immediacy of access to games and other *Boys' Love* texts that can take months or years to reach the United States.[18]

Additionally, the website *Boys' Love Game Headquarters* operates an online forum where gamers can exchange information and resources, including "capture guides" that provide players with the patterns of choices to make in games that will allow them to reach specific sex scenes and narrative endings. Pooling the knowledge and resources of fans in this manner speaks to Henry Jenkins's concept of "collective intelligence." Drawing from Pierre Lévy's notion that "no one knows everything, everyone knows something, all knowledge resides in humanity," Jenkins argues that collective intelligence is "th[e] ability of virtual communities to leverage the combined expertise of their members."[19] The collective intelligence of fans displayed on forums and websites like *Boys' Love Game Headquarters* has the advantage of enabling a wider number of participants with varied levels of experience and familiarity to acquire, circulate, and play these games.

At the same time, these websites and online forums provide fans with the means to privately access and play *Boys' Love* games free of charge. Privacy is of particular importance to young adult fans that may wish to keep their interest in erotic media secret from adults who attempt to police the sexual "innocence" of minors.[20] Similarly, because *Boys' Love* games focus on queer sexual scenarios, adolescents may be even more reluctant to have adults aware of their erotic fantasies and interests. The desire for privacy in consuming erotic media, however, can also carry specific gendered associations. Jane Juffer argues that women are culturally conditioned and often required to "carve out spaces" to consume erotic media "within a particular, constantly redefined space called the 'home.'"[21] Juffer explains the paradox inherent behind this, however, when "women's access to the production and consumption of erotic materials also occurs as part of a larger political context in which visual pornography is regularly demonized as a threat to the home."[22] Negotiating these barriers and conflicting messages about erotic media can be a difficult endeavor for adult women, let alone adolescent girls attempting to explore their burgeoning sexual desires and fantasies. Not surprisingly, therefore, young adults who are fans of the *Boys' Love* genre may prefer using the Internet to acquire and play related games in private because the visual nature of the medium, along with its queer sexual content, already carries a cultural stigma of taboo no doubt felt even more strongly by minors. Precisely because the demographic for these games, much like the manga, consists largely of adolescent girls who are at a liminal stage between childhood and adulthood,

> They powerfully showcase certain cultural anxieties about sexual control surrounding bodies, and specifically female ones, that do not satisfactorily fit into the binary taxonomy of child or adult. Indeed, the counterpublic itself queers such understandings, troubling the lines between adolescent and adult in much the same way it complicates gender and sexual identity among readers and even characters in the texts themselves. This in itself is presumably what is so worrying to those who want to enforce such distinctions in order to restrict access to erotic media.[23]

In light of such sentiments, it is easy to see how technology can become a gateway for shared exploration and communication among many adolescents and teens that are part of *Boys' Love* fandom, while at the same time serving as a restrictive barrier to their parents and other adults.

In contrast to the many *Boys' Love* games available in Japan, only two have been translated and sold to gamers in North America by the company JAST USA. The first of these two games that I will be discussing is *Zettai Fukuju Meirei: Absolute Obedience*. As a fantasy game text, the setting of the game world suggests an obvious fascination with Western European culture of the past, which becomes an exoticized symbol of difference. This is a fairly common occurrence in *Boys' Love* texts, for as Mark McLelland explains, "The stories are usually set in an ill-defined 'other' place (often Europe or America), in another historical time period (more often the past but sometimes the future) and often deal with boys who are somehow 'other', being aristocrats, historical figures, vampires, angels or even aliens."[24] Consistent emphasis on the alterity of setting as well as characters in *Boys' Love* texts denotes a queer privileging of difference and the nonnormative at the heart of these narratives. *Zettai Fukuju Meirei: Absolute Obedience* is no different; situated in an imaginary post–World War II Germany, the game revolves around a series of missions that the player must complete while playing as one of two possible avatars—Kia Welbehenna or Louise Hardwich—both of whom are members of an undercover spy agency. The double entendre of their agency motto—"Got a problem with certain people? Call us, and we'll bring 'em to their knees"—already lets the player anticipate the kinds of sexual scenarios to expect in the game.

Once the player has chosen her avatar, she selects from a list of possible missions with specific "targets" that her character will attempt to seduce. Kia and Louise each have six different targets: a thief, an Arab prince, a young priest-in-training, a male prostitute, a vigilante / gang leader, a wealthy playboy, a soccer player, a military man, a KGB spy, and so on. These targets are nonplayer characters (hereafter NPCs), and a fundamental part of their erotic characterization, I would argue, revolves around their costumes. Thus, most of these "targets" wear fetishized uniforms or outfits that appeal to a particular erotic imaginary—a point to which I will return shortly. In addition to his distinctive costume, each male character in the game has a Japanese voice actor, known as a *seiyuu*,[25] who performs his audio dialogue throughout the game. Although the player is informed of specific client requests that she must meet in order to accomplish each mission, the implicit and primary goal is to seduce the "target" and unlock all the possible erotic vignettes punctuating each individual storyline.

On the whole, *Boys' Love* games revolve around the player's sexual conquests, and the emphasis on visualizing these moments often transcends language barriers that might impede play in other games. Indeed, since few *Boys' Love* computer games have been translated in English, fans often resort to downloading and playing Japanese versions even if they do not understand the language. This mode of playing is entirely possible, especially if a user obtains an English capture guide that indicates which choices to make at specific junctures in a game. Furthermore, in most instances in which a player must pick a course of action, there are only two options to choose from. Thus, a simple binary system of choices makes it easy for players to simply select the first or second option regardless of whether they can read and understand what that choice is. Consequently, the decision-making process in *Boys' Love* games can be incredibly random and arbitrary, especially if one is playing without a capture guide, and the player may have to perform a long trial-and-error process in order to find and unlock the various sexual scenarios or story endings that are possible in a game. I would argue that, in some respects, it is this "play" between expectation and delayed gratification in the trial-and-error decision-making process that generates one kind of ludic pleasure for the player. Indeed, for some, the pleasures of pursuing a variety of narrative choices that lead to unexpected sex scenes and story resolutions, is very similar to the enjoyment many readers experience with "Choose Your Own Adventure" novels, especially if they elect to explore all the narrative possibilities and endings rather than reading to achieve only one specific or "correct" ending. Despite the didactic function on the surface of "Choose Your Own Adventure" novels, the texts remain open to different reading styles and strategies that resist the structure readers are encouraged to follow.[26] Subversive reading and game playing opportunities available in *Boys' Love* games reflect Eve Sedgwick's notion of "perverse" strategies for reading and making meaning out of texts that can appeal to queer desires and fantasies of the player.[27]

Making connections between "Choose Your Own Adventure" novels and *Boys' Love* computer games is not far-fetched, despite the fact that the former are Western cultural products and the latter are Japanese. Nick Montfort contextualizes the origins of "Choose Your Own Adventure" novels and explains their early relationship to gaming:

> The juvenile fiction series name Choose Your Own Adventure . . . began in 1979 with Edward Packard's *The Cave of Time*. . . . it was one of

several series of children's books (in many languages) that asked readers to choose the next step to take after each page or so of text. There were more than two hundred such books published in the two main Banta series, Choose Your Own Adventure and Choose Your Own Adventure for Younger Readers. *The Cave of Time* itself was made into a graphic adventure game by Bantam Software and published in 1985.[28]

The fact that, from the beginning, "Choose Your Own Adventure" novels were linked with computer games that employed a similar interactive narrative function is significant. Indeed, Japanese game developers were probably not unaware of early interactive U.S. computer games like *The Cave of Time*. Similarly, "Choose Your Own Adventure" books did not remain isolated to a North American context and were in fact translated and serialized in Japan with considerable popularity in the 1980s.[29]

Eroticizing and queering the "Choose Your Own Adventure" model, especially in *Boys' Love* games designed primarily for adolescent girls and young women, can generate incredibly polemic reactions. On the one hand, the problem for some may be the fact that these games are not simply smutty versions of alphabetic text-based "Choose Your Own Adventure" novels, but rather games that use a similar model and employ explicit visual computer graphics and audio accompaniment to illustrate and highlight their sexual content. Similarly, as erotic media, *Boys' Love* games can obviously serve as a visual fantasy aid or titillating inducement to self-pleasure. Erotic media, from literature to film, have a long history of employment as masturbatory aids. Undoubtedly, the suggestion that adolescents could be using erotic media (in this case computer games) for such purposes might generate discomfort with the overlap between real and symbolic pleasures that can be derived from such texts. Objections about adolescents accessing erotic media often speak to a larger cultural investment in "protecting" idealized notions of adolescent sexual innocence[30] rather than critically engaging with the idea that adolescents may want to explore erotic media as they begin to take ownership of their sexuality and their sexual fantasies. Hence, Gayle Rubin argues that in America "our culture denies and punishes erotic interest and activity by anyone under the local age of consent" so that minors "are forbidden to see books, movies, or television in which sexuality is 'too' graphically portrayed."[31] Despite such policing efforts, however, young adults remain curious about erotic media not only due to the age-restrictive cultural taboos placed on it, but also because they are often searching for information about and representations of sex and sexuality. This has become an even more salient point for queer adolescents given the rise of abstinence-only programs, which are particularly dismissive of and ignorant about LGBTQ sexual orientations, in the K–12 public education systems of many states.

Boys' Love games, with their provocative and explicit sexual imagery, may seem extreme to some audiences—however, sex has long been a fundamental aspect of computer and video games. Indeed, Maria Consalvo argues that "sex and sexuality have been integral (if subtextual) parts of many games, and their expression generally reifies conservative religious beliefs about heterosexuality and 'proper' romance."[32] Contrary to this heteronormative typicality in mainstream games, *Boys' Love* games resist such paradigms and present queer views of sex, sexuality, and erotic fantasies that destabilize normative understandings of these terms. First and foremost, these games, much like their manga and anime counterparts, trouble gender in some significant ways. In *Zettai Fukuju Meirei: Absolute Obedience,* queerness often intersects with a camp aesthetic that is evident in the CG images and overall game narrative. Camp can reflect a number of sensibilities, but as Susan Sontag argues, "The essence of Camp is its love of the unnatural: of artifice and exaggeration."[33] Most obviously, artifice and exaggeration are manifested in *Boys' Love* games in CG images of androgynous *bishōnen* (beautiful boy) characters. Sontag suggests that "as a taste in persons, Camp responds particularly to the markedly attenuated and to the strongly exaggerated. The androgyne is certainly one of the greatest images of Camp sensibility."[34] *Boys' Love bishōnen* characters—typically "tall, slim, elfin figures with big eyes, long hair, high cheekbones, and pointed chins"[35]—embody an exaggerated and androgynous pictorial abstraction that corresponds with Sontag's description. Indeed, many scholars have emphasized the gender ambiguity surrounding these characters as a defining feature of the *Boys' Love* genre.[36]

In a similar fashion, the camp aesthetic in *Zettai Fukuju Meirei: Absolute Obedience* extends to characters' clothing in the game's emphasis on fetishized costumes: police, military, and athletic uniforms; exotic garments of foreigners; religious vestments; and so forth. Part of the fantasy dynamic of this game hearkens to subcultural fan practices of "cosplay" (an abbreviation for "costume-play") and the sexual undercurrents that often operate behind such performances. Sharon Kinsella explains cosplay, in a Japanese context, as a practice whereby fans "dress up in the costumes of well-known manga [and anime] characters and perform 'live *parody.*'"[37] Importantly, Kinsella connects Japanese notions of parody (as associated with manga and anime fandom) with "the Anglo-American sensibility of 'camp'" and argues that "both of these cultural modes are based on the subversion of meanings carried in original, and frequently iconic, cultural items . . . [and] this playful subversion is focused particularly on cultural items which contain strongly identified gender stereotypes."[38] *Zettai Fukuju Meirei: Absolute Obedience* employs parody in this manner when it plays with and brings to the surface some of the homoerotic undercurrents evident in the cultures of patriarchally affiliated professions (like the military, the police, and the church).

The game also subverts roles of masculine power by allowing the player's avatar to bring a number of male authority figures under her/his sexual control. Costumes become a critical part of this fantasy, and thus NPCs are often visualized in eroticized states of dress and undress that voyeuristically fetishize their outfits. At the same time, costumes frequently serve the function of facilitating sexual role-playing in the erotic vignettes. For instance, one figure depicts Louise engaging in light BDSM sexual activity with one of his targets, a military officer. Particular attention is given to the target's military uniform in a highly eroticized context (he is nude except for his formal hat and part of his shirt). His position of power has turned into one of vulnerability as he is now tied up with a whip (a symbol of discipline and violence) and physically submissive to Louise, who is fondling his erect penis. In contrast, Louise retains more of his clothing—a visual signal of his control in the scenario—wearing an outfit that is in fact a parody of a military uniform chosen as his undercover disguise. This costume, which Louise wears throughout the game, also humorously reflects his personal predilections for sexual role-playing and light bondage and submission. *Zettai Fukuju Meirei: Absolute Obedience*, with its many costume-focused sexually explicit scenarios, offers players a wide spectrum of possible pleasures associated with cosplay performativity in a context that enables them to voyeuristically gaze upon *bishōnen* in a variety of fantasy role-based costumes and sexual situations.

Sexually explicit sequences in this and other *Boys' Love* games bring together both queer and camp sensibilities in their emphasis on exaggeration and excess. While graphics in other parts of the games are often mediocre at best, it is only during the sex scenes that players are shown high-quality CG anime-style images of fantastically beautiful and androgynous male characters in various stages of seduction, coitus, and orgasm. As the player watches these static images presented in sequence,[39] accompanying audio dialogue punctuated by pornographically performative breathy gasps and exclamations of pleasure plays in the background. At the culmination of each interlude the viewer is typically shown a "money-shot" CG image, which invariably features a virtual explosion of semen so exaggerated in its excess that it parodies the conventions of mainstream pornography's emphasis on this moment, which Linda Williams (1989) has described as the ultimate "frenzy of the visible."[40]

Kia and Louise are very different characters, but in their sexual encounters both tend to be take on the role of *seme* (top) in their missions with occasional turns as *uke* (bottom). As a result, *Zettai Fukuju Meirei: Absolute Obedience* demonstrates an awareness of not only the performative nature of gender, but also sex roles. The two characters embody very different representations of masculinity, which plays a direct part in how they interact with and pursue their targets in the game. Kia is bold, energetic, and always on the lookout for danger and adventure. Throughout the game, he is constantly trying to assert his idea of macho masculinity by cruising around on his motorcycle and getting into fights. Not surprisingly, his actions and dialogue at many points in the game are quite humorous, and the player is made keenly aware of the performative nature of Kia's masculinity and its frequent ridiculousness. In contrast, Louise is represented as a suave and sophisticated man who seduces his targets with subtlety and charm rather than brash or lewd advances, as is Kia's wont. On the surface, Kia and Louise seem to embody attributes of what R. W. Connell has described as "exemplary masculinity." Cultural productions of "exemplary masculinity" have often employed and valorized the imagery of masculine heroism, the sexual hero, and masculinity by violence.[41] These images have been, and continue to be predominantly figured as resolutely heterosexual. In *Zettai Fukuju Meirei: Absolute Obedience*, Kia and Louise often perform to aspects of this cultural imaginary but within a queer context. This major difference reveals one way in which the game emphasizes that the derivative masculinities Kia and Louise perform are unstable and in flux. Thus, while Kia and Louise often share a desire to appear in control, the fact that they relinquish sexual power to other men or to each other at certain moments of the game (and take erotic pleasure in such submission) suggests that they are not satisfied with a static or singular notion of masculinity. Therefore, although both men usually take the role of *seme* in their sexual pursuits, there are a number of times when targets try (with occasional success) to persuade them to take the bottom role of *uke*. In this game, like many *Boys' Love* texts, "The *possibility* of changing roles often serves as a point of teasing humor and even sexual excitement between partners"[42] and, I would argue, a point of queer pleasure for players as well. Such moments in the game also open different possibilities for player-identification—which I will discuss in more detail shortly—as well as working to sustain a player's erotic investment and ludic pleasure in the game by keeping her guessing about what may come next.

Most obviously, the player will wonder about whether or not Kia and Louise will have a sexual encounter together during the course of the game. Indeed, the two are depicted as "partners" in their spy agency, and the game develops a clear homoerotic undercurrent between them from the start. During the interludes between missions, Kia and Louise always meet up back at the agency. These brief, almost domestic moments typically show Kia and Louise playfully arguing or exchanging humorous banter with one another, but the game resists allowing the player to immediately explore the possibilities behind their relationship. Instead, if one successfully completes all of the primary missions, then two extra hidden missions are unlocked at the end of the game that temporarily pair the two men together. Thus, if the player chooses Kia as her avatar for the first of these unlocked missions, she has the opportunity to seduce Louise; alternatively, if she chooses Louise, she has the chance to seduce Kia. Significantly, however, the game resists a clichéd or normative "happily ever after" ending, because at the end of every mission, even if Kia or Louise receives or shares a love confession with a target (or with one another), they do not enter into a monogamous or romantic relationship. Thus, although missions are completed in the game, their narratives remain somewhat open-ended creating spaces for fans to imagine further adventures for their favorite couple pairings in the game.[43]

Demonstrating an awareness of its young adult audience, the game evaluates a player's performance when each mission is given a grade upon completion. Employing a parodic representation of the student "report card," the game ranks the player's mission as follows: An A is achieved if the player completes the mission successfully (this usually involves a combination of meeting the client's requirements and securing a love confession from the target); a B is received for "satisfactory" performance (most, but not all objectives are met); a C is earned if the mission ends badly or if the target escapes; and a D is given to missions that end too early or very badly. Comprehensive capture guides are available online so that players can achieve all of these rankings for any mission, but some players may enjoy the more time-consuming process of earning these grades through several different trial-and-error runs of different missions.[44]

Boys' Love Games, Gendering Sexual Play, and Concerns about "Virtual" Child Pornography

In contrast to the relatively vanilla content and lighthearted tone of *Zettai Fukuju Meirei: Absolute Obedience,* JAST USA's first Boys' Love release in 2004 was the rather infamous game *Enzai: Falsely Accused,* which focuses on a young boy living in a fictional Napoleanic France who is convicted and sent to prison for a murder he did not commit. Dark and far more disturbing than some Boys' Love games, *Enzai: Falsely Accused* is "infamous" among fans for several reasons, but most notably for the fact that it features characters who are of dubious legal age involved in sexually explicit, and sometimes violent and nonconsensual, scenarios within a prison setting. Completely fantastical and soap operatic in nature, the main character Guys's quest is described by JAST USA:

> In prison, Guys is made to endure a world of violence and betrayal as he fights desperately to survive. Inside that world of fear and loathing, he endures in his quest for justice for himself. He finds help in unlikely places—from alcoholic lawyers and insane men in the prison with him. Eventually he begins to realize the scope of the diabolical plot he's fallen into, but even as he works to uncover the truth, he despairs of that which he has lost. And every day, he struggles for dignity and survival, while the powerful interests who put him here look on with smirking amusement.

Will his strength and determination be enough to break through the hearts of his fellow prisoners? Will he be able to finally uncover the truth and find salvation?[45]

As JAST USA's description of the game demonstrates, *Enzai: Falsely Accused* is highly melodramatic, engendering hyperbolic and fantastical modes of excess that have very little grounding in reality. Nonetheless, the age question surrounding some of the characters—especially Guys—becomes an issue of contention in an American context. JAST USA's decision to translate and release *Enzai: Falsely Accused* was a brave one considering the fact that the noticeably young characters in the game could easily be classed as falling into the *shotacon* subgenre of *Boys' Love,* which focuses on underage boys (usually between eight and twelve years old) in homoerotic relationships with other boys their age or older. Accuracy and the ethics of translation become murky issues here, as JAST USA takes some liberties in claiming that the main character Guys is over eighteen when the Japanese version of the game clearly states that he is only fourteen. This tendency of U.S. publishers to "age-up" characters in *Boys' Love* games, a practice that also occurs with English translations of manga and anime, is often done to avoid associations with what might legally be classed as virtual child pornography. However, as I have discussed elsewhere,[46] characters in Boys' Love texts often appear rather young in part due to their androgynous features but also because of certain aesthetic conventions of manga that often veer toward abstraction rather than realism in their pictorial representations of people.

Japan does not share the same cultural discomfort surrounding age and sexuality as the West, especially when it comes to erotic expression in fictional art forms like manga and anime. For instance, a popular genre of manga and anime (which also has connections to certain video games) is *Lolicom.* Sharon Kinsella explains that *Lolicom* is an "abbreviation of Lolita complex" and "is widely used to refer to the theme of sexual obsession with young pre-pubescent girls." [47] Manga and anime from the *Lolicom* genre ranges from sexually suggestive to pornographically explicit, and although there have been debates surrounding these fictional texts,[48] they are still a distinct part of the cultural marketplace in Japan. McLelland demonstrates that "whereas in Anglophone culture homosexual narratives are highly segregated and excluded from children's media, in Japan, homosexuality is an 'essential feature' and 'part of the everyday landscape' of girls' comic books."[49] I do not want to suggest that consumption of sexually explicit media is universally condoned for adolescents in Japan, but I believe it is necessary to illustrate that adolescents encounter far fewer barriers to accessing and actually buying such media in Japan than they do in the West.

Japan and the United States do generally share many of the same legal views, however, on what is known as virtual child pornography. Indeed, McLelland notes that both countries' legislation addressing virtual child pornography (text and images that are purely imaginary and fictional) has been fairly similar, although not always consistent. He explains that while both countries have clear-cut no-tolerance policies regarding real child pornography,

> There is much less uniformity in the treatment of "virtual" images and text-based descriptions that are purely fictional. US legislation in particular draws a clear distinction between real and "virtual" child pornography. In several recent test cases, the US Supreme Court has found it unconstitutional to prohibit the possession and distribution of child-pornography when the images are purely "fictional," since such a ban would violate an individual's First Amendment right to free speech. In accounting for its decision, the court explained that the government may not legislate to control people's thoughts: "The government cannot constitutionally premise legislation on the desirability of controlling a person's private thoughts." The dissemination of these fantasy narratives via the internet is thus not legally prohibited in the US providing the authors are over the age of 18 and have taken steps to ensure that their material cannot be accessed by minors (i.e. they are treated in the same manner as other pornographic text/images).[50]

However, adolescents with sufficient technological acumen and experience within fandom can easily sidestep these barriers and access erotic media online. While the visual imagery and sexual content of certain *Boys' Love* media, like *Enzai: Falsely Accused,* may be objectionable to some, potentially more problematic than the fact they sometimes feature characters that appear to be younger than eighteen is the idea that actual minors are consuming this media. It is the visual nature of the *Boys' Love* genre that makes it far more threatening,[51] for as Jane Juffer demonstrates, culturally there has been a persistent social and cultural legitimization of "the literary—broadly defined—as juxtaposed to the threat of the image."[52] Significantly, however, *Boys' Love* texts (and games in particular) have remained hidden on the subcultural media margins thus far, enabling adolescents to pursue their interest in the genre online with little fear of adult monitoring or intervention.

Keeping in mind some of these cultural disagreements surrounding age, sexuality, and erotic media, I would like to consider how one actually "plays" *Enzai: Falsely Accused* and some of the game's differences from *Zettai Fukuju Meirei: Absolute Obedience*. As with most erotic computer games, *Enzai: Falsely Accused* contains primarily still anime-style CG artwork rather than moving images. The game opens with a short narrative sequence that explains how Guys became involved in a murder and was wrongfully convicted for the crime; thereafter, game play begins once Guys enters prison. As Guys (there are no other player characters), the player progresses through the game and must make decisions at certain junctures in the story in an effort to prove his innocence and escape the dreary, dangerous space of the prison. Although this objective is ostensibly the player's main goal for "successful" narrative closure and completion of the game, far more critical to the experience of "play" in *Enzai*, as with *Zettai Fukuju Meirei: Absolute Obedience*, is making decisions that will "unlock" the sexually explicit sex scenes. As a result, the game becomes something of an erotic scavenger hunt as the player seeks to uncover a seemingly endless array of sexual encounters between Guys and other male characters in the prison. However, in contrast to *Zettai Fukuju Meirei: Absolute Obedience*, a significant number of these sex scenes involve molestation or rape as power dynamics in the prison hierarchy unfold.

Sex sequences in the game pause and disrupt the overall narrative flow, altering the visual dynamic of the player's experience in provocative ways that make possible a number of different and shifting identifications. Initially, after the opening story background, point of view in the game is aligned with that of the player and her avatar, Guys. Thus, when encountering other NPCs the player's avatar will appear in miniature icon form next to a dialogue box that appears on the monitor/screen when he is speaking. Other NPCs will appear in full body image while talking to Guys, along with a dialogue box, but the game's point of view generally comes from Guys's gaze. Thus, apart from the dialogue talking-head box, the player does not often see her character embodied on screen while moving through the game. Sex scenes, however, change this pattern. Queerness manifests at these moments in the game when the explicit vignettes, although not unrelated to the game story, temporarily stop the flow of the narrative. Such breaks with continuity and narrative reflect a privileging of nonlinear time and space that is inherently queer. Similarly, during sex scenes the camera eye shifts to that of an outside view as the player's avatar is fully embodied on screen in all manner of sexual situations. This establishes a temporary break between the player and her male avatar, as the former is now positioned as a voyeuristic outsider watching and listening to the sexual scenarios that ensue.

Such distancing efforts in the game may be a deliberate way of separating the player's identification with her avatar to allow possible pleasure in viewing fantasy sexual scenarios that are nonconsensual. Indeed, Aoyama has argued that when sex in *Boys' Love* texts is situated in a violent context it becomes "an act of revenge" for female readers who act as spectators "rather than . . . prey."[53] While I am reluctant to agree with the applicability of this claim to all readers' or players' experiences with such scenarios, I do think that gendered consumption of these media becomes a critical issue for consideration. Indeed, adolescent girls and young women playing these games have undoubtedly experienced constant media exposure to sexually saturated female bodies treated as objects of heterosexist male desire. Witnessing sexually vulnerable male bodies may be a relatively new experience for some players, and *Boys' Love* games can potentially provide a safe space in which to fantasize about and even critically interrogate sexual dominance and submission outside of more common heterosexual representations in mainstream media. What I find most provocative in the sexual scenarios depicted in *Enzai: Falsely Accused,* and other *Boys' Love* games, is the fact that players have opportunities "to participat[e] in and restag[e] a scenario in which the subject can hold a number of identificatory positions."[54] Mark McLelland claims that "situations of sexual subjugation" depicted in *Boys' Love* texts are "modelled upon roles traditionally fulfilled by female victims" and that "the reader is clearly supposed to identify with the youth, who, as victim, is placed in a subordinate (read, feminine) position."[55] While such an identificatory expectation may be the objective of some authors and game creators, I consider the gender roles and sexual scenarios of *Boys' Love* texts to be more fluid and ambiguous than this. Even in "situations of sexual subjugation," *Boys' Love* narratives often open spaces and possibilities for different reading and viewing experiences that require us to develop, as Constance Penley argues with respect to popular narratives more broadly, a "more complex account of identification and sexual difference in fantasy" that can engage with "the multiple possibilities of identification and numerous pleasures" found in *Boys' Love* texts.[56] It is problematic to assume that female readers necessarily identify with "feminine" roles or characters. *Boys' Love* texts resist reifying the gender and sexuality of characters; thus I believe it is necessary for us to resist doing so in our analyses of readers of these narratives, especially young adults who often still confound the coherent gendering of the self. In contrast, the editors of *GenderQueer* argue, "As we age, the web [of gender conformity] tightens. The gender transgressions of infancy are no longer amusing or accepted in childhood; childhood's are increasingly unwelcome by puberty; and the gender experimentation of puberty must be abandoned by early adulthood."[57] I would argue that *Boys' Love* games provide narrative environments in which young adults can experiment with gender and explore the genderqueer through *bishōnen* characters. Illustrating the genderqueer potential of these characters, James Welker has gone so far as to argue that the *bishōnen* is "visually and psychically neither male nor female: his romantic and erotic interests are directed at other beautiful boys, but his tastes are not exclusively homosexual; he lives and loves outside the heteropatriarchal world inhabited by his readers. He seems a queer character indeed."[58] Because of the shift in point of view that takes place during sex scenes, it is entirely possible for the player to identify in ways that do not adhere to a binary understanding of gender. Consequently, the claim that contemporary youth know "gender is the new frontier: the place to rebel, to create new individuality and uniqueness, to defy old, tired, outdated social norms, and yes, occasionally drive their parents and sundry other authority figures crazy"[59] already reflects one of the myriad possible pleasures afforded through a *Boys' Love* computer game.

The sexual content in *Enzai: Falsely Accused* is transgressive and at times paradoxically titillating as well as disconcerting. Age discrepancies between characters become far more discernable when viscerally embodied in still panels depicting *bishōnen* in the throes of sexual passion, and even violence, with one another. While Guys does enjoy a number of more romantic and mutual sexual experiences while incarcerated, he is also confronted with the problematic hierarchical power dynamics of an all-male prison in which rape becomes a very real and constant threat. In this regard, *Enzai: Falsely Accused* raises more complex questions about how the fantasies presented in the game may speak to anxieties and material concerns in actual adolescents' lives. Indeed, many of the power hierarchies in the prison system in the narrative are structured around age. Because Guys is one of the youngest inmates, he is often subjected to the power and control of older boys and adult prison officials. Consequently, the game demonstrates a critical awareness of how age plays a key factor in cultural understandings and depictions of sex and sexual autonomy. For instance, in one early scene Guys is overpowered by an older boy named Jose when he returns to his cell one night. Guys initially tries to resist Jose's sexual advances and call the guards but the older boy threatens to tell them that Guys was the instigator. Jose makes it clear that calling the guards would inevitably result in solitary confinement for both boys. Guys does not want to take this chance because he is hoping that his lawyer Lusca will be able to convince a judge to grant him a retrial. As a result, Guys decides to play along and see what Jose really wants. The present-tense narration during this sequence is telling. "Jose violently flicks his tongue over mine, despite my attempts to avoid it. It resembles a battle more closely than it does a kiss." Guys recognizes a power hierarchy at work and the fact that Jose derives pleasure in having sexual power over others. Although physically unable to repel the stronger Jose, Guys verbally resists and ultimately wins a degree of Jose's respect. Guys is able to diffuse the violence of the moment by demonstrating that he is not a passive player in the prison power hierarchy. At the same time, he keeps himself alive and does not jeopardize his chance for a retrial.

Despite Guys's many trials and tribulations, on the whole, *Enzai: Falsely Accused* sides with the young and vulnerable protagonist. "Correct" endings for the game usually involve Guys successfully proving his innocence or escaping from the prison to find freedom and love. The more tragic endings turn him into a martyr of an unjust and corrupt "adult" system, for it is in fact the adult detective Guildias who frames Guys for murder at the beginning of the story. As a result, despite its dark and unsettling content, *Enzai: Falsely Accused* has the potential to resonate with young adults who feel oppressed by adult power and authority, especially in regard to sex and sexuality.

Boys' Love games like *Zettai Fikuju Meirei: Absolute Obedience* and *En-*

zai: Falsely Accused raise new and provocative questions about the genre and the sexual politics of visual play at work in these computer games. Much like other texts of the genre, *Boys' Love* games demonstrate queer sensibilities about gender and sexuality that leave open a range of possible readings and identifications among participants in this diverse online counterpublic. Although by no means queerly utopian in their overall understandings of homosexuality, many of the games do contain significant moments that articulate a discernable support for progressive queer politics. In *Zettai Fukuju Meirei: Absolute Obedience,* for instance, one of the missions involves a priest in training who, in one of the "correct" endings, comes to question his profession and identity— ultimately leaving the church and embracing his homosexuality. Small moments like these carry significant weight as they present players with queer affirmations and representations of coming out that they may strongly desire, and which, by and large, are not common in the realm of computer or video games. Although some adults in the West may be less than accepting of the idea that adolescents are attracted to erotic (and specifically queer) computer games, the fandom clearly shows that adolescents are a key demographic for these games, and their investment in them is worthy of further study.

NOTES

1. Chris Kohler demonstrates the strong impact Japanese games have had in the United States, noting that "in their January 2002 issue, editors of the popular video game magazine *Electronic Gaming Monthly* voted for their favorite 100 games of all time" and of those 100, "93 were Japanese in origin." Chris Kohler, *Power Up: How Japanese Video Games Gave the World an Extra Life* (Indianapolis: Brady Games, 2004), 8.

2. In this essay I will be referring to games played on personal computers as "computer games" and those played on console systems as "video games."

3. A Japanese transliteration for "erotic games."

4. The *H* refers to *hentai,* a polyvalent Japanese term that often denotes sexual perversion and has become an umbrella category for media texts (like manga, anime, and video games) with sexually explicit content.

5. Often abbreviated as BL in Japan and the West.

6. Mark McLelland, "The World of *Yaoi:* The Internet, Censorship and the Global *'Boys' Love'* Fandom," in *Australian Feminist Law Journal* 23 (2005): 66–67.

7. More recent research in both Japan and America suggests that there is a small but evident demographic of male consumers for this genre. At the same time, it is erroneous to assume that all female readers of the genre are hetero-

sexual. Recent online studies show that many *Boys' Love* fans do not identify in these terms. Communications scholar Dru Pagliassotti's online study of 478 English-language speakers revealed that 47 percent identified as heterosexual, 25 percent as bisexual, 4 percent as gay, 3 percent as lesbian, 2 percent as other, 7 percent as not interested in sex, 10 percent as not knowing, and 2 percent as preferring not to say." Dru Pagliassotti, "Reading *Boys' Love* in the West," *Particip@tions* 5.2 (2008), http://www.participations.org/Volume%205/Issue%202/5_02_pagliassotti.htm. Although I focus primarily on girls and women as players of *Boys' Love* games, I do not want so suggest that they are uniform or homogenous, especially in terms of their sexuality. At the same time, I want to acknowledge that boys and men are also part of this counterpublic, thus suggesting the appeal of *Boys' Love* games is not as gender segregated as some scholars have previously claimed.

8. Andrea Wood, "'Straight' Women, Queer Texts: Boy-Love Manga and the Rise of a Global Counterpublic," *Women's Studies Quarterly* 34.1–2 (2006): 394–414.

9. Several examples include the PC game *Gakuen Heaven: Boys' Love Scramble* (2002), which inspired a thirteen-episode anime spin-off series, a novel, several manga, and at least two Playstation 2 video games; the PC game *Angel's Feather* (2005), which inspired a two-episode original video animation (OVA) series; and *Enzai: Falsely Accused* (2002), which led to the creation of two-episode OVA.

10. http://www.jastusa.com.

11. McLelland, "The World of *Yaoi*," 68.

12. In terms of *Boys' Love* manga, most texts are shrink-wrapped and come with additional disclaimers inside the books that indicate all characters are eighteen or over, thus labeling them as "adults" as determined by current legal definitions.

13. Although JAST USA's *Boys' Love* games are primarily available for purchase (hard copy or immediate download) online, a credit card is required in order to buy the games, which would prove to be a restrictive barrier for most young adults. As a result, many adolescent fans turn to illegal downloading or file-sharing as alternative means of access.

14. "Scanlation" refers to the fan-based practice of digitally scanning manga onto computers, translating the written text into another language, and editing out the original text and replacing it with the translated material inserted into the necessary frames and dialogue bubbles. These versions of the manga texts are then made available to fans, for free, on the Internet. See Wood, "Straight Women."

15. There are also many scanlation groups that translate *Boys' Love* texts into other languages such as Chinese, French, German, Italian, Korean, and Spanish.

16. http://blgames.ukepile.com.

17. *Dōjinshi* refers to amateur fan-created and self-published manga, novels, games, etc., which often parody original commercially published texts. Some *dōjinshi*, however, do present original narratives and characters.

18. In general, these groups of dedicated fans strongly advocate purchasing texts once they become commercially available in order to support the original authors and artists.

19. Henry Jenkins, *Convergence Culture: Where Old and New Media Collide* (New York: New York University Press, 1998), 27.

20. This is an already conflicted ideal, for as Jacqueline Rose has shown, such a notion of innocence is not purely "a property of childhood but . . . a portion of adult desire." Jacqueline Rose, *The Case of Peter Pan, or the Impossibility of Children's Fiction* (Philadelphia: University of Pennsylvania Press, 1992), xii.

21. Jane Juffer, *At Home with Pornography: Women, Sex, and Everyday Life* (New York: New York University Press, 1998), 5, 3.

22. Ibid., 7.

23. Wood, "Straight Women," 408.

24. Mark McLelland, "The Love Between 'Beautiful Boys' in Japanese Women's Comics," *Journal of Gender Studies* 9.1 (2000): 18.

25. In Japan, many *seiyuu* have major fan followings and can achieve levels of popularity akin to that of celebrity screen actors. Kia is voiced by Yusei Oda, who also does character voices in the *Enzai* computer game and OVA feature. Louise is voiced by Ken Takeuchi, who has done the voices of characters in the *Boys' Love* anime *Gakuen Heaven* and the tamer *shonen-ai* anime *Loveless*.

26. For instance, one could read the books in linear order or backward rather than following the page directions.

27. Eve Kosofsky Sedgwick, "Queer and Now," in *Tendencies* (Durham: Duke University Press, 1993), 1–20.

28. Nick Montfort, *Twisty Little Passages: An Approach to Interactive Fiction* (Cambridge: MIT Press, 2003), 71.

29. The first series, "Kimi nara dou suru?" (a literal English translation of this title is "If It Were You, What Would You Do?"), was first published in 1980. It was then followed by "Adobenchaa Bukkusu" (a Japanese transliteration of "Adventure Books"), which ran from 1985 to 1986. Both series are currently out of print but remain important artifacts that speak to the history of the transnational appeal of "Choose Your Own Adventure" narratives.

30. James R. Kincaid, *Erotic Innocence: The Culture of Child Molesting* (Durham, NC: Duke University Press, 1998).

31. Gayle Rubin, "Thinking Sex: Notes for a Radical Theory of the Politics of Sexuality," in *The Lesbian and Gay Studies Reader*, ed. Henry Abelove, Michele Aina Barale, and David M. Halperin (New York: Routledge, 1992), 20.

32. Maria Consalvo, "Hot Dates and Fairy-Tale Romances: Studying Sexuality in Video Games," in *The Video Game Theory Reader*, ed. Mark J. P. Wolf and Bernard Perron (New York: Routledge, 2003), 171.

33. Susan Sontag, "Notes on Camp," in *Against Interpretation* (London: Vintage, 2001), 275.

34. Ibid., 279.

35. Mark McLelland, "No Climax, No Point, No Meaning? Japanese Women's Boy-Love Sites on the Internet," *Journal of Communication Inquiry* 24.3 (2000): 277.

36. Anne Allison, *Permitted and Prohibited Desires: Mothers, Comics, and Censorship in Japan* (Berkeley: University of California Press, 1996); Tomoko Aoyama, "Male Heterosexuality as Treated by Japanese Women Writers," in *The Japanese Trajectory: Modernization and Beyond*, ed. Gavan McCormack and Yoshio Sugimoto (Cambridge: Cambridge University Press, 1988), 186–204; Maiko Behr, "Undefining Gender in Shimizu Reiko's *Kaguyahime*," *U.S.-Japan Women's Journal* 25 (December 2003): 8–29; Sharon Kinsella, *Adult Manga: Culture and Power in Contemporary Japanese Society* (Honolulu: University of Hawaii Press, 2000); Kazumi Nagaike, "Perverse Sexualities, Perverse Desires: Representations of Female Fantasies and *Yaoi Manga* as Pornography Directed at Women," *U.S.-Japan Women's Journal* 25 (December 2003): 76–103; McLelland, "No Climax"; James Welker, "Beautiful, Borrowed, and Bent: 'Boys' Love' as Girls' Love in *Shjo* Manga," *Signs: Journal of Women in Culture and Society* 31.3 (2006): 841–70; Wood, "Straight Women."

37. Kinsella, *Adult Manga*, 113.

38. Ibid., 120.

39. In this respect, the CG images in most *eroge* sometimes operate in a fashion similar to panels in comics.

40. Linda Williams, *Hard Core: Power, Pleasure, and the "Frenzy of the Visible"* (Berkeley: University of California Press, 1989).

41. R. W. Connell, *Masculinities* (Berkeley: University of California Press, 1995), 214–15.

42. Wood, "Straight Women," 401. For example, there are a number of humorous instances in which Kia argues with targets over who gets to be the "top" in the bedroom.

43. On the Internet one can easily find fan fiction and art related to this game, and there are even a number of online Zettai *Fikuju Meirei: Absolute Obedience* role-playing game (RPG) groups.

44. In some instances, replaying completed missions may require reinstalling the game and starting over from scratch.

45. JAST USA, http://www.jastusa.com/shop/falsely-accused-enzai .html.

46. JAST USA website.

47. Kinsella, *Adult Manga*, 122.

48. Kinsella specifically notes the moral panic surrounding amateur manga subculture that arose in Japan in the late 1980s and early 1990s after the arrest and high-profile case of the "serial infant-girl killer" Miyazaki Tsutomu. Specific connections between the murders and amateur manga were made when "camera crews and reporters arriving at Miyazaki's home discovered that his bedroom was crammed with a large collection of girls' manga, *Lolicom* manga, animation videos, a variety of pornographic manga, and a smaller collection of academic analyses of contemporary youth and girls culture." Kinsella, *Adult Manga*, 126–27.

49. McLelland, "The World of *Yaoi*," 67.

50. Ibid., 65.

51. It is worth noting that in the West, some fans have taken to referring to

eroge as "visual novels" because conventional game "play" is very limited. Thus one spends a great deal of time reading through the game, which incorporates written and audio text with visual images.

52. Juffer, *At Home with Pornography*, 104.

53. Aoyama, "Male Heterosexuality," 196.

54. Constance Penley, "Feminism, Psychoanalysis, and the Study of Popular Culture," *Cultural Studies* (London: Routledge, 1992), 480.

55. McLelland, "Love Between Beautiful Boys," 22.

56. Penley, "Feminism, Psychoanalysis," 480.

57. Riki Anne Wilchins, Joan Nestle, and Clare Howell, *GenderQueer: Voices from Beyond the Sexual Binary* (Los Angeles: Alyson Books, 2002), 12.

58. Welker, "Beautiful, Borrowed, and Bent."

59. Wilchins, Nestle, and Howell, *GenderQueer*, 12.

Contributors

MICHELLE ANN ABATE is an Associate Professor of English at Hollins University, where she teaches both graduate and undergraduate courses in children's and adolscent literature. She has published on a wide range of subjects, from the role of race in *Little Women*, to the connections between a contemporary YA novel and Cold War work of lesbian pulp fiction, to the representation of Gender Identity Disorder of Childhood in a recent illustrated book for preadolescent readers, to the partisan politics driving a series of millennial-era picture books. Her book *Tomboys: A Literary and Cultural History* was released by Temple University Press in 2008.

JES BATTIS is an Assistant Professor in the Department of English at the University of Regina, specializing in fantasy, children's literature, and gender studies.

ROBIN BERNSTEIN is an Assistant Professor at Harvard University, where she teaches in the Program in Studies of Women, Gender, and Sexuality and the Program in History and Literature. Her research in U.S. cultural history focuses on childhood, race, sexuality, and performance in the nineteenth and twentieth centuries. She has published articles on Lorraine Hansberry, Angelina Weld Grimké, and Anna Deavere Smith, and she recently edited an anthology, *Cast Out: Queer Lives in Theater*, for the University of Michigan Press. She is currently completing a book manuscript titled *Racial Innocence: Performing Childhood and Race from Uncle Tom's Cabin to the New Negro Movement*.

THOMAS CRISP is Assistant Professor of Reading at the University of South Florida–Sarasota/Manatee. He teaches undergraduate- and graduate-level courses in children's and adolescent literature and methods of reading and writing instruction. His research and scholarship is primarily focused on depictions of traditionally marginalized populations, gender and queer theory, LGBTQ literature, and children's media, culture, and film.

JUNE CUMMINS is an Associate Professor in the Department of English and Comparative Literature at San Diego State University, where she specializes in children's literature and Jewish-American literature. Her articles engage a wide array of texts and tend to focus gender, ethnic, and national identities. While working on a biography of Sydney Taylor, author of the All-of-a-Kind Family books, June is currently concentrating on Jewish children's literature.

ELIZABETH A. (BETSY) FORD was lucky enough to be a student of Dr. Carol Gay at Youngstown State University in the 1970s; Dr. Gay's enthusiasm for and dedication to children's literature sparked her continuing interest. She was also lucky enough to teach at Westminster College in a department that provided her with the freedom to create courses that kept alive her love of the genre. It gave her great satisfaction to write this essay and to deliver it as part of the first session considering gay themes in children's literature at the 1996 MLA conference chaired by Kenneth Kidd. She is honored to have it included here, which demonstrates the distance the study of children's literature has traveled since Carol Gay fought for its scholars to have a permanent session at the MLA.

SHERRIE A. INNESS is Professor of English at Miami University in Ohio, where she specializes in nineteenth- and twentieth-century American literature and culture, children's literature and childhood studies, and gender and food culture. Sherrie has published numerous articles, books, and edited collections, including *Action Chicks: New Images of Tough Women in Popular Culture* (2004), *Delinquents and Debutantes: Twentieth-Century American Girls' Cultures* (1998), and, most recently, *Secret Ingredients: Race, Gender, and Class at the Dinner Table* (2006).

CHRISTINE A. JENKINS is associate professor on the faculty of the Graduate School of Library and Information Science (GSLIS) at the University of Illinois at Urbana-Champaign, where she teaches courses in youth literature, literacy, and history. She is the author of more than three dozen critical articles and chapters on children's and young adult literature, youth services librarianship, library history as women's history, and LGBTQ issues, especially among young people. Her work has appeared in *Library Quarterly, Libraries and the Cultural Record, Library Trends, Horn Book Maga-*

zine, *School Library Journal,* and *Booklist.* She is coauthor (with Michael Cart) of *The Heart Has Its Reasons: Young Adult Literature with Gay/Lesbian/Queer Content, 1969–2004* (2006). She was head of the admissions committee that admitted Mo (in Alison Bechdel's *Dykes to Watch Out For*) to the GSLIS LIS program.

KENNETH KIDD is Associate Professor of English and Associate Director of the Center for Children's Literature and Culture at the University of Florida. He is the author of *Making American Boys: Boyology and the Feral Tale* (University of Minnesota Press, 2004) and coeditor with Sidney Dobrin of *Wild Things: Children's Culture and Ecocriticism* (Wayne State University Press, 2004). He is Associate Editor of the *Children's Literature Association Quarterly.*

VANESSA WAYNE LEE earned her MA in children's literature from Illinois State University. Her interests include youth culture and critical theory.

BIDDY MARTIN is a distinguished scholar of German studies and author of two books, one on Lou Andreas-Salomé, and the second on gender theory. Having served as Provost at Cornell University from 2000 to 2008, she is now Chancellor of the University of Wisconsin–Madison.

ROBERT McRUER is Professor of English at George Washington University in Washington, DC. He is the author of *Crip Theory: Cultural Signs of Queerness and Disability* (New York University Press, 2006) and *The Queer Renaissance: Contemporary American Literature and the Reinvention of Lesbian and Gay Identity* (New York University Press, 1997). He is coeditor, with Abby L. Wilkerson. of *Desiring Disability: Queer Theory Meets Disability Studies,* which appeared as a special issue of *GLQ: A Journal of Lesbian and Gay Studies* (2003). His articles have appeared in *Genders, PMLA, Radical History Review,* the *Journal of Medical Humanities,* and other locations.

CLAUDIA NELSON is Professor of English at Texas A&M University. The author of *Family Ties in Victorian England* (Praeger, 2007), *Little Strangers: Portrayals of Adoption in America, 1850–1929* (Indiana University Press, 2003), *Invisible Men: Fatherhood in Victorian Periodicals, 1850–1910* (University of Georgia Press, 1995), and *Boys Will Be Girls: The Feminine Ethic and British Children's Fiction, 1857–1917* (Rutgers University Press, 1991), she has also coedited three collections of essays and is the series editor for Ashgate Studies in Childhood, 1700 to the Present.

JODY NORTON was a lecturer in the Department of English and the Women's Studies program at Eastern Michigan University. S/he was the author of *Narcissus "Sous Rature": Male Subjectivity in Contemporary American Poetry* (Bucknell University Press, 2000) and a number of essays on American literature and queer/transgender studies.

TISON PUGH is an Associate Professor in the Department of English at the University of Central Florida. He is the author of *Queering Medieval Genres* and *Sexuality and Its Queer Discontents in Middle English Literature,* as well as articles on children's literature in such journals as *Childrenïs Literature, Children's Literature Association Quarterly,* and *The Lion and the Unicorn.* His edited volumes include *Approaches to Teaching Chaucer's "Troilus and Criseyde" and the Shorter Poems; Race, Class, and Gender in"Medieval" Cinema; Men and Masculinities in Chaucer's "Troilus and Criseyde";* and *Queer Movie Medievalisms.*

CATHERINE TOSENBERGER is Assistant Professor of English at the University of Winnipeg, where she is attached to the Centre for Research in Young People's Texts and Cultures. She wrote her dissertation on Harry Potter fanfiction, and her research interests include children's and YA literature, folklore, and fandom studies.

ERIC L. TRIBUNELLA is an Assistant Professor of English at the University of Southern Mississippi, where he teaches children's and young adult literature. His research interests also include gay studies and queer theory, and he has written several articles about gender and sexuality in children's literature. He is the author of *Melancholia and Maturation: The Use of Trauma in American Children's Literature* (2010).

ROBERTA SEELINGER TRITES is Professor of English at Illinois State University, where she teaches children's and adolescent literature. She is the author of *Twain, Alcott, and the Birth of the American Adolescent Reform Novel* (2007), *Disturbing the Universe: Power and Repression in Adolescent Literature* (2000), and *Waking Sleeping Beauty: Feminist Voices in Children's Novels* (1997). With Betsy Hearne, she is the coeditor of *A Narrative Compass: Stories That Guide Women's Lives* (2009).

ANDREA WOOD is an Assistant Professor of English at Winone State University. Her research interests include LGBTQ literature and film, transnational and digital media, popular genres, and feminist and queer theory.

Publication History

{a.

"David and Jonathan—and Saul—Revisited: Homodomestic Patterns in British Boys' Magazine Fiction, 1880–1915," by Claudia Nelson, originally appeared in *Children's Literature Association Quarterly* 23.3 (1998): 120–27. Reprinted by permission of the Children's Literature Association.

"Queer Performances: Lesbian Politics in *Little Women*," by Roberta Seelinger Trites, originally appeared in *Little Women and the Feminist Imagination: Criticism, Controversy, Personal Essays,* ed. Janice M. Alberghene and Beverly Lyon Clark (New York: Garland, 1999), 139–60. Reprinted by permission.

"Understood Betsy, Understood Nation: Dorothy Canfield Fisher and Willa Cather Queer America," by June Cummins, originally appeared in *Children's Literature* 32 (2004): 15–40. Copyright 2004 Hollins University. Reprinted with permission of The Johns Hopkins University Press.

"There lived in the Land of Oz two queerly made men": Queer Utopianism and Antisocial Eroticism in L. Frank Baum's *Oz* Series," by Tison Pugh, originally appeared in *Marvels & Tales* 22.2 (2008): 217–39. Reprinted with the permission of Wayne State University Press.

"The Queerness of *Harriet the Spy*," by Robin Bernstein, is a revised version of "Too Realistic' and 'Too Distorted': The Attack on Louise Fitzhugh's *Harriet the Spy* and the Gaze of the Queer Child," which appeared in *Critical Matrix* 12.1–2 (2001): 26–47. Reprinted by permission of the author.

"Refusing the Queer Potential: John Knowles's *A Separate Peace*," by Eric L. Tribunella, originally appeared in *Children's Literature* 30 (2002): 81–95. Copyright 2002 Hollins University. Reprinted with permission of The Johns Hopkins University Press.

"Young Adult Novels with Gay/Lesbian Characters and Themes 1969–92: A Historical Reading of Content, Gender, and Narrative Distance," by Christine A. Jenkins, originally appeared in *Journal of Youth Services in Libraries* 7.1 (1993): 43–55. Reprinted with permission of the author.

" 'Unshelter Me': The Emerging Fictional Adolescent Lesbian," by Vanessa Wayne Lee, originally appeared in *Children's Literature Association Quarterly* 23.3 (1998): 152–59. Reprinted by permission of the Children's Literature Association.

"Reading and Writing 'Immunity': Children and the Anti-Body," by Robert McRuer, originally appeared in *Children's Literature Association Quarterly* 23.3 (1998): 134–42. Reprinted by permission of the Children's Literature Association.

"H/Z: Why Lesléa Newman Makes Heather into Zoe," by Elizabeth A. Ford, originally appeared in *Children's Literature Association Quarterly* 23.3 (1998): 128–33. Reprinted by permission of the Children's Literature Association.

"The Trouble with *Rainbow Boys*," by Thomas Crisp, originally appeared in *Children's Literature in Education* 39.4 (2008): 237–61. Reprinted with permission.

"The Hobo, The Fairy, and the Quarterback," by Biddy Martin, first appeared in Biddy Martin, *Femininity Played Straight: The Significance of Being Lesbian* (Routledge: New York, 1997), 33–44. Reprinted with permission.

"Is Nancy Drew Queer? Popular Reading Strategies for the Lesbian Reader," by Sherrie A. Inness, originally appeared in *Women's Studies* 26.3–4 (1997): 343–72. Reprinted with permission.

"Transchildren and the Discipline of Children's Literature," by Jody Norton, originally appeared in *The Lion and the Unicorn* 23.3 (1999): 128–33. Copyright 1999 The Johns Hopkins University Press. Reprinted with permission of The Johns Hopkins University Press.

"Trans Magic: The Radical Performance of the Young Wizard in YA Literature," by Jes Battis, originally appeared under a slightly different title in *The Looking Glass* 10.1 (2006), http://tlg.ninthwonder.com/rabbit/v10i1/alice3.html. Reprinted with permission of the author.

"Homosexuality at the Online Hogwarts: Harry Potter Slash Fanfiction," by Catherine Tosenberger, was originally published in *Children's Literature*

36 (2008): 185–207. Copyright 2008 Hollins University. Reprinted with permission of The Johns Hopkins University Press.

"Choose Your Own Queer Erotic Adventure: Young Adults, *Boys' Love* Computer Games, and the Sexual Politics of Visual Play," by Andrea Wood, debuts in this volume.

Index

❧

Page numbers followed by letter *f* indicate figures.